DOING COMPARATIVE EDUCATION RESEARCH
issues and problems

DOING COMPARATIVE EDUCATION RESEARCH
issues and problems

Edited by
Keith Watson

SYMPOSIUM
BOOKS

Symposium Books
PO Box 65, Wallingford, Oxford OX10 0YG, United Kingdom
www.symposium-books.co.uk

Published in the United Kingdom, 2001

ISBN 1 873927 83 5

Typeset in Melior by Symposium Books
Printed in Great Britain at the University Press, Cambridge

Contents

Preface and Acknowledgements

The chapters that appear in this book on *Doing Comparative Education Research: issues and problems* are based on a series of papers that were first presented at the inaugural conference of the British Association for International and Comparative Education (BAICE) held at the University of Reading in September 1998. BAICE was formed out of an amalgamation of the British Comparative and International Education Society (BCIES) and the British Association of Teachers and Researchers in Overseas Education (BATROE). It was most apt that the University of Reading should have been chosen since it was here that the original Comparative Education Society in Europe (CESE) (British Section) was formed in September 1965.

The differences between the 1960s and the beginning of the twenty-first century are all too apparent in the chapters that follow. Then, most comparative education studies were concerned with the 'advanced' industrialised nations of the world, including Japan and the then Soviet Union. In the early 2000s, with so many of the educational issues, concerns and reforms having a global dimension, it is right that comparative education should have moved to a focus on the problems facing Less Developed Countries (LDCs) as well as those of Europe and North America. Some of the chapters in this volume, therefore, look back as well as forward into the new century, highlighting what different authors see as the key problems to be encountered.

This is not a 'Proceedings' as such, but the chapters offered in this book do reflect some of the issues that were discussed at Reading. It is hoped that they will generate new ideas and further discussion about the purpose and importance of doing comparative studies in education and society in an increasingly 'globalised' world.

Several of the chapters, appeared in a slightly different format in *Compare*, Volume 29, Number 3, October 1999.[1] Copyright remains with BAICE. A modified version of Leon Tickly's chapter will appear in a forthcoming issue of the *International Review of Education*. Joanna Le Métais's chapter appeared in Volume 3, Number 15, June 1999, of the *International Electronic Journal for Leadership in Learning*, but is allowed to be reproduced in this volume.

Much work has gone into compiling this volume, especially chasing up authors and following up missing articles. I would like to thank

Margaret King and Julia De Faveri for all their assistance, both great and small, in helping to expedite this process.

Keith Watson
Director, Centre for International Studies
in Education, Management and Training,
University of Reading, United Kingdom

Note

[1] The chapters by Watson, Crossley, Broadfoot, Phillips & Economou, Osborn, Schweisfurth, McGrath, Stuart, and Lowe.

Introduction: rethinking the role of comparative education

KEITH WATSON

The Changing Environment for Comparative Education Studies

There was a time, in the 1960s and early 1970s, when comparative education was asserting itself as a new 'educational discipline' on university campuses throughout North America, western Europe and east Asia. Specialist journals and societies were launched. Governments, bent on reforming their education systems, sought to glean ideas from developments and innovations elsewhere in the world. Then, during the late 1970s and 1980s, it went through a 'crisis of confidence'. It came under attack from academics in the social sciences as to its relevance: in what ways did it differ from sociology, curriculum studies, educational administration and planning, policy-making and so on? Was there anything special about a comparative research methodology and was there any underpinning theory? What was its relevance to trainee teachers, policy-makers and educational administrators? Numbers studying comparative education at undergraduate level in the United Kingdom fell dramatically (Watson, 1982) but in the USA at least there was a fightback. Comparative education was classified as a 'field of study' whose relevance was both unique and important (Altbach et al, 1982; Altbach & Kelly, 1986). At the beginning of the twenty-first century, the picture has changed yet again. There is no longer any need to justify comparative educational studies; there is, however, a need to refocus its orientation; to ensure that classic mistakes of misinterpretation are avoided; and to seek new areas for research. How and why has this change come about?

The growing 'globalisation' of the world's economic systems and the apparent triumph of neoliberal, free market economics (Roberts, 1985; Fukuyama, 1992; Colclough, 1997) have led many, if not all, governments to recognise that the future success of their countries, even their survival, in the global market place depends less upon their natural resources than upon their human resources. The overwhelming evidence would now suggest that it is increasingly the creation, acquisition, manipulation and use of knowledge that constitutes the basis for international competition, especially with the growth of information technology. Singapore provides a shining example of this thesis. The better the education and training provided, the higher the levels of skills acquisition and the greater the knowledge base offered to the next generation, the more likely is it that a country, or region, will thrive and be able to compete economically. The converse is also true.

It is this recognition that has led international agencies such as the World Bank (1995), the Organisation for Economic Cooperation and Development (OECD), UNESCO (1996) and the United Nations Development Programme (UNDP) to re-emphasise the importance of education and training for both human resource development as well as for socio-economic development, especially in the poorer countries of the world. This was the thrust of the 1990 Jomtien Conference on Education for All, and of the World Bank's emphasis on the necessity to develop primary education as the foundation for all other developments:

> *Education, especially at primary level, has a vital role to*
> *play in the process of socio economic development. It is even*
> *more true to-day and in the next century with advances in*
> *technology, micro technology and computer related industry*
> *that a nation's capacity for development hinges as much on*
> *the ability of its people to acquire, adapt, and then to*
> *advance knowledge as it does on its natural resources.*
> *Literacy, numeracy, communications and problem solving*
> *skills – higher order thinking among the workforce – are*
> *essential for economic survival, let alone development.*
> *(World Bank, 1990, p. 1)*

At the same time, the industrialised countries have been looking askance at the economic challenge posed by the growth of the Newly Industrialising Countries (NICs) such as Mexico, Malaysia, South Korea and Taiwan, especially as the Asian countries have consistently outstripped the USA, Australasia and western Europe in the International Evaluation of Achievement (IEA) surveys in mathematics and science. Just as the launch of Sputnik by the Soviet Union in 1957 led to some soul-searching and educational reforms in the USA, so has the continuing growth of the Asian economies (Lewin, 1998) led many of the industrialised country leaders and businessmen to focus on the role education has played in their sluggish economic performance compared to the ongoing high rates of growth in Asia. It has frequently been suggested that the inspiration for many of the educational reforms in Australia and New Zealand and the United Kingdom during the last two decades of the twentieth century had their origins in a misreading of developments in Asia.

Certainly, the World Bank's advocacy of greater private sector involvement in higher education drew much of its inspiration from Asia and Latin America (World Bank, 1994). Unfortunately, this line of argument was based on a somewhat superficial and decontextualised reading of the situation because it chose to play down the role of state regulation and intervention in favour of playing up the place of the private sector (Watson, 1995).

One of the main purposes of comparative education has always been that of reform, learning from other situations with the express intention of borrowing ideas that might enable reform in one's own country context (Hans, 1964; King, 1968). This is no less true now than it was fifty, or even a hundred, years ago. As the UNESCO World Education Report of 1993 so aptly put it:

> *At a time such as the present, when profound changes*
> *are occurring in the whole structure of global economic,*
> *social and cultural relations, and the role of education in*
> *these changes is coming to be recognised as fundamental,*
> *all countries can only benefit from knowing more about*
> *the cultural premises of each other's education. (UNESCO,*
> *1993, p. 89)*

The willingness on the part of governments and policy-makers to seek ideas from other countries and to recognise the importance of looking comparatively, using comparative data and ideas to inform policy decisions, cannot be underestimated in the newly emerging global economic order but there are challenges that need to be recognised.

New Challenges and Opportunities

The first of these challenges is that more comparative studies are being undertaken than ever before, but by non-specialists, by consultants and by politicians or by educationists from quite different backgrounds, many of whom have a preconceived policy agenda rather than looking longer term and objectively. A classic example of this was the work done by Reynolds on primary school teaching in Taiwan (Reynolds & Farrell, 1996). Another has been the work done on school effectiveness across cultures (Reynolds, 1993). Both have largely ignored the cultural differences between countries.

A second challenge is that of speed. Because democratically elected governments might only have a limited lifespan before new elections, they are often in a hurry. They are committed to educational reforms but over a short time span, unlike the reform in Japan, following the Meiji restoration, or in China, following the Boxer Rebellions at the beginning of the twentieth century, or even the long gestation period for the reforms introduced in Sweden during the long period of control by the Social Democratic Party from the 1930s to the 1970s. The result is that 'quick fix' ideas or principles are 'borrowed' from one society and transferred to another without thinking through the consequences. Examples of this would be the 'mentoring' system for new teachers, tried in Singapore and Australia and transferred across to England and Wales; decentralisation of decision-making without necessarily transferring financial responsibility to the local level, as is happening in many parts of Sub-Saharan Africa; or the experimentation with student loans in many countries, both advanced and developing.

The biggest challenge of all is linked to the use of decontextualised data, and statistics, gathered from many countries and used for policy decisions. There has been a danger in this approach ever since the International Bureau of Education was founded in the early 1930s in Geneva. Subsequently, OECD, UNESCO and the World Bank have published international 'educational indicators'. Unfortunately, the raw data give no information about the underlying educational philosophy of a country, nor any details about the social, economic or cultural context of a country, which, ever since Michael Sadler's famous Guildford Speech of 1900 (Sadler, 1900), comparativists have recognised as essential both for meaningful comparison as well as for contextual analysis. An education system is shaped and moulded by the cultural context in which it develops. If nothing else, the recognition of this simple truth, which largely accounts for the 'difference' between systems and the uniqueness of every system of education, is one of the central contributions of comparative education. Failure to recognise what causes system A to be different from system B and failure to recognise that not every idea or 'system' can be successfully transplanted from one society to another was highlighted in Noah's classic piece on 'The Use and Abuse of Comparative Education' (Noah, 1984). It is timely to be reminded of this, especially since the viability of nation states has been called into question with the growth of 'globalisation', particularly of the media, which can undermine many of the values and curriculum ideals that individual governments may seek to protect. It is also worth being reminded of this because of the growing importance of other players in the provision of education, namely the Trans National Corporations (Ilon, 1994; Heyneman, 2001). Given that traditionally international comparisons used the nation state as the basic unit of comparison, one of the new challenges is clearly what points of reference should be used for meaningful comparison in the future.

Perhaps the biggest challenges lie in how comparative education faces up to what the Delors Report (UNESCO, 1996, pp. 15ff.) calls the 'Tensions of the Twenty-first Century'. These are between the global and the local, perhaps highlighted best in Rolland Paulston's work on social cartography (Paulston, 1996); between the universal and the individual; between diversity and uniformity, or in the comparativists' sense, between difference and similarity; between tradition and modernity; between long-term and short-term considerations; between competitiveness and equality of opportunity; between the extraordinary expansion of knowledge and the ability of individuals to absorb, let alone use, only a fraction of it; and between the spiritual and the material. How to make sense of the proliferation of ideas and values, and the rejection of commonly accepted norms and traditional values, will be a test for comparative educators in the decades ahead.

It is likely that traditional areas for comparative study will continue for the foreseeable future, given that formal structures of education are set to remain. Inevitably, therefore, there will be studies on raising the quality of schooling, through school improvement, staff development and headship training; on patterns of administration, especially relating to decentralisation, financial devolution and local community participation; on the educational provision for minority groups, whether they are ethnic, linguistic or religious. How governments seek to 'control' or 'regulate' education through examinations, national curricula and inspections in the face of pressures, both philosophical and geopolitical, which are of necessity undermining national boundaries and allegiances, will also be crucial areas for comparative research. To some extent, this will ensure a continuity of research interests.

However, it is the new avenues for research which will necessitate both a redefinition of the field as well as provide different parameters for undertaking comparative studies. The weakening of the nation state means that alternative providers will move in, or new types of educational provision will gather apace. There is already a growing network of private schooling and universities run by companies, often not-for-profit organisations that have been able to undercut state provision, that have found niche markets, or that have begun to use a brand name, together with clever marketing, to win over students (Tooley, 1999). The National Institute for Information Technology in India, Objectivo in Brazil or EDUCOR in South Africa would be examples of a new brand of private education, as opposed to the privatisation of education (Bray, 1995).

Competition for the limited number of places in higher education has long been acknowledged in countries such as Greece, Japan, Mexico and Sri Lanka (Dore, 1976) but as demand continues to exceed supply, the number of private tutors has increased dramatically, with considerable ramifications for family incomes and the 'pecking order' of the existing institutions. Mark Bray (1999) has called this development 'the shadow education system'. The scope for fruitful comparative work in this area is considerable.

There is, however, another 'shadow system', which is based less on tutorial and cramming schools: the private school system beyond, or outside state control. Schools that fit into this category would be specialist language schools, especially given the growth of English as the dominant global language (Watson, 1999); specialist institutions offering courses in computing and information technology, business administration, accounting and entrepreneurship; and religious schools that have grown up as a result of disillusionment with the declining moral values offered in the public schools. These schools have sometimes been referred to as education 'beyond the state' (Watson, 1994; Watson & Mackenzie, 1996).

The growth and influence of global Trans National Corporations are also having a profound influence on the shape of education. Not only are they having an influence on the curriculum being taught in mainstream education (Ilon, 1994; Heyneman, 1999a), but increasingly they are establishing their own 'universities' as, for example, Motorola University in Beijing. How these 'universities' operate, whether they are little more than specialist company training institutes, and how far they are developing a 'corporate image' that largely exists irrespective of local cultures will take comparative education research into very different locations and will, certainly, challenge assumptions about the role of 'universities' in the new global era. This kind of education is clearly very 'different'.

So, however, are the new approaches to teaching and learning that are being developed as a result of new information technology. Video conferencing, electronic mail, access to the Internet, inevitably mean that classroom boundaries, let alone national boundaries, are becoming meaningless. To some extent, this has always been the case. Some knowledge has always transcended both cultural and state boundaries. The development of distance learning and 'open universities' during the past 30 years has meant that people living in remote, or isolated, communities could still have access to education beyond their immediate environment, provided that they had access to a radio receiver, a tape recorder, or a television screen and a good postal service. The creation of the Internet has opened up horizons that are truly global so that it is now possible to develop 'virtual' university systems such as the British Aerospace Virtual University in the United Kingdom. The scope for undertaking comparative studies on these institutions, which is far more exciting than simply examining quality control mechanisms over overseas 'franchised' courses, is breathtaking in its implications. For example, comparisons could be made of the courses offered, where students come from and what they do with their qualifications. So, of course, is the realisation that education now is truly lifelong since much of the world's population, living well beyond retirement age, is still eager to learn and develop new skills. Education for the Third Age is bound to increase. Over 20 years ago, Edmund King talked about 'Education for Uncertainty' (King, 1979). That uncertainty is greater now than ever before, given the speed of scientific developments, the creation of new 'knowledge' and the development of new technologies. There may be an element of continuity in the research methods involved in comparative studies, but the new world order will require a greater focus on change.

Continuity and Change

These themes of change are largely picked up in the following chapters. The first four are devoted to reconceptualising the field of comparative education. Watson stresses the need to re-examine the historical roots of the field and suggests six reasons *why* comparative studies should be refocused. Crossley suggests *how* this can be done, emphasising the need to stress the contexts in which different educational systems have grown up, together with the need to understand other social science analyses of postmodernism, post-colonialism and globalisation. Preston argues that there is growing differentiation within and between states, in spite of the pressure to conform to similar ideologies, and she shows that non-formal provision is just as important as formal systems of delivery. She believes that this aspect of education has been overlooked, though Carr-Hill, in a later chapter, explains, to some extent, why this has been so. Broadfoot's chapter, originally delivered as the presidential address at the inaugural meeting of the British Association for International and Comparative Education in 1998, traces the tension between qualitative, culturally focused studies and more positivist research approaches, and argues for what she calls a 'neo-comparative' approach which embraces a wide range of social science perspectives. The term that she originally coined was 'comparology', a term designed to be all-embracing, yet stressing that lessons can only be learned by comparing; and indicating that all learning in society, not only that which takes place in formal institutions, is worthy of study.

The issue of context as a means of explaining and understanding both differences and similarities is picked up in several of the chapters, most notably by Osborn in her research on different approaches to learning in England, France and Denmark and by Schweisfurth in her comparison of teachers' experiences of educational reform in Russia and South Africa. Sanchez also explores context but in a somewhat different way. His research poses questions arising from the integration of children from the Maghreb region of North Africa into Spanish schools. Whose cultural values should predominate? With the increase in migration within and across countries as a result of economic globalisation, this is an issue that is bound to gain in importance.

Sweeting raises a question that has long been debated in comparative education circles: is it feasible to do comparative education research while focusing on a single society? He clearly argues that it is not only possible, especially if comparisons are made of different historical periods, but that valuable lessons and insights can be learnt. In this way, he strengthens Watson's argument that we must not forget our historical roots and traditions. He uses Hong Kong as a case study to develop this line of thinking, much as Phillips (1994) used Germany and England and Wales to develop a similar argument some years ago. Gellert also takes these countries, Germany and England and Wales for his more contemporary analysis of the differences in access to, the courses studied at, and the undergirding philosophies regarding higher education and society in both countries, if England and Wales are classified as one, which, for administrative and legal purposes, they have been until a degree of devolved government was introduced in 1998.

Moving away from national contexts, Le Métais highlights some of the problems facing comparativists, especially if they are concerned with large-scale cross-national studies such as those undertaken by the European Commission or the National Foundation for Educational Research. She clearly recognises that different terminology, different concepts of time, different expectations, and above all, unrealistic expectations on the part of governments and policy-makers can, and frequently do, add to the constraints. Her plea is that researchers should also be part of the policy-making process if misinterpretations and costly mistakes are not to be made.

Phillips & Economou develop these concerns in a more practical way as they describe the preliminary details of the PRESTIGE project (Problems of Educational Standardisation and Transitions in a Global Environment) funded by the European Commission. They show how a large-scale project across six European countries has divided up areas for inquiry while at the same time it has thrown up problems of realistic comparison which, even now, have not been adequately resolved.

Bunt-Kokhuis's study of academic migration across Europe, especially from the former eastern European countries, not only brings out the imperatives for improving career opportunities, arising from globalisation and the freeing up of markets, but also develops a rationale for comparing why academics migrate. The reasons are not always very different from those of the Maghrebi migrants outlined by Sanchez.

One passport to migration and seeking better job opportunities is internationally recognised qualifications. Lowe's preliminary investigations into what qualifications are sought, and how they are used, could be the forerunner of many similar studies, given that international companies and organisations are now fishing in a global pond for the best employees, rather than relying on a national or regional labour force. This develops a theme that was identified by Ilon in the early 1990s and more recently in connection with gender equity in schooling (Ilon, 1994, 1998).

Migration is not only a part of globalisation but is also a part of the post-colonial experience. As Tikly's chapter shows, post-colonialism is also a field that is ripe for comparative analysis. He highlights several areas that could be of interest to comparative researchers – racism and educational policy; language and culture; knowledge and the curriculum in post-colonial societies. Up to the present, much of the research in these fields has been undertaken by historians, sociologists and policy analysts. The scope for comparative educational research is, nevertheless, plentiful.

Problems of undertaking international and cross-cultural comparisons are widely recognised, which is why the more complex and detailed the studies become, the more realistic they become. Unfortunately, there is less likelihood of governments taking note of the small print. It is easier to seize on the headlines and, as Le Métais rightly reminded us, for policy-makers to be selective in their use of comparative studies. Where consultancy is used as part of a research project, there is frequently a conflict of interests between the different parties involved in the project. McGrath points out that there are dangers of 'schizophrenia', especially when scholars of the North are working with scholars in the South and when research agendas are set by funding agencies with their own policy and time frameworks. Inevitably, there are conflicts of interests; different audiences need to be addressed and theories become subordinate to practical day-to-day realities.

These problems can lead to frustrations and considerable difficulties for those involved in undertaking cross-cultural comparative studies, as Stuart's brief chapter illustrates only too well. She describes the background to an imaginative, and rather complex, research project called the Multisite Teacher Education Research Project (MUSTER). This is a collaborative venture involving researchers in Ghana, Lesotho, Malawi, South Africa, Trinidad and Tobago and coordinated by a team from the University of Sussex in the United Kingdom. It is concerned with both exploring the costs of conventional teacher training and what would-be teachers are taught in the curriculum of training colleges as well as with developing a research capacity within the countries concerned. Unfortunately, because the driving force has been a United Kingdom-based research team, and because it has been funded by the British overseas development agency, the Department for International Development (DFID) there have been conflicts over 'ownership' of the research. As similar large-scale comparative research projects become the norm, such conflicts will probably increase. In an age of multimedia information, it becomes increasingly difficult to control the 'ownership' of knowledge!

It is also apparent that frustrations arise over the lack of 'corporate memory' or 'corporate will' with regard to development aid agencies. Lacey & Jacklin's account of their dealings with DFID, over what use was made of the evaluation reports of aid projects over the period 1987-98, touches on raw nerves. Not only is there a sense that local ownership is largely ignored, but an even greater sense that provided the evaluation has been done, and the respective boxes have been ticked, there is little incentive to follow up any of the recommendations made in the reports. This is partly because career civil servants move to different jobs; that new personnel might have different interests, or different projects to become involved in; or that government agendas might have changed. It might simply be that appearances are more important than substance. It does, however, come back to the conflicting interests highlighted by McGrath, and it does make it difficult to ensure that lessons have been learnt so as to avoid future mistakes.

Comparative educators have traditionally used both qualitative and quantitative data collection techniques but problems often arise in the quantitative field when it comes to using national and international statistics. The reliability of, and the difficulties of making sense of, international statistics have been commented on by several writers (e.g. Puryear, 1995; Heyneman, 1999). In this volume, Carr-Hill, Carron & Peart explore in some detail the difficulties of getting agreed definitions of what is meant by non-formal, formal and adult education, and hence the difficulties of fitting statistics into meaningful classifications. The fact that there are at least 17 different terms for non-formal education does not help. The result has been that agencies like UNESCO usually end up by collecting all data outside the formal education system and classifying this as 'non-formal'. However, they explain that there have been significant improvements in recent years and discuss the developments in the International Standard Classification of Education (INSCED). Once this standard classification becomes widely used, it should make comparative analysis considerably easier.

The final chapter is written by one of the doyens in the field of comparative education, 'Harry' Higginson. It is fitting that a scholar who has specialised in analysing the works of Michael Sadler, whose contributions to comparative studies in education spanned the late nineteenth century and the first four decades of the twentieth, should end the century by reflecting upon the developments in thinking and focus of comparative education, by looking at the journal *Compare*, the journal of the British Association for International and Comparative Education. Clearly, a 'discipline' or more appropriately, 'field of study' that can periodically reflect on the changes that have taken place in education and refocus itself in the light of these changes is not only healthy but is capable of facing up to the challenges of the new century. Continuity and change are but two sides of the same coin. It is hoped that the following chapters will both encourage the reader and will focus their attention on the new opportunities that are opening up.

References

Altbach, P.G. & Kelly, G.P. (1986) Introduction: perspectives on comparative education, in P.G. Altbach & G.P. Kelly (Eds) *New Approaches to Comparative Education*, pp. 1-10. Chicago: University of Chicago Press.

Altbach, P.G., Arnove, R.F. & Kelly, G.P. (Eds) (1982) *Comparative Education*. New York: Macmillan.

Bray, M. (1996) *Privatization of Secondary Education: issues and policy implications*, Edc/5/11. Paris: UNESCO.

Bray, M. (1999) *The Shadow Education System: private tutoring and its implications for planners*. Paris: UNESCO, International Institute for Educational Planning.

Colclough, C. (1997) *Marketizing Education and Health in Developing Countries. Miracle or Mirage?* Oxford: Clarendon Press.

Dore, R. (1976) *The Diploma Disease*. London: George Allen & Unwin.

Fukuyama, F. (1992) *The End of History and the Last Man*. Harmondsworth: Penguin.

Heyneman, S. (1999) The Sad Story of UNESCO's Education Statistics, *International Journal of Educational Development*, 19, pp. 53-63.

Heyneman, S. (2001) The Growing International Commercial Market for Educational Goods and Services, *International Journal of Educational Development*, 21(4) (forthcoming).

Ilon, L. (1994) Structural Adjustment and Education: adapting to a growing global market, *International Journal of Educational Development*, 14(2), pp. 95-108.

Ilon, L. (1998) The Effects of International Economic Trends on Gender Equity in Schooling, *International Review of Education*, 44, pp. 335-356.

King, E. J. (1979) *Education for Uncertainity*. London: Sage.

Lewin, K.M. (1998) Education in Emerging Asia: patterns, policies and futures into the 21st century, *International Journal of Educational Development*, 18(2), pp. 81-118.

Noah, H.J. (1984) The Use and Abuse of Comparative Education, *Comparative Education Review*, 28, pp. 550-562.

Paulston, R.G. (Ed.) (1996) *Social Cartography: mapping ways of seeing social and educational change*. New York: Garland Press.

Phillips, D. (1994) Periodisation in Historical Approaches to Comparative Education: some considerations from the examples of Germany and England and Wales, *British Journal of Educational Studies*, 42, pp. 261-272.

Puryear, J.M. (1995) International Education Statistics and Research: status and problems, *International Journal of Educational Development*, 15(1), pp. 79-91.

Reynolds, D. (1993) School Effectiveness: the international perspective, Unpublished paper.

Reynolds, D. & Farrell, S. (1996) *Worlds Apart? A Review of International Surveys of Educational Achievement including England*. London: HMSO.

Roberts, J.M. (1985) *The Triumph of the West*. London: BBC Publications.

Sadler, M. (1900/1964) How Far Can We Learn Anything of Practical Value from the Study of Foreign Systems of Education? *Comparative Education Review*, 7, pp. 307-314 (reprinted from his speech of 1900 delivered in Guildford).

Tooley, J. (1999) *The Global Education Industry. Lessons from Private Education in Developing Countries*. London: Institute of Economic Affairs.

UNESCO (1993) *World Education Report, 1983*. Paris: UNESCO.

UNESCO (1996) *Learning: The Treasure Within*, Report to UNESCO of the International Commission on Education for the Twenty-First Century (The Delors Report). Paris: UNESCO.

Watson, K. (1982) Comparative Education in British Teacher Training Institutions, in R. Goodings, M. Byram & M. McPartland (Eds) *Changing Priorities in Teacher Education*, pp. 193-225. London: Croom Helm.

Watson, K. (1994) The Church and State Debate Revisited with Special Reference to the New Christian School Movement: education beyond the state or intertwined with the state? in D. Turner (Ed.) *Education Beyond the State*, pp. 15-32. London: University of East London.

Watson, K. (1995) Redefining the Role of Government in Higher Education: how realistic is the World Bank's prescription? in L. Buchert, & K. King (Eds) *Learning from Experience: policy and practice in and to higher education*, pp. 125-144. The Hague: Centre for the Study of Education in Developing Countries (Ceso) Paperback No. 24.

Watson, K. (1999) Language, Power, Development and Geopolitical Changes: conflicting pressures facing plurilingual societies, *Compare*, 29, pp. 5-22.

Watson, K. & Mackenzie, P. (1996) The New Christian Schools in England and Wales: an analysis of current issues and controversies, *Journal of Research on Christian Education*, 5, pp. 179-208.

World Bank (1990) *Primary Education*. Washington, DC: World Bank.

World Bank (1994) *Higher Education: the lessons of experience*. Washington, DC: World Bank.

World Bank (1995) *Priorities and Strategies for Education: a World Bank review*. Washington, DC: World Bank.

PART ONE

Reconceptualising Comparative and International Education

Comparative Educational Research: the need for reconceptualisation and fresh insights

KEITH WATSON

Introduction

It was highly appropriate that the launch of the new British Association for International and Comparative Education (BAICE) should have taken place at the University of Reading in September 1998 since it was in Whiteknights Hall at the same university that Vernon Mallinson, one of my predecessors, helped to launch the British section of the Comparative Education Society in Europe (CESE) in September 1965. It was also highly appropriate that the first session of the BAICE conference should have been on the theme of 'Reconceptualising Comparative Education' since the world at the end of the 1990s is very different from that of the mid-1960s. Then, nation states were not only viable and competing political entities, but new ones, often with quite arbitrary and artificial boundaries, were being created as a result of decolonisation. Regional groupings such as the European Union, the Association of South East Asian Nations (ASEAN), the North American Free Trade Association (NAFTA) and the Southern African Development Community (SADC) were but distant ideals. Governments were largely responsible for educational provision at every level. Indeed, they presided over the biggest increase in educational enrolments ever seen (Coombs, 1985; World Bank, 1971). Educational planning was in the ascendancy. Comparative Education as a discipline was growing: its brief was to compare national education systems and to observe the experiments and reforms that were being undertaken in many formal education systems in both east and west Europe (Robinsohn, 1992; Mitter, 1997). International understanding and goodwill were part of the justification for comparative studies, especially in seeking to understand the Soviet bloc countries and China. This was a period of optimism and certainty (Watson, 1988). Changes were taking place in social and sexual mores, at least in the West, but there was still a sense of certainty about what was socially acceptable and what was right and wrong. There was a core of religious beliefs that, while not necessarily adhered to by a large minority, nevertheless was still a cement holding together most societies.

Now, as the twenty-first century begins, not only have the post-war certainties dissolved into confusion, socially and politically, not only have value systems become fragmented and individualised (Cook, 1996), but economic systems and political entities are breaking up, being challenged and being reformulated under the pressures of globalisation (Watson, 2000). The break-up of the Soviet Union and the eastern bloc was widely welcomed in the late 1980s; now the implosion of Russia is greeted with alarm and uncertainty. Whereas Fukuyama (1992) in his famous book, *The End of History and the Last Man*, was able to proclaim the triumph of Western democratic capitalism in the early 1990s, the financial and economic collapse in much of Asia and parts of Latin America in the 1990s make this appear to be a hollow claim. Just as Horowitz (1985) saw ethnic groups in conflict as an inevitable expression of unequal power relationships, Huntington's (1993) *Clash of Civilisations* foresees only conflict in the future between fundamental Islam and post-Christian Western democracies. This is already happening, as can be seen from the growing anti-American sentiments expressed by many Islamic groups.

Whereas comparative educators with a long historical sweep, such as the late William Brickman (1985), Nicholas Hans (1964) or Harry Higginson's (1979 and 1995) commentaries on the insights of Sir Michael Sadler, could perhaps have hinted at what might happen from previous experience, the danger is that we now ignore these historical perceptions and insights to our cost (Theisen, 1997; Watson, 1998). Unfortunately, there are too many pressures from governments and aid agencies for research to be focused on the present or for the immediate future rather than taking a longer time perspective. Our time frames are too short, say, 5-10 years at the most. They are often far less. Comparative historical experience of what has been tried elsewhere and with what success or failure, such as in the fields of community education or the vocationalised curriculum, is rarely called upon in policy recommendations, often with depressing consequences. This is particularly true in regional experiments such as in South-east Asia, southern Africa or Latin America, where lessons for future policy can be learned from past mistakes. *There is a real challenge for comparative education to re-establish its unique role in providing comparative historical insights for future policy action.* The tragedy is that, as Hobsbawm (1994, p. 3) has observed, there is no longer 'a historical memory'. As he says:

> The destruction of the past, or rather of the social mechanisms
> that link one's contemporary experience to that of earlier

*generations, is one of the most characteristic and eerie
phenomena of the late twentieth century. Most young men and
women at the century's end grow up in a sort of permanent
present, lacking any organic relation to the public past of the
times they live in.*

Jameson (1988, p. 29) talks about 'the disappearance of a sense of history' and of people living 'in a perpetual present and in a perpetual change that obliterates traditions of the kind which all earlier social formations have had in one way or another to preserve'. Postmodern thinking, which denies any overarching meta-narrative to explain the present, makes the problem worse. The new Labour Government in Britain epitomises this shallow and disturbing rejection of the past. The danger is that comparativists who become influenced by postmodern thinking cease to have anything relevant to say on policy matters (e.g. Paulston, 1996; Paulston et al, 1996). Fortunately, there are a few who have challenged this as a direction in which comparative education should go, arguing that its position would be further undermined (Torres, 1996; Masemann & Welch, 1997; Watson, 1998).

Unfortunately, postmodernist approaches merely provide ammunition for the growing chorus of criticism that too much educational research is of little value for policy-makers, a view that is becoming widely voiced in the United Kingdom (e.g. Reynolds, 1998). While governments are no longer so ready to commit ever-increasing funds to education, they are concerned that they get value for money for their investment. Hence, the strong emphasis on school improvement and school effectiveness and on research that will apparently provide easy answers to complex problems. The dangers of this approach to research are that too much state-funded research is expected to provide arguments to justify government policies. At the same time, international agencies are perceived as dominating much of the research in developing countries (Samoff, 1993, 1996; Little & Wolf, 1996; Watson, 1996a; Jones, 1997; Crossley, 1998). Surely, a key aspect of comparative education research should be to challenge misguided government or agency policies as and when these occur?

These are a few introductory points. The thrust of this chapter will be to argue that as we reach the end of one century, and move into another, not only is there a unique opportunity to look afresh at the twin disciplines of comparative and international education, but there is also a need to reconceptualise their rationale and purposes for the future. Although comparative and international education are terms that are used throughout this chapter, with greater emphasis on comparative, it needs to be stressed that they are both interlinked and that they have different origins and purposes (see Wilson, 1994; Watson, 1998).

The Rationale for Reconceptualisation

There are many reasons for the need to reconceptualise comparative and international education at this time. It is almost a century after Michael Sadler's famous Guildford speech on 'How far can we learn anything of practical value from the study of foreign systems of education?' (Sadler, 1900/1964). A new society, BAICE, has just been formed out of two distinct professional associations, the British Association of Teachers and Researchers of Overseas Education (BATROE) and the British Comparative and International Education Society (BCIES). More people than ever before are involved in some form of educational consultancy work but with little or no formal training in the dangers and pitfalls of undertaking comparative studies (Thomas, 1990). There is a requestioning of the place of educational research and of the place of formal education systems in the twenty-first century (Cummings & McGinn, 1997). Above all, at a time of great confusion and growing similarities between education systems and their problems, there is a need for more comparative insights than ever before. As Stephen Heyneman, a former World Bank staff economist, recently observed:

> *What is different today (from 30 years ago) is that there is no longer such a thing as a 'developed country.' There is no part of the world which does not need to modernise in the field of education. All countries are deeply concerned with difficult, controversial, educational policy reforms. This requires them to learn from wherever insightful experience might emerge. In my opinion this spells the end of development education as we know it. It represents a new era in which all countries are borrowers and all are donors. This is a refreshing change. (Heyneman, 1999a, p. 190)*

This is perhaps the biggest justification for comparative studies. However, for the purposes of this chapter, six justifications for the reconceptualisation of both comparative education as a discipline and as a key area for educational research are identified as follows. The justifications have been defined as 'needs'.

(1) The need to challenge wrong assumptions.
(2) The need to stress the unique contribution of comparative educational research.
(3) The need to understand the implications of globalisation.
(4) The need to understand the economics of education.
(5) The need to move beyond the economy and to analyse spiritual and philosophical values.
(6) The need to prepare for the future.

1. The Need to Challenge Wrong Assumptions

It is widely believed that comparative education as an academic discipline is in a state of decline (Mitter, 1997). At one level, this is true. As Altbach (1997) and Theisen (1997) have shown in the context of the USA, and Watson (1982) showed in the context of the United Kingdom, there has been a decline in the number of academic staff teaching comparative education studies as hard-pressed finance officers and administrators have made savings in those areas deemed to be less 'relevant' to the political needs of the paymasters, namely, governments. However, a forthcoming survey will show that there is something of a resurgence in British higher education, especially at master's and doctoral levels, and especially in the 'new' universities, which see comparative education as a means of attracting overseas students and their fees and as a means to undertaking lucrative overseas consultancies (Watson, 2001). Moreover, Thomas (1990) has argued that there were more people involved in some form of comparative and international education in the early 1990s than ever before, while Altbach & Tan (1995) have shown that there is a worldwide growth in comparative education centres. The perceived decline is therefore no longer true from the evidence.

The widely held criticism that comparative education is too fragmented and irrelevant for policy-makers is harder to refute (Farrell, 1979; Psacharopoulos, 1990). There are many reasons for this: personality clashes, arguments over terminology, too much emphasis on methodology and not enough on substance. These points have been analysed elsewhere (Altbach et al, 1982; Watson, 1996b). Suffice it to say, as Theisen (1997, p. 339) did in his CIES Presidential Address in 1997, that we need to recognise the inadequate impact comparative education has had in much of the international policy field except in certain areas. We need to acknowledge that the perceptions of comparative education as a discipline are often negative; that we have allowed international bodies to develop policies based on inadequate data (Chapman & Boothroyd, 1988; Walberg & Zhang, 1998; Spaulding & Chaudhuri, 1999); that we have allowed too much of the educational debate to be hijacked by economists, planners and efficiency experts; and that comparative educators 'as a body, are fragmented, underrepresented at the policy and program formation level, and are inexcusable in their complacency ... the CE community is a small voice in the cavernous hall of development and intellectual exchange' (Theisen, 1997, p. 399).

If comparative and international education is to have any hope of impacting on the challenges facing education in the twenty-first century, then not only must it take stock of its current position but it must be less exclusive and it must be prepared to build alliances in terms of research with other disciplines such as economics, political science, international relations and sociology. It needs to reassert its unique contribution in terms of historical and comparative research. Above all, comparative educators need to build alliances with the wider educational community outside the comfortable area of comparative and international education.

Moreover, as Theisen (1997, p. 400) suggests, comparativists need to recognise the growing importance of non-governmental organisations (NGOs), not only in areas like community development and literacy (e.g. Action Aid and Education for Development) (Rogers, 1994; Archer & Cottingham, 1996) but also in the role played by NGOs in providing basic schooling, as with the Aga Khan Foundation in India, Pakistan and Tanzania, or the Centre for British Teachers (CfBT) in inspection and careers advice, and the likely intervention in the running of failing schools in England and Wales. NGOs increased their percentage share of service delivery in education from 2% in 1980 to 4.5% in 1994 (Edwards & Huime, 1994) and bodies like the Department for International Development (DFID) (1997) and the Commonwealth Secretariat (1998) increasingly see NGOs as key players, alongside government and the private sector, especially in those communities and regions where governments do not successfully reach. Apart from greater collaboration, therefore, the effectiveness of NGOs in different communities and societies could prove to be a useful area for comparative education research.

2. The Need to Stress the Unique
Contribution of Comparative Educational Research

Given, as Raivola (1985) has argued, that 'all research that seeks to offer general explanations must be comparative' and that 'comparative education is a field of study that covers all the disciplines that seek to understand and explain education' (Le Than Khoi, 1986), not only must it relate to other disciplines like sociology, politics and international relations, which, to be fair, it often has done, but it must reassert its unique contribution to research. This has nothing to do with research methodologies, which are much the same as in other social sciences (Thomas, 1990, 1998; Watson, 1996b), though as Crossley (1998) and Crossley & Vulliamy (1997) argue, there is justification for greater emphasis on qualitative and ethnographic research rather than quantitative and deterministic research when it comes to explaining much of what happens in communities in Less Developed Countries (LDCs), as it is to do with approaches and areas of inquiry.

Given the financial pressures brought about by globalisation and the need to remain competitive in world markets, many governments are seeking ways of cutting back on social services expenditure, including that of education. They want value for money. They are concerned about raising quality and about preparing students for the labour market. They want cost-effective solutions to their problems and they want research that will either offer quick solutions for policy, or they will only commission research that will support policy commitments already made, for example, over student loans or headship training or school improvement.

The dangers of this approach are that the research data upon which policies are based are too often superficial to be really meaningful, as, for example, with the very broad International Association for the Evaluation of Educational Achievement (IEA) studies; or they fail to take into account local cultural and contextual issues, as with Reynolds & Farrell's (1996) work on primary schooling in Asia, especially Taiwan. Cheng (1997), for example, has highlighted the folly of international consultants failing to understand the local situation in a rural minority area in China, while Hayhoe (1989) has noted that Western approaches to China have so often failed because of a lack of understanding of Chinese culture. Comparativists from Sadler onwards, at least those within the historical/cultural stream as opposed to the scientific stream (Watson, 1996b), have stressed the need to understand the cultural, social and historical setting of individual societies if they are fully to understand the reasons why education systems are as they are, and the values they seek to transmit.

As David Phillips (1997) has rightly observed, and as many poorer countries know to their cost, educational policies cannot easily be transplanted from one national and social context to another. Principles can be used, but they must be modified and adapted according to the local context. Yet, the World Bank (1994, 1995) has appeared to ignore this axiom in its reform proposals for both higher education and basic education, which would appear to have a universal applicability. It has rightly been criticised by academics (e.g. Lauglo, 1996; Samoff, 1996; Watson, 1996c). Most of the school effectiveness/school improvement literature emanates from the USA and the United Kingdom and is being applied, with some modifications, to Commonwealth Africa (Commonwealth Secretariat, 1993/1996). Yet how relevant is this literature to the realities of running a school in much of Sub-Saharan Africa? (e.g. Yanni, 1996; Harber & Davies, 1997).

Comparativists *must* re-establish their unique role in seeking to understand different cultural contexts if (a) government or agency policies are to be challenged, and (b) costly mistakes are to be avoided in the future. To achieve this properly not only means working alongside colleagues from other disciplines but it also means closer collaboration and research partnerships with colleagues in other countries who understand the nuances of their own particular cultures (Oxenham & Watson, 1985; Crossley & Vulliamy, 1997; Crossley, 1998). This is easier done in advanced countries than in LDCs, where, in spite of the rhetoric of the World Bank (1995) and DFID (1997) in favour of closer collaboration and partnerships with recipient country governments, each partner clearly has its own agenda. Good examples of this would be the World Bank's support for basic education and primary school management in Pakistan, and DFID's support for the District Primary Education Progamme in various Indian states.

The fundamental question is: on whose terms does the partnership operate? Preston & Arthur (1996) have observed that consultancy work, whether or not it has a research element, frequently involves conflicting agendas, and it is not always easy to maintain a research integrity. It is certainly nigh on impossible to provide a longitudinal and historical contextual analysis in the time frame that many consultancies have to operate within. This is why the development of networks and partnerships becomes so important (McGinn, 1996). As Michael Crossley (1998) commented at the World Congress of Comparative Education Societies (WCCES) Meeting in Cape Town, when thinking about the need for closer collaboration with researchers in LDCs and the need for greater capacity building:

> We have much to gain from listening more carefully to the
> voices from the South, and from international research and
> development work conducted by 'insiders' and 'outsiders'
> working together. (Crossley, 1990; Reimers & McGinn, 1997)

An added complication arises, especially in the United Kingdom context, with research assessment exercise demands, which mean that more and more individuals, and institutions, are moving into international consultancies and research, largely because it is perceived that this brings in revenue as well as research kudos, but with little or no training about the dangers and pitfalls of doing comparative research (Noah & Eckstein, 1998, pp. 57-67). Part of the purpose of the inaugural BAICE conference was to address some of these issues. Equally, it must be acknowledged that comparative education does not have a monopoly and does not have all the answers. It must recognise that there are new methodologies and insights to be drawn from the social science research foundations. At the same time, it must reassert the value of drawing upon comparative and historical insights. It is interesting to note that of all the comparative education societies, it is the Southern African Comparative and History of Education Society (SACHES) that brings together the two disciplines.

As Heyneman (1999a, p. 190) has pointed out, 'Insight (on any sector) requires a marriage between those whose professional devotion is without question with those whose analytic techniques are profound. If either partner is absent, results can prove dysfunctional. No matter how compelling the evidence, new policies breed their own distortions and will required adjustments'. The role of the comparativists is to provide insights into the policy-making process.

3. The Need to Understand the Implications of Globalisation

This is not the place to enter into a long discourse on the meaning of 'globalisation', a term which is frequently used but which is rarely defined. This has been covered elsewhere (Kofman & Youngs, 1996; Pettman, 1996; Stewart, 1996; Watson, 1998). Suffice it to say that it is an attempt to explain that in many areas of life, especially those connected with banking, finance, economic production, the division of labour, migration and the media, we are dealing with influences that transcend national boundaries, over which individual governments have little or no control. The collapse of the financial markets of East and South-east Asia and the inability of governments to do anything about it, let alone to prevent pornography being broadcast on the Internet, or to prevent satellite television broadcasting and international advertising from penetrating remote parts of countries, are all illustrative of this weakness. As Reich (1991) has observed, globalisation also 'entails the privatization and marketization of economic and political structures', the weakening of central government control over planning or the running of public services such as health and education and the growing inability of the state to control all the activities within its borders. The growth of ever larger Trans National Corporations, the top 250 of which have larger annual turnovers than the gross national products of the 90 poorest countries; the influence of multilateral organisations like the World Bank and the International Monetary Fund and the growth of supra-national bodies such as the European Commission all have influences that transcend national borders (McGinn, 1994). While globalisation is not necessarily a new phenomenon, is not strictly global (Green, 1997), is only related to certain aspects of life, and is far from benign, since, while it has led to increased wealth for many, it has also led to increased poverty and marginalisation for millions. Above all, it does have implications for the ways in which comparative education research is conducted (Watson, 2000).

Traditionally, comparative education has compared educational policies and systems on the basis of nation states, but with the growth in privatisation and marketisation within education, and the lack of readily available data on the private sector, especially in countries like India or even the USA, how reliable is the nation state as the unit for comparison? It is still used by the World Bank, UNESCO and the Organisation for Economic Cooperation and Development (OECD) amongst others as the main source of data collection for comparative purposes, but the reliability of this data collection needs to be checked very carefully (Puryear, 1995; Walberg & Zhang, 1998; Heyneman, 1999b).

Moreover, the growth of regional, political and economic groupings, which have implications both for labour markets, and hence educational training courses and forms of assessment, as well as for curriculum content, provide new challenges for the comparativist. A few comparativists like Nigel Grant (eastern Europe), Mark Bray, Paul Morris and Tony Sweeting (East Asia), Thompson (Sub-Saharan Africa) and Watson (South-east Asia) have taken the region as a point of reference. In the future, it looks as if regional studies may become the norm rather than the exception.

While the effects of globalisation may have been to weaken the nation state in certain areas of control, they have also, ironically, led to the break-up of federations like the USSR or Yugoslavia, and to the creation of many new states – e.g. Bosnia, Croatia, Tadjikistan – or to the re-establishment or independence of others – e.g. Albania, Mongolia, Namibia, South Africa and the Baltic States. A discussion of the development of these 'transitional' or 'transforming' states would require a paper in its own right (e.g. Mebrahatu et al, 2000). Suffice it to say that, in spite of the chaos, confusion and uncertainty surrounding the developments in many of these 'new' countries, there is a key role for the comparativist to use historical, as well as political and sociological, insights to try to map the reforms and developments that are taking place.

There are two more ironies resulting from the process of globalisation: the rise in migrant labour crossing national boundaries at a global level (Castles & Miller, 1993; Bunt-Kokhuis, 1997) and the strengthening of government control in key areas such as assessment, the curriculum and quality control through inspection. The presence of many minority groups within different countries poses threats to the concept of national unity, curriculum development, language policies and policies towards minority groups. Some of these have long been areas of interest to comparativists but the scope for tracking the educational performance of different ethnic and cultural groups in different settings becomes considerable. Likewise does work on the use of inspection, assessment (Little & Wolf, 1996) and other forms of government control.

4. The Need to Understand the Economic Aspects of Education

It has been argued in the 50 years or so since the end of the Second World War that educational development has a major spin-off on economic growth. There have been numerous studies trying to show whether the benefits are to the individual or to society as a whole (e.g. Denison, 1962), though as Cummings & McGinn (1997) argue, the evidence is patchy. Most of these studies have been carried out by economists. The arguments in favour of investment in basic education, or in technical education, or in higher education have been considerable and contentious. For example, the World Bank's (1994, 1995) arguments in favour of diverting funds from higher education to basic education have been challenged by numerous academics (e.g. Bennell, 1996; Lauglo, 1996; Samoff, 1996) or for their different approaches to technical and vocational education and training (TVET) (e.g. King, 1994; McGrath & King, 1997). However, with the growth of new, and flexible, labour markets, there need to be many more studies not only on how governments and firms plan their training programmes but also to explore, comparatively, where the advantages lie in TVET provision. Moreover, with the growth of privatisation and marketisation, not only is there scope for numerous comparative studies to explore different approaches to the use of both these terms, technical and vocational, but also to explore how far students benefit from the private sector as opposed to the public sector, especially given the decline in public expenditure. To be fair Mark Bray (1996) has done much work in this field, but there needs to be more, especially if government policies are to be challenged – or substantiated. There is even scope for some historical work on the place of private, as opposed to public, provision of education since J.S. Mill, writing *On Liberty* in 1859, was probably an early exponent of the free market and, maybe, even vouchers.

> *If government would make up its mind to require for every child a good education, it might save itself the trouble of providing one. It might leave to parents to obtain the education where and how they pleased, and content itself with helping to pay the school fees of the poorer classes of children, and defraying the entire school expenses for those who have no-one else to pay for them. An education established and controlled by the State should only exist, if it exists at all, as one among many competing experiments, carried on for the purpose of example and stimulus to keep the others up to a certain standard of excellence.*

This is certainly ammunition for those who oppose the notion of compulsory education!

5. The Need to Look Beyond the Economy

For 40 years, economic thinking has dominated approaches to education in terms of policies, funding, curriculum development, planning and the like. Somehow, the cultural, moral, religious and idealistic dimensions became overlooked. Reading the texts of Michael Sadler (Higginson, 1979), or Nicholas Hans (1964), or even Vernon Mallinson (1975), let alone the reports of many post-war writers, one is struck by their sense of idealism and optimism for education. Now, those certainties and ideals seem to be lost. UNESCO, and especially ·the recent Delors Report (UNESCO, 1996) on Education in the Twenty-First Century, have tried to redress this balance, but the failures of neo-liberal economic policies in

Asia, Latin America and Russia, and the growth of postmodernism, with different, competing value systems, provide a challenge, and an opportunity, for comparativists to reassert that educational systems cannot be divorced from their religious, cultural and social contexts. If, as Huntington (1993) has argued, the future can no longer be seen in terms of nation states per se, but can only be viewed in terms of 'civilizations' e.g. Islamic, Hindu, Confucian, Christian (Orthodox, Catholic and Protestant), liberal democracies, etc., which transcend national identities, and which will inevitably lead to conflict because the underlying value systems are so different, comparativists need to look again at how traditional education systems have shaped group outlooks and identities. This might mean working closely with cultural and religious specialists but if we are truly to understand alternative Islamic, Russian, Chinese or Japanese paths to development and economic understanding, there are great opportunities. Ruth Hayhoe (1997) sees this as a key role for Western universities into the new millennium.

It should also be noted that amongst the fastest growing groups of private schools in recent years, in Australia, Canada, the United Kingdom, the USA and several of the central and east European countries, has been special religious schools, mostly Christian (Cookson, 1989), and that in Malaysia and Indonesia, a similar group of Islamic private schools has also emerged (Thomas, 1994). The reasons are largely the same – a reaction against secular schooling provided by governments. Comparative studies of the development of those schools would provide insights into why many parents are so dissatisfied with existing state provision.

6. The Need to Prepare for the Future

Finally, with the beginning of the new millennium, at least in the Western calendar, though it needs to be acknowledged that the Chinese and Muslims have their own calendar systems, let us look at some of the possible developments in the future. This is a legitimate role for comparativists. Most of the early pioneers of the twentieth century – Sadler, Kandel, Bereday, Hans, Holmes, Mallinson, King – all regarded a key purpose of comparative education as one that looked into the future. As Hans (1959, p. 300) pointed out:

> *Comparative education is not only to compare existing systems but to envisage reform best suited to new social and economic conditions ... comparative education quite resolutely looks into the future with the firm intent of reform.*

Unfortunately, as Theisen (1997, p. 397, pp. 404ff.) reminds us, comparative educators have been 'careless and unimaginative' in thinking about the future or in using the legitimacy of past experiences and their intellectual tradition to comment about the future. One exception to this is a recent volume from Cummings & McGinn (1997) on *Preparing Schools, Students and Nations for the Twenty-first Century.* Another is the Delors Report, previously alluded to. Not only does a new millennium provide opportunities for us to think about the future, but there are certain imperatives as to why we need to think about the future.

The first comes about because of changing demographic patterns. As the recent United Nations Report on Population (UN, 1998) has pointed out, on current levels of growth, in spite of a slowdown, and in spite of regional variations, the world's population will almost double from 6.8 billion to between 10 and 12 billion by 2050. India, China and Pakistan will be the three most populous nations (Figure 1).

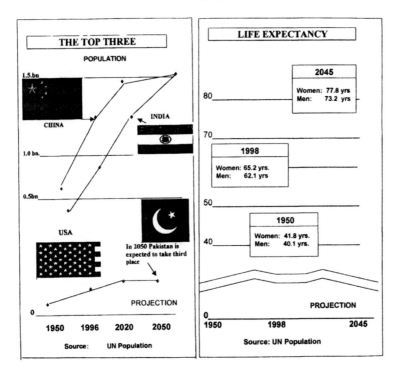

Figure 1. Source: United Nations (1998) Report on Population.

The global population is increasing by 80 million per annum; nearly 95% of this is in the poorest countries of the South. These figures have implications for both poor and rich countries, but in different ways.

In the poor countries, the question to be asked is whether the existing systems can cope with this expansion, or whether alternative approaches to formal schooling will have to be considered. For example, between 1990 and 1995, the number of primary-aged children rose from

496 million to 545 million, yet over 55% of primary-aged children in Sub-Saharan Africa are still not enrolled in schools (UNESCO, 1996). Is it simply a matter of alternative sources of funding or should there be greater emphasis on community-based learning or on new forms of delivery through information technology and the Internet? What experiments have been tried, or are being tried, in different parts of the world?

At the other end of the scale are those over 60. Do they cease to learn because they have come to the end of their formal working lives? According to a US Agency for International Development (USAID, 1985) report, the global population was due to rise by 76% between 1980 and 2000 but those over 60 would rise by 160%. In the High Income Countries (HICs), those over 60 would rise by 73% but in the LDCs by over 230%. Breaking this down by region, the increase in those over 60 would be 500% in Latin America and nearly 600% in Africa and South Asia. Not only are these figures staggering in themselves, but they are likely to increase during the next few decades even more dramatically (UN, 1998). The demographic increase will bring enormous pressures on governments across the globe in terms of pensions, healthcare and social services, let alone education.

In what ways could comparative educationists help to suggest and pioneer new approaches to education? New ways of funding education have been studied comparatively (Bray, 1996; Watson, 1991), but new ways of learning and teaching are growing apace. Already there is a wide range of delivery systems for higher education courses across the globe. It is possible for a South African or a Malaysian student with access to a modem, a television screen and the Internet to enrol for a course in many American universities without ever leaving his/her own country. This interface between education, technology and teaching/learning is bound to increase in the years ahead (Orozco-Gomez, 1997; Schiefelbein, 1997). In many senses, the real ways of learning for the next generation may be through computer-related developments.

Likewise, if education for all is to mean anything, it is not simply provision of basic schooling for primary-aged children. Nor is it simply related to gender issues. Education for all must address the educational needs of the Third Age, the needs of disabled and handicapped people, as well as those of minority groups. It is these latter groups that are so often marginalised in society, are ignored by governments and have not really attracted the interest of comparativists, yet how they are treated reveals the true nature of many societies. A recent paper on how mentally retarded children have been treated in Bengal over the past 150 years might be a catalyst for further research and debate (Miles, 1998).

The future poses enormous problems, the consequences of which can hardly be foreseen. The masterly study of Paul Kennedy (1993) on *Preparing for the Twenty First Century* is already out of date because of recent developments in Asia and Russia. Nevertheless, the future also presents great challenges for all those involved in education. Comparativists in particular should be prepared to respond to some of these challenges.

This chapter has taken a broad look at 'why' there needs to be a reconceptualisation of the role and purposes of comparative and international education. The 'hows' of developing comparative research and 'what' areas should be researched will be developed in subsequent chapters.

References

Altbach, P.G. (1997) The Coming Crisis in International Education in the United States, *International Higher Education*, 8, pp. 4-5.

Altbach, P.G. & Tan, E.T.J. (1995) *Programs and Centers in Comparative and International Education: a global inventory*. Buffalo, State University of New York Press.

Altbach, P.G., Arnove, R.F. & Kelly, G.P. (Eds) (1982) *Comparative Education*. New York: Macmillan.

Archer, D. & Cottingham, S. (1996) *Regenerated Freirean Literacy through Empowering Community Techniques*. London: Overseas Development Administration.

Bennell, P. (1996) Using and Abusing Rates of Return: a critique of World Bank priorities and strategies for education, *International Journal of Educational Development*, 16, pp. 235-248.

Bray, M. (1996) *Counting the Full Cost: parental and community financing of education in East Asia*. Washington, DC: World Bank.

Brickman, W.W. (1985) *Educational Roots and Routes in Western Europe*. Cherry Hill, NJ: Emeritus Inc. Publishers.

Buchert, L. (1999) Educational Reform in the South in the 1990s. Paris: UNESCO.

Bunt-Kokhuis, S.G.M. van de (1997) *Academic Pilgrims: determinants of international faculty mobility*. Tilburg: Tilburg University Press.

Castles, S. & Miller, M.J. (1993) *The Age of Migration*. Basingstoke: Macmillan.

Chapman, D. & Boothroyd, R.A. (1988) Threats to Data Quality in Developing Country Settings, *Comparative Education Review*, 33, pp. 2-39.

Cheng, Kai-Ming (1997) Qualitative Research and Educational Policy Making: approaching the reality in developing countries, in M. Crossley & G. Vulliamy (Eds) *Qualitative Educational Research in Developing Countries: current perspectives*. New York: Garland Press.

Commonwealth Secretariat (1998) *Action for Human Resource Development: partnership between government, the private sector and NGOs in education, training and employment*. London: Commonwealth Secretariat.

Commonwealth Secretariat (1993/96) *Better Schools, Resource Materials (and Modules) for School Heads*. London: Commonwealth Secretariat.

Cook, D.C. (1996) *Blind Alley Beliefs*. Leicester: N.P. Press.

Cookson, P.W.J. (1989) United States of America: contours of continuity and controversy in private schools, in G. Walford (Ed.) *Private Schooling: tradition, change and diversity*. London: Paul Chapman.

Coombs, P.H. (1985) *The World Crisis in Education: the view from the eighties*. Oxford: Oxford University Press.

Crossley, M. (1990) Collaborative research, ethnography and comparative and international education in the South Pacific, *International Journal of Educational Development*, 10, pp. 37-46.

Crossley, M. (1998) The Place of Research and Evaluation in Educational Transformation: cross-cultural issues and research capacity building in Belize, Central America, paper presented to the Tenth World Congress of Comparative Education Societies (WCCES), Cape Town, South Africa, 12-17 July.

Crossley, M. & Vulliamy, G. (Eds) (1997) *Qualitative Educational Research in Developing Countries*. New York: Garland Press.

Cummings, W.K. & McGinn, N.F. (Eds) (1997) *International Handbook of Education and Development. Preparing Schools, Students and Nations for the Twenty-first Century*. Oxford: Pergamon.

Denison, E.F. (1962) *THe Sources of Economic Growth in the United States*. Washington, DC: The Brookings Institution.

Department for International Development (1997) *Eliminating World Poverty: a challenge for the 21st century*. London: The Stationery Office.

Edwards, M. & Huime, D. (1994) *From Non-governmental Organisations – performance and accountability*. Paris: Organisation for Economic Cooperation and Development.

Farrell, J. (1979) The Necessity of Comparisons in the Study of Education, the Salience of Science and the Problems of Comparability, *Comparative Education Review*, 23, pp. 3-16.

Fukuyama, F. (1992) *The End of History and the Last Man*. Harmondsworth: Penguin.

Green, A. (1997) *Education, Globalisation and the Nation State*. London: Macmillan.

Hans, N. (1959) The Historical Approach of Comparative Education, *International Review of Education*, 5, pp. 299-309.

Hans, N. (1964) *Comparative Education*, 3rd edn. London: Routledge & Kegan Paul.

Harber, C. & Davies, L. (1997) *School Management and Effectiveness in Developing Countries: the post-bureaucratic school*. London: Cassell.

Hayhoe, R. (1989) A Chinese Puzzle, *Comparative Education Review*, 33, pp. 153-175.

Hayhoe, R. (1997) Universities and the Clash of Civilizations, in W.K. Cummings & N.F. McGinn (Eds) *International Handbook of Education and Development. Preparing Schools, Students and Nations for the Twenty-first Century*, pp. 741-756. Oxford: Pergamon.

Heyneman, S. (1999a) Development of Aid in Education: a personal view, *International Journal of Educational Development*, 19, pp. 183-190.

Heyneman, S. (1999b) The Sad Story of UNESCO's Education Statistics, *International Journal of Educational Development*, 19, pp. 65-74.

Higginson, J.H. (Ed.) (1979) *Selections from Michael Sadler.* Liverpool: Dejall & Meyorre.

Higginson, J.H. (1995) Michael Sadler's Groundwork as Research Director, *Compare*, 25, pp. 109-114.

Hobsbawm, E. (1994) *The Age of Extremes: the short twentieth century, 1914-1991.* London: Abacus.

Horowitz, D. (1985) Ethnic Groups: a study in conflict. Berkeley: University of California Press.

Huntington, S. (1993) The Clash of Civilizations? *Foreign Affairs*, 72, pp. 22-49.

Jameson, F. (1988) Postmodernism and the Consumer Society, in E.A. Kaplan (Ed.) *Postmodernism and its Discontents.* New York: Verso.

Jones, P.W. (1997) On World Bank Education Financing Policies and Strategies for Education: a World Bank review, *Comparative Education*, 33, pp. 117-129.

Kennedy, P. (1993) *Preparing for the Twenty First Century.* London: Harper Collins.

King, K. (1994) Technical and Vocational Education and Training: an overview, in T. Husen & N. Postlethwaite (Eds) *The International Encyclopedia of Education.* Oxford: Pergamon.

Kofman, E. & Youngs, G. (Eds) (1996) *Globalisation: theory and practice.* London: Pinter.

Lauglo, J. (1996) Banking on Education and the Uses of Research. A Critique of World Bank Priorities and Strategies for Education, *International Journal of Educational Development*, 16, pp. 221-233.

Le Than Khoi (1986) Towards a General Theory of Education, *Comparative Education Review*, 30, pp. 12-39.

Little, A. & Wolf, A. (1996) *Assessments in Transition.* Oxford: Pergamon.

Mallinson, V. (1975) *An Introduction to Comparative Education.* London: Heinemann.

Masemann, V. & Welch, A. (Eds) (1997) Tradition, Modernity and Post-modernity in Comparative Education, Special Issue of *International Review of Education*, 43, pp. 393-395.

McGinn, N.F. (1994) The Impact of Supranational Organisations on Public Education, *International Journal of Educational Development*, 14, pp. 289-298.

McGinn, N.F. (Ed.) (1996) *Crossing Lines, Research and Policy Networks for Developing Country Education.* London: Praeger.

McGrath, S. & King, K. (1997) The Future of Technical and Vocational Education and Training, in W.K. Cummings & N.F. McGinn (Eds) *International Handbook of Education and Development. Preparing Schools, Students and Nations for the Twenty-first Century*, pp. 865-878. Oxford: Pergamon.

Miles, M. (1998) Professional and Family Responses to Mental Retardation in East Bengal and Bangladesh, 1770s–1990s, *International Journal of Educational Development*, 18, pp. 487-499.

Mill, J.S. (1859) *On Liberty*. London: Everyman.

Mitter, W. (1997) Challenges to Comparative Education: between retrospect and expectation, *International Review of Education*, 43, pp. 401-412.

Noah, H.J. & Eckstein, M.A. (1998) *Doing CE: three decades of collaboration*. Hong Kong: Comparative Education Research Centre, Hong Kong.

Orozco-Gomez, G. (1997) Schools and Television, in W.K. Cummings & N.F. McGinn (Eds) *International Handbook of Education and Development. Preparing Schools, Students and Nations for the Twenty-first Century*, pp. 845-864. Oxford: Pergamon.

Oxenham, J. & Watson, K. (Eds) (1985) Research, Cooperation and Evaluation Programmes in the Third World, special issue of the *International Journal of Educational Development*, 5(3).

Paulston, R.G. (Ed.) (1996) *Social Cartography: mapping ways of seeing social and educational change*. New York: Garland Press.

Paulston, R.G., Liebman, M. & Nicholson-Goodman, J.V. (Eds) (1996) *Mapping Multiple Perspectives: research reports of the University of Pittsburgh Social Cartography Project*, 1993-1996. Pittsburgh: University of Pittsburgh.

Pettman, R. (1996) *Understanding Political Economy*. London: Lynne Rienner.

Phillips, D. (1997) Policy Borrowing in Education, in W.K. Cummings & N.F. McGinn (Eds) *International Handbook of Education and Development. Preparing Schools, Students and Nations for the Twenty-first Century*, pp. 283-290. Oxford: Pergamon.

Preston, R. & Arthur, L. (1996) *Quality in Overseas Consultancy: understanding the issues*. London: The British Council.

Psacharopoulos, G. (1990) Comparative Education: from theory to practice, or are you a A:/neo* or B:/disc? *Comparative Education Review*, 34, pp. 369-380.

Puryear, J.M. (1995) International Education Statistics and Research: status and problems, *International Journal of Educational Development*, 15, pp. 79-91.

Raivola, R. (1985) What is Comparison? Methodological and Philosophical Considerations, *Comparative Education Review*, 29, pp. 261-273.

Reich, R.B. (1991) *The Work of Nations: preparing ourselves for 21st century capitalism*. New York: Vintage Books.

Reimers, F. & McGinn, N.F. (1997) *Informed Dialogue: using research to shape education policy around the world*. Westport, CT: Praeger.

Reynolds, D. (1998) *Teacher Effectiveness*, Teacher Training Agency, Corporate Plan Launch, 1998-2001. London: Teacher Training Agency.

Reynolds, D. & Farrell, S. (1996) *Worlds Apart? A Review of International Surveys of Educational Achievement including England*. London: HMSO.

Robinsohn, S.B. (1992) *Comparative Education: a basic approach*. Jerusalem: The Magnes Press, Hebrew University.

Rogers, A. (1994) *Using Literacy*. London: Overseas Development Administration.

Rust, V.D., Soumaré, A., Pescador, O. & Shibuya, M. (1999) Research Strategies in Comparative Education, *Comparative Education Review*, 43, pp. 86-109.

Sadler, M. (1900/1964) How Far Can We Learn Anything of Practical Value from the Study of Foreign Systems of Education? *Comparative Education Review*, 7, pp. 307-314 (reprinted from his speech of 1900 delivered in Guildford).

Samoff, J. (1993) The Reconstruction of Schooling in Africa, *Comparative Education Review*, 37, pp. 181-222.

Samoff, J. (1996) Which Priorities and Strategies for Education? *International Journal of Educational Development*, 16, pp. 249-273.

Schiefelbein, E. (1997) Trends in the Provision and Design of Self-learning Models of Education, in W.K. Cummings & N.F. McGinn (Eds) *International Handbook of Education and Development. Preparing Schools, Students and Nations for the Twenty-first Century*, pp. 813-829. Oxford: Pergamon.

Spaulding, S. & Chaudhuri, R. (1999) UNESCO's World Education Report: its evolution, strengths and possible futures, *International Journal of Educational Development*, 19, pp. 53-63.

Stewart, F. (1996) Globalisation and Education, *International Journal of Educational Development*, 16, pp. 327-333.

Theisen, G. (1997) The New ABCs of Comparative and International Education, *Comparative Education Review*, 41, pp. 397-412.

Thomas, R.M. (Ed.) (1990) *International Comparative Education: issues and prospects*. Oxford: Pergamon.

Thomas, R.M. (1994) Religious Education, in T. Husen & T.N. Postlethwaite (Eds) *International Encyclopedia of Education*, 2nd edn. Oxford: Pergamon.

Thomas, R.M. (1998) *Conducting Educational Research: a comparative view*. London: Bergin & Garvey.

Torres, C.A. (1996) Social Cartography, Comparative Education and Critical Modernism; An After thought, in R.G. Paulston (Ed.) *Social Cartography*, pp. 417-433. New York: Garland Press.

UNESCO (1996) *Learning: the treasure within*, Report to UNESCO of the International Commission on Education for the Twenty-first Century (The Delors Report). Paris: UNESCO.

United Nations, (1998) *Population Report*, 1998. New York: United Nations.

US Agency for International Development (USAID) (1985) *Aging Populations in Developing Nations*. Washington, DC: USAID.

Walberg, H.J. & Zhang, G. (1998) Analyzing the OECD Indicators Model, *Comparative Education*, 34, pp. 55-70.

Watson, K. (1982) Comparative Education in British Teacher Training Institutions, in R. Goodings, M. Byram & M. McPartland (Eds) *Changing Priorities in Teacher Education*, pp. 193-225. London: Croom Helm.

Watson, K. (1988) Forty Years of Education and Development: from optimism to uncertainty, *Education Review*, 40, pp. 137-174.

Watson, K. (1991) Alternative Funding of Education Systems: some lessons from Third World experiments, in D. Phillips (Ed.) *Lessons of Cross-national Comparison in Education*, pp. 113-146. Wallingford: Triangle Books.

Watson, K. (1996a) Educational Provision for the 21st Century: who or what is shaping the agenda and influencing developments? *Southern African Review of Education*, 1, pp. 1-19.

Watson, K. (1996b) Comparative Education, in P. Gordon (Ed.) *A Guide to Educational Research*, pp. 360-397. London: Woburn Press.

Watson, K. (1996c) Banking on Key Reforms for Educational Development: a critique of the World Bank Review, *Mediterranean Journal of Educational Studies*, 1, pp. 43-61.

Watson, K. (1998) Memories, Models and Mapping: the impact of geopolitical changes on comparative studies in education, *Compare*, 28, pp. 5-31.

Watson, K. (2000) Globalisation, Educational Reform and Language Policy in Transitional Societies, in T. Mebrahatu, M. Crossley & D. Johnson (Eds) *Globalisation, Educational Transformation and Societies in Transition*. Oxford: Symposium Books.

Watson, K. (2001) Comparative and International Education in British Higher Education: the state of the art (forthcoming). University of Reading.

Wilson, D. (1994) Comparative and International Education: fraternal or Siamese twins? A Preliminary Genealogy of Our Twin Fields, *Comparative Education Review*, 38, pp. 449-456.

World Bank (1971) *Education Sector Policy Paper*. Washington, DC: World Bank.

World Bank (1994) *Higher Education: the lessons of experience*. Washington, DC: World Bank.

World Bank (1995) *Priorities and Strategies for Education: a World Bank review*. Washington, DC: World Bank.

Yanni, A. (1996) Leadership in the Management of Secondary Schools in Sierra Leone, unpublished PhD thesis, University of Reading.

Reconceptualising Comparative and International Education

MICHAEL CROSSLEY

Introduction

Educational research and educational research communities are currently facing concerted challenges worldwide. Critiques are being generated within professional circles (Hargreaves, 1996; Kennedy, 1997; Furlong, 1998) as well as by governmental agencies, policy-makers, funders, practitioners and a wide spectrum of other stakeholders (Gray, 1995; Teacher Training Agency [TTA], 1996; Sroufe, 1997; Tooley, 1998). At the heart of this highly charged debate are calls for educational research to be more cumulative and authoritative – to be more directly relevant, useful and accessible to both policy-makers and practitioners – and to be more cost-effective as budgets tighten and accountability is ever more emphasised.

Similar challenges are being faced by researchers in the field of comparative and international education, with critics such as Reynolds & Farrell (1996) adding to familiar analyses of problems that have long been recognised within the field itself (Noah, 1986; Crossley & Broadfoot, 1992; Reimers & McGinn, 1997; Watson, 1998). In addition, the rapidly increasing pace of globalisation, and related cross-cultural issues and tensions associated with the advance of the 'global century', have generated a new set of powerful and complex challenges. These impact most dramatically upon comparative and international studies of all kinds as:

> *The world has changed dramatically – borders have become fluid, culture has acquired a global dimension, economic models share similar basic orientations – and yet politics remain stubbornly local. (Hawkins et al, 1998, p. 1)*

This chapter reflects upon the implications of these trends and developments for the reconceptualisation of comparative and international education, paying particular attention to opportunities for renewed growth and the future research potential of our field.

A Multidisciplinary Field of Study

While writers such as Halls (1977), Watson & Williams (1984) and Altbach & Tan (1995) have documented the changing fortunes of comparative and international education, it is, today, re-emerging as a vibrant multidisciplinary field that is attracting increased attention from researchers and policy-makers worldwide (Alexander, 1996; Ball, 1998; Bray, 1998). Why this is so is sketched out briefly here, but explored in more detail in related work (Crossley, 1990; Crossley & Broadfoot, 1992). Given this resurgence of interest in comparative and international studies of education, it is argued that the time is now ripe for a comprehensive reconceptualisation of the field as a whole. Influential factors include dramatic changes in geopolitical relations; the intensifying pace of globalisation; growth of international consultancy and exchange programmes; advances in information and communications technology; demand for strengthened linkages between educational research, policy and practice; growing tensions between the economic and cultural dimensions of social reform; postmodern challenges to dominant theoretical frameworks; and the symbolic impact of the turn of a new century. These all call for urgent and critical reflection, and for a repositioning of our field to better address contemporary priorities and meet the emergent needs of the future.

In doing this, we should not overlook the very real strengths that have characterised our field, from its positivistic origins in the nineteenth-century plans and aspiration of Jullien (Fraser, 1964), or Sir Michael Sadler's (1900) benchmark lecture, delivered, appositely, at the last turn of the century (see Higginson, 1979). Sadler, for example, inspired many generations of comparativists on both sides of the Atlantic, including his student, Isaac Kandel (1933), with his then pioneering and interpretative social, historical and cultural studies of education. Significantly, Sadler warned that:

> *We cannot wander at pleasure among the educational systems of the world, like a child strolling through a garden, and pick off a flower from one bush and some leaves from another, and then expect that if we stick what we have gathered into the soil at home, we shall have a living plant. (1900, p. 49)*

Many are familiar with this often cited lecture but, in the present context, it justly deserves reconsideration in view of the post-war reassertion of positivistic social science in the field (Noah & Eckstein, 1969) – and the more recent renewal of interest in interpretative and sociocultural analyses of education (Wertsch, 1995; Bruner, 1996;

Masemann & Welch, 1997). This is especially pertinent in a global community where rationalistic and economic imperatives have dominated much research in the social sciences, but where critical theory and postmodern perspectives (Morrow & Torres, 1995; Cowen, 1996) help to highlight the (multi)cultural forces and factors that underpin human progress – even in the technological world of the twenty-first century (Mazrui, 1990; UNESCO, 1998). Sadler's influence on scholars such as Kandel (1933), Hans (1959) and Mallinson (1960) emphasised 'the things outside the school' and the philosophical, historical and religious contexts and traditions in which differing education systems are embedded. Similar, but reconstructed, perspectives are now attracting renewed efforts to 'bring culture back in' to contemporary research in the process of rediscovering 'the intellectual, methodological and theoretical premises upon which the foundations and traditions of comparative and international education have been built' (Hawkins et al, 1998, p. 1). These same foundations also celebrate a 'time-honoured commitment to policy-oriented research relevant to the world around it' (King, 1997, p. 90).

In related ways, mainstream educational research is today increasingly adopting cross-disciplinary frameworks and recognising that, while we can learn much from the experience of others, there are very real dangers in the uncritical transfer of policy and practice. With this has come renewed recognition of the fact that context (in its multiple dimensions) matters. These developments are reflected in, for example, the growth of cross-disciplinary and cross-faculty research centres, and in the changes in core research disciplines, such as the growth in attention given to 'socially-situated' and cultural psychology (Bruner, 1996). As discussed at length elsewhere (Crossley & Broadfoot, 1992), such action-oriented perspectives, core issues and multidisciplinary research strategies have long characterised much of the most reputable work carried out in the field of comparative and international education – along with recognition of the fact that studies of other systems can do much to 'tutor our judgement' (Stenhouse, 1979) and, paradoxically, help us to better understand education at home – wherever that may be. We therefore have much to be proud of in the traditions of our field, and much to benefit from in building creatively upon these foundations as we look to the future.

Reconceptualising the Field

New developments and challenges to the established traditions of comparative and international education are already visible but, to date, their cumulative impact and potential has not been coherently articulated in a framework related to the socio-economic transformations, intellectual shifts and research priorities characteristic of the emergent twenty-first century. Further work on this meta-analysis is under way (Crossley & Watson, 2001, forthcoming; Crossley & Jarvis, 2000) but, collectively, this body of work is intended as a stimulus and benchmark for others to build upon in shaping what could be a new phase of development for the field as a whole. In saying this, the teleological limitations of attempts to demarcate phases of development (see, for example, Brickman, 1988) can imply that the methods and concerns of early phases of any field inevitably become superseded and outdated. The reconceptualisation proposed here avoids such dangers by focusing upon the future, while recognising current trends and rebuilding upon the strengths of previous phases of scholarship and research. This, as already indicated, can help us to forge valuable linkages with fundamental social, cultural and historical traditions – in a way that acknowledges the implications and complexities of globalisation in a postmodern world where issues of culture and identity are heightened.

Early efforts to synthesise challenges to the post-war 'social sciences' phase of comparative and international education were made by Altbach & Kelly (1986) in their compilation of relevant articles, drawn from the *Comparative Education Review*. Reflecting upon what they saw as the theoretical dominance of structural functionalism, combined with positivist methodological assumptions, Altbach & Kelly identified four main challenges that had emerged since the last 'state of the art' reviews of the field in 1977 (see *Comparative Education Review*, 21, 1977; *Comparative Education*, 13, 1977). These were:

challenges to the nation state as the exclusive research framework;
challenges to input–output models and total reliance on quantification;
challenges to structural functionalism; and
the emergence of new substantive concerns, most notably gender research, institutional studies and critiques, the content and processes of education and the legitimisation of educational knowledge.

According to Kelly & Altbach (1988, p. 14), 'Prior to 1977 these issues scarcely entered the discourse of the field and were not promoted through its major journals or texts'.

Since then, however, much has changed with the impact of work such as Carnoy's (1974) *Education as Cultural Imperialism* stimulating varieties of world systems analyses that argue that education is affected more by external factors than those found within the country in question. Alternatively, other scholars have, since 1977, drawn attention to the importance of within-country comparisons and micro-level ethnographic studies (Heyman, 1979; Masemann, 1982; Crossley & Vulliamy, 1984). Moreover, the systematic application of qualitative research helped to challenge the dominance of theoretical frameworks derived from structural functionalism, and reinforced early advances in the application of interpretative traditions, critical theory and conflict studies (Apple, 1978; Arnove, 1980; Weiler, 1983).

Although Kelly & Altbach (1988) also pointed to the 'new realism' influencing more conservative perspectives that were emerging in the 1980s, the theoretical, methodological and substantive developments that have followed have been significant across a broad spectrum of inquiry. To some extent, the fourfold framework for analysis remains useful, and much contemporary work can still be located within the main categories. The challenge to the nation state as the unit of analysis, for example, has been pursued through a multilevel strategy by Bray & Thomas (1995), a comparative, subregional, format by Fry & Kempner (1996) and through detailed qualitative studies by a new generation of advocates (see the contributors to Crossley & Vulliamy, 1997). Similarly, theoretical challenges to structural-functionalism have advanced considerably through the work of scholars such as Paulston (1996) on social cartography; Cowen (1996) and Masemann & Welch (1997) on postmodernity; and Watson (1996), Green (1997) and others on globalisation and internationalism. Kelly's (1984) pioneering call for more substantive work on gender is now well represented in studies documented and conducted by researchers such as Stromquist (1998) and Sutherland & Cammish (1997), while influential comparative studies of international institutions and agencies (Jones, 1992, 1994; Leach, 1994; Arthur & Preston, 1996), the processes of teaching and learning (Broadfoot et al, 1993), privatisation, marketisation and globalisation (Colclough, 1997; Whitty et al, 1998) and school management and effectiveness in developing countries (Levin & Lockheed, 1993; Harber & Davies, 1997; Bush, 1998) demonstrate considerable attention to the once emergent themes identified by Altbach & Kelly.

It is pertinent, however, to return to the contemporary critique of educational research outlined at the outset, and to the implications of more recent socio-economic trends and developments. In this light, it is argued that much more remains to be done if the reconceptualisation of comparative and international education is to benefit from the recent resurgence of interest; and if we are to capitalise upon the current visibility, application and potential of the field for the improvement of educational policy and practice – and for the advancement of theory relating both to education and to the social sciences more generally. It is to ways in which such reconceptualisation can be achieved that we now turn.

New Priorities for Comparative and International Education

A Research Orientation

Perhaps, above all, it is clear that it is the research dimension and research potential of comparative and international education that currently underpins the contemporary resurgence of interest in the field. Moreover, it is research activity, and related research training, that has played a strategic part in the re-establishment of the institutional base. New research centres in comparative and/or international education have, for example, been established at the universities of Oxford, Bristol and Warwick in the United Kingdom (Schweisfurth, 1998); at the University of Hong Kong and elsewhere in South-east Asia (Bray, 1998) and at the University of Oslo and Oslo College in Norway and throughout Scandinavia (Tjeldvoll & Smehaugen, 1998).

Directories such as those by Dyer & King (1993) and Altbach & Tan (1995) usefully document the nature, extent and changing fortunes of institutional bases in the United Kingdom and USA; and the emergence of new comparative and international education societies and journals within, and especially beyond, the English-speaking world further testify to global growth and expansion (see Bray, 1998; Assié-Lumumba, 1998). Indeed, increasingly:

> *international organisations are also major producers of*
> *comparative education research. This includes the UNESCO*
> *Principal Regional Office for Education in Asia and the*
> *Pacific, which during the 1980s and early 1990s had declined*
> *in visibility but which is making renewed efforts to play an*
> *active role. It also includes the Asian Development Bank,*
> *which has emerged as a major figure in the education sector.*
> *Thus considerable work is being conducted outside*
> *universities as well as within them. (Bray, 1998, p. 8)*

Development agency involvement in the process of research and evaluation capacity-building in the South is strategically significant in strengthening the comparative and international constituency. This is demonstrated by the work of UNESCO (Buchert, 1998), the Commonwealth Secretariat (Crossley & Holmes, 1999) and the Norwegian Development Assistance Agency (NORAD) (1995) – and the United Kingdom Department for International Development's (DFID) enhanced commitment to research-based policy development (King, 1998; Allsop, 1998). Similarly, the growth of international research networks such as the European Union-funded PRESTIGE (Training and Mobility of Research) initiative coordinated by the Institute of International Education at Stockholm University (Fagerlind, 1998), the ongoing work of the International Association for the Evaluation of Educational Achievement (IEA) (Postlethwaite, 1999), and the various African Educational Research Networks (Mwiria & Wamahiu, 1995) represent innovative forms of research collaboration and partnerships within the field. Reflecting the shift from traditional academic teacher education courses, training and research that is carried out today often emphasises policy-oriented issues and evaluation activities, aimed at the specialist postgraduate level and acknowledging governmental interest in the efficacy of selected foreign policy and practice (Reynolds & Farrell, 1996; *Assessment in Education*, 1996). There are, of course, influential and distinguished exceptions, but this emergent pattern of action-oriented activity reveals the strategic importance for the field of comparative and international education to engage more centrally with contemporary professional and intellectual debates – while repositioning itself in ways that will more effectively realise the full potential of its distinctive perspectives and collective expertise.

Evidence-based Policy and Research

In addressing the ongoing critique levelled at educational research, comparative and international education can justifiably point to its traditional strengths as an applied, problem-oriented field (King, 1989). New ways, however, must be found to engage both directly, and critically, with the contemporary concerns and priorities of mainstream educational research and with the worldwide call for cumulative and professionally-oriented, evidence-based research and policy-making. As Goodson (1997) recently argued, in speaking at the British Educational Research Association's annual conference, it is time for educational researchers to reposition themselves closer to practice. Since mainstream educational researchers and policy-makers have also taken renewed interest in international trends, the potential for a distinctively strategic contribution, in this respect, from comparative and international education has increased. Noah (1986, p. 161), for example, pointed out some time ago that:

> comparative education is an applied field of study that finds
> particular justification in the service of evaluation,
> management, administration and policy-making. [But] like all
> fields, it is open to potential abuse by those who wish to use its
> results to support (or oppose) a specific program of change.

Secondary analyses and politically inspired interpretations of the influential IEA (International Association for the Evaluation of Educational Achievement) Studies illustrate such dangers well in a global context where relative positions on international league tables often tempt decision-makers to consider the adoption of apparently successful pedagogic practice from foreign cultural contexts. Comparativists can thus make a uniquely valuable contribution when reports of foreign educational policy are considered by reminding decision-makers that they can be:

> fully and fruitfully used in discussion only if they are seen as a
> part of a much broader enterprise, with HMIs [inspectors]
> contributing their particular insights along with others:

> *scholars, researchers and students whose job it is to take more*
> *sweeping views, not necessarily tied to this month's policy*
> *problem ... the health of policy-making in an interdependent*
> *world must depend in part on the health of comparative*
> *education research in the broadest sense. (Beattie & Brock,*
> *1990, p. 4)*

The explicitly comparative IEA studies are particularly pertinent examples of the sort of large-scale, cumulative and evidence-based research that is advocated by contemporary stakeholders in education. Ironically, however, criticism of this highly influential, and still evolving model, has come more from within the field of comparative and international education than it has from without. Dialogue and discourse across such boundaries can thus be much improved. This critique is also valuable because it draws attention to the limitations of policy transfer and to further lessons that can be learned from the comparative perspective. It is in considering such issues that distinctive implications for theory, context and culture re-emerge with renewed force and relevance.

Theoretical Implications of Context and Culture

It should, perhaps, not be too surprising that the IEA comparisons of school achievement should have gained widespread recognition in the broader arena of policy-making. The sequence of assessment studies produced, since their origins in the early 1960s, have focused upon issues relating to the quality of teaching and learning that have increasingly come to dominate the priorities and agendas of decision-makers worldwide. Data have been systematically quantified on a large scale, core school subjects such as science and mathematics have received concerted attention, and substantial resources have been invested in the research enterprise in countries drawn from a wide spectrum of developed and developing nations (Goldstein, 1996; Postlethwaite, 1999).

The critique noted earlier relates as much to the way in which findings have been used as it does to the methodological and theoretical limitations of the IEA studies themselves. Acknowledging this, Goldstein (1996) draws attention to the contextual relevance of IEA findings and the dilemmas encountered when attempts are made to focus upon comparisons of achievement across national systems of education. Such critiques draw more directly upon the core concepts of context and culture – concepts that remain central to the work of those specialists in the field of comparative and international research that have long questioned the methodological rationale of the IEA model. It is possible, however, to argue, as does Cumming (1996), that useful policy results can be more realistically derived from comparisons of differing groups within the same national education system data set – and that such findings can be related to differences in social and cultural factors. In the light of such issues, Kellaghan (1996) draws upon many insights and perspectives central to the comparative canon in outlining key parameters for those involved in the disciplined application of IEA findings in the policy arena. In doing this, Kellaghan helps to add renewed legitimacy to the distinctive characteristics of comparative and international research in education, in a policy context central to the management and performance concerns of governmental agencies worldwide. This discussion also draws attention back to the importance of contextual and cultural factors in cross-national research and to the dilemmas, long recognised by comparativists, associated with international transfer in all dimensions of educational research and development.

Rapprochement between Comparative and International Research

A useful irony is embedded in the foregoing analysis. Revealingly, the contextual critique emerges more strongly from the theoretically-oriented comparative tradition of the combined field of comparative and international education than it does from the more explicitly applied and action-oriented expertise associated with international education. This, it is argued, is one of the most fundamental issues for consideration in the reconceptualisation of the combined field; for it simultaneously demonstrates the weaknesses of *both* established traditions, while identifying priorities for future attention in a way that is of considerable theoretical and methodological significance. In broad scope, this relates to long-standing criticism of much 'international education' for being too closely related to policy agendas of the day, and to the implementation of reform projects tied to development assistance agency assumptions and priorities (Buchert & King, 1996; Samoff, 1996; Jones, 1998). Counterpoising this perspective is the critique of the more explicitly 'comparative' dimension of the field for being too preoccupied with abstract theoretical scholarship divorced from the real world of educational policy and practice (*International Journal of Educational Development*, 1995; Watson, 1998). While the polarisation of this analysis may oversimplify the issues involved, it is helpful, and the latter critique is reminiscent of the broader challenge to educational research that calls for cumulative, applied and professionally relevant research that is clearly, and unambiguously, communicated to policy-makers and practitioners.

Experience within the international education arena also points, somewhat ironically, to the very real limitations of undue reliance upon applied, policy-oriented studies (Crossley, 1998). In developing countries, greater degrees of austerity (Lewin, 1987) have long accentuated accountability, evaluation, project relevance and generalisability in research but, despite this, the success rate of many intended reforms has been disappointing, particularly with regard to their sustainability beyond periods of external funding (King, 1991; Buchert, 1998). Moreover, it is argued here that it is the failure of many international development initiatives to give sufficient weight to the broad spectrum of theoretical insights, and to contextual and cultural issues, that lies at the heart of this dilemma. It is only rarely that those working within the research culture of international development assistance are able to apply the literature, experience and perspectives characteristic of the more detached comparative social science constituency in any challenging and sustained way. Unfortunately, the irony is greater still, for, while the comparative dimension of our combined field accords particular premium to such issues, it is this constituency that is most open to the ongoing challenge to mainstream educational research for not adequately addressing the policy issues and practical concerns of the day. In this context, initiatives such as the amalgamation in 1997 of the former British Association of Teachers and Researchers in Overseas Education (BATROE) and the British Comparative and International Education Society (BCIES) to form the combined British Association for International and Comparative Education (BAICE), represents important structural and organisational bridge-building. This is a positive movement in itself, and one that helps to further consolidate efforts made to unite comparative and international education societies in the 1980s, while providing a foundation for more fundamental interpersonal, subcultural and intellectual advances in the future.

Perhaps, more intractably, the task of rapprochement will be more complex than this somewhat oversimplified portrayal and analysis implies, for there are often sound reasons for the persistence of intellectual and organisational divisions between research cultures and communities. There are also well-established traditions and 'political' and 'territorial' imperatives to negotiate; and, as Furlong (1998, p. 23) points out, educational research is 'constantly subject to fads and fashions, to competing, ill-defined and sometimes contradictory goals'. Moreover, to be realistic, we should recognise the limitations of research and not expect the impossible, or forget that:

> *The connection between research and practice is not one in*
> *which research influences practice, as many researchers might*
> *hope, nor one in which practice influences research as many*
> *might hope, but rather one in which both research and*
> *practice are influenced by and are perhaps even victims of*
> *the same shifting social and political context. (Kennedy, 1997,*
> *pp. 9-10)*

Recognition of the impact of such changing socio-political trends, nevertheless, points to a more profound rationale for concerted efforts towards reconceptualisation and rapprochement in comparative and international education. This arises because we now approach the new 'global' millennium, when old conceptual divisions between developed and developing countries are increasingly problematic, when global forces influence the educational arrangements of all nation states, and when issues relating to culture, identity and context are challenging rationalism and modernist assumptions and development priorities worldwide. In such times, the bridging of traditional divisions, the challenging of old certainties and the forging of new discourses is essential for the advancement of all fields of enquiry.

Widening the Discourse in Comparative and International Education

Central to the thesis developed here is the argument that the increasingly rapid pace of socio-economic change demands vastly improved forms of communication and interchange between human groups, organisations and cultures worldwide. This includes professional cultures, international agencies, specialists, policy-makers, practitioners, the public, and researchers across all disciplines and fields. Such cross-cultural bridging is essential if we are to better conceptualise and understand the dramatic changes that contemporary globalisation processes have set in train. Indeed, in tune with Huntington (1993), it is argued that the changes now being faced across the globe are as profound as any previously encountered. Globalisation, spurred on by 'appeals to unfettered capitalism' [1] is, however, progressing hand in hand with postmodern challenges to the Enlightenment project, positivistic science, modernisation theory, and rationalism itself. Tensions between ideas and developments that underpin globalisation on the one hand, and postmodernism on the other, thus generate what may be the most fundamental of all intellectual challenges of the present day. Dealing with such challenges will demand the bridging of much more than intellectual traditions and cultures. It will require fundamental social change and new discourses that recognise the limitations of deeply embedded ways of thinking about the world; for, as Giddens (1997, p. 2) points out, globalisation 'describes the increasing inter-penetration between individual life and global futures, something which ... is relatively new in history'. Giddens goes on to say that 'it is a wholly contradictory process' and that 'we are the first generation to enter a global age' (1997, p. 2). Discourses that can help improve our conceptualisation of globalisation processes while engaging with the diverse challenges raised by postmodern critiques of meta-narratives have the potential to go beyond the well-known limitations of deconstruction, and to contribute to advances that may be both affirmative and more effectively tuned to the cultural differences and multipolar geopolitics of the twenty-first century (Norris & Benjamin, 1996).

Within the field of comparative and international education, the reconceptualisation thesis articulated here suggests that there is much to be gained from a fundamental challenge to the barriers that limit wider debate and interchange, especially between what Altbach & Kelly (1986) labelled the 'new realists' and the postmodern proponents of critical scholarship. This is not to imply that comparative and international education should be too disparaging of itself for, within the parent field of education, it has always been particularly well placed to advance genuinely multidisciplinary research across cultural boundaries – with an inherent concern for contextualisation and respect for differing social constructions of reality. Nevertheless, given the turbulence of the times in which we live, there remains, as already expressed, much to be done – and it is to the potential of a number of the more significant possibilities that we now turn in more specific detail.

Research and Scholarship

The broad epistemological issues raised in the previous section help to highlight the significance of strengthening linkages between the predominantly action-oriented, applied, international constituency of the field, and the more traditionally theoretical, comparative dimension. This also points to the importance of forging a more substantial dialectic between empirical research from all paradigmatic foundations – and critical, in-depth scholarship. Unfortunately, intensified financial, managerial and micro-political imperatives have in recent years been notorious in increasing the pressures on researchers to compete rather than collaborate, and to seek new externally-funded projects before sustained reflection upon the findings of 'completed' studies has been possible. Such missed opportunities and conflicts of interest can be costly in themselves, and undue haste, often generated by external pressures, does little to improve the range and quality of research dissemination repeatedly called for by concerned stakeholders. Efforts to bridge the research and scholarship divide also draw attention back to the limitations of prevailing research cultures that separate the study and conceptualisation of education in 'developing countries' from other dimensions of comparative and international research – all the more so in a world where global forces have an increasingly influential impact in all socio-economic contexts. Despite encouraging organisational trends, barriers between the personnel, networks and literatures of researchers working on 'European' and 'development' studies, for example, remain pervasive and detrimental to the field as a whole, even when faced with the questionable legitimacy of long-established socio-economic classifications, and the dramatic impact of major socio-economic transformations characteristic of the late twentieth century.

Cross-disciplinary Studies

Discourses and studies that build upon the multidisciplinary traditions of the field are particularly apposite in times when 'cultural forces' (Mazrui, 1990) and political transformations (Bray & Lee, 1997) are repeatedly demonstrating the limitations of linear, teleological assumptions about national and international development strategies. Holding significant potential for comparative and international education at this time are studies that combine the field's long engagement with language, literacy and culture (Masemann & Welch, 1997), with the advancement of the post-colonial critique (Tikly, 1998). This has the potential to stimulate new developments that more firmly recognise the contemporary significance of intellectual frameworks that deal with issues of identity, culture, race, gender and class. Compatible with multilevel analyses, post-colonial applications can be advanced, for example, through critical ethnography (Masemann, 1982) and through further applications of the meta-level studies of critical theorists such as Bourdieu & Passeron (1977), Habermas (1978, 1990), Apple (1993) and Giroux (1997). Post-colonial frameworks could also do much to challenge the Eurocentric profile of much postmodern theorising and the colonialist image of some ethnography, in a way that could help to better demonstrate their contemporary potential for applied, policy-oriented research. The relevance of this for the reconceptualisation and widening of the discourse of international education is, perhaps, especially pertinent in line with the broader components of reconceptualisation outlined earlier. Indeed, as documented by Torres (1998), for many years, comparativists have sustained interest in the work of Freire (1974) and Freire & Macedo (1987) and its implications for development activities. The cultural critiques of Mazrui (1990, 1992), Thaman (1993) and other non-Western analysts have also been acknowledged within the field – but the consistent application of such perspectives within the mainstream of international education discourse and development work remains limited or confined to the activities of Non-governmental Organisations (NGOs), detached theorists or polemical critics. On the other hand, there are some shifts in thinking and praxis inspired by the work of Freire, Chambers (1992) and others, that demonstrate ways in which more concerted post-colonial analyses may help to advance theory while contributing in a productive way to the improvement of educational policy and practice in pluralist and multicultural communities. As with the postmodern critique and associated literature, however, the dangers of inaccessible theorising obscuring the applied potential of such cross-discipline and cross-cultural research deserve attention in their own right.

The mainstream challenge to what Becher (1989) has called 'academic tribes and territories', and reconsideration of the philosophical and historical traditions of Sadler's approach to comparative education also have much in common with the rationale and goals of contemporary sociocultural studies of education (Wertsch, 1995). Closer working relationships between social scientists from different fields thus have much to offer, as acknowledged by the Association of Learned Societies in the Social Sciences' recent efforts to demonstrate the benefits to be gained from multidisciplinary work through the recently established British Academy of Learned Societies for the Social Sciences.

Indeed, methodologically fruitful advances could arise from more focused studies of the theory and practice of comparative methodology across the social sciences. Øyen's (1990) work, for the International Sociological Association, is indicative of the methodological lessons that may be learned from other comparative fields, and this is appropriately related to Galtung's (1990) plea for pluralism in theory formation for social research. At a more specific level, the potential for innovative cross-disciplinary comparative and international research is demonstrated by studies of cognition and culture that are beginning to open up new insights into the nature and implications of legitimate 'ways of knowing' in differing cultural contexts (Oatley, 1992). Masemann (1990) echoed such principles on a broader platform in her Presidential Address for the American Comparative Education Society, and Noah (1986, p. 161) reminds us that:

> A comparative approach enlarges the framework within which
> we can view the results obtained in a single country: by
> providing counter instances, it challenges us to refine our
> theories and test their validity against the reality of different
> societies; and, by providing parallel results, it can yield
> important confirmation of results obtained elsewhere.

Multiple Frames of Reference and Units of Analysis

The initial challenge to the nation state as the primary unit of analysis has been sustained and reinforced in more recent years by the ethnographic movement at the micro-level and by the rapidly changing socio-political events of the 1990s. To Bray & Thomas's (1995) rationalistic plea for multilevel analysis, writers such as McLeash & Phillips (1998) have thus focused upon the distinctive issues relating to educational reconstruction in societies facing rapid socio-political transition. Others have seen potential in comparative studies of Pacific Rim contexts (Sullivan, 1998), and of small states (Bray & Packer, 1993;

Crossley & Holmes, 1999). Thus, Cowen (1996, p. 150) refers to 'transitology' and the need to give attention to forces beyond the nation state, and to 'international and global structures associated with tendencies towards "post-modernity"' in his search for a 'new' comparative education. Paulston (1998, p. 9) too endorses the opening up of the comparative and international discourse to the debate of postmodern ideas, noting that: 'letting go of modernity's language, let alone its essentialist and instrumental vision is easier advocated than achieved'. Building on Rust's (1991) postmodern challenge, Paulston's (1996, 1998) advocacy of social cartography as a framework for comparative studies of education suggests that:

> *as comparativists we are ... well positioned to ... become*
> *social cartographers, to compare and map multiple*
> *interpretations of social and educational life ... we are*
> *learning to recognise and include views from the margins,*
> *thus enlarging the scope of our vision and the diversity ... of*
> *our representations. (1998, p. 23)*

Miller (1991) captures the importance of recognising the 'other' in similar terms when he applies place theory to the dilemmas faced by small states at the periphery of international decision-making, and argues that:

> *Marginal countries and marginal groups within these*
> *countries are in the most favourable position to take ... risk.*
> *They can convert disadvantage into opportunity and move to a*
> *more central place in the continued development of human*
> *civilisation. (Miller, 1991, p. 290)*

From this perspective, it can be seen that much can be learned from alternative units of analysis and from intellectual frameworks that apply postmodern notions of, for example, place theory and social cartography. Watson's (1998) plea for clear applications remains important, however, if the advantages of such theoretical frameworks and units of analysis are to be realised and communicated in a way that is accessible to those seeking assistance in the qualitative improvement of education policy and practice. This returns the debate to the initial critique of mainstream educational research, and to the call for more substantial, cumulative, applied and relevant evidence-based policy and research.

Educational Research, Policy and Practice

In many ways, the present analysis began with the call for a strengthening of the relationship between educational research, policy and practice. Much has already been said on this core theme to demonstrate how comparative and international experience can make a distinctive contribution to the broader debate. In particular, it is argued that the tendency for much traditional comparative research to focus upon detached theory, or, at best, comparisons of policy – and for much international work to eschew theory or implicitly adopt a modernist perspective, deserves concerted attention in the future. The postmodern debate articulated earlier, for example, helps to demonstrate the potential and legitimacy of detailed qualitative research carried out within the field, of the opportunities presented by critical ethnography and of the centrality of cultural context in reputable studies designed to contribute to improved policy and practice (see, for example, Masemann, 1982, 1990; Alexander, 1996). In this arena, the strengths of collaborative studies carried out by combinations of insiders and outsiders are enhanced (Crossley, 1990; Dyer & Choksi, 1997). This is well demonstrated by the policy relevance of Broadfoot et al's (1997) studies of perceptions of teaching in England and France and Stuart et al's (1997) efforts to improve classroom practice through action research in Lesotho. Strengthening partnerships between insiders and outsiders, researchers and practitioners, and policy formulators and analysts could thus play an integral part in the reconceptualisation of the field as a whole. However, while the case for the practitioner researcher is strong, Jarvis (1999) calls for broader scope within the field of education, and King (1997, p. 85) warns that 'part of our conceptual reorientation lies in escaping from a purely pedagogical preoccupation: our "constituency" today includes not just other academics but a limitless array of participants'. Research strategies such as Participatory Rural Appraisal (Chambers, 1992) are thus finding increased favour in international development work focused upon non-formal education and other community empowerment activities (NORAD, 1995; DFID, 1997). Research must also encompass a much wider spectrum of teaching and learning sites and issues if it is to deal effectively with the uncertainties, technologies and imperatives of the future.

Moreover, as mainstream educational researchers engage with comparative and international studies, many additional insights and benefits, both intellectual and professional, may accrue. This is evident in recent policy work by Ball (1998, p. 117) in which he highlights the political motives for many cross-national studies where 'proposals and justifications for reform in one country provide resources for advocates and politicians interested in promoting change in others'. While Ball goes on to argue that 'This is not so much a matter of policy exchange but the reinforcement of shared assumptive worlds', he also calls for 'more research and more theoretical development in the field of international policy' (p. 117). Clearly, this identifies an important vein for future comparative studies but it also re-emphasises the dangers of inadvertently reinforcing policy studies in a subfield where a detailed knowledge of educational context and practice is often limited, and when evidenced-based research is given a high premium by policy-makers and other key stakeholders.

Finally, fundamental reconceptualisation must undoubtedly take greater cognisance of the advances in the field beyond the English language literature or dominant European discourses. As already argued, increased recognition of differing social constructions of reality, different cultural conceptions of development priorities (Cheng, 1997) and innovative work on teaching and learning in contrasting sociocultural contexts (Little, 1988; Watkins & Biggs, 1996) can all help to improve our impact upon specific policy and practice, while strengthening genuinely global theoretical insights and understandings. As Hawkins et al (1998, p. 1) point out:

> To accomplish a truly democratic education, it is necessary to promote dialogues among and across different perspectives and academic communities around the world.

Conclusions

In the light of a critique of the nature and evolution of comparative and international education, the discussion articulates ways in which the fundamental reconceptualisation of this multidisciplinary field could be advanced. As the turn of a new century takes place, it is argued that increasingly rapid socio-economic changes make such reconceptualisation essential. Tensions stimulated by the pace of globalisation, and the simultaneous impact of postmodern critiques of the Enlightenment project, generate the most fundamental intellectual challenges of the present day. These tensions underpin the case for reconceptualisation in our field, although it is further enhanced by the contemporary emergence of a sustained challenge to the nature and worth of mainstream educational research – and to its relevance and accessibility to those engaged in the improvement of policy and practice worldwide.

Looking to the future, it is argued that the multidisciplinary traditions of the field make it especially well placed to deal with the increasingly complex, global and cross-cultural issues that will characterise the twenty-first century. It is, for example, a field that has long recognised the significance of global forces in educational research and development, and one that has consistently examined the dilemmas associated with the transfer of educational policy and practice from one cultural context to another. While some of the traditional strengths of the field provide a foundation for renewed growth, the case for fundamental critique and reconstruction, nevertheless, demands priority attention – if its potential to contribute to the improvement of policy and practice, or to advance theory in the educational and social sciences, is to be fully and effectively realised.

This process must necessarily involve a reconsideration of long accepted assumptions and subcultures within the field, and a reconceptualisation that engenders new priorities, discourses and modes of operation that are more closely in tune with the exigencies of the contemporary world. Of primary importance in this respect is the need for fundamental reconceptualisation and rapprochement relating to the comparative and international dimensions of the field. The significance of this is explicated with reference to the need for new or revitalised forms of discourse; for greater integration between empirical research and theoretical scholarship; for the advancement of cross-disciplinary studies; for the application and development of new frames of reference and units of analysis and – perhaps above all – for a strengthening of the relationship between educational research, policy and practice.

A research orientation for the field, if systematically but creatively constructed, is especially pertinent in a world marked by increasingly powerful global trends, and cross-cultural tensions founded upon issues of culture, identity and difference. Such turbulent times will also generate their own research issues and priorities, which will, in turn, influence the nature of the work conducted. While it is not the place here to anticipate substantive trends in detail, the analysis conducted so far suggests that these will inevitably be influenced by international and local agendas and include studies of the further advancement and critique of the neo-liberal performance model of education; increased focus on culture, identity and learning in differing contexts; policy implications of the cross-cultural transfer of educational innovations; large-scale cross-national studies building upon the IEA model and increasingly funded by international agencies; the extension of mainstream/national studies into the international arena; the changing nature and role of international agencies; the impact and potential of information and communication technologies; studies of power, gender and marginalised groups, such as refugees, the disadvantaged, or small states; and the relationship between education and poverty across all levels of society. Consideration of such substantive issues and of the nature and place of specialist teaching in a repositioned comparative and international education will be pursued elsewhere, but it is clear from the analysis so far that challenging advantages and problems may arise from the bridging of discourses.

While closer linkages with mainstream educational research communities, debates and agendas may, for example, help to strengthen comparative and international education, the dangers of the uncritical transfer of dominant research paradigms, theories and agendas also arise, and help to re-emphasise the field's distinctive strengths and expertise that relate to the study of the two core concepts of context and culture.

Indeed, for these reasons, it is argued that a reconceptualised field of comparative and international education will be especially well placed for the future study of issues relating to globalisation, culture and identity, and of the continued emergence and impact of international educational agendas. To some extent, this further challenges the nation state as the primary unit of analysis without, as demonstrated by Green (1997), denying its continued relevance. A case is therefore made for the reconceptualised field to be more explicitly associated with the sociocultural study of education in context. This reaffirms the principle that context matters; but repositions the field to study education in all its varied and new forms, with regard to contextual factors operating at all levels, ranging from the organisational to the global.

Returning to theoretical and methodological themes and to the debate relating to policy and practice, it is clear that there is much to learn about the interrelationship between theoretical scholarship and applied research from, and within, the field of comparative and international education. Firstly, the dangers of an either/or conceptualisation tempting researchers to abandon culturally sensitive theoretical studies in the face of the contemporary 'applied' critique are well demonstrated by the cautionary experience of much policy-oriented research carried out in developing countries. However, tensions long existing between the comparative and international traditions also help to reinforce criticism of too much research becoming *too* divorced from the needs of policy and practice.

The plea here is therefore for greater recognition of the interdependence between improved theory, policy and practice, and of the potential of related bridge-building between the various research discourses and professional cultures involved.

As I have demonstrated, the field of comparative and international education can add much to broad social science debates in this respect, and it can, and should, do this confidently in the light of its own distinctive experience and traditions. This will, in itself, contribute to the process of strengthening its own institutional base through the professional networks and research capacity-building initiatives that it is equally well placed to support. This need not imply that there is one 'definitive' path to follow, for, in sympathy with King (1989, p. 37), it is argued that such proposals could 'divide comparative education's scholars from each other while distracting attention from urgent tasks, from new opportunities, and indeed from the need to continue our growth'. A strengthened institutional base may, therefore, be best seen as a core component of a thoroughly reconceptualised field, that welcomes the incorporation of multiple research discourses, and simultaneously supports further advancement through disciplined comparative and international initiatives conducted in collaboration with mainstream educational researchers and their frameworks and organisations. Such a

Michael Crossley

combined strategy for development and repositioning may well help the field to accommodate the systematic and rational impulse for renewed growth – with the inevitable strategic and political imperatives of all fields of study – in a way that is compatible with the respect for identity and difference that is so characteristic of the postmodern era.

Acknowledgement

This article is based upon a keynote presentation made at the Inaugural Conference of the British Association for International and Comparative Education (BAICE), University of Reading, 11 September 1998.

Note

[1] I owe thanks to Phillip Jones, University of Sydney, for this evocative phrase.

References

Alexander, R. (1996) *Other Primary Schools and Ours: hazards of international comparison*. Warwick: University of Warwick, Centre for Research and Evaluation in Primary Education.

Allsop, T. (1998) Seeking after Partnerships in Research, *NORRAG News*, 23, pp. 30-31.

Altbach, P.G. & Kelly, G.P. (Eds) (1986) *New Approaches to Comparative Education*. Chicago: University of Chicago Press.

Altbach, P.G. & Tan, J. (1995) *Programs and Centres in Comparative and International Education: a global inventory*. Buffalo: State University of New York.

Apple, M. (1978) Ideology, Reproduction and Educational Reform, *Comparative Education Review*, 22, pp. 367-387.

Apple, M. (1993) *Official Knowledge: democratic education in a conservative age*. London: Routledge.

Arnove, R. (Ed.) (1980) *Philanthropy and Cultural Imperialism: the foundations at home and abroad*. Boston: G.K. Hall.

Arthur, L. & Preston, R. (1996) *Quality in Overseas Consultancy: understanding the issues*. Warwick: University of Warwick/The British Council.

Assessment in Education (1996) Special Issue: The IEA Studies, 3.

Assié-Lumumba, N.T. (Ed.) (1998) *Journal of Comparative Education and International Relations in Africa*, 1.

Ball, S. (Ed.) (1998) *Comparative Perspectives in Education Policy*, Special Issue of *Comparative Education*, 34.

Beattie, N. & Brock, C. (1990) Editorial, *Compare*, 20, pp. 2-4.

Becher, T. (1989) *Academic Tribes and Territories*. London: Longman.

Bourdieu, P. & Passeron, J.C. (1977) *Reproduction in Education, Society and Culture*. London: Sage.

Bray, M. (1998) Comparative Education Research in the Asian Region: implications for the field as a whole, *Comparative Education Society of Hong Kong Bulletin*, No. 1 (May), pp. 6-10.

Bray, M. & Lee, W.O. (Eds) (1997) Education and Political Transition: implications of Hong Kong's change of sovereignty, Special Issue of *Comparative Education*, 33.

Bray, M. & Packer, S. (1993) *Education in Small States: concepts, challenges and strategies*. Oxford: Pergamon.

Bray, M. & Thomas, R.M. (1995) Levels of Comparison in Educational Studies: different insights from different literatures and the value of multi-level analyses, *Harvard Educational Review*, 65, pp. 472-490.

Brickman, W.W. (1988) History, Concepts and Methods, in T.N. Postlethwaite (Ed.) *The Encyclopaedia of Comparative Education and National Systems of Education*. Oxford: Pergamon.

Broadfoot, P., Osborn, M., Gilly, M. & Bucher, A. (1993) *Perceptions of Teaching. Primary School Teachers in England and France*. London: Cassell.

Bruner, J. (1996) *The Culture of Education*. Cambridge, MA: Harvard University Press.

Buchert, L. (Ed.) (1998) *Education Reform in the South in the 1990s*. Paris: UNESCO.

Buchert, L. & King, K. (1996) *Consultancy and Research in International Education*. Bonn: German Foundation for International Development.

Bush, T. (Ed.) (1998) *School Management in the People's Republic of China*, Special Issue of *Compare*, 28.

Carnoy, M. (1974) *Education as Cultural Imperialism*. New York: Longman.

Chambers, R. (1992) Rural Appraisal: rapid, relaxed and participatory, Institute of Development Studies Discussion Paper. Brighton: University of Sussex.

Cheng, K.M. (1997) Qualitative Research and Educational Policy-making: approaching the reality in developing countries, in M. Crossley & G. Vulliamy (Eds) *Qualitative Educational Research in Developing Countries*. New York: Garland.

Colclough, C. (Ed.) (1997) *Marketizing Education and Health in Developing Countries*. Oxford: Clarendon Press.

Comparative Education (1977) *Comparative Education – its present state and future prospects*, 13.

Comparative Education Review (1977) *State of the Art Review*, 21.

Cowen, R. (Ed.) (1996) *Comparative Education and Post-modernity*, Special Issue of *Comparative Education*, 32.

Crossley, M. (1990) Collaborative Research, Ethnography and Comparative and International Education in the South Pacific, *International Journal of Educational Development*, 10, pp. 37-46.

Crossley, M. (1998) The Place of Research and Evaluation in Educational Transformation: cross-cultural issues and research capacity building in

Belize – Central America, paper presented to the Tenth World Congress of Comparative Education Societies, Cape Town, South Africa.

Crossley, M. & Broadfoot, P. (1992) Comparative and International Research in Education: scope, problems, potential, *British Educational Research Journal*, 18, pp. 99-112.

Crossley, M. & Holmes, K. (1999) *Educational Development in the Small States of the Commonwealth*. London: Commonwealth Secretariat.

Crossley, M. & Jarvis, P. (Eds) (2000) *Comparative Education for the 21st Century*, Special Millennium Number of *Comparative Education*, 36.

Crossley, M. & Vulliamy, G. (1984) Case-study Research Methods and Comparative Education, *Comparative Education*, 20, pp. 193-207.

Crossley, M. & Vulliamy, G. (Eds) (1997) *Qualitative Educational Research in Developing Countries*. New York: Garland.

Crossley, M. & Watson, K. (2001) *Comparative and International Research in Education*. London: Routledge (forthcoming).

Cumming, A. (1996) IEA's Studies of Language Education: their scope and contributions, in Special Issue of *Assessment in Education: The IEA Studies*, 3, pp. 143-160.

Department for International Development (1997) *Eliminating World Poverty: a challenge for the 21st century*. London: HMSO.

Dyer, C. & Choksi, A. (1997) North–South Collaboration in Educational Research: reflections on Indian experience, in M. Crossley & G. Vulliamy (Eds) *Qualitative Educational Research in Developing Countries*. New York: Garland.

Dyer, C. & King, K. (Eds) (1993) *The British resource in International Education and Training*. Edinburgh: University of Edinburgh.

Fagerlind, I. (1998) *Prestige Newsletter*, 1.

Fraser, S.E. (1964) *Jullien's Plan for Comparative Education – 1816-1817*. New York: Bureau of Publications, Teachers College Columbia.

Freire, P. (1974) *Pedagogy of the Oppressed*. London: Penguin.

Freire, P. & Macedo, D. (1987) *Literacy. Reading the Word and the World*. London: Routledge & Kegan Paul.

Fry, G. & Kempner, K. (1996) A Sub-national Perspective for Comparative Research: education and development in North-east Brazil and North-east Thailand, *Comparative Education*, 32, pp. 333-360.

Furlong, J. (1998) Educational Research: meeting the challenge, An Inaugural Lecture. Bristol: University of Bristol.

Galtung, J. (1990) Theory Formation in Social Research: a plea for pluralism, in E. Øyen (Ed.) *Comparative Methodology*. London: Sage.

Giddens, A. (1997) Excerpts from a keynote address at the UNRISD Conference on globalization and citizenship, *UNRISD News*, 15, pp. 1-3.

Giroux, H. (1997) *Pedagogy and the Politics of Hope: theory, culture and schooling*. Oxford: Westview Press.

Goldstein, H. (1996) Introduction, in Special Issue of *Assessment in Education: The IEA Studies*, 3.

Goodson, I. (1997) The Educational Researcher as a Public Intellectual, The Lawrence Stenhouse Lecture, presented at the Annual Conference of the British Educational Research Association.

Gray, J. (1995) Education: a review of ESRC supported work (unpublished).

Green, A. (1997) *Education, Globalization and the Nation State.* London: Macmillan.

Habermas, J. (1978) *Knowledge and Human Interests.* London: Heinemann.

Habermas, J. (1990) *Moral Consciousness and Communicative Action.* Cambridge: Polity Press.

Halls, W.D. (1977) Comparative Studies in Education: a personal view, *Comparative Education*, 13, pp. 81-86.

Hans, N. (1959) *Comparative Education.* London: Routledge & Kegan Paul.

Harber, C. & Davies, L. (1997) *School Management and Effectiveness in Developing Countries.* London: Cassell.

Hargreaves, D. (1996) Teaching as a Research Based Profession: possibilities and prospects, The Teacher Training Agency Annual Lecture 1996. London: Teacher Training Agency.

Hawkins, J., Rust, V., Stromquist, N. & Torres, C.A. (1998) *Comparative Education Review* Editorship Changes Hands after Ten Years, *Comparative and International Education Society Newsletter*, 118, pp. 1-4.

Heyman, R. (1979) Comparative Education from an Ethnomethodological Perspective, *Comparative Education*, 15, pp. 241-249.

Higginson, J.K. (Ed.) (1979) *Selections from Michael Sadler.* Liverpool: Dejall & Meyorre.

Huntington, S. (1993) The Clash of Civilizations? *Foreign Affairs*, 72, pp. 22-49.

International Journal of Educational Development (1995) Special Issue: *Globalisation and Learning*, 16.

Jarvis, P. (1999) *The Practitioner-Researcher.* San Francisco: Jossey–Bass.

Jones, P. (1992) *World Bank Financing of Education. Lending, Learning and Development.* London: Routledge.

Jones, P. (1994) United Nations Agencies, in *Encyclopaedia of Educational Research*, 6th edn. New York: Macmillan.

Jones, P. (1998) Globalisation and Internationalism: democratic prospects for world education, *Comparative Education*, 34, pp. 143-155.

Kandel, I.L. (1933) *Studies in Comparative Education.* Boston: Houghton & Mifflin.

Kellaghan, T. (1996) IEA Studies and Educational Policy, *Assessment in Education: principles, policy and practice*, 3, pp. 143-160.

Kelly, G. (1984) Women's Access to Education in the Third World: myths and realities, in S. Acker (Ed.) *World Yearbook of Education 1984. Women in Education.* New York: Kogan Page.

Kelly, G.P. & Altbach, P.G. (1988) Alternative Approaches in Comparative Education, in T.N. Postlethwaite (Ed.) *The Encyclopaedia of Comparative Education and National Systems of Education.* Oxford: Pergamon.

Michael Crossley

Kennedy, M.K. (1997) The Connection between Research and Practice, *Educational Researcher*, 26(8), pp. 4-12.

King, E. (1989) Comparative Investigation of Education: an evolutionary process, *Prospects*, XIX, pp. 369-379.

King, E.J. (1997) A Turning point in Comparative Education: retrospect and prospect, in C. Kodran (Ed.) *Essays in Honour of Wolfgang Mitter*. Bonn: Böhlan Verlag.

King, K. (1991) *Aid and Education in the Developing World*. London: Longman.

King, K. (Ed.) (1998) *Knowledge Generation in Higher Education, NORRAG News*, 23, pp. 2-4.

Leach, F. (1994) Expatriates as agents of cross-cultural transmission, *Compare*, 24, pp. 217-232.

Levin, H.M. & Lockheed, M.E. (Eds) (1993) *Effective Schools in Developing Countries*. London: Falmer Press.

Lewin, K.M. (1987) *Education in Austerity: options for planners*. Paris: UNESCO International Institute for Educational Planning.

Little, A. (1988) *Learning from Developing Countries*. London: University of London Institute of Education.

Mallinson, V. (1960) *An Introduction to the Study of Comparative Education*. London: Heinemann.

Masemann, V.L. (1982) Critical Ethnography in the Study of Comparative Education, *Comparative Education Review*, 26, pp. 1-15.

Masemann, V.L. (1990) Ways of Knowing, *Comparative Education Review*, 34, pp. 463-473.

Masemann, V. & Welch, A. (Eds) (1997) *Tradition, Modernity and Post-modernity in Comparative Education*, Special Double Issue of *International Review of Education*, 43.

Mazrui, A.A. (1990) *Cultural Forces in World Politics*. London: James Currey.

Mazrui, A.A. (1992) Towards Diagnosing and Treating Cultural Dependency: the case of the African university, *International Journal of Educational Development*, 12, pp. 95-111.

McLeash, E.A. & Phillips, D. (Eds) (1998) *Processes of Transition in Education Systems*. Oxford: Symposium Books.

Miller, E. (1991) *Men at Risk*. Kingston: Jamaica Publishing House.

Morrow, R.A. & Torres, C.A. (1995) *Social Theory and Education. A Critique of Theories of Social and Cultural Reproduction*. Albany: State University of New York.

Mwiria, K. & Wamahiu, S. (Eds) (1995) *Issues in Educational Research in Africa*. Nairobi: East African Educational Publishers.

Noah, H.J. (1996) The Use and Abuse of Comparative Education, in P.G. Altbach & G.P. Kelly (Eds) *New Approaches to Comparative Education*. Chicago: University of Chicago Press.

Noah, H.J. & Eckstein, M.A. (1969) *Towards a Science of Comparative Education*. New York: Macmillan.

NORAD (1995) *NORAD's Support to the Education Sector. Basic Principles. Oslo:* NORAD.

Norris, C. & Benjamin, A. (1996) *What is Deconstruction?* Boston: Academy Editions.

Oatley, K. (1992) *Best Laid Schemes: the psychology of emotions.* Cambridge: Cambridge University Press.

Øyen, E. (Ed.) (1990) *Comparative Methodology. Theory and Practice in International Social Research.* London: Sage.

Paulston, R.G. (1996) Mapping the Post-modernity Debate in Comparative Education Discourse, University of Pittsburgh (unpublished).

Paulston, R.G. (Ed.) (1998) *Social Cartography. Mapping Ways of Seeing Social and Educational Change.* New York: Garland.

Postlethwaite, T.N. (1999) *International Studies of Educational Achievement: methodological issues.* Hong Kong: Comparative Education Research Centre, University of Hong Kong.

Reimers, F. & McGinn, N. (1997) *Informed Dialogue. Using Research to Shape Education Policy around the World.* Westport: Praeger.

Reynolds, D. & Farrell, S. (1996) *Worlds Apart? A Review of International Surveys of Educational Achievement Including England.* London: HMSO.

Rust, V.D. (1991) Post-modernism and Its Comparative Implications, *Comparative Education Review*, 35, pp. 610-626.

Sadler, M. (1900) How Far Can We Learn Anything of Practical Value from the Study of Foreign Systems of Education? in J.H. Higginson (Ed.) (1979) *Selections from Michael Sadler.* Liverpool: Dejail & Meyorre.

Samoff, J. (1996) Which Priorities and Strategies for Education? *International Journal of Educational Development*, 16, pp. 249-271.

Schweisfurth, M. (1998) Resilience, Resistance and Responsiveness: comparative and international education at UK universities, University of Warwick (unpublished).

Sroufe, G.E. (1997) Improving 'the Awful Reputation' of Educational Research, *Educational Researcher*, 26(7) pp. 26-28.

Stenhouse, L. (1979) Case-study and Comparative Education. Particularity and Generalisation, *Comparative Education*, 15, pp. 5-11.

Stromquist, N. (Ed.) (1998) *Women in the Third World. An Encyclopaedia of Contemporary Issues.* New York: Garland.

Stuart, J., Morojele, M. & Lefoka, P. (1997) Improving our Practice: collaborative classroom action research in Lesotho, in M. Crossley & G. Vulliamy (Eds) *Qualitative Educational Research in Developing Countries.* New York: Garland.

Sullivan, K. (Ed.) (1998) *Education and Change in the Pacific Rim.* Oxford: Symposium Books.

Sutherland, M.B. & Cammish, N.K. (Eds) (1997) *Aspects of Gender, Education and Development*, Special Issue of *Compare*, 27.

Teacher Training Agency (TTA) (1996) *Teaching as a Research-based Profession: promoting excellence in teaching.* London: TTA.

Thaman, K.H. (1993) Culture and the Curriculum, in M. Crossley (Ed.) Special Issue of *Comparative Education: Education in the South Pacific*, 29, pp. 249-260.

Tikly, L. (1998) Post-colonialism and Education, paper presented to the Tenth World Congress of Comparative Educational Societies, Cape Town, South Africa.

Tjeldvoll, A. & Smehaugen, A. (1998) *Scandinavian Comparative Education Research in Progress*. Oslo: Nordic Network of International and Comparative Education (NICE).

Tooley, J. (1998) *Educational Research. A Critique*. London: Office for Standards in Education.

Torres, C.A. (1998) Paulo Freire, paper presented to the Tenth World Congress of Comparative Education Societies, Cape Town, South Africa.

UNESCO (1998) *Our Creative Diversity. Report on the World Commission on Culture and Development*. Paris: UNESCO.

Watkins, D.A. & Biggs, J.B. (Eds) (1996) *The Chinese Learner. Cultural, Psychological and Contextual Influences*. Hong Kong: Comparative Education Research Centre.

Watson, K. (Ed.) (1996) *Globalisation and Learning*. Special Issue of *International Journal of Educational Development*, 16.

Watson, K. (1998) Memories, Models and Mapping: the impact of geopolitical changes on comparative studies in education, *Compare*, 28, pp. 5-31.

Watson, K. & Williams, P. (1984) Comparative Studies and International Awareness in Teacher Education: the need for reappraisal, *Journal of Education for Teaching*, 10, pp. 249-255.

Weiler, H.N. (1983) Legislation, Expertise and Participation: strategies of compensatory legitimisation in educational policy, *Comparative Education Review*, 27, pp. 254-277.

Wertsch, J. (1995) *Socio-cultural Studies of Mind*. Cambridge: Cambridge University Press.

Whitty, G., Power, S. & Halpin, D. (1998) *Devolution and Choice in Education*. Buckingham: Open University Press.

Contextual and Methodological Influences on Trends in Comparative and International Educational Research [1]

ROSEMARY PRESTON

This chapter discusses the ways in which international and global trends are influencing educational development and associated research, substantively, methodologically and in terms of outcomes achieved. The chapter refers to contemporary research into educational development, which is seen as a response to the transition to a technologically driven, neo-liberal global market with new regional substructures, its impact on the structure of labour markets and widening social differentiation. Substantively, it cites studies in the politics, economics and sociology of educational adjustment to the market for more and less included categories. In the case of the former, there is the shift to competency-based assessment, international accreditation systems and decentralised educational management. With considerable blurring of boundaries, there is for the latter, in all parts of the world, the complex business of education for the alleviation of poverty, funded through different types of aid system and implemented by voluntary service organisations. In terms of methods, referring to education in either mode, the chapter relates contemporary interest in multidisciplinarity, qualitative techniques, evaluation and accountability to the changing infrastructures of international educational research, within these global influences. Here it cites collaborative, team-based cross-national comparative studies and consultancy. It goes on to discuss the implications of this for organic and mechanistic dissemination, at different levels of analysis, challenging recent criticisms of adequacy. In conclusion, consideration is given to the social and intellectual outcomes of the trends and processes described and the extent to which they may serve to widen or reduce differentiation within and between states.

In doing this, the intention is to construct some modest conceptual coherence out of observed trends in international educational development research over the last decade and a half. A working assumption of the chapter is that there is little that is essentially new in the practices currently being promoted. It is the changing contextual influences that explain their present configuration. Another assumption is that, as globally inspired, the differential language of the description of these changes in different kinds of state is a political mechanism for maintaining other forms of inter-state differentiation. It is not necessarily based on different national characteristics and experiences.

Internationalising Educational Research

It seems appropriate to clarify what one understands by international education (see Table I).

	Inspiration, locus, resource	
Learners	Local	International
	1	2
A. Local	Local	International
B. International	International	International

Table I. Internationalising education.

Taking 'local' to refer to activities within the territories in question, and categorising education as informal, non-formal and formal, it would seem that if we are talking about the acquisition of locally inspired knowledge, with local resources, by local people, within their locality (A1), we are not (at face value) talking about anything international. When any one of these parameters is not local, the educational experiences in question have international characteristics (A2, B1–B2). Students and teachers of different nationalities bring the culture of their nations to incidences of teaching and learning which take place in other states (B1). Learning by local people and in-migrants through international institutions (local and cross-national children attending international schools, watching internationally inspired television programmes) goes beyond that encouraged by national educational and other media (A2, B2). If research [2] into educational experiences designated as local is undertaken by expatriate researchers, then the process and outcomes of that research are internationally informed, as are all the other permutations of the process.

In so far as Comparative Education purists are concerned with the description and analysis of educational processes in more than one state (Altbach et al, 1982), their work by definition is international. For those who perceive the essence of all research to be both comparative and educational, this is far from the case (Arthur & Preston, 1996; Preston, 1997a). Beyond doubt, there is a renewed interest in cross-national comparative research. It is being undertaken in new ways, within new structures, with reference to education and other fields of social analysis. Tracking the dynamic for this through the fusion of contextual and methodological inspiration is complex, as is an appraisal of its implications for the themes under investigation and their interpretation. Whether it is made harder or easier to discern by the contemporary cannons of the explanatory discourse for the wonders or (depending on perspective) evils of our time, is a matter for debate (World Bank, 1994; United Nations Research Institute for Social Development [UNRISD], 1995; Watkins, 1995). Among these cannons, the forces of globalisation and technological change in a neo-liberal market are dominant. Within them are the processes of democratisation, urbanisation and demography, gender and other lesser guns. Along with the passage of time, each has implications for education, more and less formal, for the ways in which it is researched and why.

Contextual Inspiration

Being highly selective, I want to focus on the implications of a neo-liberal global market, facilitated by instantaneous transnational communications, for the creation of a new international division of labour focused increasingly on the production of knowledge and services, rather than on manufactured outputs. The processes of economic reform or, depending on geography, adjustment to the new structures, mediated by international financial institutions (IFIs), transnational corporations (TNCs) and other supra-national authorities have refined the stratification of states according to their capacity and autonomy to compete on the international market and also, integrally related but not necessarily consonant with this, the stratification of the force of the world's labour within and between them (Reich, 1995a, 1995b). For Reich, it is far from clear whether the ownership of capital and business is as critical to the well-being of states in which they are registered as ensuring the availability of suitable labour which will disperse internally the incomes it generates. It is clear that for decades regional alliances of states have been formed and held together by complex cross- and supra-national bureaucracies and that over a similar period, a new, increasingly numerous, category of very poor nations has emerged (World Bank, 1990). Instability, conflict, war and displacement are a feature of the times, as resistance to a global process of emiseration becomes endemic. Everywhere the expectation of (secure) employment has evaporated, with massive casualisation of professional as well as manual workers (Castells, 1997). The pervasive managerial culture is part of a process of what some Chinese perceive as the face of a cultural revolution (Cheng, 1998) and others fear will become total bureaucratisation (Wallerstein, 1991). It is also a response to the outsourcing of work and the need to ensure that tasks are completed according to increasingly prescribed specifications and that they are complementary to those undertaken before, simultaneously or at a later date (Preston, 1999). Outcomes management has become a guiding principle, accompanied by the adoption of tools to facilitate worker compliance and client satisfaction. Project planning frameworks are global management tools. They specify aims, objectives, outcomes, tasks, indicators of performance achieved and possible threats to the process, and allow management to monitor development of progress to what may have been self-imposed (certainly accepted) targets at all phases of project and programme cycles, from pre-planning to post-hoc evaluation (Overseas Development Administration [ODA], 1995). A punitive ethic within these structures allows those with power in central locations to obfuscate their errors, leaving people at the work periphery ever more vulnerable (Lutz, 1988).

Within all this, education is acquiring extended roles and, in rich and poor countries, is increasingly funded by internationally-oriented institutions. These include the IFIs and other multilaterals, regional governments and parastatal institutions, as well as an exponentially increasing number of small private, not-for-profit and voluntary organisations offering specialist training and professional development services. It remains the key mechanism for socialisation into national and international modes of thinking and culture (Usher & Edwards, 1995). More and more, it determines eligibility to compete for labour market entry, wherever relevant. It continues to be the criterion determining the level of initial and continuing access to the formal sector of national and international labour markets. To maintain eligibility for such work, in a context of high international unemployment, professional development is becoming mandatory and universally similar (Preston, 1999). This may occur in the workplace or externally, with evidence of specified competency in recent work-related training becoming a prerequisite, at hitherto undifferentiated occupational levels (Preston, 1999). For those without work but aspiring to it, there is a de facto similar requirement. In these circumstances, national and international markets for educational commodities and services are diversifying and flourishing. Simultaneously, in rich and poor countries alike, lack of any prospect of returns to investment in education is causing poor people to question its relevance and to withhold or withdraw children from school (UNRISD, 1995; Watkins, 1995; Le Monde, 1997), by implication leaving them to achieve their socialisation and acculturation through less formal experiential learning.

These processes are part of contemporary global experience. States are differentiated according to their autonomy to introduce measures of economic adjustment or having to suffer their imposition, although the measures taken have proved to be similar worldwide (Ilon, 1994). They are distinguished by the proportions of their populations with greater or lesser capacities to withstand the effects of the market, by their ability to maintain stability, providing safety nets for the destitute, by exporting in their own interests educationally differentiated categories of surplus labour, by meeting their need for varying kinds of imported expertise and determining the conditions under which they acquire it.

Methodological Inspiration

Associating changing research and development practice with each of these processes does not imply abandonment of previously popular themes and approaches. The educational changes associated with the structural changes described earlier have generated research that is substantively different from that of pre-liberal social welfarism, although research with welfarist assumptions continues to be important. There has been an augmentation and integration of approaches, facilitating access to informant interpretation, as well as to more factual responses. The extent to which research using new approaches serves the same goals as more conventional modes, regardless of their different intermediary objectives, remains a matter for debate (Preston, 1997a). The same is the case of research, at whatever levels, which adopts seemingly conflicting (mainstream and counter-stream) epistemological perspectives.

Substance

We have long been familiar with league tables comparing the wealth of nations, rich and poor, including their educational performances. We now find education well to the fore in their multivariate alternatives, the Human Development Index (HDI), the Gender Index (GI) and the Human Poverty Index (HPI) (United Nations Development Programme [UNDP], 1997). The implication is that these indices, which are based on multiple sources of secondary data, will set targets of achievement on chosen parameters for those concerned to monitor and improve national performances. Events suggest that one implication is that this will be done through interacting research and development in different parts of the world, with those who produced indices (the World Bank and UNDP) incidentally playing a key role as the funders or managers of initiatives. In a different genre are carefully researched but small-scale, global-level analyses of the influence of multilaterals and IFIs in standardising and stabilising national educational policies (Mundy, 1998) and the characteristics of the global education elite (those who attend the top 50 conferences) who inspire this (Chabbott, 1998). At regional levels are cross-country comparisons of strategies to reduce social and educational investment, for example, Reimers in Latin America (1992) and Samoff in Africa (1994). Others are investigating these decision-making processes at national levels (Schultze-Kraft, 1997) and their implications at institutional levels in different parts of the world (Shattock, 1989; Benjamin, 1995; Charles, 1997).

Challenging the idea that there are essential differences in response in richer and poorer states, there are now, among copious others, comparative studies by poor country researchers of non-governmental organisations (NGOs) and literacy in the United Kingdom and South Africa (Sigodi, 1996) and of the financing of literacy in the United Kingdom and Lesotho (Jele, 1997). Concern with managing outcomes has led internationally to a slew of cross-national studies on school effectiveness (Preston, 1985; Reynolds, 1999; Alexander, 1999), the relevance and ethics of criterion-referenced competency-based assessment (Hyland, 1995) and the global, regional and national implications of systems of accreditation for career mobility and development (Preston, 1998a). Although the vocabulary varies, aid-funded, development-oriented research targets poor people in remarkably similar ways, in poor and rich countries alike. It prioritises poverty alleviation through pro-market strategies (Preston, 1996; Love, 1994), incidentally focusing attention on women, in part on egalitarian grounds but also, because they are likely to give better returns to outlay than men (King Herz & Khandker, 1991). Decreasing investment in physical infrastructure means that inputs favour skill development for self-sufficiency, community integration and stability (Arthur & Preston, 1996). The recent shift by some organisations, away from short-term project investment, back to large-scale, national, sectoral programme investment may in due course achieve measurable social outcomes, but it should not be forgotten that the number of countries receiving donor support has dwindled (German & Randel, 1997, p. 249), with levels of that support declining to below those of 1950 (Curtis, 1997, p. 5). Nor should it be forgotten that under the new structures of funding, spending requirements stipulate the proportion to be invested in donor country goods and services. Ranging between 0 and 70% (New Zealand and Canada respectively), with investment in basic education across donor states at an average of 1.2% of Official Development Assistance (ODA) (German & Randel, 1997, p. 249), some writers speculate the demise of untied grant aid and its conversion to exclusively trade-oriented transactions (Curtis, 1997).

Methods

The institutionalisation of a multiplicity of alternative qualitative and participative techniques as means through which to throw new light on the meaning and significance of observed behaviour may be as much associated with fatigue at the limitations of survey data, top–down planning and the normalisation of modernisation processes, as it is with the cost of large-scale statistical research (Preston, 1997a). The narratives legitimating these techniques, associated with educational research and development, may have geographically, socially and politically different expressions in different types of state, but the convergence of practice within them is palpable. Social and gender planning in poor states may refer to a participatory process of project design, implementation and evaluation (Conyers, 1982; Moser, 1996). Perhaps thought to be attributable to thinkers such as Paolo Freire, it assumes the development of critical cognitive approaches to change. In richer parts of the world, where participation is measured in terms of enrolments (McGivney, 1993; Bourgeois et al, 1999; Bond & Merrill, 1999), the anatomical metaphor is of 'bums on seats', rather than of 'between the ears' activity. Here, research involvement terminology referring to intellectual participation may refer to end-user consultation. Whatever, participatory approaches are being promoted universally in connection with educational research, in their own right and in association with a growing number of regional-level and international multimethod case study analyses (Preston, 1997a). This is to the point of them being a mandatory requirement of most project funding applications, national and international, however mainstream their substance and methods.

Whatever the context, the project planning frameworks of applied international research, using diverse sources of primary and secondary information, have a considerable influence on the ways in which questions are asked at different stages and on the information being sought. (Training) needs analysis in the pre-planning stages has been formatised, while research into the most appropriate forms of provision to be made is constrained by the predetermined range of options known to be available. Monitoring and evaluation is increasingly according to prescribed schedules, sometimes at precise and controlled times, against criteria already indicated in project documents (Becker, 1997), as contemporary emphasis on accountability imposes a realpolitik on endeavour (Harland, 1996). It may also use familiar techniques of cost–benefit and effectiveness analysis, as well as newer systems-impact approaches and tracer studies of longer-term effects.

Making the link between trends such as these in international social and educational research and the contextual changes already described is not problematic. Increased participation (in educational and research processes alike) may be seen as a reflection of libertarian commitment to democracy. Such is its popularity among hitherto non-mainstream

75

researchers that for some, the use of these and other qualitative techniques is seen to be a statement of political commitment (Dingwall, 1997). This ascribes oppositional political positions to those not using or recognising them. Cases in point would be the United Kingdom reports by Hillage et al (1998) and Tooley & Darby (1998). Similarly, preoccupation with process and outcomes through diverse techniques of monitoring and evaluation becomes consonant with mangerialism, and the regulatory tendencies of a fragmented labour market. Its implication for the routinisation, regularisation and commodification of intellectual creativity is already apparent.

Infrastructure

If the changes in substance and methods of internationally-oriented educational research can be linked to changes in the wider structures of society, so too can the infrastructure of the work being done. Utilitarianism means that funding for research is forthcoming if it seeks to produce tangible, directly applicable results. Researchers increasingly work to short-term contracts with tightly specified terms of reference, to the extent of setting themselves up in this way to initiate work that will eventually lead to major theoretically-oriented outcomes (Preston, 1996c). If fulfilled, the desired results will be produced. In development-related international educational research, the shift has long since been away from hands-on, long-term, expatriate technical assistance, favouring instead local implementation teams, with short-term advisory consultancy to supplement this capacity (Arthur & Preston, 1996). The emphasis on multidisciplinary consultancy teams coming together for a few days, with a coordinator integrating their different inputs, has grown in popularity, although little is known about the effectiveness of stakeholder communications under these circumstances (Preston & McCaffery, 1999). While daily rates for such work may appear to be generous, they mask large discrepancies between the number of days paid and the number of days worked. This in turn has implications for motivation, the quality of contribution being made and the opportunity, between jobs, for personal development to cutting-edge levels. With consortium funding and the possibility of several businesses being involved in project administration, there is increasing complexity at all levels of programme and project structures throughout their cycles. The extent to which at funder levels this serves as a strategy to obfuscate higher-level channels of blame in a punitive global culture should be seriously contemplated (Preston, 1997).

With less applied research, similar managerial requirements are apparent, with cross-national collaboration expected of comparative studies. This occurs in school-based research conducted by international teams (Alexander, 1999; Osborn & Planel, 1999; Reynolds, 1999). It is also true of post-school educational studies such as those of Barbara Merrill at Warwick on access and participation in higher education in western Europe (Bourgeois et al, 1995). Those describing their experiences of such work stress the seemingly endless amount of time needed for the creation of a communications infrastructure and its maintenance, as efforts are made to ensure common conceptualisations, methods and effective communication between team members (Merrill, 1997). This raises the question of how far these maintenance activities consume resources intended for other purposes and what they imply for the quality of comparability of the information obtained. Research into international educational consultancy as a multi-stakeholder activity has begun to investigate some of these processes (Preston & Arthur, 1997), but there is a case for a great deal more to be done. Certainly, this dimension of cross-national research is a product of the geopolitical changes of the last 20 years already described.

Also, at the level of an evolving international research infrastructure and bureaucracy, studies are being commissioned to propose government and non-government organisational research agendas. Seeking to take account of contemporary thinking on substantive and methodological issues as well as the restrictions of organisational missions (Preston, 1996a), they have led to studies which compare the policies and strategies of peer organisations in respect of overarching common goals, presumably for multiple reasons, among them non-duplication, compatibility, competitiveness, etc. Examples would include the studies commissioned by the Overseas Development Institute (ODI) on the approaches to poverty alleviation being adopted by bilateral organisations of western Europe (Rhi-Sausi & Zupi, 1997; Udsholt, 1997; Weidnitzer, 1997; Randel & German, 1997). In these, the shift to thinking of multisectoral social development as the term to include support for social welfare, health and educational development reduces the former prominence of the language of education, although training is well to the fore within them (Preston, 1996a).

Finally, often working in teams, intra- and inter-organisational practitioner research into community development and social movement support is increasingly important (Hart & Bond, 1995). Unlike the post-war years, staff of such organisations are likely to have had some basic or even advanced research training, developed a commitment to its worth and some skill in its execution. Adding to arguments made in respect of the quality of information to be obtained through such insider research and the economics of doing so, it is easy to understand the growth of practitioner research, in this case in the international voluntary sector committed to education and development. This has occurred to such an extent that it has in its turn generated the production of simplified practitioner research manuals (Marsden & Oakley, 1990; Nichols, 1991) and a new tier in the organisational structure of support organisations dedicated to building research, training and management capacities in those working at the community level. The International NGO Research and Training Centre in Oxford would be an example. Again, the organisation of civil society organisations in this way is a product of the influences of the neo-liberal economy on the labour market. Without the combined effects of impoverishment and the displacement of people with high levels of professional expertise from formerly secure employment, there would not have been either the incentive or the capacity for such initiatives, which have far-reaching implications for the nature of research and the quality and dissemination of its outcomes.

Dissemination

This global popularisation of research combines with the utilitarian requirement that research enhance lay understanding of its issues, processes and infrastructures. Of itself, it provides a challenge to the pandemic stereotype that research, presumably including internationally relevant educational research, is poorly disseminated (Hillage et al, 1998; Tooley & Darby, 1998) and warrants scrutiny. As with everything else, dissemination is a socially constructed process. As with earlier stages of the research, it is politically informed, by and large serving the interests of included categories, however defined. Dissemination depends on multiple categories of people, this time those who have an interest in sharing information between themselves and, if appropriate, arranging for its further distribution. On one side of a binary divide are the contractors, producers and publishers of research. On the other are those who might be expected to respond to it as policy-makers, teachers, learners and other customers. In practice, the divide may be illusory from start to finish of the process, with stakeholders from either side integrally committed to all developments. They include those with specialist and technical commitment and those with more general and lay interests. While there is an argument to include people with no hitherto declared interest in the information net (seemingly the tenor of much of today's complaint), unless they can perceive its relevance, their interest is unlikely to be aroused. What seems certain is that the increased cross-national complexity of much international educational research lends itself to more far-reaching dissemination than that undertaken in other modes. This occurs everywhere, at all stages of the ever more tightly controlled project and policy cycles with which it may be associated.

Heuristically, this chapter differentiates organic and mechanistic dissemination. Organic dissemination is that which occurs incidentally through the interaction of those involved with a project and others within their many personal and institutional networks. They include funders, contractors, clients, researchers, informants and all those to whom they relate. Mechanistic dissemination is that planned and organised as project activity. It includes the preparation of project documents and reports; project meetings, workshops, seminars and conferences; publication through the media, practitioner, community and specialist outlets; and the use of new international global communications systems. It infers that the more technical, regularised and comprehensive the mechanistic communication strategies, in either research or development activities, associated with the need to meet targets and be accountable, the wider the organic dissemination process will be as well. Outcomes-oriented management and accountability have already been linked to globalisation and the neo-liberal economy. They assume dissemination strategies which allow these to be measured. In the case of contemporary trends in research into international education, they will assume dissemination of analyses of the parameters of contextual and methodological inspiration already discussed, including analyses of the dissemination that occurs in association with them. Necessarily, they will take account of the purpose of the study being undertaken and what this implies for its levels of analysis and presentational modes (Reimers & McGinn, 1995). These might include oral, printed and other media of communications in policy arenas, potential user arenas, research and academic arenas. In any of these, it might be hypothesised that contracted policy-oriented research will in the first instance be reported at different stages positivistically. Later (subject to barrier removal [Crossthwaite & Curtis, 1994; Arthur & Preston, 1996]), it might be reconstructed, by the researchers themselves or other secondary analysts, and presented with a more critical conceptualisation. Present-day utilitarian expectations of studies envisaged at higher levels of abstraction mean that the same is likely to occur. Overall, an enormous amount of unpublished research documentation is being produced in all parts of the world. There is every case for investing heavily in synthetic studies which seek to generalise its contribution.

Impact

Attempting to conceptualise the impact of the contemporary internationalisation of educational research is as complex as the entity itself. Such an analysis has to account for the contributions being made to understanding of the substantive issues under analysis, the underlying assumptions of the methods being used in their interpretation and the political intentions of the new international research infrastructures. It also has to take account of the implications of all this for a very greedy international market, with abundant surplus labour, and its needs to commoditise what it can. For example, the case for research into processes of incidental learning may be made on the grounds that understanding of the micro-conditions that make it effective will allow them to be simulated and applied to increase work efficiencies and productivity. The implications of this objectification include: (i) that learning under such conditions will no longer be incidental but planned, as with increasingly formalised processes of coaching and mentoring in organisational learning environments; and (ii) if incidental learning is an essential element of the human condition, there is the probability of the autonomous emergence of new forms of incidental learning associated with the objectified forms of those that have been already appropriated and, in part, to compensate for those that no longer qualify. These new forms would in their turn have to be objectified to further enhance organisational efficiencies, ad infinitum. The commodification of this increasingly objectified personal knowledge occurs via self-help publications, training and training manuals, and longer formal courses. All of these are being produced in forms which seek to reduce cost and maximise profit in a global market. This includes the need to minimise media of communication to internationally common languages, with a dwindling number of publishing houses and software companies in control. The use of English as the global language is vital to the international economics of education at the end of the second millennium. It generates a profitable industry as nine-tenths of the world's people have to learn to navigate some aspect of their lives in English, however unwillingly, allowing it to undermine their fluency in their indigenous tongues. Nor should it be forgotten that the new internationalisation of research, in this case educational research, creates job opportunities for those whose livelihoods depend on such work.

As a reaction to social trends, this chapter suggests that the processes discussed in the previous paragraphs are part of the institutionalisation of these trends, at the level of both narrative and practice. In providing analyses of the fragmentation of knowledge, the reduction of language repertoires, the new alienation of labour, educational research (as any other) validates them all and, by implication, their affirmation of the widening social differentiation with which they are associated, within and most importantly between states.

In this, research, as any part of institutional process, facilitates adjustment to the cultural economic and political characteristics of global reforms. Without restructuring, it can do no more.

Notes

[1] A version of this paper was presented to the symposium, 'International Education: research and its contribution', at the annual conference of the British Educational Research Association, Queens University Belfast, 27-30 August 1998.

[2] This chapter takes research to refer to a systematic process of gathering, interpreting and communicating information (Preston, 1997a, p. 35).

References

Alexander, R. (1999) Culture and Pedagogy: pedagogy across cultures, in R. Alexander, P. Broadfoot & D. Phillips (Eds) *Learning from Comparing: new directions in comparative educational research, Vol. 1, Contexts, Classrooms and Outcomes.* Oxford: Symposium Books.

Altbach, P., Arnove, R.F. & Kelly, G. (1982) *Comparative Education.* New York: Macmillan.

Arthur, L. & Preston, R. (1996) *Quality and Overseas Consultancy: understanding the issues*, p. 86. Manchester: British Council/Warwick: University of Warwick, International Centre for Education in Development.

Becker, H. (1997) *Social Impact Assessment: method and experience in Europe, North America and the developing* world. London: UCL Press.

Benjamin, E. (1995) A Faculty Response to the Fiscal Crisis: from defense to offense, in M. Berube & C. Nelson (Eds) *Higher Education under Fire: politics, economics and the crisis of the humanities*, pp. 52-72. London: Routledge.

Bond, M. & Merrill, B. (1999) Advertising, Information and Recruitment to Return-to-learning in Six European Countries: looking at the findings, *Journal of Access and Credit Studies*, 1, pp. 204-213.

Bourgeois, E., Duke, C., Guyot, J-L. & Merrill, B. (1999) *The Adult University.* Buckingham: Open University Press and the Society for Reseach in Higher Education.

Buchert, L. & King, K. (Eds) (1996 *Consultancy and Research in International Education: the new dynamics.* Bonn: NORRAG/DSE.

Castells, M. (1997) *The Rise of the Network Society, vol. 1: The Information Age, Economy, Society and Culture.* Oxford: Blackwell.

Chabbott, C. (1997) Constructing Educational Concensus: international development professionals and the World Conference on Education for All, *International Journal of Educational Development*, 18, pp. 207-218.

Charles, D. (1997) Progress or Regress? Structural Adjustment and Its Impact on Tertiary Education: a case study of Cave Hill campus, unpublished MA thesis, University of Warwick, Department of Continuing Education.

Cheng, K-M. (1998) Personal communication, University of Warwick, May.

Clark, B.R. (1998) *Creating Entrepreneurial Universities: organisational pathways of transformation.* Oxford: Elsevier.

Conyers, D. (1982) *An Introduction to Social Planning in the Third World.* London: Wiley.

Curtis, M. (1997) Development Co-operation in a Changing World, in J. Randel & T. German (Eds) *The Reality of Aid: an independent review of development co-operation*, pp. 4-20. London: Earthscan/EUROSTEP ICVA.

Dalichow, F. (1996) Culture and Procedures for the Recognition of Foreign Qualifications, *Higher Education in Europe*, 21(4), pp. 28-38.

Department for International Development (DfID) (1998) [Approaches to impact analysis]. London: DfID.

Dingwall, R. (1997) The Moral Discourse of Interactionism, in G. Miller & R. Dingwall (Eds) *Context and Method in Qualitative Research*, pp. 198-205. London: Sage.

German, T. & Randel, J. (1997) Trends in Aid and Development Co-operation, in J. Randel & T. German (Eds) *The Reality of Aid: an independent review of development co-operation*, pp. 247-257. London: Earthscan/EUROSTEP ICVA.

Harland, J. (1996) *Evaluation as Realpolitik*, in D. Scott & R. Usher (Eds) *Understanding Educational Research*, pp. 91-105. London: Routledge.

Hart, E. & Bond, M. (1995) *Action Research for Health and Social Care*. Buckingham: Open University Press.

Hillage, J., Pearson, R., Anderson, A. & Tankin, P. (1998) *Excellence in Research on Schools*, Research Report, 74. London: Department for Education and Employment.

Hyland, T. (1995) Morality, Work and Employment: towards a values dimension in vocational education and training, *Journal of Moral Education*, 24, pp. 445-456.

Ilon, L. (1994) Structural Adjustment and Education: adapting to a growing global market, *International Journal of Educational Development*, 14, pp. 95-108.

Jele, D. (1997) Financing Literacy Programmes in England and Swaziland, unpublished MA thesis, University of Warwick, Department of Continuing Education.

King Herz, B. & Khandker, S.R. (Eds) (1991) *Women's Work, Education and Family Welfare in Peru*, World Bank Discussion Paper 116. Washington, DC: World Bank.

Love, A. (1994) *Development Cooperation Report, 1993*. Paris: OECD.

Lutz, F.W. (1988) Witches and Witchfinding in Educational Organisations, in A. Westoby (Ed.) *Culture and Power in Educational Organisation*. Milton Keynes: Open University Press.

Marsden, P. & Oakley, P. (1990) *Evaluating Social Development Projects*, Oxfam Development Guidelines, 5. Oxford: Oxfam.

McGivney, V. (1993) Participation and Non-participation: a review of the literature, in R. Edwards, S. Sieminski & D. Zeldin (Eds) *Adult Learners, Education and Training*. London: Routledge/Open University.

Merrill, B. (1997) Working Teams: implications for method in cross-national contexts, *International Journal of University Adult Education*, 36(3), pp. 1-8.

Miller, G. & Dingwall, R. (Eds) (1997) *Context and Method in Qualitative Research*. London: Sage.

Moser, C. (1996) *Gender Planning and Development: theory, practice and training*. London: Routledge.

Mundy, K. (1998) Educational Multilateralism and World (Dis)order, *Comparative Education Review,* 42, pp. 448-478.

Nichols, P. (1991) *Social Survey Methods: a field guide for development workers,* Oxfam Development Guidelines, 6. Oxford: Oxfam.

Overseas Development Administration (1995) *A Guide to Social Analysis for Projects in Developing Countries.* London: HMSO.

Osborn, M. & Planel, C. (1999) Comparing Children's Learning, Attitude and Performance in French and English Primary Schools, in R. Alexander, P. Broadfoot & D. Phillips (Eds) *Learning from Comparing: new directions in comparative educational research, Vol. 1, Contexts, Classrooms and Outcomes.* Oxford: Symposium Books.

Preston, R. (1985) *Attainment and Community in Managalas Schools.* Waigani: University of Papua New Guinea.

Preston, R. (1996a) *Social Policy and Education: towards a research agenda,* p. 45. London: Overseas Development Administration.

Preston, R. (1996b) Consultancy, Research and Human Development, in L. Buchert & K. King (Eds) *Consultancy and Research in International Education: the new dynamics,* pp. 139-152. Bonn: NORRAG/DSE.

Preston, R. (1996c) Restricting Freedom: international credit transfer and skill recognition in the late twentieth century, conference report, International Centre for Educational Development, University of Warwick.

Preston, R. (1997a) Integrating Paradigms in Educational Research: issues of quantity and quality in poor countries, in M. Crossley & G. Vulliamy (Eds) *Qualitative Educational Research in Developing Countries: current perspectives,* pp. 31-64. New York: Garland.

Preston, R. (1997b) Working with the British Resource: partner and client perspectives, report of a colloquium held at the Commonwealth Secretariat, United Kingdom Forum for International Education and Training, Occasional Paper 4.

Preston, R. (1998a) Cross-national Credit Compatibility and Global Stratification, paper presented to the international conference, 'Credit Accumulation and Transfer Systems', University of Derby, June.

Preston, R. (1998b) *Stability and Chaos: new lenses in educational analysis.* University of Warwick: International Centre for Education in Development.

Preston, R. (1999) Returns to Investment in Refugee Education: comparing tracer studies, *Journal of International Education,* 10, pp. 38-45.

Preston, R. & Arthur, L. (1997) Knowledge Societies and Planetry Cultures: international consultancy in human development, *International Journal of Educational Development,* 17, pp. 3-12.

Preston, R. & McCaffery, J. (1999) Organisations, Communication and Poverty: researching partnerships in the international aid sector, report of the first phase of the CfBT funded project, *Improving Partnership: consultancy-related communication in complex projects. Case studies of international educational development,* p. 50f.

Randel, J. & German, T. (Eds) (1997) *The Reality of Aid: an independent review of development co-operation.* London: Earthscan/EUROSTEP ICVA.

Reich, R. (1995a) Who Is Us? in K. Ohmae (Ed.) *The Evolving Global Economy: making sense of the new world order*, pp. 141-160. Harvard: Harvard Business School.

Reich, R. (1995b) Who Is Them? in K. Ohmae (Ed.) (1995) *The Evolving Global Economy: making sense of the new world order*, pp. 161-182. Harvard: Harvard Business School.

Reimers, F. (1992) *Deuda externa y financiamiento de la educación: su impacto en Latinoamerica*. Paris: UNESCO.

Reimers, F. & McGinn, N. (1995) Using Research in Educational Policy and Administrative Decision-making, in F. Reimers & N. McGinn (Eds) *K. Wild Confronting Future Challenges: educational information, research and decision-making*. Paris: International Bureau of Education.

Reynolds, D. (1999) Creating a New Methodology for Comparative Educational Research, in R. Alexander, P. Broadfoot & D. Phillips (Eds) *Learning from Comparing: new directions in comparative educational research, Vol. 1, Contexts, Classrooms and Outcomes*. Oxford: Symposium Books.

Rhi-Sausi, J.L. & Zupi, M (1997) *Italian Aid Policies for Poverty Reduction*. London: Overseas Development Institute.

Samoff, J. (Ed.) (1994) *Coping with Crisis: austerity, adjustment and human resources*. London: Cassell.

Schultze-Kraft (1997) Adjustment and Reform: educational policy in Latin America: the case of Chile, Nicaragua and Venezuela, University of Oxford, mimeo.

Shattock, M. (1989) Thatcherism and British Higher Education, *Change*, 21(5), pp. 30-39.

Sigodi, P. (1996) Delivering Literacy: the impact of organisational policies and structures on practice, University of Warwick, Department of Continuing Education, unpublished MA thesis.

Tooley, J. & Darby, J. (1998) *Educational Research: a critique*, report presented to the Office for Standards in Education (OFSTED). London: OFSTED.

Udsholt, L. (1997) *Danish Aid Policies for Poverty Reduction*. London: Overseas Development Institute.

United Nations Research Institute for Social Development (UNRISD) (1995) *States of Disarray: the social effects of globalisation*. Geneva: UNRISD.

Usher, R. & Edwards, R. (1995) *Post-modernism and Education: different voices, different worlds*. London: Routledge.

Wallerstein, I. (1991) *Geo-polities and Geoculture: essays on the changing world system*. Cambridge: Cambridge University Press.

Watkins, K. (1995) *The Oxfam Poverty Report*. Oxford: Oxfam.

Weidnitzer, E. (1997) *German Aid and Policies for Poverty Reduction*. London: Overseas Development Institute.

World Bank (1990) *The World Development Report*. Washington, DC: World Bank.

Stones from Other Hills May Serve to Polish the Jade of This One: towards a 'comparology' of education [1]

PATRICIA BROADFOOT

I want to start with a picture. Four people are sitting around a table. It is lunchtime. They are discussing comparative education:

'Has comparative education a unique role to play?' asks one. 'If so, what is it?' 'Couldn't it be subsumed as a methodological device within other social science disciplines?' asks another.

'Perhaps it is, after all, dispensable', says a third.

'But can we even define what comparative education is?' says the fourth after some reflection.

The setting is a seminar on comparative education methodology. The discussants are established, even distinguished, scholars in the field. In the light of the theme of this book – 'Doing comparative education research: issues and problems' – the conversation prompted me to reflect on these fundamental questions concerning our common endeavour. At a meta-level, it prompted me too, to consider whether other fields of enquiry are subject to the same insecurities about their area of study. Do physicists or archaeologists similarly agonise about the very existence of their discipline? I doubt it. Do they grapple with debilitating internal debates about purpose and methodology? I doubt it. Do they have to defend their field against the incursions of carpetbaggers who are only too ready to jump on any fashionable bandwagon? I doubt it. Even closer to home, I doubt whether either other comparative fields – comparative anatomy or comparative theology, for example – or other social science fields are so much given to such fundamental and frequent 'omphalopsychics' – that is, collective disciplinary-navel-gazing.

If comparative education seems to be more subject to difficulty in defining its particular identity and mission than other fields, it nevertheless appears to share with many others, at the present time, a desire to review this role. The infectious Zeitgeist of the millennium has prompted a period of reflection and review in many areas of life; a sense of standing on the verge of a new era that as yet can still only be dimly perceived but one which presents an urgent challenge to clarify how we will respond. But for us here today, the impact of this more general watershed is greatly strengthened by the knowledge that we are entering a very much more specific new era as well with the launch of BAICE. The birth of a new comparative and international education society on the verge of the millennium makes this an ideal opportunity to reflect on our joint endeavour and to generate a new vision for the years to come.

In the relatively short time available to me today, this is my intended goal. I want my address to complement Keith Watson's masterly presidential address to the last British Comparative and International Education Society (BCIES) conference last year, which was recently published in *Compare*. It was entitled 'Memories, Models and Mapping', a title that gives a clue to both its content as a comprehensive review of past and present trends in comparative education, and to its valedictory tone. At that time, it was appropriate, among other things, to reflect on the achievements of the 30 years of first, the Comparative Education Society in Europe (CESE), (British Section) later to become BCIES. Watson's theme was the prevailing *historical amnesia* which he argued to be one of the most characteristic features of late twentieth-century society and his talk urges us to rediscover:

> *the roots, origins and purposes of the discipline of*
> *comparative education [p. 6] ... instead of anguishing over the*
> *value and justification for comparative education we need to*
> *re-find its roots in historical and cultural analysis, and we*
> *need to stress its ability to critique policy, drawing from the*
> *experience of different societies, and its ability to explain and*
> *identify themes and trends across the globe. Above all the*
> *work undertaken should have purposeful, reformist and*
> *practical goals and should be used to inform and advise*
> *governments. (Watson, 1998, p. 28)*

However, at this time, it is appropriate to look forward. I have already used the metaphor of new life to introduce the tone that I want to set today – to challenge us to think about the future, about a vision to guide the work of the new Society and what it might achieve.

But I also want to mount a more general challenge for us to think about our field as a whole as we face the prospect of radical, if not unprecedented, change in the nature of education itself. I draw your attention to the introductory paragraph in the publicity for this conference, which provides a succinct summary of some of these changes:

*In a world of growing uncertainty and continuing rapid
change, interrelated developments in telecommunications,
together with the impact of globalisation on labour markets,
patterns of migration and cultural norms mean that basic
assumptions about education are being challenged. New
patterns of learning shaped by media that transcend national
boundaries, and transformed by the demands of the market,
call into question the structure of existing systems of
education and the content of national curricula. There is no
longer any certainty about the place of national values, or
state control, in the development of education and training
systems as the competing interests of the market and civil
society influence forms of provision and the process of
learning. As a result there is renewed interest in comparative
research across the social sciences and its implications for
policy and practice in education in different parts of the
world. (Conference Publicity, BAICE Conference, 1998)*

When the use of printing began to become widespread after Caxton set
up his printing presses in the grounds of Westminster Abbey in 1476,
even its most enthusiastic proponents, such as William Caxton in this
country, could have had little idea what its eventual impact would be on
life and culture throughout the world. Equally, it is clear that when the
chairman of IBM announced in the 1940s that the world would only ever
need four computers, he too had little idea of the significance of that new
technology. Both our natural inclinations and the intellectual tools our
culture has developed mean that we are better at looking back and
learning lessons from the past, or analysing the present, than anticipating
the future. This may, in the end, prove the ultimate undoing of our
civilisation as we fail fully to anticipate the future impact of our current
technologies on the natural world on which we depend; on our social
and economic relations, on our political structures.

The potential ramifications for our global society of the current
'revolution' may perhaps best be envisaged by employing – appropriately
enough – a comparative perspective. Drucker (1993), for example,
suggests that we are living through one of the great 'transformations' of
history equivalent to that of the thirteenth century when the European
world became centred in the new city, the Renaissance of the fifteenth
century and the Industrial Revolution in the 40 years between 1775 and
1815:

*every few hundred years in Western history there occurs a
sharp transformation. We cross what in an earlier book I
called a 'divide'. Within a few short decades, society
rearranges itself – its world view, its basic values; its social
and political structure; its arts; its key institutions. Fifty years*

> *later there is a new world. And the people born then cannot*
> *even imagine the world in which their grandparents lived and*
> *into which their own parents were born. (Drucker, 1993, p. 1)*

If, as Drucker suggests, life for us in the future is likely to be almost unrecognisably changed – a view shared by many other contemporary commentators – there can be no more fundamental challenge than for us to begin to engage with what such change is likely to mean for education; for scholarship in general and for comparative and international education studies in particular.

This, then, is my theme for today. Like Christopher Columbus arriving in what subsequently became known as the West Indies, I want to consider the new world that we are just discovering. As yet, we have little idea of anything more than the outlying islands of change – the impact of information technologies and geopolitical currents which, like El Niño, promise significant upheavals in the social and political climate across the globe. The existence of the great landmass of the Americas may be projected but its nature, as yet, can hardly be envisaged. Indeed, we have hardly begun to try to do so while the familiar landscape of the school remains the norm around the world. As Rogers, (1997) suggests, 'Walk into most any classroom in most any school in America today and you'll walk into a time warp where the basic tools of learning have not changed in decades'. Aspirations to provide for open education and lifelong learning, though much talked about, have as yet made little impact.[2]

We find ourselves thus still in the early stages of a voyage of discovery and my slightly quaint choice of an ancient Chinese proverb, 'Stones from other hills may serve to polish the jade of this one', as a title for this talk reflects this. I came across this old Chinese saying during a visit to Shanghai earlier this year. It was a context pertinent to our conference theme since it evoked some of the issues and problems in doing comparative (and international) education research. The visit involved my colleague and me, as British educators, with all the cultural baggage that this represents, advising Chinese colleagues about how to introduce personal, social and moral education to address the current problems of childhood socialisation which have been brought about by the uniquely Chinese 'one-child' family policy. Equally distinctive and significant to that context is the pervasive Confucian tradition which provides both that country's moral foundation for education and a powerful element in Chinese cultural discourse more generally. Can these two worlds of East and West usefully meet? Can educators in one cultural context usefully learn from the experiences of another? In what way is it true to say that 'Stones from other hills may serve to polish the jade of this one', as not only the Chinese, but governments around the world, appear increasingly to believe? This is the first of the two defining themes that will provide the 'warp' and weft' of my talk today, the two I will weave into what I hope will emerge as a useful and perhaps even attractive final product.

Since we are celebrating here today a 'marriage' between two societies, as well as the birth of their 'offspring', BAICE, to which I have already alluded, I have chosen another old saying, this time drawn from Western culture and the powerful symbolic context of a major social institution, to serve as the other metaphor to guide our common thinking. I have borrowed a well-known prescription for good luck in their marriage that is given to brides in Britain on their wedding day – to wear 'Something old, something new, something borrowed, something blue'. The metaphor has both expressive and instrumental aspects. The first can be dealt with quite readily since it concerns the aspiration that the union or 'marriage' of the two societies will prove to be both happy and fruitful. However, the rest of my address will be devoted to the more instrumental implications of the prescription. What needs to be done to ensure such a happy marriage?

Two Metaphors and Four Stages: a matrix of possibilities

Thus, my talk will be structured in four parts – something old, something new, something borrowed, something blue – in which I explore the implications of this prescription for comparative education. Through each part I shall weave my second, Chinese, theme in order to highlight and refine the argument.

Something Old: the heritage of comparative education

The *Oxford English Dictionary* defines 'jade' as 'a material of instruments and ornament valued for its hardness'. Its ubiquitous use in many ancient cultures, such as the Maori in Aotearoa (New Zealand) as well as China, provides a symbolic reminder both of the many different civilisations and cultures that have come and gone and of the technologies and values that characterised them. The nuances jade evokes as a cultural artefact make it well suited to represent the core qualities of comparative education. It has long been valued for its utility as a tool because of its hardness; it can be used to make decorative objects of high quality because of its subtlety, adaptability and varied forms. It is thus a fitting symbol to represent the fine and varied traditions of comparative education; its core commitment to being a useful tool in the goal of improving education; its commitment to rigour in both empirical enquiry and the generation of theory; and its use in many different cultures. A brief review of the heritage of comparative education may serve to highlight these core values and characteristics.

Comparative education has a long and distinguished history, which goes back at least as far as the ancient Greek and Roman era (Brickman,

1965). A number of commentators have suggested that comparative education has evolved through three stages. After the pre-history of 'travellers' tales', came Jullien's 1817 call for the collection of data on national education systems by an international agency (Wolhuter, 1997). This is commonly regarded as the beginning of the use of the term 'comparative education' and of at least one of the field's two major genres that subsequently developed. It was the beginning of a positivist approach, which emphasised the systematic gathering of empirical, statistical data to inform policy-making.

Schriewer (1999) suggests that the development of comparative education epistemologies and methodologies borrowed from those of the natural sciences explains the long-standing emphasis on comparison as a quasi-experimental mode which assumes principles of causality, i.e. the same cause always produces the same effect, other things being equal. Durkheim, in his *Rules of Sociological Method* (1982), regarded comparative research as the basis for 'proof'' of sociological questions. Such neo-scientific approaches have continued to gain strength in the field, particularly in the period post-World War II with the work of scholars such as Brian Holmes in the United Kingdom and Noah and Eckstein in the USA. More recently, the work of international agencies such as the World Bank has served greatly to strengthen this tradition, with its emphasis on the rigorous collection and interpretation of statistical data across countries – a concern for 'measuring' different aspects of education as a guide for policy-makers (Psacharopoulos, 1990).[3]

The other major strand in the history of comparative education is the cultural-interpretative tradition pioneered by Michael Sadler and others. This approach emphasises the need to understand educational systems and practice as part of their wider context – as the following quotation from Kandel makes clear:

> *The comparative approach demands first an appreciation of the intangible, impalpable, spiritual and cultural forces which underlie an educational system; the forces and factors outside the school matter even more than what goes on inside it.*
> *Hence the comparative study of education must be founded on an analysis of the social and political ideas which the school reflects, for the school epitomises these for transmission and for progress. In order to understand, appreciate and evaluate the real meaning of the educational system of a nation, it is essential to know something of its history and traditions, of the forces and attitudes governing its social organisations, of the political and economic conditions that determine its development. (Kandel, 1933, p. xix, cited in Crossley & Broadfoot, 1992)*

This, then, is the broad heritage of comparative education – a commitment to collecting data systematically across cultures and countries, 'drawing from the experience of different societies ... to explain and identify themes and trends across the globe ... to inform and advise Governments' (Watson, 1998a, p. 28). However, as I have already suggested, things are changing and we now need to consider 'something new'.

Something New: postmodernism and its scholarly implications

Many of us have been pleased to welcome the recent upsurge of interest in comparative education, among policy-makers in particular. There is evidence around the world of a very real desire to learn from the experience of other countries and education systems as a means of bringing about improvement. However, it has been wisely said, 'timeo Danae dona ferentes' and we would do well to consider the implications of this sudden surge of interest. Interestingly, 'jade' has another meaning – that of a contemptuous name for a horse or a woman – another metaphor that can provide us with important insights about the nature of comparative education. For it is arguable that the field's current prominence is being achieved at a price.

At a recent comparative education seminar, which focused on aspects of international comparisons of student achievement, a policy-maker expressed his need for guidance in terms of the need to know the following.

Are we getting the best return for our money?
Are children doing as well as in the past?
Are they learning the right things?
How competitive are we as a country?
What are the social consequences of our policies?

To help answer these questions, he suggested that we needed good quality data, good analysis, sensible pointers concerning what ought to be done; and caution against drawing conclusions too swiftly.[4] Whilst these questions are eminently reasonable in themselves, they reflect the emergence of a discourse in which data have become increasingly detached from considerations of context. Even more fundamentally, they fail to raise any more general consideration of the ends of education. They reflect a situation in which, I would argue, the nature of 'the good life' has become subsumed within a discourse of means.

Elsewhere, I have argued (Broadfoot, 1996) that we are witnessing an international trend towards the domination of a 'technocratic consciousness' in our cultural life. One manifestation of this is that issues concerning the relative effectiveness of educational systems are discussed in almost entirely technical terms; they are addressed by the

91

'purposive rational application of techniques assured by empirical science' (Habermas, 1976).[5] It is a discourse dominated by the notion of standards and competition; of efficiency and accountability. It finds its clearest expression in the ubiquitous and still growing use of performance indicators and surveys of national and international standards.[6] The recently published 'Third International Mathematics and Science' study (TIMSS) provides a good example in this respect, provoking, as it did, a storm of national and international debate among policy-makers and the media concerning the relative apparent performance of different countries. In the United Kingdom and the USA in particular, the carefully reasoned analyses by scholars went unheard in the rush to condemn teachers and schools for having failed the nation's children.[7]

The result has been substantial 'policy-borrowing', notably of alternative pedagogic techniques such as whole class teaching, which in England, for example, has now become embodied in the high-profile national 'Literacy Hour' and 'Numeracy Hour' initiatives. Not only is such 'policy borrowing' not being subjected to the careful cultural analysis that comparative educationists would regard as essential to any judgement about the potential utility of such techniques in a different context; it is also not informed by any more fundamental theoretical understanding of the factors that influence learning. But if such use of comparative data is flawed pragmatically, it is arguably even more fundamentally flawed by not being informed by an overall vision of the purposes of education. It is a debate defined only in its own terms of relative efficiency.

We live in an age dominated by rationalist assumptions. The current international obsession with measurement underpins the assumption that it is possible to describe, compare and evaluate all the different aspects of educational activity. It is an age that assumes it is desirable to measure the quality of education using quantitative techniques; an age that is willing to invest very considerable resources in so doing in the belief that such studies will elucidate whether the education system is both providing value for money and the necessary infrastructure of skills to ensure future economic competitiveness on the international stage. Thus, countries around the world are putting in place mechanisms for both the *intra-national* comparison of standards – of schools, of regions and even, sometimes, of individual teachers – as well as *international* comparisons of relative standards.

However, as Steedman (1999) suggests, the enthusiasm for this kind of comparison has overtaken the instruments available for doing it. We are trying to reach Mars with a rocket built for going to the moon. Our technology is at best dangerously meaningless, at worst, pernicious, in its effects. Like all technologies, international surveys are neutral in themselves and it is *the use to which the products are put* which requires extreme caution if the overall effect is to be beneficial. For, whatever the innovation in question, its effects will only endure if it is linked to a more fundamental understanding of learning and how this, in turn, is influenced by the prevailing culture.

Moreover, the significance of the growing obsession with evaluative data goes well beyond its implications for comparative education alone. If it largely reduces comparative education to a more or less rigorous data-collection exercise, it also reduces education itself to a *commodity*, the role and value of which is closely tied to economic goals. Lyotard (1979) describes this trend in which notions of the social good have been subsumed by a more instrumentalist orientation as one in which knowledge itself is being commodified in the extension of 'performativity ... optimising the system's performance becomes the ultimate goal and the technology is found within the discourse of business and management' (p. 7). Indeed, Hartley (1997) has suggested that:

> *the school is a monument to modernity. Virtually everything is*
> *arranged rationally ... It purports to render everything as*
> *certain, as objectively recognisable, as measurable and*
> *therefore as comparable ... It spawns masses of data, allegedly*
> *valid data, which can be used to inform the customer or to set*
> *the pay of the producer. These data purport to be true*
> *representations of what they measure ... the crucial question is*
> *what do these facts mean and what is to be done about them.*
> *These are masters of value, of interpretation, of ideology.*
> *[p. 49] ... This growing obsession with 'data' flies in the face of*
> *profound shifts towards both epistemological uncertainty*
> *within academe and moral uncertainty at large. (p. 54)*

Whatever, their cause, these developments have prompted a significant and growing backlash. Hanson (1993) is one among many scholars who have argued that the divorce of economic reasoning from its roots in moral philosophy is like 'a grammar without language' and sees an urgent need to put social, moral and political activity back as an indicator of school quality. However, the attack against this trend in society as a whole has been mounted by the critical theorists, most notably Habermas. Again, it involves the reassertion of the older goals of human and social enlightenment and emancipation (Welch, 1998).

If, as Watson (1998a) and others have argued, comparative education has lost its way in losing sight of its roots in historical and cultural analysis, I suggest that this is because it is largely a victim of the prevailing discourse, a discourse in which modernist notions of science have become shorn of their underpinning meta-narrative of social progress and have, as a result, become elevated into becoming the goals, as well as the means, of progress. Thus, 'getting the scores up' becomes the focus for international educational activity, given the assumed link with economic performance, with the latter defined as the end, the vision of the good life, as well as the means of achieving it.

Thus, it may fairly be said that the tension between the interpretive and positivist research traditions in comparative education, between qualitative and quantitative methodologies, is an echo of a more general tension in the philosophy of social science itself. However, it is a tension that now finds expression in the much more fundamental changes that are overtaking society as a whole as we move from a modern to a postmodern era. For this is a change in which social life itself is also characterised by the struggle between the power exerted by an increasingly international discourse of economic efficiency and that of the 'micro-discourses' of individual cultures which are struggling to survive (Castells, 1998).

Huntington (1996), for example, suggests that it is possible to identify eight 'major civilisations' in the world today – Western, Confucian, Japanese, Islamic, Slavic-Orthodox, Hindu, Latin American and African – each characterised by its own view of life and relationships, God and authority, the state and power. Whilst we may not agree with Huntington's definition of these distinctions as 'civilisations' rather than cultures, the way in which the contemporary global economic discourse and technological systems are interacting with older, differently-generated world-views is likely to be one of the defining characteristics of the twenty-first century and perhaps the most significant basis for conflict. In an extreme form, we can see this struggle illustrated in the rise of Islamic fundamentalism and the efforts, even if we may deplore them, of, for example, the Taliban in Afghanistan, to outlaw all modern Western artefacts such as television and even formal schooling for girls.

A great deal has been written about postmodernism (not least the 1996 special issue of *Comparative Education* edited by Bob Cowen) and I do not intend to reiterate the arguments again in detail here. Suffice it to say that comparativists have been in the forefront of attempts to explore the nature of the international changes in our common social, economic and political context which are currently taking place. Dale (1996), for example, refers to the implications of 'globalisation' in terms of the trend towards economic deregulation and the associated growth of consumerism which has led in many countries to the advent of corporatism even at classroom level. Others have referred to 'globalisation' (Green, 1996) and the need for a 'globology' (Schriewer, 1999) to study it. The causes that lie behind these trends are complex and difficult to unravel. However, Ball identifies five key themes that underpin 'the new orthodoxy in the relationship between politics, Government and education' (1998, p. 122) – the ideologies of the market; new institutional economics based on devolution, targets and incentives;

performativity; public choice theory and new managerialism and the cult of quality. But, he suggests, 'the new orthodoxies of education policy are grafted onto and realised within very different national and cultural contexts and are affected, inflected and deflected by them' (1998, p. 127).

Undoubtedly, we live at a time when the old 'modernist' certainties are breaking down: the belief in science as the neutral harbinger of progress. The institutions of the nuclear family, the nation state, the school – all arguably modernist creations – are breaking down into more fluid arrangements that reflect the decline of earlier relationships and taken-for-granted assumptions (Quicke, 1998). The national unit – so long the primary focus of much comparative educational research – is increasingly having to yield its place as the prime unit of analysis in the light of the growing salience of groupings of all kinds and sizes, from huge multinational agglomerations to small local communities. Between the 15 countries of the European Union, for example, there are more than 50 education systems, with Belgium alone having five and Germany 16 (Vaniscotte, 1996). By the same token, what does national identity mean for a country such as Australia, in which one in four of its citizens was born in another country and one in two has at least one parent from overseas? Although it remains true that the national context is still deeply significant in influencing the conduct of education, as my colleagues and I have shown in a series of studies, it is also the case that, as Claude Thelot has recently remarked, 'autant les réponses sont nationales, autant les questions sont internationales'.[8]

But if it is important for comparative education to be willing to engage with new units of analysis such as Cowen's 'transitologies' (Cowen, 1999), for example, and to develop new methodologies such as Paulston's 'social cartography' (Paulston, 1996), it must also be ready to engage with new theoretical perspectives which can provide some counterbalance to the power of the prevailing evaluative discourse. Thus, not only do we need to trace the increasingly common educational trends around the world – trends such as institutional downsizing; the downstreaming of information systems using new technologies; the outsourcing of services; the mainstreaming of pupils with special needs; the proliferation of feedback mechanisms for accountability purposes (Blackmore, 1996) – we also need to recognise that all these trends and others like them are manifestations of an increasingly global 'text', a discourse which embodies within it the power to define both problems and their solutions in a way that makes alternative goals, as well as means, almost literally unthinkable (Wittgenstein, 1965; Dale, 1996).

It is a discourse that reflects international changes in the mode of economic regulation from mass individual and collective consumption to more differentiated production and distribution of health, education and other previously public services, replacing the highly stratified forms of curriculum and pedagogy linked to a hierarchical division of labour

(Bernstein, 1990) with education provision segmented vertically rather than horizontally by type not status. It reflects too, the advent of more complex patterns of political, economic and cultural differentiation, which have replaced the traditional class divisions on which previous educational arrangements were typically predicated, 'the multiple cultural identities of modern society' (Hartley, 1997). Such changes imply the emergence of qualitatively new modes of social solidarity.

The need for comparativists to recognise the scale of the international changes which are currently taking place, to understand their implications and to develop appropriate theoretical and methodological approaches so that they can engage with them, is an urgent one if comparative education is not to become the 'jade' of policy-makers. If the current interest in international comparisons results in the pursuit of data divorced from a deeper understanding of its meaning, we shall be open to the legitimate criticism of having failed to mount a critique of the current instrumentalist discourse at the very time it is most needed – when the familiar landscape of schools and teachers, lessons and textbooks, curriculum and assessment – the whole apparatus of formal educational provision as it developed in the industrialising societies of the Western world and which was subsequently exported, initially by means of colonialism and subsequently through international pressures to compete – is about to change out of all recognition. When schools may have to reconstruct their role in society as the coordinating centres of electronically-based learning systems; into networks which are open and flexible to inputs from learners faced with the task of constructing their own futures. For:

> *The idea that the outputs of learning can be determined*
> *independently of pupil inputs, and pre-specified in terms of*
> *clusters of trained abilities linked to a set of stable and*
> *unchanging productive enterprises, is already becoming*
> *obsolete as a basis for curriculum design and being replaced*
> *by the idea of a core of generic personal abilities; cognitive,*
> *interpersonal and motivational. The individualisation process*
> *in advanced societies challenges schools to develop an*
> *education which enables pupils to take active responsibility—*
> *to locate the development of their natural talents within a*
> *personally- constructed vision of a life worth living. (Hanson,*
> *1993, p. 223)*

I suggest that it is the field of comparative education that should be at the heart of trying to make sense of the new role of education and how it may best be achieved in a myriad of diverse contexts linked by their common location in a global society. And, to the extent that this is so, it brings me to my third section – 'something borrowed'. What 'stones from other hills may serve to polish the jade' of comparative education and so make it ready to meet this challenge?

Something Borrowed

One of the biggest problems facing comparative education is its diversity of subject matter. The most recent issue of *Comparative Education*, for example, contained articles on key skills, special needs, denominational schools, pedagogical movements, organisational cultures, and the impact of war. At first sight, the articles would seem to have little in common. Their subject matter represents as great a diversity of educational issues as might ever be found inside the cover of one journal issue. The contexts which provide the setting for these various analyses are equally diverse, from the sophisticated economies and highly-developed education systems of Europe – England, Sweden, Germany, Austria, the Netherlands and France – at one end of the continuum, to the desperate struggle within a developing country – Somalia – to preserve any formal educational provision at all in a country racked by war and internal conflict, at the other. In a recent review of the range of articles published over the last 5 years in one leading journal in the field of comparative education, I found that it was possible to classify the articles in terms of their broad methodological approach as follows.

(i) Studies which provide detailed empirical documentation of educational phenomena in a particular, typically national, setting.
Studies which provide (1) above but which are contextualised in terms of the broader international debates/theoretical frameworks/empirical accounts of the issue.
(ii) Studies which are designed as explicitly comparative, based on a coherent rationale for their selection in order to illuminate 'constants and contexts'.
(iii) Studies in which the contexts being compared are themselves theorised as part of wider social science debates on, for example, the relationship between system and action, power and control, culture and the creation of meaning.
(iv) Studies which use comparative research to inform theory. (Broadfoot, 1999).

This diversity of both subject matter and methodology provides a clear illustration of the difficulties facing comparative education in defining its distinctive contribution and field of activity. It might reasonably prompt outsiders to ask whether comparative education studies do indeed have a distinctive contribution to make to the study of education or whether they are merely a 'pot pourri' of topics linked only by the variety of their national settings.

As comparativists, we would undoubtedly welcome any such challenge and the opportunity it would present to explain the profound importance of the comparative approach. As Epstein has argued in an editorial of the *Comparative Education Review*:

> the traditional disciplines always will be essential; they
> furnish much of the theoretical and methodological base for
> scholarship generally. Yet the kinds of skills that individuals
> who face directly the challenges driven by changes in the
> global order need to have – 'how to think and act flexibly and
> strategically, how to move readily from one project or region to
> another, how to grasp a new situation quickly, and how to
> start solving pragmatic problems' (Goodman) – derive from
> interdisciplinary and comparative study.
>
> The time has come for a change in emphasis, and that change
> must be demanded by policy-makers and students alike. Our
> field, which draws knowledge from multiple disciplines and
> focuses it on the problems at hand, is well positioned to be a
> major resource in meeting that demand. (1997, p. 119)

Whether the setting is at the macro-level of international comparisons of educational achievement and national policy-making or at the micro-level of classroom processes, the process of education can arguably only be fully understood in the light of the impact of the context in which it is taking place. The role of comparative education is therefore the study of 'social practices and how they vary according to cultural and ideological content' (Lindsay & Parrott, 1998, p. 11). The unique contribution of comparative studies is to underline the importance not only of recognising this, but also of providing the possibility of a more systematic and theorised understanding of the nature of the relationship *between* context and process, structure and action. Too often, in social science in general and educational studies in particular:

> imputation dispenses with analysis of social interaction and
> the interests actually salient in it at the time. For these are the
> real processes that drive the system – which are responsible for
> structuring it and for its re-structuration ... to deal only with
> abstract interests (e.g. parents seek the best for their child; the
> State has an interest in a minimum level of civil disobedience
> within the total population) prevents interests from (a) ever
> being seen as vested interests in a particular structure that is
> firmly anchored in time and space and conditioned by that
> specific educational reality and (b) as elements whose results
> depend exclusively upon interaction taking place in that
> context. (Archer, 1981, p. 213)

Although Paulston (1996) suggests that the majority of 'the social sciences today are like flies stuck in amber' in their continued association with positivism, the assumptions that Archer critiques are now increasingly being challenged. As even the natural sciences come to terms with the implications of chaos theory, so the impetus to reject traditional Western models of rationality and to replace them with the more relativist perspectives of postmodernism is growing (Welch, 1998). For, if chaos theory teaches us that even in the natural sciences the smallest change can exert a profound influence on subsequent events, how much more true must this be in the social world where human perceptions and traditions, values and desires, influence everything that happens. To the extent that it is possible to trace patterns through such social chaos – the patterns of culture and human behaviour which have been identified by the various social science disciplines – comparative education provides us with the vehicle to apply them systematically to different educational contexts. As such, it offers what must arguably be one of the most rigorous forms of analysis as the basis for both understanding educational processes and predicting the potential outcomes of different forms of intervention.

But if this is so, it means, as Althusser so famously said, 'holding on to both ends of the chain' of social life. We need to engage with the reflexive relationship between structure and action that has long been the central challenge of social science; to explore how far individuals create reality and how far they are created by it. Central to the process of what Giddens (1976) calls 'structuration', whereby action is progressively transformed into system, is the role of culture. As Wertsch (1991) suggests, individuals construct their personal, group and national identities through a stock of narratives which are the result of particular historical and cultural contexts. Such 'mediated action' is the product of the interaction of a range of mediational means – cultural tools which both facilitate and constrain how individuals engage with the situation in which they find themselves. Such tools are associated with power and authority and as such are potential sources of individual and social control (i.e. systems).

Marceau 1977 makes a very similar point:

> Culture is not only a set of symbolic goods but also a picture of
> the world; it involves a hierarchy which is normative as well as
> 'factual' and people who 'own' (or control in the sense of
> understanding in particular) most of the cultural goods have a
> moral worth denied to those who 'own' least. (Marceau, 1977,
> p. 176)

Power to define the way issues are conceptualised is embodied in the key cultural tool of language. Discourse analysis of this kind offers a potentially rich harvest for comparative scholars who can use it to explore the different formulations of educational priorities in different cultural settings and hence the constraints influencing who gets what, in what form, for what purpose, within the education system. The recent advent of the discourse of the market in a number of Western countries provides a very clear example of the power of discourse to constrain thinking.

Such broad cultural differences are reflected in notions of, for example, citizenship and 'the good society'. They in turn provide the informing principles of the culture and organisation of, for example, schools. They influence both the goals imposed on schools either through central directions or through consumer pressure. These expectations are in turn mediated through the particular organisational culture and ethos of the school to shape the environment in which individual learners develop a sense of themselves socially and intellectually.

The adoption of a comparative perspective establishes the sociocultural organisational setting of educational provision – whatever it might be – as the starting point to explore the way in which different approaches to the organisation of education impact on the development of individual identity and learning. By the same token, it is essential that comparativists should both be able to study education in all its increasingly diverse forms and to recognise the importance of culture as an informing principle of what takes place. The cultural perspective of individual actors such as teachers and pupils mediates the reality they experience, both to give it meaning and to provide them with the 'tools' they need to act effectively within it. Equally important, however, is the culture of the organisation within which this education is delivered – both at the level of the institution and of the system itself. But, as Ouchi & Wilkins (1988) suggest: 'rarely do [studies] attempt to explain the relationship between an organisation's internal culture and its larger cultural or socio-economic environment' (p. 237).

I have suggested that comparative education needs to be, and arguably already is, at the forefront of change in recognising the implications of the analytic problems caused by an increasing complexity of interacting international and intercultural variables and in its consequent willingness, therefore, to embrace an interdisciplinary approach (Brock & Cammish, 1998). Nevertheless, much more needs to be done in reconceptualising the culture of comparative education itself if stones from other disciplinary hills are truly to polish the jade of this one. There needs to be a progressive recognition that a search for one absolute truth or route to progress is doomed and that there is no overarching grand meta narrative to explain the world, only a multiplicity of perspectives and fragmentations. Watson (1998b) suggests that though recent efforts by comparativists to 'map' the interactions between power, knowledge or control of knowledge and local communities has given an important boost to establishing the legitimacy of a phenomenological perspective and has usefully served to open up debates about values, this, on its own, is not enough to underpin a significant challenge to current ways of thinking about education. It is not the radical vision with comparative education as a significant force for change to which I hope we could aspire. Articulating what such a radical vision might look like will take us even further into unknown, and possibly dangerous, intellectual waters – into my last, rather more speculative section of 'something blue' – the blue yonder! But then, if earlier explorers had been content to play it safe and stay at home, where would we be now?

Something Blue: the Fourth Age of comparative education

'Has comparative education a unique role to play?' asks one. 'If so, what is it?' 'Couldn't it be subsumed as a methodological device within other social science disciplines?' asks another.

'Perhaps it is, after all, dispensable', says a third.

'But can we even define what comparative education is?' says the fourth ...

In this final section, I want to return to these questions with which I began. In the first section, 'Something Old', I outlined some of the distinctive perspectives and traditions in the field of comparative education which constitute its new unique qualities – the 'jade' which is prized for its usefulness as a tool. In the second section, 'Something New', I outlined some of the new intellectual and practical challenges that face us in the light of current social, political and economic trends and suggested that our field must move to embrace these new developments both theoretically and empirically if it is not to become 'jaded'. In the third section, 'Something Borrowed', I suggested that we need to 'borrow' from other social science disciplines to enrich the quality of our enterprise, especially the burgeoning field of sociocultural studies. If we do not, the growing interest in comparative studies on the part of policy-makers internationally is likely to reduce it to mere number-crunching and the application of half-baked hunches borrowed indiscriminately from other contexts. To the extent that this is so, comparative education is likely to become regarded increasingly contemptuously, as a 'jade' (a broken down horse) – fit for little.

In the light of all these considerations, we need to consider the way forward for our field. I want to suggest that, not only does comparative education have a unique role to play, it is a role that is potentially so comprehensive, so powerful, that it can not only answer all the preceding questions but also explain why we have traditionally found them so difficult. Accepting that comparative education is something of a cornucopia when it comes to methodologies, that its application can

101

range from complex statistical analyses based on huge quantitative databases at one extreme through to intensive ethnographic studies on the other, that it addresses all manner of topics and contexts at different levels and through different theoretical filters, I want to suggest a new conceptualisation of its role. Such a 'neo-comparative education' would be characterised by three main features.

Firstly, while it would be characterised by rigour, it would not be regarded as a discipline. Disciplines are characterised by specialist theory and often an associated language and terminology; they are likely to develop a particular set of concepts, methodology and subject matter. The various scholarly fields have, in the past, been rightly called 'disciplines' because they represent the cumulative wisdom concerning how best to pursue truth which has been built up patiently and painstakingly through the development over the years of a particular subject specialism. However, many were the product of a different, modernist, world and are associated with methodologies rooted in that conceptualisation. Comparative education, like other more interpretive social science approaches, is not, in this sense, a discipline, but rather, needs to be seen as the expression of a more generally conceived social science perspective. Its particular contribution, if we take the pervasive influence of culture as a starting point, is to document salient cultural features in a given context, to compare cultures in order to generate insights about variables whilst recognising the integrity of the cultural whole. It thus represents a profoundly interdisciplinary, or rather, meta-disciplinary, approach in which other specialisms combine to illuminate the complex and interrelated realities of our changing world. As the boundaries between education itself and other activities in life themselves break down – and the worlds of work and home, leisure and study become inextricably related – the erosion of modernist conceptions of education as a defined and organised form of activity need to be matched by similar evolutions in our tools of study.

Secondly, it will be radical. Let us for a minute consider that in the 49 Least Developed Countries of the world, 50% of children are not in school; 50% do not finish the first 4 years of schooling; 60-80% of these have no place to sit or write, and 90% learn in a strange language (Ordonez, 1996). There are very many countries where the provision of formal education cannot keep pace with the rising birth rate and others where, even if this were possible, the economy could not usefully absorb the products. The intractable problems associated with trying to provide Western-style formal schooling as a right for every child in the world are the daily concern of many of you in this audience today. Perhaps, like Lindsay & Parrott, comparative studies have led you to recognise the need to 'rethink the delivery of education in today's societies'; that moreover, although:

> *stable economies are a keystone to democratic societies ...*
> *concentration on material prosperity creates an indifference to*
> *communal life and encourages docility. If democratic societies*
> *are to be sustained and expanded, an educated populace that*
> *acknowledges values related to human dignity is a necessity.*

We need to reintroduce 'virtue' into the equation (Macintyre, 1981), that is, the consideration of the fundamental goals of our life together and the discourse associated with such debates. Intellectuals arguably have a particular responsibility in this respect, since they have the necessary insights to tease out the issues and the skills to articulate them. Dubet's (1996) criticism of the laissez-faire perspective of postmodernist stances is relevant here:

> *la critique intellectuelle est aussi portée par une éthique de la*
> *responsibilité, celle qui n'analyse pas seulement la subjectivité*
> *des acteurs, mais qui s'interroge sur les conséquences de leur*
> *action ... mais si nous voulons vraiment que quelque chose*
> *change, il import que nous rompions avec la défense d'un*
> *modèle qui n'est que la témoin d'une grandeur passé. C'est*
> *pour cela qu'il nous faut refuser de nous laisser enfermer dans*
> *la dialectique des 'vrais amis' du peuple, celle qui a si souvent*
> *préfère la beauté des principes a la réflexion sociale. (p. 139)*

I suggest that in recognising that there is an implicit value position in any conceptualisation of a problem and in the choice of method to study it (Weiler, 1990), comparative educationists should be willing to engage in fundamental debates about the nature of 'the good life' and about the role of education in relation to this in a world where, increasingly, nothing can be taken for granted. In our unique role that enables us to straddle cultures and countries, perspectives and topics, we have a responsibility to carry the debate beyond the discussion of means alone – and towards ends.

Third, and finally, I suggest that this calls for a new name for our field, a name that recognises both the blurring of boundaries between education per se and other areas of life, and equally, the necessity to blur the boundaries between the various social science disciplines in order to provide for a more integrated approach to the study of issues. If we redefine our field as being about 'learning in society' rather than education systems and practices, we might better conceptualise it as 'comparology'. Whether this name appeals to you or not, I suggest that the conception it represents is more than worthy of our new society. Ours would be firstly, a field of study which is internationally and interculturally focused; secondly, it would be in tune with the diverse currents of politics, economics and social life; and last but not least, it would be dedicated to improving the quality of our corporate life through the promotion of more effective and more important forms of learning.

It is when academics break out of the safe closet of scholarly enquiry to engage with the powerful and urgent agendas of policy-making that they are likely to encounter both their greatest opportunities and their greatest challenge. To be fruitful, such a development requires a degree of collective maturity which permits a positive response to the new opportunities which are now opening up for scholars in our field to make a positive contribution. It also requires a clear and confident vision of what we want to achieve and the principles of enquiry that are the foundation of high quality research in the field.

Comparative education has arguably never before been presented with such potentially fruitful avenues to contribute to international and national policy debates. It is pertinent to remind ourselves that 'jade' – our many-faceted metaphor – also means fortune. Comparative education is at a crossroads in its long history. If we take the right road, we may find ourselves on a major new highway. If we do not, we shall find ourselves trapped in a blind alley from which there may be no escape. As we enter a new millennium, with all the changes that it represents, there can be no greater challenge. Research that anticipates the future is typically termed 'blue skies' research. I hope we shall find that 'something blue' is the most important thing of all to the happy and fruitful marriage of our two societies.

Notes

[1] A version of this chapter was originally given as the Presidential Address at the inaugural meeting of the British Association for International and Comparative Education (BAICE), University of Reading, September 1998.

[2] See, for example, the British Government's 1998 Green Paper, *The Learning Age* and the Organisation for Economic Cooperation and Development's current commitment to lifelong learning as a key policy focus.

[3] Cited in Watson, 1998a.

[4] D. Hawker from the English Qualifications and Curriculum Authority, speaking at an Economic and Social Research Council-funded seminar on international comparisons, University of Bristol, 1999.

[5] See Broadfoot, 1996.

[6] See, for example, the recent major suite of OECD projects such as Indication of National Education Systems (INES) aimed at developing internationally applicable analytic tools for this purpose.

[7] See, for example, L.C. Stedman (1997).

[8] Comparative Education Societies in Europe Conference, Groningen, the Netherlands, September, 1998.

References

Alexander, R. (1996) Other Primary Schools and Ours: hazards of international comparison, Centre for Research and Evaluation in Primary Education occasional paper, University of Warwick.

Archer, M.S. (1981) On Predicting the Behaviour of the Educational System, *British Journal of Sociology of Education*, 2, pp. 211-219.

Ball, S. (1998) Big Policies/Smallworld: an introduction to international perspectives in education policy, *Comparative Education*, 34, pp. 119-131.

Bernstein, B. (1990) *Class, Codes and Control*, vol. IV. London: Routledge.

Blackmore, J. (1996) Follow-up from the 'Gender and Restructuring Education and Work' Plenary Address, 9th World Congress of Comparative Education Societies, University of Sydney.

Brickman, W.W. (1965) Prehistory of Comparative Education to the End of the Eighteenth Century, *Comparative Education Review*, 10, pp. 30-47.

Broadfoot, P. (1996) *Education, Assessment and Society*. Buckingham: Open University Press.

Broadfoot, P. (1999) Not So Much a Context, More a Way of Life? Comparative Education in the 1990s, in R. Alexander, P. Broadfoot & D. Phillips (Eds) *Learning from Comparing: new directions in comparative educational research, Vol. 1, Contexts, Classrooms and Outcomes*, pp. 21-31. Oxford: Symposium Books.

Brock, C. & Cammish, N. (1998) Paper given to Economic and Social Research Council seminar, University of Warwick, June.

Castells, M. (1998) *The Information Age: end of millennium*. Oxford: Blackwell.

Cowen, R. (1999) Late Modernity and the Rules of Chaos: an initial note of transitologies and rims, in R. Alexander, P. Broadfoot & D. Phillips (Eds) *Learning from Comparing, vol. 1: Contexts, Classrooms and Outcomes*, pp. 73-88. Oxford: Symposium Books.

Crossley, M. & Broadfoot, P. (1992) Comparative and International Research in Education? Scope, Problems and Potential, *British Educational Research Journal*, 18, pp. 246-260.

Dale, R. (1996) The Effects of Globalisation on Educational Systems and Practices, paper presented at the 9th World Congress of Comparative Education Societies, University of Sydney.

Department for Education and Employment (1995) *The Learning Age*. London: The Stationery Office.

Drucker, P. (1993) *Post-capitalist Society*. New York: HarperCollins.

Dubet, F. (1996) in A. Touraine, F. Dubet, D. Lapeyronnie, F. Khosrokhavar, & M. Wieviorka (Eds) *Le Grand Refus: réflexions sur la grève de décembre, 1995*. Paris: Libraire Fayard.

Durkheim, E. (1982) *Rules of Sociological Method*. London: Hutchinson.

Epstein, E. (1997) Editorial, *Comparative Education Review*, 41, pp. 117-120.

Giddens, A. (1976) *New Rules of Sociological Method*. London: Hutchinson.

Green, A. (1996) Education and State Education in an Era of Globalisation: some European and Asian Comparisons, paper presented at the 9th World Congress of Comparative Education Societies, University of Sydney.

Habermas, J. (1976) *Legitimation Crisis*. London: Heinemann.

Hanson, A. (1993) *Testing, Testing: social consequences of the examined life*. Berkeley: University of California Press.

Hartley, D. (1997) The New Managerialism in Education: a mission impossible? *Cambridge Journal of Education*, 27, pp. 47-59.

Huntington, S.P. (1996) *The Clash of Civilisations and the Remaking of World Order*. New York: Simon & Schuster.

Kandel, I.L. (1933) *Studies in Comparative Education*. New York: Houghton–Mifflin.

Lyotard, J.F. (1979) *The Post-Modern Condition: a report on knowledge*, pp. xxv, 31-37. Manchester: Manchester, University Press.

Macintyre, A. (1981) *After Virtue*. London: Duckworth.

Marceau, J. (1977) *Class and Status in France: 1945-75*. Oxford: Clarendon Press.

Ordonez, B. (1996) Paper presented at the 9th World Congress of Comparative Education Societies, University of Sydney.

Ouchi, W.G. & Wilkins, A.L. (1988) Organizational Power, in A. Westoby (Ed.) *Culture and Power in Educational Organizations*, pp. 223-255. Milton Keynes: Open University Press.

Paulston, R. (Ed.) (1996) *Social Cartography: mapping ways of seeing social and educational change*. New York: Garland.

Psacharopoulos, G. (1990) Comparative Education: from theory to practice or are A:* or B:/disc? *Comparative Education Review*, 34, pp. 369-380.

Quicke, J. (1998) Education for Democracy, seminar presented at the Graduate School of Education, University of Bristol, June.

Rogers, A. (1997) The Failure and the Promise of Technology in Education; online at: http://www.gsn.org/gsn/articles/promise.html

Schriewer, J. (1999) Coping with Complexity in Comparative Methodology – issues of social causation and processes of macro-historical globalisation, in R. Alexander, P. Broadfoot & D. Phillips (Eds) *Learning from Comparing, vol. 1: Contexts, Classrooms and Outcomes*, pp. 201-216. Oxford: Symposium Books.

Stedman, L.C. (1997) International Achievement Differences: an assessment of a new perspective, *Educational Researcher*, 26, pp. 4-15.

Steedman, H. (1999) Measuring the Quality of Educational Outputs: some unresolved problems, in R. Alexander, P. Broadfoot & D. Phillips (Eds) *Learning from Comparing, vol. 1: Contexts, Classrooms and Outcomes*, pp. 201-216. Oxford: Symposium Books.

Vaniscotte, F. (1996) *Les Ecoles de L'Europe*. Toulouse: Institut Universitaire du Formation des Maîtres (IUFM). Paris: Institut National de Recherche Pedagogique (INRP).

Watson, K. (1998a) Memories, Models and Mapping: the impact of geopolitical changes on comparative studies of education, *Compare*, 28, pp. 5-31.

Watson, K. (1998b) Review of 'Mapping Multiple Perspectives' by R. Paulston, *Compare*, 28, pp. 107-108.

Welch, A. (1998) The End of Certainty: the academic profession and the challenge of change, *Comparative Education Review*, 42, pp. 1-15.

Wertsch, J.V. (1991) *Voices of the Mind: a sociocultural approach to mediated action*. Cambridge, MA: Harvard University Press.

Wittgenstein, L. (1965) Lecture in Ethics, *Philosophical Review*, LXXIV.

Wilson, D. (1996) The History of Comparative Education, paper presented at the 9th World Congress of Comparative Education Societies, Sydney.

Wolhuter, C.C. (1997) Classification of National Education Systems: a multivariate approach, *Comparative Education Review*, 41, pp. 161-187.

PART TWO

Aspects of Research on Europe

Conducting Research into EU Education and Training Policy: some theoretical and methodological considerations

DAVID PHILLIPS & ANASTASIA ECONOMOU

The purpose of this chapter is threefold. It introduces a new project funded by the European Commission within its Training and Mobility of Researchers (TMR) programme; it describes the research design of the Oxford part of that project and of a comparative study being undertaken in Oxford on the implementation of the 'European Dimension' in education in England, Scotland and Wales; and it poses a number of theoretical and methodological problems we anticipate having to address as the studies proceed.

1. PRESTIGE

The Centre for Comparative Studies in Education in Oxford, together with centres and institutes with a comparative focus in Stockholm, Berlin, Dijon, Lisbon and Madrid, has funding from the European Commission for a joint project with three principal aims:

to examine critically the explanatory power of theories, assuming the global spread of standard models of educational provision and organisation;

to identify the complex interplay between the necessity to ensure excellence and the preservation of cultural traditions;

to provide policy-oriented information for European policy-makers at both the public and the firm (company) level on the implementation of reforms in all areas of education and training that both meet the challenges of global transition and preserve cultural identities, while ensuring high levels of excellence.

The project, using the acronym 'PRESTIGE' (Problems of Educational Standardisation and Transitions in a Global Environment) began its work in January 1998 and will continue for 4 years. Each contributing centre/institute is engaged on a project reflecting its own particular area of expertise. Thus, Berlin will focus on educational knowledge, Stockholm on educational structures and content, Dijon on macro-level education indicators, Lisbon on patterns of educational organisation, Madrid on the 'Europeanisation' of political concepts and values, and Oxford on educational policy analysis.[1]

The aim of the TMR programme is to enable young researchers from European Union (EU) member states to receive training in countries other than their own, and so PRESTIGE envisages a constant interchange and interaction of pre- and post-doctoral students between the six institutions over the 4-year period of its activities.

The Oxford part of the project will be concerned with an analysis of EU education and training policy in its relationship to the national identity and cultural traditions of the several member states. The focus will be on a comparison of factors affecting the implementation of policy in selected member states of the EU. Education and training policy in the EU is, of course, subject to so many provisos as to render much of it (apparently) technically ineffective. In Annexe 1, we give the full text of the relevant sections of the Treaty on European Union (the Maastricht Treaty). It is clear that the sovereignty of individual member states is protected to a clear and unambiguous degree. But there is consensus about the spirit of cooperation in education and training matters, and the Commission issues statements and guidelines from time to time which we might expect member states to follow.

The first task has been to identify the route of policy implementation through the educational structures of member states. We began with the schema shown in Figure 1.

Not all the countries with which we shall be concerned will have education systems whose structures fit this particular chain of policy implementation, but all will allow us to follow the transmission process from macro- to sub-macro- to micro-level. At this stage, we envisage selecting four member states for the purposes of our research: the United Kingdom – as an exemplar of traditionally decentralised systems; Germany – as an exemplar of a federal system; France – as an exemplar of a centralised system; and Sweden – as an exemplar for the 'new' member states.[2]

The principal questions to be addressed are as follows.

How big is the gap between the ideals of EU education and training policy and the reality of its interpretation and implementation in member states?
How can differences in the extent of interpretation and implementation of EU policy within the member states be explained?

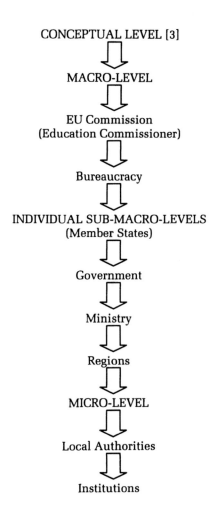

CONCEPTUAL LEVEL [3]

MACRO-LEVEL

EU Commission
(Education Commissioner)

Bureaucracy

INDIVIDUAL SUB-MACRO-LEVELS
(Member States)

Government

Ministry

Regions

MICRO-LEVEL

Local Authorities

Institutions

Figure 1. Paths of policy implementation.

In attempting to find answers to these questions, use will be made of a number of tentative theories and hypotheses, which will be tested empirically. These are:

cultural traditions (including what some comparativists have called 'national character'), and national political will, will significantly affect interpretation;

vested interests at all levels will affect transmission and implementation by creating resistances;

commitment of 'significant actors' will contribute to effective implementation at the various levels;

institutional ignorance will impede all processes of interpretation, transmission and implementation;
processes of reception of policy will inevitably result in a transformation (distortion) of the policy in question;
standardisation of policy within the member states is likely to prove unrealistic in theory and unworkable in practice.

There will be three phases to the study:

(1) collection and analysis of documents; development of an understanding of the role of various actors at various levels; design of research instruments (questionnaires, interview schedules); preliminary visits to ministries and regional and local governmental and non-governmental bureaux;
(2) semi-structured interviews (some conducted in German and French) with politicians, civil servants, administrators and teachers at the various levels; discussions with academics and other researchers;
(3) detailed analysis of the data collected.

We shall be particularly interested in three domains. They are ideas, processes and resistances.

In the *ideas* domain, our focus will be on formation, interpretation, transmission and implementation. The *processes* domain will cover enablement, enforcement, encouragement, and enhancement of policy as it is interpreted and transmitted through the various levels of the education systems of the sample member states. As far as *resistances* are concerned, we shall expect them to be bureaucratic, 'cultural'/'traditional', technical/legalistic or ignorant in character.

Because education and training policy covers such a vast field, we shall in the first instance concentrate on one area which has already received considerable attention from researchers (and for which a significant corpus of literature exists [4]) and one in which there is already research expertise in Oxford. That area is the 'European Dimension' in education. The Treaty of Maastricht places the European Dimension at the forefront of its list of aims for Community action in Article 126, which deals with 'quality education':

Community action shall be aimed at:
– developing the European dimension in education,
particularly through the teaching and dissemination of the
languages of the Member States ... [5]

We turn now to experience of investigating the European Dimension within a comparative study of implementation in England, Scotland and Wales.

2. Investigating the European Dimension

The study undertaken by Anastasia Economou has been concerned:

to investigate the interpretation and implementation of EU policy on the European Dimension by the United Kingdom (excluding Northern Ireland, i.e. Great Britain);

to identify the actors involved and procedures followed in the formulation, acceptance and implementation of the European Dimension in compulsory schooling in Great Britain;

to identify the obstacles faced in those processes and to suggest solutions to the problems identified;

to compare the approaches followed within Great Britain in regard to the European Dimension and to suggest a model for its successful and effective implementation.

Considerable data have so far been collected in the form of documents; interviews with officials, teachers, and pupils; and questionnaire returns from local education authorities (LEAs) and pupils.

Documents analysed have come from a wide variety of sources, among them the European Community, the United Kingdom Government, the Scottish Office, LEAs, the Qualifications and Curriculum Authority, the Office for Standards in Education (OFSTED), the Scottish Consultative Council on the Curriculum, the Curriculum Council for Wales, the Welsh Joint Education Committee, the Central Bureau for Educational Visits and Exchanges, and various interest/pressure groups (political parties, teachers' unions and associations).

Semi-structured interviews have been conducted with officials from the European Commission and the European Parliament representation in the United Kingdom, from the Department for Education and Employment (DfEE), the Welsh Office and the Scottish Office, and from the various organisations listed above.

Semi-structured group interviews have been conducted with pupils aged 11 and 16 in three primary and three secondary schools, one of each school type in England, Scotland and Wales, selected as examples of various forms of practice in implementing the European Dimension.

Questionnaires with open-ended questions have been sent to all LEAs in Great Britain (a 60% return rate has been achieved), and a pupil questionnaire with open-ended and closed questions has been completed by 11 and 16 year old pupils in the sample schools.

Detailed analysis of the data collected will be reported in due course. For the moment, it can be reported that models for transmission of policy for England, Scotland and Wales have been constructed on the basis of analysis of documents and information from interviews. These models, which will be of some help with the Oxford part of the PRESTIGE project (see Figure 1), are given in Figures 2, 3 and 4; they demonstrate the complex and divergent paths of policy transmission and implementation in the three parts of the United Kingdom covered in the study.

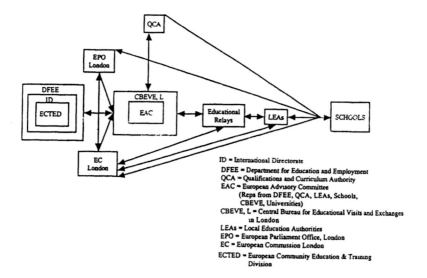

DFEE = Department for Education and Employment
QCA = Qualifications and Curriculum Authority
EAC = European Advisory Committee
(Reps from DFEE, QCA, LEAs, Schools, CBEVE, universities]
CBEV = Central Bureau for Educational Visits and Exchanges in London
LEAs = Local Education Authorities

Figure 2. England

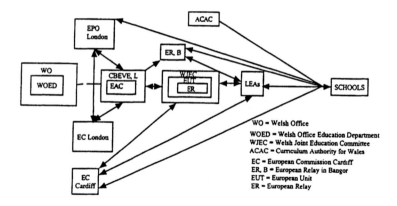

WOED = Welsh Office Education Department
WJEC = Welsh Joint Education Committee
ACAC = Curriculum Authority for Wales

Figure 3. Wales

SOED = Scottish Office Education Department
IRB = International Relations Branch
HMI = Her Majesty's Inspectorate
SIEAG – Scottish International Education Advisory Group
SCCC = Scottish Consultative Council on the Curriculum
SSTA = Scottish (Secondary) Schools Teacher Association
ADES = Association of Directors of Education for Scotland
EC = European Commission, Edinburgh
CBEVE = Central Bureau for Educational Visits and Exchanges, Edinburgh
PAT = Professional Association of Teachers
SHA = Secondary Heads Association for Scotland

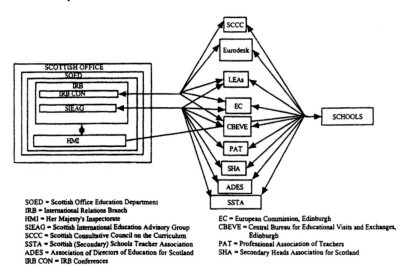

SOED = Scottish Office Education Department
IRB = International Relations Branch
HMI = Her Majesty's Inspectorate
SIEAG = Scottish International Education Advisory Group
SCCC = Scottish Consultative Council on the Curriculum
SSTA = Scottish (Secondary) Schools Teacher Association
ADES = Association of Directors of Education for Scotland
IRB CON = IRB Conferences

EC = European Commission, Edinburgh
CBEVE = Central Bureau for Educational Visits and Exchanges, Edinburgh
PAT = Professional Association of Teachers
SHA = Secondary Heads Association for Scotland

Figure 4. Scotland

A number of practical and methodological problems have emerged during the first 3 years of the study on the European Dimension. They can be listed as follows.

Access to senior officials. There is considerable reluctance among senior civil servants in particular to agree to be interviewed and to reveal information; often they are protected by fearsome secretaries. Great persistence has been necessary; appointments are sometimes brief and long-delayed.

Recording of information. When interviewees declined to be recorded there were considerable problems – especially for an interviewer whose first language is not English – in writing sufficiently detailed notes which would result in a report comparable to those produced from transcriptions of taped interviews.

Addressees of questionnaires. Identifying the person(s) responsible for the European Dimension in each British LEA was something of a problem. To achieve a high percentage return it was essential to ensure that as far as possible the questionnaires reached the right desk in each authority, but often there was no obviously identifiable person with the appropriate responsibility. Nevertheless, the return rate of 60% was satisfactory.

Sample interviews. A subjective judgement had to be made based on information culled from LEAs as to which LEA officials to interview on the basis of their authority's good practice regarding the European Dimension. Among the 40% of LEAs which did not send in returns, there might, of course, be examples of good practice that it would be useful to investigate.

Sample schools. Identification of the six schools in the sample depended on information from such European and International Coordinators as it was possible to identify within the LEAs with which contact was established. Therefore they form an opportunity sample rather than an ideal sample.

Pupil questionnaires and interviews. The questionnaire was administered by the researcher in the presence of class teachers. One particular problem concerned a teacher prompting pupils during their completion of it and then proceeding to teach her class about Europe so that they would be prepared for the group interviews held on the following day.

The experience to date of researching the complexities of interpreting and implementing the European Dimension in schools in three parts of the United Kingdom has prepared the ground for the new project within PRESTIGE and serves both to provide models for the research design and to indicate some of the difficulties the larger project will encounter.

3 . Some Problems

As the Oxford part of the PRESTIGE project begins its work (described in Part 1), we face a number of methodological questions on which we would welcome advice and comment from the research community. They can be divided into four groups.

Definitions

In investigating the European Dimension, we shall use as a starting point the definition used by the European Commission in its 1988 Resolution (See Annexe 2).

This will at least provide a basic point of comparison of different ways in which policy formulation is interpreted, linguistically and conceptually, in the member states with which we shall be concerned. Here detailed textual analysis can be attempted, together with a survey of individuals' personal understanding of the document in its different language forms.

We can expect that some terms will be differently understood simply at the level of linguistic equivalence; there will be considerable differences at a conceptual level in interpreting some of the ideas conveyed in the Resolution ('European identity', 'European civilisation', 'democracy, social justice and respect for human rights'); and the 'European Dimension' will prove to be susceptible to at least as many interpretations as there are member states of the EU. Linguistic and conceptual problems are, of course, fundamental to the comparativist's concerns when approaching any cross-national study. But irrespective of the anticipated complexities, we might attempt:

> to produce a definition of the European Dimension that will be commensurate with the reality of its linguistic and conceptual interpretation in the four member states in our survey, that will satisfy the principal actors in policy implementation, and that will comply with the spirit of the 1988 Resolution;
> to explore with interviewees their own perceptions of problems of definition;
> to confront interviewees with alternative definitions and interpretations identified from the experience of other countries.

Sample

A full assessment of the extent of the awareness and implementation of the European Dimension – at all levels – could only properly be undertaken by ministries or other authorities with the power to require the completion of survey instruments. We shall be limited to an investigation of proxies for larger entities. We shall seek to identify:

> those who might be taken to be key figures in the facilitation or prevention of policy transmission at various stages of the kinds of paths illustrated in Figures 1-4;
> those who – in our terms – might be considered 'significant actors', whether or not they are 'key figures' in terms of their official positions;
> institutions which represent examples of good or bad practice.

The identification of individuals and institutions can be random, but given our time constraints, we shall have to depend upon recommendations from national and local politicians, administrators, teachers and other researchers about whom to contact. There are clearly dangers with this approach, but experience (especially with Anastasia Economou's research) has shown that personal recommendation can initiate a kind of chain reaction of contacts willing to help with an investigation of this kind. The problem with random sampling (particularly in the case of administrators and teachers) is that it is quite possible to miss, through the vagaries of randomising, those significant actors in whose role we are especially interested and who – we might expect – will help us shed light on the processes of policy interpretation, transmission and implementation.

Another problem we face is that of matching the roles of individuals across the systems of the four member states. We shall have to devise a schema for analysing the powers and functions of individual actors that will enable us to equate them across the various systems.

Access

Having identified our key actors, there will be the problem of gaining access to them. It might be expected that those with a function in public life and all the responsibilities that go with it should be willing to answer reasonable questions about their role, to reveal their opinions on important issues and to defend their decisions and actions. But we have encountered those among the 'powerful' in education who will not give time to researchers. Among them is a well-known British Member of the European Parliament who does not reply to letters and whose secretary protects her on the grounds that she only has time to deal with inquiries from her constituents. Other people with positions of responsibility say that they will only be interviewed by senior academics (i.e. not by doctoral students, for example). Some will give only very little time; some prove haughty and supercilious. As with all research involving interviews, there are those who refuse to allow tapes to be made of interviews with them, however many assurances are given about the use to be made of the material.[6]

It is self-evident that the more powerful and important the interviewee is – or likes to think he or she is – the more difficult it will be to arrange an interview. Even where we have secured permission to interview staff in a particular division by the head of that division, we have encountered resistance, perhaps for the very reason that a superior has – in their perception – virtually required an inferior member of the staff to assist us.

We shall aim:

to provide each potential interviewee with a full account of the PRESTIGE project and what it is trying to achieve;
to include with that account a personal letter from the Project Director who will in as many cases as possible participate in the interviews;
to follow up this letter with a telephone conversation to respond to questions and make interview arrangements;
to conduct interviews where possible in the interviewee's first language;
to give the usual assurances about confidentiality; and
to provide each interviewee with project newsletters and a copy of our interim and final reports.

Comparison

This is not the place to rehearse all the problems involved in attempting cross-national comparison. Many comparative endeavours result only in the identification of contrasts, and we have chosen – deliberately – four member states whose education systems are quintessentially contrastive.

But we shall be investigating an educational phenomenon (the European Dimension) which can be expected to be common to each, and in analysing our data we shall be concerned to identify significant contrasts and to highlight commonalities between systems which might help us to identify good practice which could inform future policy implementation processes. As we have indicated in Part 1, one of the aims of PRESTIGE is 'to identify the complex interplay between the necessity to ensure excellence and the preservation of cultural traditions', and so we shall be concerned to analyse the *efficacy of significant difference* as it is manifested in the four member states of our sample.

Notes

[1] See PRESTIGE Newsletter 1, June 1998, available from the Institute of International Education, Stockholm University, 10691 Stockholm, Sweden. The total budget of the PRESTIGE project is 1.25 million ECU. Further information is to be found at: www.interped.su.se/prestige/

[2] Sweden joined the EU in 1995.

[3] We began, not entirely tongue-in-cheek, to call this the 'stratospheric' level.

[4] Among the most significant studies on or including the European Dimension are those listed in Annexe 3.

[5] Quoted from the text in: Bernard Rudden & Derrick Wyatt (Eds) (1994) *Basic Community Laws*, 5th edn, p. 92. Oxford: Clarendon Press.

[6] A key publication in this whole domain is: Geoffrey Walford (Ed.) (1994) *Researching the Powerful in Education*. London: UCL Press.

ANNEXE 1

The Treaty on European Union
Chapter 3. Education, Vocational Training and Youth
Article 126

1. The Community shall contribute to the development of quality education by encouraging cooperation between Member States and, if necessary, by supporting and supplementing their action, while fully respecting the responsibility of the Member States for the content of teaching and the organization of education systems and their cultural and linguistic diversity.

2. Community action shall be aimed at:

– developing the European dimension in education,
particularly through the teaching and dissemination of the
languages of the Member States;
– encouraging mobility of students and teachers, inter alia by

encouraging the academic recognition of diplomas and periods of study;
– promoting cooperation between educational establishments;
– developing exchanges of information and experience on issues common to the education systems of the Member States;
– encouraging the development of youth exchanges and of exchanges of socio-educational instructors;
– encouraging the development of distance education.

3. The Community and the Member States shall foster cooperation with third countries and the competent international organizations in the sphere of education, in particular the Council of Europe.

4. In order to contribute to the achievement of the objectives referred to in this Article, the Council:

– acting in accordance with the procedure referred to in Article 189b, after consulting the Economic and Social Committee and the Committee of the Regions, shall adopt incentive measures, excluding any harmonization of the laws and regulations of the Member States;
– acting by qualified majority on a proposal from the Commission, shall adopt recommendations.

Article 127

1. The Community shall implement a vocational training policy which shall support and supplement the action of the Member States, while fully respecting the responsibility of the Member States for the content and organization of vocational training.

2. Community action shall aim to:

– facilitate adaptation to industrial changes, in particular through vocational training and retraining;
– improve initial and continuing vocational training in order to facilitate vocational integration and reintegration into the labour market;
– facilitate access to vocational training and encourage mobility of instructors and trainees and particularly young people;
– stimulate cooperation on training between educational or training establishments and firms;
– develop exchanges of information and experience on issues common to the training systems of the Member States.

3. The Community and the Member States shall foster cooperation with third countries and the competent international organizations in the sphere of vocational training.

4. The Council, acting in accordance with the procedure referred to in Article 189c and after consulting the Economic and Social Committee, shall adopt measures to contribute to the achievement of the objectives referred to in the Article, excluding any harmonization of the laws and regulations of the Member States.

ANNEXE 2

Resolution on the European Dimension in Education by the Council and Ministers of Education, 24 May 1988

The objectives were restated and defined as follows, to:

– strengthen in young people a sense of European identity and make clear to them the value of European civilisation and of the foundations on which the European peoples intend to base their development today, that is in particular the safeguarding of the principles of democracy, social justice and respect for human rights;
– prepare young people to take part in the economic and social development of the Community and in making concrete progress towards European union, as stipulated in the Single European Act;
– make them aware of the advantages which the Community represents, but also of the challenges it involves, in opening up an enlarged economic and social area to them;
– improve their knowledge of the Community and its Member States in their historical, cultural, economic and social aspects and bring home to them the significance of the cooperation of the Member States of the European Community with other countries of Europe and the world.
[Quoted from: *Commission of the European Communities: Green Paper on the European Dimension of Education*, Brussels, 29 September 1993, pp. 17-181]

ANNEXE 3

Select Bibliography of Material on the European Dimension

Adams, A. & Turner, K. (1993) *The Changing European Classroom: multi-cultural schooling and the New Europe*. Cambridge: University of Cambridge Department of Education.

Antonouris, G., Bonner, H., Keane, M., Peck, B. & Ramsay, H. (1995) *The Training of School Directors for the European Dimension: School Directors and the European Dimension. Towards a Training Programme*. Glasgow: University of Strathclyde.

Bartel, H., Bambey, D., Cseh, G., Fahrwinkel, H. & Wicker, K. (1996) *Bibliographie zur europdischen Dimension des Bildungswesens 1994/95* [Bibliography on the European Dimension of Education]. Berlin: Verlag für Wissenschaft und Bildung.

Bell, G.H. (1989) *Europe in the Primary School: a case review report*. Cambridge: Pavic.

Bell, G.H. (1991) *Developing a European Dimension in Primary Schools*. London: David Fulton.

Byram, M. (1996) Education for European Citizenship, *Evaluation and Research in Education*, 10(2&3), pp. 61-67.

Convey, A. & Speak, C. (1994) *A European Dimension in the Teaching of Geography: an introduction*. Sheffield: Geographical Association.

Convey, A., Evans, M., Green, S. Macaro, E. & Mellor, J. (1996) *Pupils' Perceptions of Europe*. London: Cassell.

Evans, M., Adams, T. & Rattan, J. (1993) *A Pilot Study of UK Co-ordinated Socrates: Comenius Action 1 School-based Partnership Programmes*, Interim Report. Cambridge: University of Cambridge Department of Education.

McLean, M. (1990) *Britain and a Single Market Europe: prospects for a common school curriculum*. London: Kogan Page and Institute of Education, University of London.

Neave, G. (1988) *The EEC and Education*. Stoke-on-Trent: Trentham Books.

Peck, T.B. & Ramsay, A.H. (1994a) *The Training of School Directors for the European Dimension: managing schools in Europe*, vol. 1. Glasgow: University of Strathclyde.

Peck, T.B. & Ramsay, A.H. (1994b) *The Training of School Directors for the European Dimension: school managers and the European Dimension*, vol. 2. Glasgow: University of Strathclyde.

Ryba, R. (1992) Toward a European Dimension in Education: intention and reality in European community policy and practice, *Comparative Education Review*, 36.

Ryba, R. (1993) Educational Resources for Teaching about Europe in Schools, Report, 61st Council of Europe Teachers' Seminar, Council of Europe, October.

Ryba, R. (1994) Developing the European Dimension in Education in European Countries, in M. Bottery, C. Brock & M. Richmond (Eds) *Politics and the Curriculum*. Hull: British Comparative and International Education Society.

Ryba, R. (1995) Is Progress towards Development of the European Dimension in Education Satisfactory? In D. Phillips (Ed.) *Aspects of Education in the European Union*, pp. 63-75. Oxford: Symposium Books.

Santos Rego, M.A. (Ed.) (1997) *Politica educativa en la Union Europea después de Maastricht* [Educational Policy in the European Union after Maastricht]. Santiago de Compostela: Escola Galaga de Administración Publica.

Shennan, M. (1991) *Teaching about Europe*. London: Cassell.

Life in School: pupil perspectives and pupil experience of schooling and learning in three European countries

MARILYN OSBORN

Introduction

In a series of comparative studies, research at the University of Bristol has documented the way in which the construction of teachers' professional identity, and hence their priorities and what they define as their responsibilities, are influenced by the national context and educational traditions within which they work. This work suggests that teachers in many different national contexts mediate the external requirements placed upon them, in terms of nationally specific professional values and understandings, to produce interpretations of both their priorities and desirable classroom practices, which are often very different from those intended by government directives. Just as schools mediate prevailing social, economic and cultural realities through their own traditions and practices, so too do the actors within them. Teachers and pupils thus interact with the institutional ethos created and through their actions, both reflect and help to shape educational priorities.

Current research is exploring further the significance of the cultural context in which learning occurs by examining pupil perspectives on the purposes of schooling and on themselves as learners. The findings from this research suggest that although pupils in different European countries share many common concerns, they also come to school with significantly different attitudes towards themselves as learners, towards school and towards achievement. As a result, their expectations of themselves and of their teachers are also different.

The research traces the relationship between national educational values (as represented in official policy documents and policy statements) and these values as they are translated into the school context, teacher beliefs, classroom processes and pupil perspectives on learning and schooling. In this chapter, the theoretical rationale for such research is examined and evidence is drawn from the first phase of the study which is taking place in secondary schools in England, France and Denmark. Using a sociocultural theoretical perspective (Vygotsky, 1978; Wertsch, 1985, 1991), the main focus of the study is to explore the social reality of schooling for pupils in the three contrasting educational systems of England, France and Denmark, and the relative significance of the factors that influence the development of a learner identity in these three national settings.

There are important theoretical reasons for a study of pupils in these three national contexts. The differences between the systems and the consequent differential impact on pupils may be decreasing in the context of a united Europe, the internationalisation of adolescent peer culture, and the effects of globalisation (Eide, 1992; Masini, 1994). The study makes it possible to examine the relative effect of trends towards homogenisation and of distinctive national cultural traditions in the light of increasingly convergent economic and social structures. The research explores whether pupils' experience of schooling is becoming more similar as they try to construct their identity as learners and as adolescents, and to negotiate pathways which lead to success on the dimensions of academic achievement, peer status and social conformity (Keys & Fernandes, 1993; Rudduck et al, 1995).

Yet, continuing differences in terms of school structure, organisation, ethos, environment and learning culture in the three countries may impinge significantly on the creation of pupils' identities and on their views of themselves as learners. Gender, socio-economic status and ethnicity are also likely to be highly significant. Current research evidence suggests that, in England, it may be difficult for children to negotiate strategies which achieve a balance between academic success as a pupil, social and peer group success as an adolescent, and success in conforming to school norms for social behaviour (Hargreaves, 1967; Lacey, 1970; Woods, 1990; Abrahams, 1995; Raphael Reed, 1996). However, the process of negotiation and the strategies required may be quite different in France and Denmark, mediated as they are by different national traditions, school ethos and structures (Charlot et al, 1992; Jensen et al, 1992; Frønes, 1995; Dubet et al, 1996). The prevailing ideological traditions in each country are very different. In England, there is an emphasis on differentiation and individualisation (Department for Education and Employment [DfEE], 1997; Best, 1998), in France, on republicanism and universalism (Corbett & Moon, 1996; Organisation for Economic Cooperation and Development [OECD], 1997; Osborn et al, 1997; Osborn & Planel, 1999) and in Denmark, on collaboration and consensus (Jensen et al, 1992; Frønes,

1995). As a result, the structures put in place by schools to deal with both the cognitive and the affective aspects of children's experience are significantly different.

In Denmark there is a strong concern with the development of the 'whole child'. In Danish schools, pastoral care is emphasised as part of the teacher's role, and there is a focus on participatory democracy and lessons in citizenship (Kryger & Reisby, 1998). Children are encouraged to make decisions jointly with teachers about the direction of lessons. In addition, children often remain with the same class teacher throughout their school careers. Paradoxically, this emphasis on collaboration and consensus may actually represent a more pervasive degree of control or influence over the child as 'person' than exists in either England or France, while at the same time giving more freedom to the child as pupil.

Arguably, in England, the school attempts to exert control over both the child as pupil and the child as 'person'. While the existence of a National Curriculum and national assessment emphasise academic objectives for pupils, structures such as the pastoral care system, the inclusion in the curriculum of personal and social education, the emphasis on behavioural and moral norms, and the wearing of uniform reflect a continuing concern with the child as 'person' or the 'whole child' (Best, 1998).

In contrast, in France, the main focus of the school is on the child as 'pupil', with a relatively weak influence over the child as 'person'. Academic objectives are emphasised as the school's main area of concern. A distinctive institutional ethos and associated behavioural norms are less important and concern with pastoral care is left to outside agencies (Cousin, 1998; Audiger & Motta, 1998).

Aims of the Research

The project therefore seeks to provide an overview of the learning cultures in secondary schools in the three different countries. It examines the extent to which these can be seen to be a product of the societal culture, and the extent to which they are negotiated by the pupils/learners within them. The following key questions will be explored.

At the level of national policy discourse in the three countries, what are seen as the main aims of secondary schooling?

How are these national policy discourses mediated by institutional structures at the school level, such as school organisation and ethos, pastoral care systems, rules and norms of behaviour?

How do teachers mediate these agendas to pupils?

In the light of the preceding questions, how do children construct an identity as a learner and as a pupil, and what are the main sources of influence on their perspectives on learning, schooling, and academic achievement?

What is the relative significance of intra-national differences in social class, gender, and ethnicity as compared with international differences?

To what extent is children's experience of secondary schooling becoming more similar or moving towards convergence in the context of Europeanisation, globalisation, and the internationalisation of adolescent/peer group culture?

This chapter reports on preliminary findings from Phase 1 of the project and seeks particularly to address issues surrounding children's experience of schooling and their perspectives on teaching and learning.

Data Collection

Data were collected during 1998 and 1999 at three levels and in three phases.

National Policy Level

Government policy documentation from each country was collected and national policy discourse analysed in order to establish what are seen as the key goals of the secondary education system, the main means of achieving these goals and the major areas of tension.

School Level

School level documentation such as prospectuses, policy documents, and school development plans were collected wherever these or comparable documents existed. Interviews took place with the headteachers of the three secondary schools in each country and the appropriate year heads or form tutors. These focused on educational priorities for the children, and on the structures and organisation in place in each school to provide for the affective dimension (for example, pastoral care systems and personal and social education) and the understandings which the staff hold about the purposes of these.

The sample of schools was selected by the researchers in each country to be as representative as possible of a socio-economic mix. In England, three comprehensives, one in an area of relatively high socio-economic status in the Midlands, one in a 'mixed' area in the south-west, and one in a highly disadvantaged area in London were selected. These were matched as far as possible with schools in Denmark – two in Copenhagen and one in the north of Denmark – and with three schools in France – one an area of relatively high socio-economic status in the south-west, one in a 'mixed' suburb of Paris, and a third in a highly disadvantaged suburb of Paris. In these schools, all the qualitative data collection, teacher and pupil interviews and observation was carried out. However, for the questionnaire phase of the study, which required a sizeable sample, since English comprehensives are considerably larger than comparable schools in France and Denmark, in order to collect comparable numbers of pupil responses we had to include 20 additional schools in Denmark and one in France. In both cases, these were drawn from areas of 'mixed' socio-economic status.

Pupil Level

Data collection at pupil level combines quantitative and qualitative approaches to provide for both generalisability and richness of data. Data were collected in three phases over the course of the study during 1998 and 1999. All the pupils in the relevant year group in each school completed questionnaires. Further details of how the subsamples were selected for interview are as follows.

Phase 1 (1 week in each school)

Phase 1 consisted of a questionnaire survey of approximately 600 12 and 13 year-old children in each country, school and classroom observation and individual interviews with a selected subsample of children. These 'target' children who were interviewed and observed three times over the 2 years, included equal numbers of boys and girls and were chosen to represent a mix of high, medium and low achievers from a range of socio-economic and ethnic backgrounds.

Phase 2

This consisted of group interviews with pupils in each country. Each group included one target pupil and four friends chosen by the individual target child. Approximately six group interviews took place in each school and 18 in each country. These were designed to elicit insights into peer group culture and the relationship of this to children's identity as learners and to school culture (Dubet et al, 1996). To extend and validate the findings of Phase 1, the researchers fed back findings about the individual interviews and questionnaires of Phase 1 to the groups, based on what children in their school, their country, and in the other countries had said about their experience of schooling. Selected quotations from children in all three countries were used to stimulate group discussion and were followed up with a series of probes designed to explore meaning and to examine some of the influences on children's perspectives.

Phase 3

Follow-up individual interviews when the children are 14 will be carried out with the same subsample of children in each country, their teachers and headteachers, in order to establish any changes in perceptions which may have taken place after four terms of secondary education. Pupil attainment data will also be collected in order to explore the relationship between achievement and pupil attitudes.

This chapter draws upon the questionnaires and interviews from Phase 1 in order to illuminate understanding of the relationship between individual personality, cultural influences and school practices in influencing pupils' behaviour and learning.

Issues of Cross-cultural Comparison

The questionnaires, which were administered to between 500 and 700 12 and 13 year-old pupils in each of the three countries, were extensively piloted and revised a number of times as a result. Production of French, English and Danish questionnaires took place simultaneously, with team members from all three countries present. Careful consideration was given to linguistic and conceptual cross-cultural differences. In each case, bilingual researchers from at least two of the three countries administered the questionnaires to children in the classroom in the presence of their teacher. They were thus able to deal with any difficulties the children had in answering the questions and to collect the questionnaires immediately.

The extensive piloting and the presence of the researchers during completion helped to minimise some of the many problems associated with the questionnaire method in a cross-cultural study. The same researchers were also able to explore in more depth many of the issues arising from the questionnaire through individual interviews with a selected subsample of children and through teacher interviews and classroom observation. In any method of researching with young adolescents, there are potential problems of authenticity of response and researchers must accept that their presence in the setting and their relationship with the children may have influenced the outcome to some extent (Connolly, 1997). However, through triangulation of the findings using multiple methods, these problems have been minimised as much as is possible.

Findings

International Differences in Pupil Experience

This chapter focuses particularly on pupils' perceptions of their schooling and of their teachers, and compares and contrasts both *inter* and *intra*-nationally, looking at children in the three countries and at the influence of gender and socio-economic differences *within* each country on pupil attitudes.

When pupils in the questionnaire were asked to agree or disagree with a set of statements about school, the impact of universal concerns with the economic function of education made itself felt very strongly. In spite of different national emphases on the link between school and the economy, almost all pupils perceived the economic function of school and its link to jobs as strongly important (Table I). Over 85% of children in all three countries saw school as 'the first step on the way to my career'. Roughly two-thirds in all three samples felt very positive 'on the whole' about their teachers. However, the Danish children emerged as the most positive overall in their feelings about school. They were the most likely to enjoy school and lessons and the least likely to want to leave school as soon as they could or to see school as getting in the way of their lives.

		Strongly agree / agree (%)		
		Denmark	England	France
1.	On the whole I like my teachers	64	69	63
2.	School gets in the way of my life	21	30	31
3.	I enjoy school	67	54	56
4.	I really enjoy most lessons	63	52	54
5.	I want to do well at school	92	96	96
6.	I feel as though I'm wasting my time at school	10	7	13
7.	The best part of my life is the time I spend in school	11	17	18
8.	I'd like to leave school as soon as I can	17	23	17
9.	School is the first step on the way to my career	85	91	85
Totals (*n*)		610	577	444

Table I. My feelings about school. Here are some statements of what you might think about your school. Please show how much you agree or disagree by filling in the appropriate bubble.

In some respects, the English children were the least enthusiastic about school. They enjoyed school and lessons the least and they were the most likely to say that they would like to leave school as soon as they could. However, the gap between English and French children in terms of positive and negative feelings towards schooling and teaching had narrowed compared with our findings at primary level (Osborn et al, 1998). French children felt equally as strongly as English children that school got in the way of their lives. French secondary pupils who completed the current questionnaire and interviews were far more negative about their teachers and schools than their 10 and 11 year-old compatriots at primary level. This suggests that perhaps the transition to secondary school and entry into adolescence might have engendered a change in French children's relationship to school, just as it has been shown to do in England (Rudduck et al, 1995).

Difference in Perceived Functions of School

Table II shows pupils' responses to a series of statements about the functions of schooling. All pupils were broadly in agreement that one of the functions of school is to teach you to learn new things and to be aware of your own strengths and weaknesses. Their general agreement that school is also concerned with 'helping you get qualifications' reflected global concerns with the economic functions of education and its links to careers and the jobs market.

However, in many respects, the differences between the responses of pupils reflected the differences in the aims of the national systems discussed earlier. There was a stronger emphasis placed on the personal development function of school by pupils in England. Some 58% of English pupils felt that school teaches you to understand other people's feelings, compared with 44% of French pupils and 33% of Danish. By contrast, in Denmark, the national emphasis is more on democratic discussion leading to consensus and on encouraging pupils to fit in with the group (Kryger & Reisby, 1998). Perhaps this is why fewer Danes (45%) felt that school is a place where you learn to obey rules. The findings suggest that group norms are more internalised in Denmark so that there is no apparent need to simply obey an externally imposed disciplinary framework. For French pupils (79%) and English pupils (78%), however, school was seen as a place where there was a high premium on obedience to institutional rules.

The results of the questionnaire present a picture of secondary school as a hard and often difficult experience for French pupils. They saw school as a place where it is difficult to succeed (43% compared with 25% of Danes and 20% of English), where rules are of paramount importance, and where there is little room for expressing your own ideas and opinions. The emphasis in England on individualism and on differentiation was reflected in English pupils' perception of school as a place where you can express your own ideas and opinions (73%), but, as for French pupils, this was less important for Danes (59%), possibly for the reasons cited earlier, the emphasis on collectivism and consensus reflected in the national goals of the system. The social function of school as a place where it is possible to socialise and meet your friends was clearly more important for English (79%) and French (86%) young people than for Danes (66%).

		Strongly agree / agree (%)		
		Denmark	England	France
1.	School teaches you to understand other people's feelings	33	58	42
2.	An important thing about school is meeting up with your friends	66	79	86
3.	School helps you to sort out your life	65	67	58
4.	School helps you to become mature	57	76	75
5.	School is boring	36	36	27
6.	An important thing about school is learning to cooperate with others	91	84	78
7.	School is all about getting jobs when you leave	75	70	84
8.	An important thing about school is that it helps you to get qualifications	80	95	75
9.	An important thing about school is learning new things	94	95	97
10.	School makes you aware of your own strengths and weaknesses	78	79	86
11.	School is a place where you learn to obey rules	45	78	80
12.	School is a place where you can express your own ideas and opinions	59	73	48
13.	School is a place where it is difficult to succeed	25	20	43
Totals (n)		610	577	444

Table II. My feelings about school. Here are some statements of what you might think of school in general. Please show how much you agree or disagree by filling in the appropriate bubble.

The results of asking the pupils in the three systems to respond to a series of statements about teachers by indicating the extent to which this applied to 'most of your teachers/many teachers/only a few teachers/hardly any teachers' are given in Tables III(a) and III(b). Danish pupils were the most likely to see most or many of their teachers as helpful with problems and worries, with building friendly relationships and with building self-esteem. Danish teachers seemed to avoid suggesting that pupils were not good enough in their work. Danish pupils also saw many of their teachers as having trust in pupils.

However, they did not feel that their teachers placed emphasis on making pupils want to work hard.

		Most / many teachers (%)		
		Denmark	England	France
	I believe teachers			
1.	aren't really interested in pupils as people.	33	24	57
2.	give challenging work.	66	74	64
3.	really want their pupils to do well.	85	79	74
4.	encourage pupils to say what they think in class.	62	65	47
5.	will have a laugh with pupils.	47	43	23
6.	make pupils want to work hard.	49	73	39
Totals (*n*)		610	577	444

Table III(a). Teachers. Please read the statements below about teachers and mark a bubble in each row to show whether you think this applies to: most of your teachers / many of your teachers / only a few of your teachers / hardly any of your teachers.

French responses once again emphasised a relatively difficult experience of school life. In the French pupils' view, they had fewer teachers who built up their confidence and self-esteem or who were helpful with pupils' problems or worries. Fewer French teachers were interested in their pupils as people or in their opinions; fewer encouraged pupils to say what they thought in class or were willing to have a laugh with pupils. Nor were most French teachers seen as concerned with helping pupils to get on well as a group. Once again, the findings reflect a national educational emphasis on the academic and cognitive functions of the educational system in France. In keeping with the more homogeneous grouping of French pupils and the existence of specialist professionals such as educational psychologists and counsellors, French teachers were less likely to be seen as spending much time with pupils who need extra help.

However, the responses suggest that the French pupils were not particularly satisfied with the way in which teachers carried out their academic role. They saw themselves as having fewer teachers who provided good guidance about how they could improve their work, or who made them want to work hard. In contrast, in our previous study of primary pupils in England and France, it was here in the academic and cognitive side of education that the strengths of French teaching seemed to emerge. At primary level, our sample of 800 French pupils saw their schools and teachers in a very positive light, emphasising that their teacher was useful and helpful to them and was there to make them work hard (Osborn et al, 1998).

		Most / many teachers (%)		
		Denmark	England	France
	I believe teachers			
1.	make pupils feel they aren't good enough in their work	24	25	58
2.	are a good example for their pupils	52	57	53
3.	are interested in pupils' opinions	68	61	42
4.	treat all pupils equally	50	53	48
5.	are more interested in pupils who can do well	43	48	57
6.	show what they really think and feel	30	43	29
7.	are interested in building friendly relationships with their pupils	71	45	49
8.	are respected by pupils	54	52	47
9.	make pupils feel they can be successful	72	67	59
10.	like and enjoy their job	69	61	65
11.	provide good guidance about how you can improve your work	72	74	58
12.	trust pupils	63	48	35
13.	do not listen to pupils	27	23	30
14.	try to make pupils get on well as a group	80	77	52
15.	spend too much time with pupils who need extra help	36	32	18
Totals (*n*)		610	577	444

Table III(b). Teachers. Please read the statements below about teachers and mark a bubble in each row to show whether you think this applies to: most of your teachers / many of your teachers / only a few of your teachers / hardly any of your teachers.

Although the two samples of French children at primary and secondary level were different, both were from schools selected to be as representative as possible of a socio-economic, ethnic and geographical spread. Any conclusions drawn from this comparison must be tentative, but this certainly suggests that there may be a very steep fall in positive perceptions of schooling between the primary and secondary phases of schooling, which should be of some concern to French educationalists. This fall does not appear to be connected to a greater prevalence of anti-school peer pressure. There is evidence from the current study that French pupils at secondary level experience less of this pressure from their peers than pupils in other countries. For example, French pupils were more likely to see doing good work as making them popular with their friends (27%) compared with 13% of English and 11% of Danish pupils.

In keeping with the English emphasis on affective education, the English pupils were most likely to have teachers who encouraged pupils to say what they think in class and who were interested in pupils as people. Teachers in England were also seen as the most likely to show pupils 'what they really think and feel'. Interestingly, English teachers also emerged as the most likely to make pupils want to work hard and to provide good guidance on how pupils could improve their work. In spite of all this, English pupils apparently had more teachers who did not enjoy their job (Tables IIIA and IIIB). This resonates with recent studies of teachers across Europe, which suggested that teachers in England perceived themselves as more stressed and disaffected than teachers in many other countries.

Intra-national Context: gender and social inequality

The findings suggest that within each country, social inequality and gender issues may be mediated differently within the three education systems so that the impact of these factors on the way in which pupils' views of themselves are structured may vary.

In terms of gender issues, in all three countries, the girls in our sample were more positive about school and about teachers than the boys. Thus, girls were less likely to see school as 'getting in the way of my life' (Table IV). However, there were variations in the size of the 'gender' gap from one country to another. For example, Danish pupils were positive about their teachers regardless of gender (there were no statistically significant differences between boys and girls), whereas, in both England and France, girls agreed significantly more often than boys that they liked their teachers.

Where the difference in the perspectives of boys and girls was statistically significant in all three countries, the gap was often smallest in Denmark and greatest in France, with England somewhere in the middle (Figures 1-4). Overall, French boys were the least likely of all the groups to be positive about school and teachers. Whereas in Denmark and England, both boys and girls enjoyed school equally, only 45% of French boys did so compared with 67% of French girls. French boys were also significantly more likely than girls to feel that they were wasting time at school, to feel bored by school and to disagree that 'the best part of my life is the time I spend in school'. Of the three countries, England was the only one where there was no statistically significant 'gender gap' in pupils' views of the future. English boys and girls were equally likely to see school as the first step on the way to their career whereas in the other two countries girls were more likely than boys to see the career uses of school.

		Strongly agree / agree (%)					
		Denmark		England		France	
		Girl	Boy	Girl	Boy	Girl	Boy
1.	On the whole I like my teachers	66.9	63.6	*71.3	66.7	*68.1	59.4
2.	School gets in the way of my life	*18.1	25.3	*22.0	37.0	*26.3	35.1
3.	I enjoy school	71.3	63.6	59.4	51.8	*66.8	44.7
4.	I really enjoy most lessons	66.9	61.0	54.9	50.6	59.7	51.0
5.	I want to do well at school	94.6	92.8	98.0	97.7	97.5	97.4
6.	I feel as though I'm wasting my time at school	6.5	12.4	3.3	9.3	*7.3	18.2
7.	The best part of my life is the time I spend in school	*7.9	13.0	15.0	19.3	*24.2	11.0
8.	I'd like to leave school as soon as I can	13.6	18.9	21.1	24.7	14.0	20.8
9.	School is the first step on the way to my career	*89.3	83.0	92.3	91.3	*87.8	83.2
10.	School is boring	31.0	42.3	34.7	38.8	*18.8	36.7
Totals (n)		280	324	244	311	233	199

* = differences within each country which are statistically significant.

Table IV. Gender and attitudes to school. Here are some statements of what you might think about your school. Please show how much you agree or disagree by filling in the appropriate bubble.

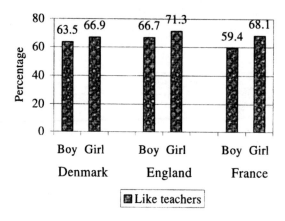

Figure 1.

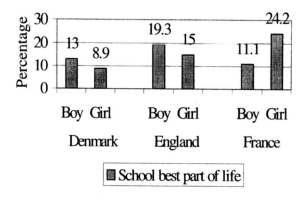

Figure 2.

School gets in the way of my life
(strongly agree + agree)

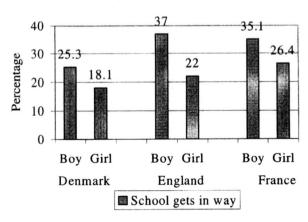

Figure 3.

I feel as though I am wasting my time at
school
(strongly agree + agree)

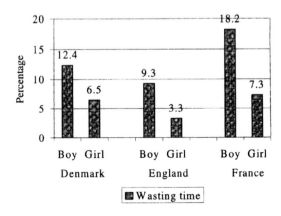

Figure 4.

		Strongly agree / agree (%)								
		Denmark			England			France		
		P/M	W/B-C	Unem.	P/M	W/B-C	Unem.	P/M	W/B-C	Unem.
1.	On the whole I like my teachers.	*80.6	58.7	62.5	*71.1	74.2	68.6	*79.1	53.8	52.9
2.	School gets in the way of my life.	*13.2	23.5	29.5	*28.0	28.8	40.0	26.4	33.8	31.3
3.	I enjoy school.	*83.9	61.0	65.1	52.7	54.9	54.3	60.2	53.6	70 6
4.	I really enjoy most lessons.	72.3	60.1	67.2	47.6	54.6	51.4	52.6	55.3	62.5
5.	I want to do well at school.	95.5	92.8	95.3	98.4	98.1	91.4	97.6	97.2	100.0
6.	I feel as though I'm wasting my time at school.	*5.8	9.6	15.6	*2.7	5 1	17.1	10.4	14.3	18.8
7.	The best part of my life is the time I spend in school.	5.2	11 3	17.2	15.0	17.6	20.0	18.1	19.0	17.6
8.	I'd like to leave school as soon as I can.	8.4	18.8	20.6	18.7	23.0	34.3	22.7	25.0	8.8
9.	School is the first step on the way to my career.	85.9	86.0	85.9	93.0	92.1	91.4	87.9	83.9	94.1
Totals:	n =	155	293	64	108	125	16	172	208	17

(* = differences which are statistically significant)

(P/M = Professional/Managerial W/B-C = White Collar Unem. = Unemployed)

Table V. Socio-economic status and attitudes to school. Here are some statements of what you might think about your school. Please show how much you agree or disagree by filling in the appropriate bubble.

In summary, for pupils of this age group, the much publicised 'gender' gap in England was not so striking as might have been expected, given the concern of English policy-makers with boys' underachievement and lack of motivation (Office for Standards in Education [OFSTED], 1998). In fact, the most significant gender differences occurred in France, where traditionally the undermotivation of boys has not been seen as an issue.

In order to examine socio-economic differences in pupil perspectives, we divided pupils into three groups according to parental employment (either father's or mother's, whichever fell into the 'highest' category). The categories were: professional/managerial, white/blue collar, and unemployed. Table V indicates how pupils in each of these three categories responded to a series of statements about school and teachers. On the whole, for each country, the pattern of difference is fairly consistent, with the children of professional/managerial parents most positive about school, teachers and learning, and the children of unemployed parents the least positive. However, there were some exceptions to this and it is striking that in all three countries, pupils from all social groups were equally concerned to do well at school and to use school as a step to a future career.

In England and Denmark, there were more statistically significant differences between social groups. The children of unemployed parents were the most likely to see school as a waste of time or as getting in the way of their lives. There were significant differences in enjoyment of school in Denmark, with the children of professional/managerial parents far more positive than the other social groups. Although, in France, this group more often liked their teachers than did the children of white/blue collar or unemployed parents, in general there were fewer significant differences in the perspectives of pupils from different social groups than was the case in the other countries (Figures 5-8). It may be that the clear understanding shared by the whole of French society about progress through the educational system, together with a national emphasis, clearly taken on board by teachers, on equal entitlement and on bringing all children to a common level rather than on differentiation and individualisation, are factors which might make a difference to the narrowing of this social gap in France.

The findings lend some support to the notion of a 'long tail of undermotivation' in both England and, perhaps more surprisingly, Denmark in relation to some more disadvantaged children.

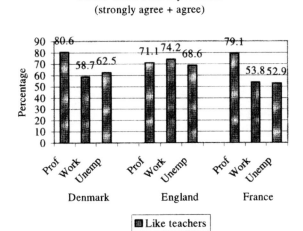

Figure 5.

The best part of my life is the time I spent in
school (strongly agree + agree)

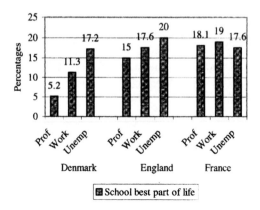

Figure 6.

I feel as though I am wasting my time at school
(strongly agree + agree)

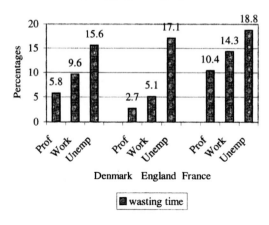

Figure 7.

School gets in the way of my life
(strongly agree + agree)

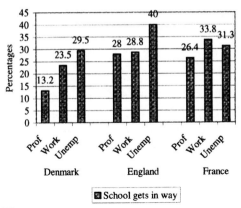

Figure 8.

Concerns of European Pupils

Thus, the study found clear evidence of difference between the three countries in pupils' views of their learning, but also many common concerns. In both the questionnaires and the individual and paired interviews, certain universal issues which suggest enduring features of the teaching/learning situation emerged. In talking about their teachers both quantitatively (responding to fixed response statements in the questionnaire) and qualitatively (responding to open-ended questions in the questionnaires and in individual interviews), English, French and Danish pupils all emphasised the same three qualities as of paramount importance. All children thought it most important to have teachers who explain things well, teachers who give interesting lessons, and teachers who are firm but above all, fair.

A strong sense came from all the children's interviews that some teachers are far more prepared than others to spend time explaining things that have not been understood. However, it was particularly noticeable in France that children had strong concerns about teachers who were unwilling to give proper explanations. These were allied with the importance of teachers having 'respect' for pupils, which it was felt was often lacking. Florence, at a collège (secondary school) in a disadvantaged outer suburb of Paris, talked of the three things she disliked about school:

> *The attitude of people, their behaviour. Pupils who don't respect teachers. Teachers who don't respect pupils. For example, at the end of the exercise, when we haven't understood. They don't explain properly what we have to do.*

145

> *There are some teachers who explain well, but there are others*
> *who, who don't really explain well.*

Daniel, in the same school, where most of the pupils were of ethnic minority, mainly North African origin, used similar concepts:

> *There are teachers who respect us and there are those who*
> *don't respect us.*

Those teachers with whom he was particularly out of sympathy were:

> *Those [teachers] who are only interested in those who get good*
> *marks. Those [pupils] who don't get good marks, they just say*
> *that they only have to listen in class.*

A Danish pupil, Mette, from a school in the north of Denmark, also talked of some teachers who 'are better at explaining than others'. However, she felt that there were a significant number of teachers where:

> *They try to kind of explain to everyone. If you don't*
> *understand it immediately then they explain it again, so ...*

If you got a wrong answer in class then 'the teacher will try to explain it and ask you to try again or something or maybe they'll pick someone else'. She felt that a good way of learning was:

> *by getting it explained and getting some problems we can sit*
> *and work out while the teacher goes round, and then if you*
> *can't manage something, you get it explained again and then*
> *... but also – there are a lot of ways, like with a report or*
> *something – there are many possible ways of presenting it.*

A concern which emerged most strongly for English pupils was the importance of having a secure and well-developed social life in school. For Ann, a pupil in an inner-city comprehensive, friendships originated, were developed and sustained by talk, chat and 'having a laugh'. Humour and having a laugh were an important aspect of lessons. While it was 'OK' to work, it was not acceptable to simply keep one's head down and get on with one's work. The maintenance of her social relationships through 'humour' often took priority over work, even lesson time:

> *The main thing is to just have a laugh. Not just get on with*
> *work and not communicate with anybody because we don't*
> *like that. It's all right to get on with work but not to not talk or*
> *not have a laugh.*

She talked disparagingly of Jon, the class 'boffin':

> *Jon the gnome. He's the class boffin. He's just the smartest in*
> *the class and he gets everything right. He's in all the top*

*groups and he's just – agh! He's just clever. He just gets
everything right and he's just good at everything. The only
wrong thing with him is his handwriting. He doesn't chat or
have a laugh. He just gets on with it.*

Similarly, she particularly valued teachers who were able to have a laugh but at the same time get the children to work. Her assessment of and reaction to her teachers was subtle and sophisticated. One of her most liked teachers was Mrs Baxter. She recognised that:

*Mrs Baxter would like Jon because he's always trying his best,
to the best of his ability. But Mrs Baxter's like, relaxed; likes a
laugh and that. But she's serious, though. She'll make sure
everyone works to the best of their ability.*

In spite of other reservations about Mrs Baxter's criticisms of her, she still liked Mrs Baxter because 'she's just funny. She makes me laugh'.

In Ann's interview, and in the remarks of many other English secondary pupils, there were echoes of the findings of a previous project, QUEST (Quality in Experiences of Schooling Trans-Nationally), carried out by three of the research team. In a comparison of pupils in the upper years of primary school in England and France, we found that in England, there was more evidence of the influence of peer group pressure in the classroom which made it not acceptable to pupils to be too successful in school. This led pupils not to want to be seen as a 'goodie', a 'keener' or a 'boffin' in class (Osborn et al, 1998). We argued that pupils' attitudes to school related to non-official criteria such as obtaining social approval and popularity with peers.

Measor & Woods (1984) and Pollard (1985) describe an 'informal' pupil culture in England which differs from the formal one and where the teacher's positive values of hard work and effort are translated by pupils into a negative one of being a 'boff', a 'goodie-goodie' or a 'keener'. In France, however, the peer culture seemed more positive towards school, at least at primary level. Pupils appeared from our observations largely to share official school values. In part, this may be a result of the separation of the person and the system, of personal and academic competences in French education (Dubet et al, 1996; Cousin, 1998). Thus, in France, at both primary and secondary level, there is a strong distinction between *la vie scolaire*, the social domain, and *l'instruction ou la pédagogie*, the learning domain, with a different structure in place, particularly within the secondary school, to develop each domain. The English system does not make this strong ideological distinction between learning and the social domain, conceptualising learning in wider terms as embracing the 'whole child' rather than being restricted to teacher instruction in the classroom. This means that pupils are controlled with a stronger hidden message that how one behaves, not only in the classroom, in the school and even outside school, affects learning.

According to this view, learning and behaviour are less easily separated, whereas in the French model they are seen as distinct. Thus, for example, in England, an emphasis on strict rules connected with uniform or dress is perceived as linked to better examination results, and there is an emphasis on a code of behaviour and discipline which extends even to outside the school gates. Possibly this stronger control over the 'whole person' in English education is related in a symbiotic way to the stronger influence of peer group pressure which we found in both our studies of primary and secondary schooling.

Conclusion

Overall, many of the preliminary findings from the questionnaires and interviews of Phase 1 of the study suggest that pupils' perceptions, filtered as they are through the mediation of teachers and the particular interpretations which pupils bring to school with them, do nevertheless resonate fairly closely with the particular emphases of the goals of the national systems. The Danish emphasis on collaboration and consensus and the concern with education for citizenship and democracy as well as with the academic goals of education emerged strongly in the pupils' responses. Danish pupils were broadly the most positive towards schooling, learning and teachers. They saw school as helping them to fit into a group situation rather than emphasising the development of the individual. They did not in general feel that their teachers placed a great deal of emphasis on making them work hard. They were less likely than the other groups to want to leave school as soon as they could or to see school as getting in the way of their lives.

In some respects, the English children, like those we studied previously at primary level, were still the least enthusiastic about school. They enjoyed school and lessons the least and were the most likely to want to leave school as soon as they could and to feel that school got in the way of their lives. However, there were a number of positive elements of teaching for this group, who emphasised their teachers' concern with pupils expressing their own ideas and with pupils as people. Encouragingly, they also felt that they had good feedback from teachers about their work and felt that teachers made them work hard. The English pupils' responses reflected the emphasis at national level on the affective dimension of education as well as the cognitive, and the stress on individualisation and differentiation. In terms of the dimension shown in Figure 1, the English findings did suggest that the dual concerns at national level with both the whole child and the child as student were equally reflected in their school experiences.

In France, with its emphasis on universalism and republicanism and on all children being treated equally, and with its separation of academic and social/personal development goals, children nevertheless had strong concerns about teachers who do not respect pupils and who do not explain things properly. The French secondary pupils in our sample did not show much evidence of having experienced an affective or social and personal dimension to their school experience. Neither did they feel that they were getting the guidance they needed to improve or an emphasis on hard work from teachers. There is some suggestion from these findings of a lowering of teacher expectations at secondary level and a drop in pupil motivation.

Although there was continuing evidence from these results of the influence of national context on pupil perceptions of schooling, there was also a clear suggestion of the globalisation of many concerns. All pupils shared a certain number of similar priorities for teaching and a similar concern with the economic function of education and its link to the job market.

Within each education system, gender and socio-economic issues were mediated differently so that the impact of these on pupils' views of themselves as learners varied. There were gender differences in perceptions of schooling in all three countries, but the differences in perceptions of schooling between boys and girls were more marked in France than in the other two countries. In general, French boys were the least likely of all the groups to be positive about school.

Socio-economic differences in perceptions of schooling were evident in all three countries, but were more significant in England and Denmark than in France, suggesting evidence of a 'long tail of undermotivation' of children from different social groups in these countries. It is possible that the French emphasis on universalism and on a clear understanding of progress through the system, aimed at bringing all children to a common level of achievement, rather than on individualisation and differentiation, may have contributed to the narrowing of this gap.

The findings presented here suggest that in spite of the many pressures towards greater homogenisation of educational systems, the national culture and educational traditions of the three European countries under study continue to lead to significant differences in the way in which pupils define their relationship to school. Overall, the study emphasises the importance of understanding how pupil attitudes to teaching, learning and schooling are situated within a wider cultural context.

Acknowledgements

This chapter is based on the Economic and Social Research Council (ESRC) funded ENCOMPASS project, Education and National Culture: a comparative study of pupil attitudes to secondary schooling. ESRC's continuing support for this work is gratefully acknowledged.

The ENCOMPASS project team, who all contributed to this chapter, are: Birte Ravn and Thyge Winther-Jensen, University of Copenhagen; Olivier Cousin, CADIS, University of Bordeaux II; Marilyn Osborn, Patricia Broadfoot, Elizabeth McNess, Claire Planel and Pat Triggs, University of Bristol.

References

Abrahams, J. (1995) *Divide and School: gender and class dynamics in comprehensive education.* London: Falmer Press.

Audiger, F. & Motta, D. (1998) The Strange Concept of Affective Education: a French perspective, in P. Lang (Ed.) *Affective Education: a comparative view.* London: Cassell.

Best, R. (1998) The Development of Affective Education in England, in P. Lang (Ed.) *Affective Education: a comparative* view. London: Cassell.

Charlot, B., Bautier, E. & Rochex, J-Y. (1992) *École et Savoir dans les Banlieues ... et Ailleurs.* Paris: Armand Colin.

Connolly, P. (1997) In Search of Authenticity: researching young children's perspectives, in A. Pollard, D. Thiessen & A. Filer (Eds) *Children and their Curriculum.* London: Falmer Press.

Corbett, A. & Moon, R. (Eds) (1996) *Education in France: continuity and change in the Mitterand years, 1981-1995.* London: Routledge.

Cousin, O. (1998) *L'Efficacité des Collèges: sociologie de l'effet établissement.* Paris: Presses Universitaires de France.

Department for Education and Employment (1997) *Excellence in Schools.* London: HMSO.

Dubet, F., Cousin, O. & Guillemet, J.P. (1996) A Sociology of the Lycée Student, in A. Corbett & R. Moon (Eds) *Education in France: continuity and change in the Mitterand years, 1981*-1995. London: Routledge.

Eide, K. (1992) The Future of European Education as Seen from the North, *Comparative Education,* 28, pp. 9-17.

Frønes, I. (1995) *Among Peers: on the meaning of peers in the process of socialisation.* Oslo: Scandinavian University Press.

Hargreaves, D. (1967) *Social Relations in a Secondary School.* London: Routledge & Kegan Paul.

Jensen, B., Nielsen, M. & Stenstrup, E. (1992) *The Danish Folkeskole: visions and consequences.* Copenhagen: Danish Council for Educational Development in the Folkeskole.

Keys, W. & Fernandes, C. (1993) *What Do Students Think About School?* Slough: National Foundation for Educational Research.

Kryger, A. & Reisby, K. (1998) The Danish Class Teacher: a mediator between the pastoral and the academic, in P. Lang (Ed.) *Affective Education: a comparative view.* London: Cassell.

Lacey, C. (1970) *Hightown Grammar: the school as a social system.* Manchester: Manchester University Press.

Masini, E. (1994) The Futures of Cultures: an overview, *The Futures of Cultures*. Paris: UNESCO Publishing.

Office for Standards in Education (1998) London: Department for Education and Employment.

Organisation for Economic Cooperation and Development (1996) *Reviews of National Policies for Education: France*. Paris: OECD.

Osborn, M. & Broadfoot, P. (1997) Proposal to the Economic and Social Research Council.

Osborn, M., Broadfoot, P.M., Planel, C., Sharpe, K. & Ward, B. (1998) Being a Pupil in England and France: findings from a comparative study, in A.M. Kazamias, with M.G. Spillane (Eds) *Education and the Structuring of the European Space*. Athens: Seirios Editions.

Osborn, M. & Planel, C. (1999) Comparing Children's Learning, Attitude and Performance in French and English Primary Schools, in R. Alexander, P. Broadfoot & D. Phillips *Learning from Comparing*, vol. 1. Wallingford: Triangle Books.

Pollard, A. (1985) *The Secret World of the Primary School*. London: Holt.

Raphael Reed, L. (1996) Working with Boys: a new research agenda, *Redland Papers no. 3*. Bristol: University of the West of England.

Richards, M. & Light, P. (1986) *Children of Social Worlds*. Cambridge: Polity Press.

Rudduck, J., Chaplain, R. & Wallace, G. (1995) *School Improvement: what pupils can tell us*. London: David Fulton.

Vygotsky, L.S. (1978) *Mind in Society: the development of higher psychological processes*. Cambridge, MA: Harvard University Press.

Wertsch, J.V. (Ed.) (1985) *Culture, Communication and Cognition: Vygotskian perspectives*. Cambridge: Cambridge University Press.

Wertsch, J.V. (1991) *Voices of the Mind: a socio-cultural approach to mediated action*. Cambridge, MA: Harvard University Press.

Woods, P. (1990) *The Happiest Days?* Basingstoke: Falmer Press.

Learners' Diversity: the integration of Maghrebi children in mainstream classrooms in Spain

PILAR ARNAIZ SÁNCHEZ, REMEDIOS DE HARO & JUAN NAVARRO

Introduction

Europe has become a true multicultural society; we are able to appreciate the presence of different cultures, races, ethnic groups, languages and religions throughout the different state members of the European Union (EU), which basically have their roots in migrations. Therefore, European society must allocate the necessary mechanisms in order to convert these differences into a useful source of enrichment and not of discrimination. Thus, it must fight against inequalities and the causes that provoke them, that is to say, the phenomenon of social rejection that so much affects immigrants (Figueroa, 1995; Hoff, 1995; Arnaiz y de Haro, 1995). Therefore, our schools should be privileged places to promote tolerance and living in harmony with other people, and should instil the positive values of diversity (de Haro Rodriguez, 1995, 1997; Díaz Aguado, 1996).

This has spawned a challenge for schools in the latter part of the twentieth century, and as a consequence, schools are expected to provide answers for the diversity of cultures, ethnic groups, races, languages, religions and ideologies present in our educational environment (Banks & McGee Banks, 1995).

Consequently, multicultural education constitutes an answer for the needs and problems of multicultural societies. Its main objective is to promote respect for diversity and the living in harmony of citizens of a state. Above all, intercultural education helps to overcome ethnocentrism, by educating citizens to become open-minded and objective and at the same time make them capable of participating in the wealth that cultural diversity provides (Olneck, 1995; Arnaiz & de Haro Rodriguez, 1997).

This means the modification of old and the presentation of new approaches. Writers such as Banks (1993) and Artiles & Larsen (1998) define multicultural education as an idea, an educational reform movement and a process whose main objective is to change the structure of educational institutions.

Nieto (1992, 1998) has provided one of the most inclusive and eclectic definitions of multicultural education as a process of comprehensive school reform, aimed at all the students. Seen from such a perspective, racism and all other types of discrimination are rejected, and he defends the pluralism that the students themselves, their communities and their teachers represent (ethnic, racial, linguistic, religious, economic and gender). His underlying philosophy is the objective pedagogy and he focuses on awareness, reflection and action (praxis) as the basis of social change. So, multicultural education goes beyond the democratic principles of social justice and does not limit itself to integrating or adding contents to some curricular areas or to programme activities for special occasions. On the contrary, the entire curriculum must be open and impregnated with diversity (King & Reiss, 1993; Gay, 1995).

In a similar way, intercultural approaches are not exclusively aimed at foreign immigrant students who come from the Third World, but at all students (Arnaiz, 1996). Bearing this perspective in mind, Besalú (1998, p. 7) states:

> *if immigration has been the socio-historic occasion that has generated interest for the intercultural aspects, the intercultural problems cannot be reduced to a question of immigration and of insertion of the children of these immigrants in schools. To limit the intercultural aspect to these terms is an expression of opposition to the deep-rooted dimensions of this concept.*

Some Comments on the Migratory Phenomenon in Murcia and Spain

Spain has experienced a notable change since 1985, from being a country of emigration to a country receiving immigrants. Before 1985, people used to leave for other countries for political and/or economic reasons. Once the Civil War ended (1939), we can clearly pinpoint two periods: first, a period of going into exile and second, the 1950s and 1960s, when emigrants went to central Europe, mainly to Germany, France and Switzerland, where there was a need for labour.

This migratory flow changed in the 1970s, on the one hand, due to the return of emigrants, and on the other hand, the arrival of other immigrants, mainly from Chile and Argentina. But it is from the 1980s onwards that the flow increased markedly. To be precise, in 1986 there were 293,202 foreign residents in Spain and in 1997 there were 609,813, and we have to add to these figures those immigrants who are not registered. The tendency is upward and progressive, as we can appreciate from Figure 1, which shows the variations in the increase in the last few years.

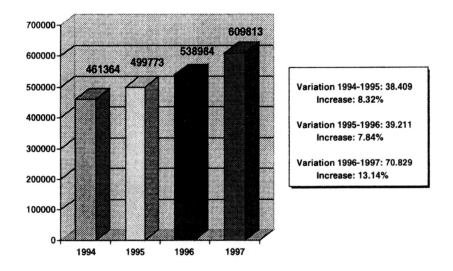

Figure 1. Variations in the total of foreign residents (1994-97). Source: Ministerio del Interior: Inter-ministerial Commission on Aliens.

The autonomous regions of Spain with most immigrant residents are Cataluña, Madrid, Andalucia and the autonomous region of Valencia. As far as the region of Murcia is concerned, it occupies tenth place on the list, registering successive arrivals of new immigrants. According to Izquierdo (1997), Moroccans constitute the largest group within the foreign labour force in Spain, highlighting their importance in the private sector's economy (see Figure 2).

We could also say that immigration and the attention paid to immigrants by non-profit making organisations are recent phenomena for Spain. According to the data for 1996 on the origin of immigrants in the region of Murcia, Moroccans occupy the first place with 3763, with the total number of African residents in the region being 4036. In second place are immigrants from the rest of Europe, followed by those from North and South America and Asia (see Figure 3).

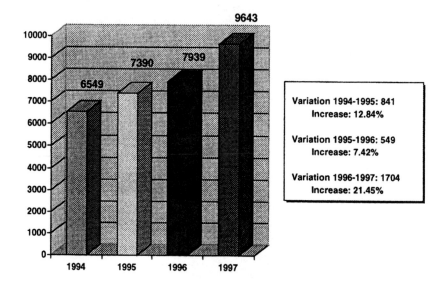

Figure 2. Variations in the total of foreign residents in Murcia. Source: Ministerio del Interior: Inter-ministerial Commission on Aliens.

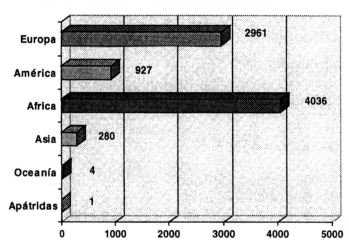

Figure 3. Distribution according to the place of origin of foreign residents. Source: Ministerio del Interior: Inter-ministerial Commission on Aliens. Total 9643.

The immigrants in the region of Murcia are mainly found in the municipalities of Cartagena and Murcia, followed by the coastal areas such as Mazarron and San Javier. This has a great impact on education in the area because the immigrants aim to bring their wives and children to Spain, that is to say, family regrouping and settlement is taking place. According to the data for the school year 1997/98, the region of Murcia had 1176 foreign students distributed across nursery schools, primary schools, secondary schools and vocational training centres; however, the primary schools had nearly half of the existing foreign students (see Figure 4).

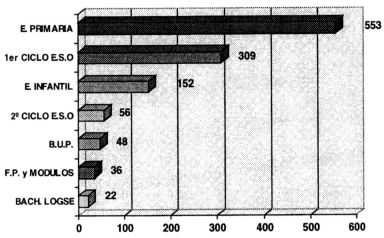

Figure 4. Distribution according to the place of origin of foreign students. Source: Ministerio del Interior: Inter-ministerial Commission on Aliens. Total 1176.

If we analyse the total number of students belonging to other cultures, races, ethnic groups and languages, the majority group is made up of Moroccan boys and girls. In second place are students from the EU, and in third place, students from South America. Thus, there is an array of cultures in the education centres in the region of Murcia, but these are distributed in different proportions (see Figure 5).

The 605 Moroccan students are distributed at different levels of non-university education. The majority (265) of these students are located at the primary school level, followed by the first cycle of the compulsory secondary school education, 'CSE' (213). There are 94 students at the nursery school level, 17 at the second cycle of CSE, 14 in the vocational training centres and modules, one student in higher secondary education in Logse (Bachillerato) [1] and one student in BUP [2] (see Figure 6).

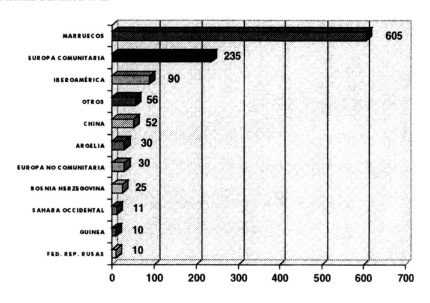

Figure 5. Distribution according to origin of foreign students with no university education, resident in the region of Murcia, 1997/98. Source: Ministry of Education and Science: Provincial Department of the Ministry of Education and Science of Murcia. Total 1176.

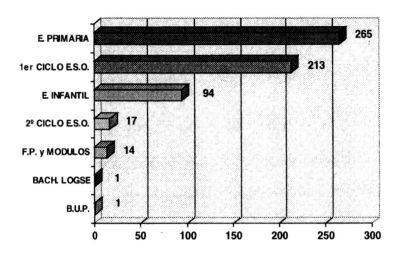

Figure 6. Distribution of the Maghrebi students resident in the region of Murcia, 1997/98. Source: Ministry of Education and Science: Provincial Department of the Ministry of Education and Science of Murcia. Total 605.

The centres with the greater numbers of foreign students are situated in the areas where their parents or families work. We have already referred to the areas that take the majority of immigrants, and in this case these coincide, and in the order of importance, from upper to lower, are as follows: Cartagena, Murcia, Torre Pacheco, San Javier and Mazarron. Thus, these places are where the majority of the foreign students attend school.

The Approach of Our Research

This report is part of a research project set up to analyse and assess the educational solutions offered in the centres of the region of Murcia, which take children from other cultures, ethnic groups and races (mainly from Maghreb). The title of the project is 'Analysis and assessment of the educational solutions offered in primary school education in the region of Murcia for a multicultural environment. Intercultural education as an answer'.

The general objective of this present work is to describe, analyse and assess the reach of the progressive incorporation of the Maghrebi children, as well as the type of educational solution that is being provided to the cultural diversity present in the schools in the region.

The Context

The population object of our study is comprised of all the primary schools in the region of Murcia that take children from other cultures, ethnic groups and races, which has allowed us to compile a multicultural map of the region.

The sample of the participating centres in the research consists of nine centres, situated in the areas of major presence of foreign immigrant students, that is to say, Murcia and agricultural area of Cartagena; it has been compiled using the following criteria:

centres with recent incorporation of students from other cultures;
centres with some experience in the treatment of these students;
centres with many years of experience in taking children from other races, ethnic groups and cultures.

The Process of Reception of Data and Techniques of Analysis

The data were obtained in the school year 1996/97 by means of a semi-structured interview directed at the parents, teachers, school management team and students. In order to analyse the interviews, we have followed Miles & Huberman's characterisation of inductive type

(Miles & Huberman, 1984), adhering to the following steps: general reading of the interviews, codification and characterisation.

Analysis of the Data

The information obtained from the interviews with the parents and students was based on the following topics.

Centres: school management team, teachers and students.

What the arrival of Maghrebi students meant for the centre, seen from the perspective of the school management team and the teachers.
If the presence of these students meant some restructuring of the learning–teaching process.
Advantages and disadvantages arising from the presence of these students in the centre.
Whether the existing resources of the centre were sufficient for the new situation.
Activities organised for intercultural education.
Teacher training.
Information on the Maghrebi students with respect to their situation in the centre.

Parents

Reason for their emigration, composition of their family and housing.
Work situation and profession.
Expectations with respect to the school: situation of their children there, participation in school life, etc.
Social interaction, participation in association groups or other organisations.

In order to analyse the interviews; we adopted inductive characterisation, using the data obtained from the interviews. Thus, the categories obtained are as follows.

The effects of Maghrebi students on the centre: in this category we obtained different viewpoints from the school management teams and teachers regarding the arrival at the centres of these students.
Organisational and curricular changes: criteria of classroom assignation for these students, application of an intercultural curriculum, realisation of activities for awareness, acceptance and respect for different cultures.
Advantages and disadvantages of the presence of Maghrebi students: the positive and negative situations that the teachers assessed with respect to the presence of the Maghrebi students.
Resources: material and human.

Teacher training
Maghrebi students: in this category, we have highlighted different aspects related to the academic and social situation of Moroccan students at the centres.
Immigration: when it happened; why; composition of the family; housing; knowledge of Spanish, maintenance of cultural identity, etc.
Work situation: labour market and work conditions.
School–parent relationship: assessment of education, relationship and participation in the school life.

Comments Obtained from the Data and Conclusions

Next, we shall evaluate some of the comments obtained in the process of analysis of the data.

At the beginning of the interviews, we encountered acceptance by the school management teams of the centres with respect to the presence of the students from other cultures, ethnic groups and races. They tried their best to show that the Maghrebi students were accepted in the same way as native Spanish inhabitants. However, three of the centres, in spite of having affirmed their acceptance at the beginning of the interviews, expressed at a later stage that there were other factors, such as fear and apprehension, that emerged due to the presence of these students in these centres. They also experienced the emergence of difficulties due to the sudden increase in the ratio of certain courses, and the situation of novelty and strangeness.

Similarly, the majority of teachers accepted the presence of students of other cultures and languages, despite the difficulties of language barriers. However, a minority of the teachers expressed, from the beginning, uncertainty and fear with respect to these students, showing concerns about problems of communication and not knowing what to do. For example:

Acceptance:
Normal, here people don't have problems ... Admittance is not based on whether the student is Moroccan or not, but if there are places, they are accepted and if there are no places, they are not accepted. (Centre 1, subsidised)

Everything is normal, whenever we have had one of these characters, the teachers have accepted them very well. (Centre 2. State owned)

Very well, we have accepted them well, no problem of any kind. Here, we do not reject. (Centre 4. State owned)

Apprehension:
Because of the expectation, surprise, uncertainty, and not
knowing how to tackle this topic, somewhat strange, it is an
awkward situation. (Centre 8. State owned)

From 34 students having enrolled including 12 or 15
Maghrebis in this classroom, just imagine the reaction when
the students were divided into two groups so that they could
be better cared for. (Centre 7. State owned)

With regard to organisational and curricular changes, we found that in eight of the centres, the criterion used for assignation of the students to a class was the level that corresponded to the age of the student. Aspects such as the level of Spanish (low or non-existent in majority of the cases) or the level of curricular competence were not assessed. However, we applied criteria such as placements in classrooms with a lower staff:pupil ratio or where the group is supposed to offer a better acceptance. At just one centre, children are sent to a lower level rather than the one they are supposed to been in according to their age. In general, the centres give precedence to the integration of these children with their peer group, instead of basing their assessment on the level of knowledge of each student.

With respect to the teachers, many consider that the Maghrebi students must preserve their identity and never abandon their culture. However, we did not find the necessary strategies to put this into practice. Thus, there is no treatment of their culture in the documents which support the institutional status of the centres (Educational and Curricular Project), nor there is anything in the classroom programmes. Therefore, we consider that intercultural education, that is to say, the dialogue between cultures based on awareness, acceptance, respect and the value of being different, is not reflected in the school curriculum. It does not characterise the practices of these centres, and is relegated to certain activities and incidental deeds, such as 'the day of peace, and no racism'.

The priority objective that the teachers are faced with for these students is the acquisition of Spanish; once this is achieved, they can be given academic tasks. If the student speaks Spanish, they can follow the same objectives as their classmates.

According to the school management team, the presence of students from other cultures, racial and ethnic groups has enriched the life of the centres; it is considered an advantage. Thus, five of the centres have considered it an asset to know other cultures, and three centres have indicated that it makes the students more tolerant, affirming that students of different races can live together. One centre has expressed the satisfaction that children get from this. And lastly, one centre states that there are neither advantages nor disadvantages, but the more students there are at the centres, the better. These statements reflect that one culture tries to assimilate the other; there is a strong desire for homogeneity and a closing of doors to the intercultural aspect, because there is no dialogue or interchange between cultures, instead there is only a monocultural dialogue:

> *Advantages, yes, these teach us many things. They teach new things that we do not know. (Centre 3)*

> *Advantages, that the children learn to live together with the whole world, with all the other kids, including those kids who live in bad conditions. (Centre 4)*

> *The same advantage that any student, having students in the centre is good thing, the more students we have, the better. (Centre 5)*

The disadvantage described by the centres is the lack of Spanish amongst the Maghrebi students, which makes it difficult to assess the academic level of the students and to establish the corresponding teaching–learning process. In some cases, the teachers and the rest of the students see the lack of hygiene in the Maghrebi students as a disadvantage. This fact appears connected in many cases to the dreadful conditions they live in.

Also, the school management team finds it difficult to carry out the enrolment procedures for these children, as these do not have legitimate documentation to verify their studies in their own countries and, at most, they have a photocopy of a family register book in Arabic, which they do not understand. For example:

> *The most serious inconvenience is the language.*

> *So, the inconvenience of us not understanding them, which could change if the things at the centre were a little bit better.*

> *When they arrive here with neither documentation, nor papers, nor with knowledge. (Centre 3)*

The existing human resources at the centres to fulfil the educational needs of these students are made up of the tutors and the teacher assistants. Just three centres had a teacher for complementary education, in charge of covering the needs of Maghrebi children regarding the teaching of Spanish as a second language and educational assistance. Thus, a centre with a high number of students (24) covered these functions by dedicating the hours of the special education teacher, while another centre with the same characteristics had a support teacher shared by all the children who needed her attention. Therefore, the necessary human resources needed to respond educationally to the Maghrebi students were scarce and depended on the goodwill of the teachers, one of whom had never undertaken such a task. The criticism directed at the administration was varied and mainly centred on the lack of support and help. For example:

> *They haven't said anything to us, they have simply said here they are; and you have to give them schooling. (Centre 6)*

> *We have here, at centre, so many Maghrebi students, but we haven't received anything, nothing whatsoever, as an extra support teacher just as any other ordinary centre without one, it is not stipulated separately. (Centre 3)*

In spite of this, we know that there is interest on the part of the education authority to solve these problems.

As far as material resources are concerned, the centres show that there is no material aimed at teaching Spanish as a second language. In all the cases, the teachers use reading/writing texts used in the initial levels of primary education or they prepare their own material. With respect to school materials (pencils, notebooks, etc.), the centres seek help from organisations such as the local town hall, parents' association, or Caritas [3], as the Maghrebi families normally lack financial stability.

With respect to teacher training, five of the centres had not received any training on intercultural education or teaching Spanish as a second language. The rest of the centres had taken part in teacher training programmes or work groups on intercultural aspects, with each one acknowledging that they had not put everything into practice, the majority arguing that they did not have enough time. In most cases, the teachers prefer the support teacher to be responsible for the care of the Maghrebi students, instead of further training for them and to be made responsible for this work.

> *During the first 3 months, every Thursday we held meetings on the training sessions with the members of the intercultural team ... Everything that you are told when you start from the beginning is positive ... But the most important need is the attention for these students and not a gentleman coming here to train me. (Centre 7)*

On other occasions, it is argued that the courses are eminently theoretical, blaming the lack of training in the classroom for being responsible for this.

> *During two courses, we have had a seminar at the centre, formed by the teachers from the centre and a person who came from the Intercultural Team ... The problem is that it did*

*not cover the expectation of fellow teachers, it was very
theoretical and little practical. (Centre 3)*

And lastly, just one centre gave high assessment marks to the training in intercultural aspects carried out by the centre, but stated that it has not been put into practice because of the lack of time.

*We had a course on intercultural aspects which was quite
complete, but if you want to know the truth, I believe that
there is no one in the centre who has put it into practice ...
Ideally there should be some time given in order to be able to
use this material. (Centre 4)*

As far as the integration of the Maghrebi students into our education system is concerned, we can make a clear distinction between those students in nursery education or the first levels of primary education and those who start their schooling in Morocco and arrive in Spain at the ages of 10, 12, 13 and 14. In the first group, the period of adaptation to the education system is better; these children follow the rest of their classmates and need little educational support, as explained by the teacher interviewee. The students themselves argued that they could not remember having difficulties. However, the group of older children, of course, remember difficulties when they first arrived at the centre; they felt as if they were alone, with no friends and with many difficulties in learning Spanish.

Their culture is always present, and they expressed their desire to receive their language and their Arabic culture in school in order to preserve and not to lose their identity. This right is being fomented in the region of Murcia by means of the presence of a teacher of Arabic language and culture in those centres where the intake of Maghrebi students is quite high. This resource may need to be extended, especially to secondary education where it is non-existent.

*We are Arabs and we have to be able to read and write in
Arabic.*

The main reason for the immigration of Maghrebis to Spain is the socio-economic situation of Maghreb, the lack of jobs and the low pay. The families are quite numerous, with an average of between 4 and 10 children, living in dreadful conditions. They maintain their cultural and religious traditions, and are followers of Islam with all that it entails.

Work Situation

With respect to the work of the Maghrebi parents, we established that they all work in agriculture and their work conditions bear a high degree of exploitation and racial discrimination.

The work in the fields is hard and with no rights. One has to put up with the boss so that he can make a contract, if he insults you or he gets upset you have to bear him and work hard in order to get your next contract and renew your residence permit, you have neither rights, nor holidays. (Interview number 3)

The expectations deposited by the Maghrebi parents in education are many; they see in schools the chance of fulfilling many of their unfulfilled dreams: that their children should be part of a fairer society where they have equal opportunities, the chance to study and have a better life. Nevertheless, we must bear in mind the social and work situation, which makes them believe that it would be impossible: the lack of knowledge of the language; the lack of money to buy school materials. We have to bear in mind that the majority have a minimum of four children; and the distance of the school from the place of residence that obliges some of the students to travel several kilometres to get the school transport.

I expect nothing from the school, they are studying and that's all. Here in Spain I cannot find them work, because we are working in the fields and they are as well; the poor are going to be working in the field for sure. (Interview number 3)

All these comments make us believe that the educational situation of these students is not seen from the same perspective by the school management teams, teachers, parents and the Maghrebi students.

The centres tend to protect themselves, arguing that it is normal behaviour while ignoring the problem of the multicultural aspect present in the centre. At all costs, they want to show that all is well; they accept the diversity and work on those lines. These initial declarations of normality and denial of problems contrast with succeeding indications of the problems and difficulties that the Maghrebi students have.

The 'problem' is reduced to the lack of Spanish as a second language and the lack of support teachers who could assume the responsibility for these students. Thus, it has been proved that the cultural identity of these students is recognised in the theoretical sense and not in an explicit sense by means of organisational and curricular criteria in the centres.

We are not considering, for example, questions such as a new vision of work in the schools in order that the diversity of the students is well cared for, the dimension of the multicultural curriculum, or support work and collaboration among teachers. Perhaps, teachers merely receive the training offered in the compensatory education programme but do not let it have any effect on school life. The family–centre relationship is another topic that is pending.

Thus, it is our duty as educators to put into practice the acceptance, the awareness and the value of different cultures present in the same educational space, that is to say, to help to build a democratic, plural and equal society, respecting at all times the individual identities of each student.

Notes

[1] Logse: The Education Law that has dominated the education system since 1990.

[2] BUP: non-compulsory secondary education, for students aged 16 to 18, that prepares them for university.

[3] Caritas: a religious organisation devoted to charity.

References

Arnaiz, P. (1996) Las escuelas son para todos, *Siglo Cero*, 27(2), pp. 25-34.

Arnaiz, P. & de Haro, R. (1995) La atención a la diversidad: hacia un enfoque intercultural, in M.J. León (Coord.) *Integración escolar: desarrollo curricular, organizativo y professional*. Granada: Servicio de Publicaciones de la Universidad.

Arnaiz, P. & de Haro, R. (1997) Educación Intercultural y atención a la diversidad, in F. Salinas & E. Moreno (Coord.) *Semejanzas, Diferencias e Intervención Educativa*. Granada: Fundación Educación y Futuro.

Artiles, A.J. & Larsen, L. (1998) Learning from Special Education Reform Movements in Four Continents, *European Journal of Special Needs Education*, 13, pp. 5-9.

Banks, J.A. (1993) Multicultural Education: approaches, developments, and dimensions, in J. Lynch, C. Modgil & S. Modgil (Eds) *Education for Cultural Diversity: convergence and divergence*, vol. 1. London: Falmer Press.

Banks, J.A. & McGee Banks, C.A. (Eds) (1995) *Handbook of Research on Multicultural Education*. New York: Macmillan.

Besalú, X. y otros (Comp.) (1998) *La educación intercultural en Europa. Un enfoque currricular*. Barcelona: Ediciones Pomares-Corredor.

de Haro Rodríguez, R. (1995) Educar desde el pluralismo, *Anales de Pedagogía*, pp. 12-13, 47-64.

de Haro Rodríguez, R. (1997) Escuela-diversidad y educación intercultural, in P. Arnaiz Sánchez. & R. de Haro Rodríguez (Eds) *10 años de integración en España: análisis de la realidad y perspectivas de futuro*. Murcia: Servicio de Publicaciones de la Universidad.

Díaz Aguado, M.J. (1996) *Escuela y tolerancia*. Madrid: Pirámide.

Figueroa, P. (1995) Multicultural Education in the United Kingdom: historical development and current status, in J.A. Banks & C.A. McGee Banks (Eds) *Handbook of Research on Multicultural Education*. New York: Macmillan.

Gay, G. (1995) Curriculum Theory and Multicultural Education, in J.A. Banks & C.A. McGee Banks (Eds) *Handbook of Research on Multicultural Education*. New York: Macmillan.

Hoff, G.R. (1995) Multicultural Education in Germany: historical development and current status, in J.A. Banks & C.A. McGee Banks (Eds) *Handbook of Research on Multicultural Education*. New York: Macmillan.

Izquierdo Escribano, A. (1997) La inmigración en las zonas rurales de España: aspectos de la integración social en el caso de los marroquíes que trabajan en la Región de Murcia, in J. Leal & C. Mayeur (Coord.) *Vivienda e integración social de los inmigrantes*. Madrid: Ministerio de Asuntos Sociales.

King, A. & Reiss, M. (1993) *The Multicultural Dimensions of the National Curriculum*. London: Falmer Press.

Miles, M. & Huberman, H. (1984) *Qualitative Data Analysis*. Beverly Hills: Sage.

Ministerio del Interior (1994-96) *Anuario estadístico de extranjería*. Madrid: Comisión Interministerial de Extranjería.

Nieto, S. (1992) *Affirming Diversity: the sociopolitical context of multicultural education*. New York: Longman.

Nieto, S. (1998). Fact and Fiction: stories of Puerto Ricans in US schools, *Harvard Educational Review*, 68, pp. 133-163.

Olneck, M.R. (1995) Inmigrants and Education, in J.A. Banks & C.A. McGee Banks (Eds) *Handbook of Research on Multicultural Education*. New York: Macmillan.

Schools, Universities and Society in England and Germany

CLAUDIUS GELLERT

Introduction

Students at German universities study more than twice as long as their fellow students in England. Whereas the normal course at an English university lasts about 3 years, German students study on average for about 7 years before they take their first degree. This is a problem which has been a major concern for university reformers and politicians. There has been a long-lasting debate about whether or not and, if yes, how to shorten the courses and generally how to reform university education in Germany. Many have, within this context, been interested in looking abroad for some possible answers, in order to determine whether, for instance, the English example makes it desirable and feasible to shorten and reorganise university courses in Germany. In this chapter, an attempt is made to highlight some of the major differences between the two systems and to explain them.

However, before we look at some of the relevant structural and normative issues involved, we need to presuppose a functional equivalence of the two university systems on a general level. We should assume that in the two countries the universities are comparable at least in so far as they essentially fulfil the major functions (professional training, research, etc.) which are vital for the survival of modern society. Only under this assumption does it make sense to compare different educational models and to search for new and possibly more efficient methods and patterns of organising them. It also needs to be pointed out that we primarily look at the situation in England and Wales. The Scottish system in many respects has always followed continental European traditions and is therefore not as dissimilar from the German one as the English system. And finally, we are not dealing with the whole tertiary sector, but only with universities. The reason is that the other institutions of higher education in Germany have shorter courses anyway and seem generally to be better organised than universities.

In the following, we shall look at three broad areas, all of which are of central importance for an understanding of the differences between the two university systems (Gellert, 1988):

aims and purposes;
transition from school to university; and
modes of instruction.

Aims and Purposes

University functions have, depending on the country and the point in history, changed in a variety of ways. Especially after World War II, universities had to undergo major upheavals. Since the 1960s, hardly any other institution has experienced such a comprehensive and rapid transformation as the system of higher education. The number of students has more than quadrupled over that period. Staff in universities, as well as government funds for teaching and research, increased at a similar rate. New universities and other forms of advanced learning were set up. Many new disciplines or subdisciplines emerged. Outdated structures of institutional authority and government were substituted by more democratic and transparent decision-making procedures. Above all, admission to tertiary levels of education and training changed from a restrictive elite-mode to varied patterns of mass higher education.

Nevertheless, some basic functions have remained stable since the nineteenth century. For England, the essential aims of universities have, for instance, been described in the Robbins Report (Committee on Higher Education, 1963). The authors first refer to 'instruction in skills suitable to play a part in the general division of labour', i.e. professional training (p. 6). They emphasise, however, that 'the aim should be to produce not mere specialists but rather cultivated men and women' (p. 6). Then follows the research function or, as they call it, 'advancement of learning': 'The search for truth is an essential function of institutions of higher education and the process of education is itself most vital when it partakes of the nature of discovery' (p. 7).

While so far there is little difference between the generally perceived aims and purposes of university education in the two countries, the Robbins Report then continues to emphasise a university aim that is rather distinct from the German tradition, namely 'the transmission of a common culture and common standards of citizenship'. More specifically, they point out, 'We believe that it is a proper function of higher education, as of education in schools, to provide in partnership with the family that background of culture and social habit upon which a healthy society depends' (Committee on Higher Education, 1963, p. 7). The key words here are 'common standards of citizenship' and 'social habit', since they refer to individual and group characteristics which cannot solely be attained by purely academic or scientific training. Also, the mentioning of schools in this context is significant, since this would be quite incompatible with the self-image of German universities and their insistence on *Wissenschaft*. As Shapiro points out, '*Wissenschaft* means knowledge and science. Because of the English equation of science and natural science, "science" is frequently too restricted a translation and "knowledge" too loose' (Shapiro, 1971, p. vii).

The concept of *Wissenschaft* and the traditional German university aims were shaped around 1800, when educationists and high-ranking administrators like Schleiermacher and W. v. Humboldt, influenced by idealist philosophy, undertook to reform the educational system of Prussia. They formulated, somewhat belatedly in comparison to France and Britain, the democratic and emancipatory intentions of the rising bourgeoisie. These included the ideal of an independent and educated individual, a person who should be enlightened enough to be able to contribute to a rational organisation of state and society. Humboldt specified this educational programme by his concept of *Bildung durch Wissenschaft* (education through academic knowledge). Also, the term '*Bildung*' needs some explanation. As Shapiro points out, 'Bildung literally means "formation". But also "education" and (cultural) "cultivation"; in German these narrower meanings always connote an overall developmental process' (Shapiro, 1971, p. vii). According to Humboldt (1964), valid academic knowledge and 'truth as such' could only be discovered by actively participating in the process of research. Each student was expected to search, together with his or her teachers, for 'objective' knowledge, thus helping to push forward the limits in his/her academic subject.

While German universities have, since Humboldt, been characterised by a strong emphasis on the research function and while this was accompanied by the task of professional training, liberal education or even character formation in the tradition of the English gentleman-ideal of education (cf. Halsey, 1962; Wilkinson, 1970) has not played an important role in the German university tradition. Humboldt's concept of *Bildung* was primarily related to the participation in a research process, but not, as in the case of England's educational tradition, to a specific communal lifestyle or to prescribed modes of behaviour and taste.

The lack of this university function in Germany explains another major difference in the aims and purposes of university education in the two countries. Whereas in Germany professional training since Humboldt has been associated with a deep penetration of *Wissenschaft*, the English intentions were always directed more to the student than to the subject (Ashby, 1967). Although traditional English university

171

courses were in a single subject and were therefore rather specialised (a fact which will be taken up again in connection with a short discussion of the transition from school to university), the overall aim has not been to educate the student to become a perfect scientist or researcher, but to develop methodological thinking, the ability to tackle new problems in a systematic manner and to adopt personality attributes which are now referred to as 'transferable skills'. English university curricula are therefore clearly circumscribed and the body of transmitted knowledge is fairly codified (although regularly revised). In Germany, in contrast, curricula are often vague (above all in the arts and social sciences) and the contents of lectures and seminars often directly reflect topical research activities of the lecturers. Whereas the English concept is directly in accordance with the expectations of prospective employers who look for broadly educated personalities who will receive their additional, necessary skills through 'on the job training', in Germany there is no common understanding about the respective aims. On the one hand, representatives from industry increasingly demand shorter courses and more 'exemplary' and practical learning. On the other hand, the universities stick to the Humboldtian inheritance – not surprisingly, since reforms towards more stringent organisational patterns would mean a lot of additional professional commitment. And the students themselves are often afraid that such reforms would leave them with the same amount of learning to be done in a shorter period of time and that universities would increasingly become like schools.

Thus, varying ideals of university education can be said to explain to a certain extent the differing length of studies in the two countries. Another major reason has to be seen in the very different relationships between universities and secondary schools, which will be briefly sketched in the following.

Transition from School to University

The relationship between English upper secondary schools and universities, and in particular the influence of the latter upon the former, are crucial for an understanding of the fact that university studies in England normally only last 3 years. The situation can be summarised in two major points.

First, universities in England are, compared to their German counterparts, fairly autonomous from state interference. They have larger degrees of freedom in the organisation of teaching and in the selection of students and staff. They admit students mostly on the basis of their own capacity calculations. Furthermore, only those students who can be expected to fit into one of the specific university courses are accepted. The German system, in contrast, is characterised by open access and a constitutionally guaranteed right of school-leavers to enter any university of their choice. The autonomy in selecting students in England has in turn led to the universities' interest in exercising some influence on what is happening at secondary school level. Because they are able to select students on the basis of ability and suitability for the course programme, it is in the interest of the university to shape, through examination boards, the curricula and examination requirements of upper secondary schools.

Secondly, upper secondary schools in England are interested in adopting one of the syllabuses offered by the examination boards, since they want their pupils to be well prepared for university entrance. As the universities require their prospective students to have passed A levels in those subjects which they intend to study (if they exist at school), schools tend to accept the curricular recommendations of the examination boards. This has led to a distinct specialisation at the upper secondary school level, which in turn ensures high entrance standards at university. This is another reason why universities can carry out rather specialised courses of acknowledged academic quality in a comparatively short period of 3 years.

In contrast to the close interdependence between secondary schools and universities in England, the traditional German *Gymnasium* is only loosely connected with the university. The *Gymnasium,* comparable to the English grammar school, is the dominant form of secondary schooling within the selective educational system of Germany. Comprehensive schools are, unlike in England, relatively rare. Although its role was defined in the early nineteenth century by the Prussian reformers as a platform for university studies, the result turned out to be completely different from the English model (Gafert, 1979). Since university education was meant to be research-oriented and highly academic, secondary education had to be as broad and comprehensive as possible. From that evolved the traditional ideal of taking approximately 10-12 subjects up to the final *Abitur* examination. *Allgemeinbildung* (general education) remained the central aim, despite a controversial debate about its usefulness which began in the early 1960s, leading to a concentration on fewer subjects at the *Reformierte Oberstufe* (reformed upper secondary school) (Lohe et al, 1980). The reform, implemented primarily in order to improve the pupils' ability to study at university, has, however, been severely criticised by the universities. They claim that despite the obligation for pupils to take at least one discipline from each of the major subject areas, they are overspecialised and reveal extensive gaps of knowledge in other fields when they enter higher education. This fact is relevant in so far as successful secondary school leavers in Germany possess a general entrance certificate for study in any disciplinary area (with the exception of some restricted fields like medicine).

This may suffice to demonstrate that secondary schools in Germany, although they have to a certain extent moved away from the traditional concept of general education, are, at least in comparison with England, far from being directly influenced by universities with respect to curricula or examination requirements. Together with the aforementioned open access principle, the lack of university influence upon the *Gymnasium* necessarily means a lengthening of courses at German universities, because school leavers with heterogeneous educational backgrounds have to be catered for, and university courses cannot be as specialised as in England.

Modes of Instruction

The last of the three broad areas which are central in a comparative analysis of English and German university education, and which are essential for an understanding of the marked difference in the length of courses in the two countries, concerns the pattern of teaching, learning and examining. Although this is probably the most important aspect for an understanding of the differing lengths of studies, we shall deal with it only briefly here, because the explanatory implications are mostly self-evident.

A general difference between the two university systems has to be mentioned first. Although we are looking at first degree courses in the two countries, it is necessary to point out that in Germany there does not really exist a distinction between undergraduate and postgraduate studies. MAs, diplomas, state examinations, etc. are all approximately on the same degree-level, and are, apart from doctorates, the only university degrees to be aspired to. And even PhDs were in the past often taken as a first degree (cf. Clark, 1992).

It is natural under these circumstances to enquire whether university courses in England are more tightly and efficiently organised than in Germany. Only a few indications of this can be given here (cf. Gellert, 1999). First, all university courses in England are clearly defined and their contents remain stable for sufficiently long periods of time for sixth-formers, students and staff to be able to receive long-term guidance and reliable information. A large variety of options and combination of subjects is usually available.

Although it is dangerous to generalise because of differences in Germany between science and arts subjects, the modes of instruction and learning in England seem to be more intensive, efficient and transparent. In Germany, curricula, if they exist at all, often remain vague and lead to all sorts of problems of orientation for students as well as for lecturers. Besides the aforementioned Humboldtian tradition of the 'unity of research and teaching', which often leads to university teachers being little interested in the elaboration of stable curricula, the students' traditional freedom to change university as often as they wish is responsible for this situation. Also, the students' freedom to choose their dates of examination, which still applies in many subjects, contributes to the organisational uncertainties.

Furthermore, teaching at English universities is usually done in small groups, i.e. tutorials or seminars. Lectures are sometimes no more than voluntary additions to these forms of instruction. The tutor is then able to require regular amounts of reading and essay-writing, thus exercising a subtle but effective kind of control. At German universities, in contrast, lectures are the predominant form of teaching, and seminars often contain 30 or more students. The amount of written work is minimal; and it is usual not to attend lectures or seminars at all.

Finally, one more of the most obvious structural differences, the amount of teaching and counselling done by English university lecturers, should be mentioned. Although this cannot be quantified here, it seems to be correct to say that most university teachers in England, regardless of their status, are heavily involved in teaching. Besides lecturing and giving seminars and/or tutorials, they usually act as 'personal tutors' for several students. This individual and time-consuming responsibility for students is alien to German universities. The students there are largely left to themselves, which no doubt adds to their numerous difficulties of orientation. Universities are often experienced by students as anonymous, uncommunicative and estranging. This may well be the most important reason for the excessively long time it takes, at least in international comparison, to receive a first degree at a German university.

Conclusion

Perhaps the situation at German universities is not quite as bleak as it appears from the above description; and perhaps the English model of university education is not altogether perfect either. Nevertheless, it is probably correct to look for an explanation of the main problem, namely the different lengths of university studies in England and Germany, in those three areas: the difference in aims and purposes; the distinct relationships between secondary schools and universities; and the actual modes of teaching, learning and examining.

It is thus not surprising that many of the current reform attempts in German universities point in the Anglo-American direction. One of the proposals which is being discussed at present is the general introduction of bachelor's and master's degrees. The usage of the English terminology in itself indicates a major break-through in the long struggle for a more structured and efficient university system.

References

Ashby, E. (1967) The Future of the Nineteenth Century Idea of a University, *Minerva*, VI, pp. 3-17.

Clark, B.R. (1992) *The Research Foundations of Graduate Education: Germany, Britain, France, United States, Japan.* Berkeley: University of California Press.

Committee on Higher Education (1963) *Higher Education* (Robbins Report). London: HMSO.

Gafert, B. (1979) *Höhere Bildung als Antiaufklärung; Entstehung und Bedeutung des preußischen Gymnasiums.* Frankfurt: Campus.

Gellert, C. (1988) *Vergleich des Studiums an englischen und deutschen Universitäten.* Frankfurt: Lang.

Gellert, C. (Ed.) (1999) *Innovation and Adaptation in Higher Education. The Changing Conditions of Advanced Teaching and Learning in Europe.* London: Jessica Kingsley.

Halsey, A.H. (1962) British Universities, *Archives Europeènes de Sociologie*, III, pp. 85ff.

Humboldt, W. (1964) *Schriften zur Politik und zum Bildungswesen*, vol. IV. Darmstadt: Wissenschaftliche Buchgesellschaft, Werke.

Lohe, P. et al (1980) Die Reform der gymnasialen Oberstufe und ihre Verwirklichung in den Ländern der Bundesrepublik Deutschland, in Max-Planck-Institut für Bildungsforschung, *Bildung in der Bundesrepublik Deutschland*, vol. 2, pp. 1177-1213. Hamburg: Rowohlt.

Shapiro, J.J. (1971) Translator's Preface, in J. Habermas, *Toward a Rational Society*, pp. vii-ix. London: Heinemann.

Wilkinson, L.H. (1970) The Gentleman and the Maintenance of a Political Elite, in P.W. Musgrave, *Sociology, History and Education*, pp. 126-142. London: Methuen.

Going Places: social, legal and fiscal aspects of international faculty mobility

SYLVIA G.M. VAN DE BUNT-KOKHUIS

Outcomes Study on International Faculty Mobility

In a study on international mobility of Dutch faculty members entitled 'academic pilgrims' (Bunt-Kokhuis, 1996), some major determinants of international faculty mobility (IFM) were investigated, namely academic position, discipline, age and gender. These determinants formed the frame of reference for a round of personal interviews, literature study and, subsequently, a national questionnaire among 1690 faculty members, including various academic staff members such as fellows, researchers, lecturers and professors. The major outcomes were as follows.

Academic position. The enthusiasm of faculty members seems to be limited if travelling abroad is planned purely for teaching activities rather than research. Teaching abroad leads to little or no academic credit for the individual and replacement of absent faculty members is complicated. IFM may offer an important boost to career advancement to juniors and those in mid-career, but some (senior) respondents said that IFM hindered their career. Other constraints were bureaucracy, lack of replacement facilities, disruption of home commitments, tiredness, and shortage of time.

Discipline. Faculty members are dedicated and loyal primarily to their discipline. Knowledge is shared with colleagues worldwide and this attitude implies a natural need for international exchange. Limited travelling was found in disciplines such as social sciences, engineering (because monetary awards outside academia are more attractive), laboratory and law sciences, particularly in the USA. Frequent travelling was found in disciplines such as natural sciences and medicine.

Life cycle. In most academic disciplines, age and academic performance seems to be linked. The productivity curve is high at 27 years of age when academics are working on their doctorates. Subsequently, there is a period of broader orientation, and personal developments may decrease their productivity. By the age of 50, new specialisations have generally been found and their career has peaked. Senior faculty members have power over the junior members. They can compel younger colleagues to serve as co-authors of publications.

Gender. Personal circumstances may hinder females even more than their male colleagues in travelling. Increasingly, IFM for longer stays is limited by the dual career factor and may therefore become a personal barrier. Spouses are less willing to disrupt their professional life.

Legal Obstacles to IFM

Various legal obstacles may hinder IFM. Here we will discuss some major barriers for academic travelling within and outside Europe.

United States of America and Japan

Severe legal obstacles may apply to faculty members travelling to the USA and Japan. The American Illegal Immigration Reform and Immigrant Responsibility Act of 1996 (IIRAIRA) established a new term in immigration law, that of 'unlawful presence'. Severe penalties, including bars to future admission into the USA, are imposed on those so-called 'aliens' who are unlawfully present in the USA for more than 180 continuous days as of 1 April 1997. Aliens who stay more than 180 continuous days but less than 1 year prior to initiation of removal proceedings are barred from admission to the USA for 3 years from the date of departure. For 1 year or more of unlawful presence, the bar is 10 years (*NAFSA* [the Association of International Education] *Newsletter*, 1997, p. 33). Japan also has a severe immigration law for foreign job-seekers in Japan or in a Japanese organisation.

Europe

Within Europe, the penalties are less severe, but the legislation is getting stricter, especially in the Netherlands. Paradoxically, in the European educational legislation, the free movement of employees (and thus faculty members) is encouraged. The European Court decided that, due to the profession of the lecturer, restrictions are not allowed. The right to stay in another member state (article 52 EU) is valid. Nevertheless, problems may occur with the acknowledgement of professional qualifications of lecturers.

The European Commission published a Green Paper (1996) on the obstacles of international mobility. It was shown that a researcher travelling to another European Union (EU) country often is confronted with various legal regulations and obstacles. These barriers will be investigated further within the Fifth Framework Programme for Research and Technological Development.

Recently, three measures were proposed by the Commission to clarify people's rights to move within the EU to look for and take up work (*The Week in Europe*, 1998). The EU makes it clear that EU job-seekers have an automatic right of residence for 6 months, and that people have the right to go to another member state to seek work or undertake training. The proposals will support the European employment strategy by tackling obstacles to greater mobility in the labour market. They will also make it easier for people to understand and take advantage of their rights to free movement within the EU. Job-seekers would be able to stay in another EU country for more than 6 months if they can prove they are actively seeking work and have a reasonable chance of finding a job. People working on a series of fixed or short-term contracts would also gain better residence rights, once they have worked for 12 months with an 18-month period.

The Netherlands

In the Netherlands, the regulations for foreigners who want to obtain a residence permit are getting increasingly strict, especially for foreigners from non-EU/EER (Norway, Liechtenstein and Iceland) countries. Foreign faculty members visiting Dutch universities are confronted with a complex set of regulations and implications. Some universities have made workable agreements with the Aliens Police, GAB (Municipality Employment Office) and GGD (Municipality Healthcare Services), though a lot of bureaucracy remains. Despite these agreements, in daily practice problems may occur, e.g. a British faculty member was taken to prison for 2 days and had to undergo an AIDS test at the local GGD.

The State University of Leyden prefers to contract visiting faculty members for a maximum of 1 year without an employment agreement. These faculty members are usually funded by international agencies such as the World Bank and the United Nations and bring their own funding with them. If the visiting faculty member is not employed by the host university, it is easier to arrange their temporary stay.

In the following, the legal implications will be discussed. An overview of the different legal restrictions is shown in Table I.

Temporary residence permits. A temporary residence permit (*machtiging tot voorlopig verblijf*, MVV) can only be obtained if one has the necessary identity documents such as a passport, birth certificate and proof of sufficient income. The MVV is a visa linked to an objective to stay in the

179

Netherlands (study, work, etc.). The application procedure can take a long time. With the MVV, it is possible to apply for a residence permit. The need to apply for an MVV depends on the nationality of the candidate and the duration of the stay.

Procedure	Group 1	Group 2	Group 3	Group 4
	EU/EER	Australia, Canada, Japan, Monaco, New Zealand, USA, Switzerland	Andorra, Argentina, Brazil, Brunei, Chile, Costa Rica, Cyprus, Ecuador, El Salvador, Guatemala, Honduras, Hungary, Israel, Jamaica, Malawi, Malaysia, Malta, Mexico, Nicaragua, Panama, Paraguay, Poland, San Marino, Singapore, Slovenia, Slovakia, Tsechia, Uruguay, Vatican City, Venezuela, South Korea	Other countries
VKV (<3 months)	No	No	No	Yes
MVV (>3 months)	No	No	Yes	Yes
TWV	No	Yes	Yes	Yes
VTV (>3 months)	Yes	Yes	Yes	Yes
Register at Aliens Office (within 3 days)	Not compulsory	Yes	Yes	Yes
TBC-check compulsory if duration of stay >3 months	No	No	Yes, except for Israel	Yes, except for Surinam
GBA	Stay >4 months	Stay >4 months	Stay >4 months	Stay >4 months
Tax number/ employment taxes	Yes	Yes	Yes	Yes
Health insurance	Transfer of insurance of home country possible	Transfer of insurance of home country possible for Australia, Switzerland		Transfer of insurance of home country possible for Turkey, Morocco, Tunisia, Cape Verde Islands

Table I. Procedures according to country of origin. Source: Netherlands Universities Foundation for International Cooperation (NUFFIC) Report Mobiliteit Geregeld, seminar, 1999.

Faculty members from most non-EU countries (see Table I, groups 3 and 4) who are seeking a job at a Dutch university are required to apply for an MVV before departure at the Dutch embassy in the home country. Dutch embassies act within the Dutch frame of reference. Thus, for example, a document such as a recent abstract from the register of births, deaths and marriages (*recent uittreksel uit het bevolkingsregister*) is requested. Often, no equivalent exists in the country of origin.[1] On arrival, the foreign faculty member is confronted with the Aliens (registration) Office. Though most universities have a good relationship with this office, the general opinion is that the bureaucracy involved is very time-consuming.

Some larger organisations such as Shell, Unilever and the University of Amsterdam, which receive visitors on a regular basis, have made a 'fast procedure agreement' with the Immigration and Naturalisation Services (IND) in The Hague. For this purpose the shortened MVV procedure has been developed. The executive tasks are in the hands of the regional authorities of the IND.

From November 1998 onwards, a faculty member from group 3 or 4 (see Table I) can only apply for a residence permit if he/she is in receipt of an MVV.[2]

Private liquidity. The availability of private funding remains a big obstacle, in particular to visitors from developing countries. If someone wants to stay in the Netherlands, they need to prove that they are able to support themselves and that they have at least hfl.14,000 going into their bank account on an annual basis (Havermans, 1997, p. 12). In 1998, this amount increased to hfl.17,000, due to increased costs of living and tuition fees.[3] Foreign faculty members employed by a Dutch university are not obliged to prove their private liquidity.

Faculty members from non-EU/EER countries. Foreign faculty members (groups 2, 3 and 4, Table I) who visit the Netherlands for a longer period of time are often employed by a Dutch university. Faculty members from groups 3 and 4 (e.g. from an African country), staying less than 3 months, may apply for a special business visa (*zakenvisum*) at the Dutch Ministry for Foreign Affairs, Department of Persons Migration, Consular/Foreigners and Visa. The applicant is required to explain the purpose of the visit and to have sufficient financial means for their stay. A faculty member on a business visa is not allowed to accept a job at the university, unless the receiving university applies for a work permit (TWV) at the Dutch Ministry of Social Affairs and Employment. In a few cases, the Dutch Ministry of Foreign Affairs provides a business visa in combination with a TWV. If the faculty member wants to stay in the Netherlands for more than 3 months, the application must be forwarded to the Dutch Ministry of Justice. In exceptional cases, the business visa can be extended for more than 3 months, and the police need to be informed.

Visiting faculty members (groups 2, 3 and 4) need to inform the Aliens Police within 3 days of arrival of their presence. On arrival, the employer needs to apply for a TWV. The application procedure takes about 5 weeks. For practical reasons, the application procedure is therefore planned long before arrival. From 1 November 1998, it has been necessary to apply for a TWV before arrival in the Netherlands.

Faculty members from EU/EER countries. This group (see group 1, Table I) is not obliged to apply for a TWV and is free to stay in the Netherlands.

Koppelingswet (the 'couple regulation'). Since 1 July 1998, the so-called *Koppelingswet* (couple regulation) has become effective. This regulation has serious consequences for incoming staff members from non-EU countries. This regulation couples the right to stay in the Netherlands with the right to use the Dutch (social/health/educational) services. National data systems are interconnected to cross-check if foreigners have legal residence. Universities firstly have to prove if the incoming person of 18 years of age or older has a valid document to stay in the Netherlands. The university has to apply for a TWV for faculty members from groups 2, 3 and 4, which may take about 2 months, or less if there is a good collaborative relationship between the Aliens Police, Employment Office and host university.

Every foreign faculty member from a non-EU/EER country has to inform the police within 3 days of their arrival. If a visitor from group 2, 3 or 4 wants to stay longer than 3 months, they must apply for a VTV (residence permit).

Faculty members who enter the Netherlands on a tourist visa are not allowed to work. If they want to work, they first have to return to their home country, to apply for an MVV (temporary residence permit). Finally, they have to prove that they have health insurance.

Several Dutch universities disagree with the couple regulation and recently expressed their opinions in the press. According to Leyden State University, a university cannot be obliged to select students and staff on criteria other than the quality of the candidate. Tilburg University said they had only very limited preparation time to execute the new regulations. According to the vice-chancellor of Leyden State University, the university has to act according to its conscience in this matter. He compared the current situation with the Second World War, whereby the university rebelled against the German regulation to exclude Jewish professors from employment. The Dutch universities agreed that illegal foreign visitors (students or staff members) would have the opportunity to get their legal documents ready before February 1999. If these visitors did not succeed, they would then be deregistered. Leyden does not agree with the 'February control', but it is unknown what sanctions may follow. It is also unknown how many illegal students and staff members study and work in the Netherlands (*De Volkskrant*, 1998). The International Institute for Asian Studies at Leyden State University does not use the TWV procedure if faculty members stay less than 3 months.

The Netherlands Institute for Advanced Study in the Humanities and Social Sciences (NIAS). NIAS is one of the Dutch institutions receiving many faculty members from abroad. The aim of the institute is to stimulate research in the humanities and social sciences and to promote interdisciplinary cooperation in an international setting. The Ministry of Education, Culture and Science mainly finances the institute. NIAS awards annual fellowships to 20 foreign scholars and a further 20 from the Netherlands. NIAS faculty members (groups 3 and 4) need permission to enter and reside in the Netherlands during the fellowship period. A work permit (TWV) is needed, this in spite of the fact that the NIAS fellowship does not imply an employer–employee relationship. The NIAS faculty members receive a stipend and remain employed by the sending university. All faculty members (groups 1-4) need to register at the Wassenaar Municipality and Aliens Police. Upon arrival in Wassenaar, all non-Dutch faculty members are required to go to the Municipal Hall to present their passport and birth certificate. These documents need to be certified copies. If these documents are not written in Dutch, English, French or German, a certified translation in one of these languages by a sworn translator is required. Sometimes original documents need to be legalised to ensure that qualified authorities issue these documents. Problems can occur with the certified copies. NIAS refers to a document of the Ministry of Justice (8 May 1996) including the agreements of the Netherlands with various countries and the implications for the incoming foreigners. Thus, for example, in Afghanistan, legalised documents are unknown, and in Ghana, pre-names are given according to the days of the week. It is doubtful, however, whether someone would be send back to their home country if they cannot present a legalised birth certificate. So far, the authorities have only threatened these cases. Subsequently the faculty members have to present at the Aliens Police Office a copy of the NIAS letter stating the amount of the stipend and the conditions of the fellowship. The faculty member also has to present a certificate of health insurance, passport and two identical colour passport photographs, and if applicable, a marriage certificate, the birth certificates of the children, a copy of the work permit provided by NIAS and the statement of registration at the Municipal Hall. The Aliens Police charges fees of hfl.35 for EU citizens and hfl.125 for citizens of other countries (1997).

There is a big gap between theory and practice. In theory, NIAS faculty members from outside the EU/EER have to report within 3 days of arrival at the Aliens Police Office, though recently the regulations have changed, and the documents of the incoming faculty members (August 1998) firstly have to be checked at the Municipal Hall.

183

Subsequently, the faculty member will get a written request or telephone call to come to the Aliens Police Office. In practice, this may take weeks. Due to this new regulation, the TWV application of group 2 is in danger, because a TWV can only be requested after the faculty member has reported at the Aliens Police Office. Group 1 does not need a TWV and groups 3 and 4 need to apply for a TWV before arrival in the Netherlands.

Faculty members from central and eastern European countries sometimes have to undergo a medical check-up. The faculty members consider this to be very humiliating. It happened once that an eastern European faculty member receeived three summons for a medical check-up during his 10 months' stay at NIAS. Though, so far there are no sanctions in the case, the faculty member will not appear at these check-ups. NIAS gives assistance to get a temporary residence permit (MVV).

Competitors' labour. One of the obstacles to visiting faculty members is the regulation of 'competitors' labour' (*arbeidsmarktverdringende werkzaamheden*). This includes research activities, which could also have been executed by a Dutch person. In the case that a foreign faculty member executes competitors' labour, he/she will be subject to labour tax and national/social insurance tax and he/she should apply for a personal tax number (SoFi-number). EU/EER faculty members can obtain a SoFi-number by presenting a registration document of a Dutch municipality and a proof of identity such as a passport. Faculty members from non-EU/EER countries also have to present a valid residence permit. Thus, the faculty member enters into a bureaucratic spiral. Sometimes the faculty member pays labour tax in his country of origin and in the Netherlands. One can apply for a SoFi-number at any tax office in the Netherlands. If faculty members from non-EU/EER countries apply for a SoFi-number, the tax office may firstly inquire about the person at the Aliens Office to get permission to issue the SoFi-number. The tax office only issues the SoFi-number if the residence permit (VTV) is presented. Due to the long waiting period for receiving a VTV, the issuing of the SoFi-number also is delayed. Subsequently, the host university can only pay the salary if the SoFi-number is attributed after about 4-8 weeks ('Mobiliteit tussen de regels door', 1997). At this NUFFIC seminar, a representative of the Dutch Ministry of Education, Culture and Science underlined the social, fiscal and legal problems (young) researchers have to face. A few years ago, a working group of the European Commission proposed to exempt this group from taxes on their salary, grant or stipend. These recommendations have not been implemented so far. Barriers have to be solved within the competencies of the Ministries of Finance and Social Affairs ('Mobiliteit tussen de regels door', 1997, pp. 7-8).

Fiscal Regulations

Unlike the legal climate, Dutch tax legislation includes various incentives for international faculty mobility. In practice, only a few faculty members involved are aware of these favourable regulations. The incentives may be used by the receiving university in negotiations with a foreign candidate and may become a trigger for accepting a job.

The 35% Regulation

The 35% regulation is an incentive to visiting faculty members. To qualify for the 35% tax regulation, the receiving university has to prove that the visiting faculty member adds quality to the existing team and that his/her quality is not available among Dutch faculty members. In this case, the faculty member will benefit from the 35% regulation, whereby he/she does not have to pay tax over the first 35% of his/her income. If the faculty member is employed full-time, this advantage may reach about hfl. 25,000 annually. The regulation is valid during 10 years of employment. An extra advantage is that the faculty member can easily convert his/her driver's licence into a Dutch driver's licence, by presenting the 35% assignment document.

E 101 Statement

The E 101 statement is a declaration of secondment executed by the Sociale Verzekeringsbank (Social Security Bank), and may act as an incentive to Dutch faculty members going abroad. A Dutch faculty member with the E 101 statement employed by a foreign university is not obliged to pay double taxes. The Dutch Government has bilateral agreements with many countries; e.g. a Dutch faculty member working at an American university does not have to pay taxes in the USA. The Dutch tax system will only assess the faculty member for his/her salary at the sending university. Usually the sending university continues paying the salary.

Recent Developments and Recommendations

In this section, recommendations are presented, based on the research findings (Bunt-Kokhuis, 1996) and more recent developments (1997-98).

International Level

International organisations such as the EU, the Organisation for Economic Cooperation and Development and the World Bank send professionals abroad on a daily basis. The mobility programmes offered should provide a sufficient level of grants, include options to combine different sources and funds, to transfer research grants and scholarships or have them extended while abroad.

IFM must allow research to be a legitimate component in foreign assignments. Simple and clear application procedures to obtain mobility grants should be created with minimum bureaucracy and paperwork. Grants for mobile faculty members with a family should include possibilities to take the family abroad or make visits home. Institutions sending their own staff abroad should have the means to pay for replacement staff. The level of mobility grants should be kept flexible in order to make up for differences between high-cost and low-cost countries as well as provinces and metropolitan areas. Income differences between countries should be balanced. The (inter)national authorities should finance a research project or study which looks at funding mechanisms and criteria to award international mobility grants. Teaching faculty members should be allowed to reserve part of their time (10%) for teaching at a foreign university. International funding agencies, and this applies also to national funding agencies, should become more flexible and open-minded about applicants wishing to combine teaching and research activities abroad. It is recommended that international funding agencies such as the EU provide incentives to national governments and local institutions to implement internationalisation strategies at the national and local level. Institutions should be allowed to allocate these funds for particular purposes, e.g. the payment of top-up grants to incoming or outgoing staff members. To avoid managerial problems, particularly those related to teaching schedules, harmonisation of the academic year worldwide is recommended. This would enable more short-term as well as long-term trips.

National Level

The implementation of successful IFM depends to a large extent on supportive action at national level. The Dutch case illustrates how contra-productive national policy measures can be. Through the recent tightening up of Dutch immigration legislation, the access of faculty members from non-EU/EER countries is seriously hindered. It is likely that more foreign faculty members will look for opportunities at universities outside the Netherlands. The case of the Netherlands demonstrates that national authorities should be aware of legal restrictions, resulting in a negative effect on the academic climate, a decrease in income for universities, and in the end, a decrease in academic quality. National Ministries of Justice, Education and Economic Affairs should actively collaborate. These authorities should note that international mobility includes costs and benefits which go far beyond the legal, educational and economic level. Export of academic knowledge through IFM is part of the larger process of globalisation. In recent literature, the interdependence between globalisation and international mobility of highly skilled personnel is discussed. Xiaonan Cao (1996, p. 269) argues that each country should create a favourable environment to attract highly skilled professionals from both home and abroad, to exploit *'brain circulation'* (in contrast to the former 'brain drain' phenomenon) for the purpose of stimulating national development. Each country should develop a *'social engineering policy'* to provide an opportunity for increased IFM.

The Dutch Government contributes in a very limited way (a few per cent) to the export of academic knowledge through IFM. The USA, on the other hand, contributes 18% of its academic staff in countries such as Korea and Israel (Welch, 1997, p. 329). Fejerskov (in H. de Boer, 1997, p. 50) recommends the establishment of national centres for research training. These centres should be supported by 'seed money' from the EU to found joint PhD programmes and organise seminars for senior researchers. This policy can be compared with NIAS, where faculty members from all over the world come together to do collaborative research for a certain period of time. In addition, Fejerskov recommends the foundation of a European committee on research training, including two representatives of each member state. This committee needs to advise on obstacles to mobility.

Institutional Level

Institutional policy should be focused not only on the faculty members going abroad, but also on visiting faculty members and their home institutions. Both groups should be treated as fully integrated members of the receiving institution and similar quality should be required. The curriculum itself should become more internationalised.

Barriers in the Dutch legal system can be diminished through better collaboration on the local level between the authorities involved, such as the university, GGD, GBA, IND, Aliens Police and municipalities. Closer collaboration is in the interest of each party involved. Thus, for example, the willingness of the Aliens Police and GBA to shorten the admittance procedure for faculty members from abroad is in line with the willingness of the university institution to give a regular overview of foreigners currently at their university. It does not make sense to try to find loopholes in the legislation. Especially where larger groups of visiting faculty members are concerned, it is recommended to formulate adequate agreements between the parties. Thus, for example, the Board of Governors of a university could pay a (lobby) visit to the head of the local GBA and, subsequently, the university's policy-makers may start negotiations with GBA representatives.

In future, more research is needed on the effects of IFM. The infrastructure at institutional level is a crucial variable. Negative IFM effects may be caused by a lack of infrastructure at the home and/or the host institution. Thus, for example, Enders (1998) describes academic staff mobility in the ERASMUS programme during 1990-91. Problems faced before going abroad were often related to an inadequate institutional infrastructure. Those mentioned by the respondents were interruptions of teaching assignments at home institutions, incompatibility between academic themes to be taught abroad and those taught at home, and conflicting schedules. In addition, administrative matters and insufficient grants were stressed as underlying problems that often caused the envisaged exchanges to be shortened or aborted.

Encouragement of International Networks

An intensive use of international networks is recommended. The network may be particularly useful for conducting faculty mobility programmes, for pooling resources, for offering foreign language instruction in less commonly taught languages, encouraging research cooperation and/or dissemination of materials.

The American Task Force for Transnational Competence (1997, pp. 89-91) supports more international exchanges with strong, self-sustaining, horizontal linkages. The bilateral, government-dominated, institution-to-institution approach of past years has gradually been dismantled as both governments and various levels of education have experienced one or more varieties of downsizing. The model that is emerging is a variation of previous approaches to international exchanges but focuses on two principal themes: linkages in the broadest sense, and tripartite alliances between government, higher education and the private sector. These alliances on a reciprocal basis are characterised by a common international strategy; the relationship is horizontal, including knowledge and resources exchanges. Each partner retains their identity and autonomy while cooperating to achieve common goals.

An example in the Netherlands is the recent merger between the Tilburg School of Management (TIAS) and its sister institute in Antwerp (IPO). According to the TIAS Director, the merger is irreversible; nowadays mergers are common practice among banks, breweries and lawyers. The business schools are the next to follow (NRC, 1998).

Human Resources Management

An institutional policy should be developed to remove professional and personal barriers to IFM. The human resources department of the sending and the receiving university should develop a financial 'bonus' system for faculty members who have shown good international academic performance. Misuse of opportunities for IFM, sometimes called 'academic tourism', is avoided in this fashion.

Welch (1997, p. 338) underlines the importance of (financial) rewards. According to Welch, the international ebb and flow of academic personnel is by no means just affected by purely intellectual concerns. He quotes Robert Macnamara: 'Brains are like hearts, they go where they are appreciated'.

In a recent study by Shaffer (1998), it is shown that in international companies international assignees struggle with great conflicts between work and family. The main cause is the interplay between work and family, or the reciprocal influence of demands that reallocate time and energy devoted to each domain. Perceived organisational support, representing the psychological contractual obligation of the employer towards the international assignee, also explain variance in assignment withdrawal and variance in work–family conflict. Similar tensions between work and family were observed by Bunt-Kokhuis (1996). Given the personal circumstances of those in mid-career and senior faculty, facilitating return visits if longer stays are required is recommended.

Senior faculty members should be given the time to transmit their international experiences to more junior faculty members. (Language) training should be offered to non-travellers to enhance their teaching skills for international activities. Special chairs for visiting professors and a system of lending experts could be implemented. The sabbatical leave arrangement and the facilitation of teaching replacement form other structural ways to create IFM opportunities. Mental barriers should be eliminated from the minds of colleagues to be able to deal with the structural absence of faculty members. A positive attitude toward substitute personnel should be developed. The home university should guarantee procedures that facilitate a smooth return.

Perkins (1997, p. 129) describes an emerging trend among business organisations in total remuneration, moving towards increased simplicity and cost and tax effectiveness. Human resources management for this group is called expatriate reward management. A similar trend is recommended in academia. Academic credits should be given to the individual who undertakes teaching activities abroad. Just like research mobility, teaching mobility should be recognised by universities and count towards academic promotion. The home university should provide language assistance, in particular to those in mid-career and senior faculty, during normal working hours, whereby replacement of faculty members is facilitated. To guarantee interaction over a longer period of time, it would be beneficial to consider some shorter visits in a given time span. Enabling accompaniment by family members may increase the success rate of academic trips of longer duration.

Finally, Perkins (1997, p. 278) observed that people are often selected for their technical ability. It leads to 'square pegs in round holes'. More attention should be paid to their social and business skills. Perkins's findings are useful to policy-makers at universities.

Departmental Level

A general improvement in the research/teaching climate at the departmental level of sending and receiving universities is recommended. The working environment should provide freedom to (visiting) faculty members to do research/teaching without bureaucratic interference. The visitors should be introduced to the international network of the department. Computer facilities should be of high quality. The international efforts of a visiting faculty member need to be recognised by the organisation. An attractive visitors' programme should be developed for accompanying spouses.

At the departmental level, a change in the driving forces of faculty mobility can be observed. The emergence of new market-driven actors such as multinational companies, the World Bank, and consultancy firms determine the business-driven objectives of IFM. An increasing number of departments have succeeded in becoming involved in (development-related) research and consultancy. A regulatory framework should be developed at the departmental level to allow faculty members to participate in this growing market of international consultancy work. Sufficient strategic incentives should be provided, including recognition of reports on consultancies in performance assessment. The salary structure should enable differentiation based on market inputs. In a market-oriented university, IFM does not take place on an ad hoc individual basis, but is incorporated in the departmental policy.

Priority Groups

Bunt-Kokhuis (1996) has shown that faculty members with a higher rank and those with a more technical background, senior members and males, have the best opportunities to travel. Faculty members from the social sciences disciplines, such as economics, law, the humanities, and languages and culture (1), juniors (2) and females (3) have limited IFM opportunities. These priority groups form the recommended core of an institutional policy towards successful IFM.

(1) Faculty members from the alpha/gamma disciplines. At the departmental level, non-bureaucratic ways should be found to extend IFM funding for these alpha/gamma groups. Opportunities should be offered to build up professional networks and to do collaborative research. More senior faculty members should use their influence and be helpful to accomplish IFM for an alpha/gamma colleague at a host university of international standing. The position of the alpha/gamma group should be improved by decreasing the teaching load and

facilitating adequate replacement during their absence. International publications by the alpha/gamma group can be encouraged through translation facilities and language courses. Another (indirect) way to encourage international publications is to stimulate alpha/gamma faculty members to become (co)editors of international journals of high standing.

(2) Juniors. Related to the outcomes of the research by Bunt-Kokhuis (1996), Welch (1997, p. 332) shows that 'peripatetic' (mobile) staff are more likely to be among the senior ranks, particular aged over 40. If juniors get the opportunity to go abroad, it often has a positive impact on their (academic) career, as shown by Teichler (1998). Teichler reports on a large-scale investigation among 2000 young research fellows and 2500 supervisors involved in the Human Capital and Mobility Programme of the EU. It is remarkable that most faculty members, after completion of the fellowship abroad, became professionally active in institutions of higher education and research bodies. The European faculty members rated the outcomes of the fellowship for themselves very positively. Some 89% stated that the fellowship period helped them to become internationally more aware, 92% noted an improvement in their general scientific and technical competence, 81% stated that it helped them to establish international research contacts, and 76% that it had helped them to establish their scientific reputation. Some 66% reported an improvement in social and communication skills. The professional value of the fellowship period was rated positively, though not as highly as the academic value. A total of 74% perceived a career advantage in academic research, 5% help in finding employment immediately after the fellowship period, and 26% a career advantage in industry. Despite these positive results, many young research fellows assume they will have better career opportunities if they find employment at home instead of taking a European fellowship. A European fellowship is often a second or third choice.

The positive outcomes described by Teichler (1998) are in line with recent experiences in industry. Perkins (1997, p. 129) indicates the emerging trend among international companies to send young employees on international assignments. This group easily develops global skills before career and family constraints limit their mobility.

Thus, opportunities need to be created for juniors. IFM gives juniors the opportunity to promote recently completed research and encourages their participation in new international projects. To encourage junior travelling, their workload should be reduced. Often juniors teach full-time. It is recommended that juniors be offered an opportunity for international experience much earlier in their careers than was the case in the past. This would help to overcome increasing problems of mobility for older faculty members (spouse's job, children's education, etc.) It would also help to increase the returns, because the return on international investment to the home university as well as the individual may well be greater with younger faculty members. If juniors have the opportunity to make useful international contacts at an early stage in their career, it will prevent them from becoming too inflexible. It will create more opportunities for employment and career development. IFM may encourage juniors to work on their dissertations and personal growth. Juniors in particular need to be assisted by senior colleagues in finding a placement abroad, because juniors cannot yet use a professional network, like seniors do. Long-term placements, up to 1 year, are encouraged in this career stage. Such placements seem to be easier at this stage because juniors often have a less secure position.

(3) Females. Welch (1997, pp. 329-330) says that the opportunity to travel and study abroad actively discriminates against women academics. He discovered that female academics were almost entirely absent at the most senior levels in the Netherlands. The Dutch system was amongst the most gender-segregated of all academic workforces.

A departmental-level policy should be designed which takes into account the care needed for young children while their mother is at work. Both at home and at the host university, childcare facilities with flexible hours should be available.

It is recommended that a policy facilitating shorter and/or return trips should be designed. If trips of longer duration are necessary, it is recommended that the accompanying spouse be assisted in finding a job in the host country.

Outlook

In this chapter, some of the social, legal and fiscal backgrounds of IFM have been highlighted. We have seen that the successful implementation of IFM is not only an institutional matter, but depends to a large extent on national and international agreements. The obstacles to international mobility need to decrease, in the interest of national governments, the participating universities and the individual faculty members. International travelling is an eminent vehicle to develop comparative skills. These skills are beneficial to everyday research and teaching after return. In absolute terms, international mobility of faculty members is even more effective than international student mobility, due to the higher multiplier effect after return. The international experiences are translated by the individual faculty member into reading or teaching material welcomely received by a large audience. The world of academia has become a global village, whereby time and distance are relative concepts. Last but not least, new technologies and an increased knowledge-offer enforce the collaboration of faculty members across borders.

Acknowledgements

Special thanks to Mrs Irene Sloof, staff member of the Communication Department of the Immigratie en Naturalisatiedienst in The Hague, Wouter Teller, Director of the Office for International Relations of the State University Leyden, Mrs Joanneke Halbertsma, project member mobiliteitsknelpunten Department Internationalisering NUFFIC, Mr J.J.M. Hooghuis, secretary of the sciences committee of NIAS in Wassenaar, Erik van Beers, HRM Department of Tilburg University, Mr van Mes, Ministry of Foreign Affairs, Directie Personenmigratie, Consular/Vreemdelingen en Visa in The Hague, and Mrs Marieke te Booij of the International Institute for Asian Studies at State University Leyden.

Notes

[1] At Tilburg University it is not necessary to show a birth certificate to the IND. Tilburg University uses a shortened procedure based on mutual trust between the authorities and the university. One needs to show a birth certificate to become an inhabitant of a municipality. Some visiting faculty members stay in a hotel and, during a shorter visit, are not known by the municipality.

[2] A faculty member from outside Europe visiting Tilburg University enters the following procedure. Tilburg University asks for an MVV at IND. After permission, the MVV document is forwarded to the Dutch embassy in the country of origin. Subsequently, the faculty member travels to the Netherlands. Within 3 days of arrival, he/she has to visit the Immigration Police. Preferably, the faculty member will visit the police accompanied by a university representative and on appointment. Otherwise, the faculty member has to wait a long time and may be threatened as a 'usual foreigner'.

[3] The requirement (hfl.17,000) is remarkably high, because the Dutch social support minimum is currently on an annual base hfl.12,415. Probably other regulations are applicable to foreigners.

[4] An earlier version of this chapter was published in *Higher Education in Europe*, XXV, 2000, pp. 117-155.

References

Boer, H. de (1997) De Europese dimensie van het hoger onderwijs, *Th@ma*, March, pp. 48-51.

Bunt-Kokhuis, S.G.M. van de (1996) Academic Pilgrims; determinants of international faculty mobility, PhD thesis, Tilburg University Press.

De Volkskrant (1998) Universiteit van Leiden boycott Koppelingswet, 26 September.

Enders, J. (1998) Academic Staff Mobility in the European Community: the ERASMUS experience, *Comparative Education Review*, pp. 46-60.

European Commission (1996) *Education, Training, Research – the obstacles to transnational mobility*, Green Paper. Brussels: European Commission.

Havermans, J. (1997) Struikelblokken van de niet-EU-Mobiliteit, *Transfer*, November, pp. 12-13.

Koppelingswet vereist (1998) *Uitleg*, 16, 17 June, pp. 16-17.

Mobiliteit Geregeld (1999) Report of Netherlands Universities Foundation for Cooperation (NUFFIC).

Mobiliteit tussen de regels door (1997) Verslag van een seminar en backgroundpaper, NUFFIC.

Mobiliteit tussen de regels door: aanbevelingen ter vergemakkelijking van de instroom van gewenste HO-vreemdelingen in het Nederlands Hoger Onderwijs, (1998), Dossier NUFFIC, 15 June.

Mobiliteitsonderzoek Nuffic roept vraagtekens en zorg op (1998) *Transfer*, January, pp. 6-7.

NAFSA Newsletter (1997) New York, October/November, pp. 33-34.

Perkins, S.J. (1997) *Internationalization – the people dimension*. London: Kogan Page.

Shaffer, M.E. (1998) Struggling with What Matters Most: conflicts between work and family on international assignments, paper presented to the Academy of Management Proceedings 1998, San Diego.

Taskforce for Transnational Competence (1997) *Towards Transnational Competence, Rethinking International Education: a U.S.–Japan Case Study*. New York: Institute of International Education.

Teichler, U. (1998) Employment Prospects for Young Researchers after Participation in European Programmes, *Journal of International Education*, 9, pp. 27-32.

The Week in Europe (1998) 30 July, p. 1. London: European Commission.

Welch, A.R. (1997) The Peripatetic Professor: the internationalisation of the academic profession, *Higher Education*, 34, pp. 323-345.

Xiaonan Cao (1996) Debating 'Brain Drain' in the Context of Globalisation, *Compare*, 26, pp. 269-285.

PART THREE

Practical Issues and New Approaches

Approaches to Comparing Education Systems

JOANNA LE MÉTAIS

Introduction

The United Kingdom Government has recently commissioned a number of evaluation studies of educational research (see Hillage et al, 1998; Tooley & Darby, 1998) which have been critical of its quality and relevance. This view has been endorsed by HM Chief Inspector (Woodhead, 1998), who blames sloppy standards. However, it could be argued that dissatisfaction with research outcomes might be caused by issues such as 'the sponsorship of research, the use to which sponsors put it, the control they have over it and the responsibility of researchers to those who sponsor them' (Pring, 1998, p. 361).

The United Kingdom Government intends to channel the funding for educational research into a more limited number of 'centres of excellence' (Clarke, 1998) and has promoted evidence-based research following the Cochrane model, which favours large-scale, replicable and largely quantitative studies. Those engaged in comparing education systems would argue that undue reliance on quantitative studies is inappropriate. This is because such research often ignores the context that goes a long way to explain the success or failure of specific teaching and learning approaches.

However, exclusive focus on case studies also has weaknesses because, as Welch (1993) argues:

> the insistent emphasis by ethnomethodologists on micro ethnographies of classroom life as providing the bedrock of hard evidence upon which any firm understanding of educational phenomena must be based, ignores the ways in which such slices of micro life are shaped by more macro structures and forces in society. (p. 11)

Recognising that a balance needs to be maintained, this chapter seeks to examine the particular constraints facing comparative researchers in trying to meet all the criteria (e.g. relating to focus, conduct and presentation) set by policy-makers. It draws primarily on the author's experience, since 1984 [1], of preparing comparative descriptions and analyses specifically intended to support education policy-making in the United Kingdom and in the European Community.

Context

Watson (1998) pointed out that the demand for comparative and international studies of education policy and practice is growing. A number of contextual factors have influenced the amount and nature of cross-national research commissioned, and progressively increased expectations.

Throughout the world, social, economic and technological changes make new demands on education. Governments have increasingly looked overseas for solutions. Fact-finding missions, intergovernmental meetings and cross-national studies result in overt and covert policy convergence (see Husén, 1982, cited by Trow, 1986, for a description of the 'percolation' process). The impact of a single personal experience, for example, a school visit, is often greater than that of the most scrupulous and detailed research. Cross-national studies create norms and affect education policy in a forceful – even disturbing – way. For example, overseas practice may be 'transplanted' without due consideration of the original context and objectives and, in some cases, it may be ineffective, inappropriate or even counterproductive within the new setting.

Another factor is the pressure for action, within an electoral cycle (commonly around 4 or 5 years) that does not allow time for detailed reflection. This may affect the type of research conducted and the nature of reports. An example of the former is an overseas government, which sought a comprehensive evaluation of its education system, covering values, purposes and student and staff performance, all within a matter of weeks. There is in increasing trend towards demanding executive summary or 'sound-bite' reports, which may not provide adequate details of methodology to allow for classification in meta-reviews or replicated studies. Hence, governments may introduce educational reforms that have not been suitably underpinned by research, and which may be widely implemented before they are evaluated. On occasions, where an evaluation of a pilot study is commissioned, the report may be required before the completion of the pilot.

Funding criteria may impose constraints in terms of scope, timescale and method and, in the case of international sponsors, a requirement that the research include members from several countries. The fact that much policy-relevant research 'is small scale and incapable of generating findings that are reliable and generalisable' (Hillage et al, 1998) may be the result of emphasis on cost as a – not always explicit – criterion for commissioning research. In contrast, sponsors may intentionally commission overlapping or replicated studies on the grounds that preceding work (which may still be ongoing) does not, or will not, fully meet their needs.

The remainder of this chapter will deal with the five stages in the life cycle of educational research: specification, conceptualisation, data collection and analysis, presentation of findings and use. Where a single individual or group manages all of these stages, a high level of consonance between intention and outcome may be expected. In practice, a mismatch may arise between the understandings and therefore expectations of sponsors, researchers and users, all of whom may come from more than one country.

Specification

Cross-national studies range from documentary analysis, through review of existing research (e.g. the studies of European Community interest funded under SOCRATES Action III.3.1), to empirical fieldwork (e.g. Osborn, 1997). However, the high cost of fieldwork and short timescales generally favour desk-based research. Studies may focus explicitly on policy development, review or implementation, or they may be wider or more wide ranging and influence the policy process indirectly.

Explicit Policy Studies

Studies to support policy formulation or review may be 'open' or 'closed'. An example of the former is the ongoing International Review of Curriculum and Assessment Frameworks (see O'Donnell et al, 2000), commissioned as part of the Qualifications and Curriculum Authority's curriculum review. Here, information about 16 systems is collected and structured within an explicitly English framework, without seeking to test any hypotheses. Linked thematic studies draw on the Review Archive, additional research and international seminars, to explore implications and consequences in specific policy areas, again without pre-empting the nature of the discussions or making value judgements. This open approach produces findings that lend themselves to analysis at different levels and for different purposes. Despite its specific English 'lens', educators in other countries have reported finding the Review useful in their reflections.

In contrast, the review of provisions for young people who have left the education system without qualifications carried out by the EURYDICE network (1997a) is an example of a closed study. The European Commission requested this study in the context of its proposals for 'second chance' schools (European Commission, 1996), which are intended to give a new opportunity for 16-25 year-olds who have left school without qualifications. The focus on remedial measures intended *solely* for this group excluded both preventative measures and provision for a wider age group, whether general (basic skills and courses which prepare students for access to higher education) or vocational. Moreover, variations in, or the absence of, national definitions of the target group mean that some national descriptions *include* post-school education and guidance services, which are *excluded* from others on the grounds that they serve a wider population. Such restrictions in scope may cause the competence or political motives of the providers of apparently incomplete information to be called into question (e.g. see Alexander [1996] for comments on the representation of primary education) and, arguably, pre-empts a full consideration of policy options.

Open evaluation studies examine the intended and unintended implications or impact of a policy or programme, whilst closed studies focus on the benefits, to confirm ideology and support the widespread implementation of programmes. In exceptional cases, research may be designed to justify political decisions already made; Hillage et al (1998) found examples 'where ... researchers felt that their research had been suppressed when it highlighted deficiencies in government policy' (p. 22).

Studies Indirectly Related to Policy

Both policy-makers and researchers have pointed to the important contribution of fundamental research, which seeks to accumulate or develop knowledge, or to 'raise unimagined and forbidden questions'. They argue that 'while not of direct significance at [any] particular time, [it] would perhaps underpin the practitioner of the future' (Hillage et al, 1998, p. 14). General comparisons are sponsored by international bodies, for example the Organisation for Economic Cooperation and Development (OECD) and the European Commission, which have no power at the national level but seek to influence national authorities. Proactive information-gathering indirectly informs policy and supports its implementation, by providing:

> examples of overseas provision which might be considered and adapted for use in the home context (e.g. EURYDICE, 1998; O'Donnell et al, 2000);
> a context for comparative surveys of provision, participation or achievement (e.g. European Commission, 1997; Centre for Educational Research and Innovation [CERI], 1998) or surveys of student performance in specific subject areas (e.g. Third International Maths and Science Survey [TIMMS] – see Keys et al, 1996a, 1996b);
> an account of changes in education systems over a given period of time (e.g. EURYDICE, 1997b);

information on institutions, courses and qualifications (e.g. ORTELIUS, 1998 and National Academic Recognition and Information Centre [NARIC], 1998) intended to facilitate and promote the mobility of students and workers within the European Union.

Some cross-national studies are inclusive (EURYDICE studies include all the countries in the network) whilst others depend on voluntary participation (e.g. TIMMS). In addition, some enjoy official status, which entails validation by national authorities (e.g. International Bureau of Education [IBE], 1998; EURYDICE and European Centre for the Development of Vocational Training [CEDEFOP] 1999-2000). However, this is a time-consuming process, which carries the risk that concurrent policy changes may invalidate parts of the publication before its appearance. The challenge of integrating all the comments on a composite draft – some of which may contradict others – into summary descriptions cannot be overestimated.

It is therefore essential to indicate the purpose and scope of a study, and thus its constraints, exclusions and other limitations; unless they do so, authors may be criticised for failing to meet subsequent users' (unforeseen) expectations.

Concepts and Terminology

The most important issue for cross-national studies is the identification of concepts and the selection of terminology and research instruments that suit all the education systems represented in the study; misunderstandings and misinterpretations may cause problems in responses which undermine the validity and reliability of the findings. However, it is notoriously difficult to create questionnaires that are understood by, and relevant to, people in different national, cultural and educational contexts. For example, it only emerged after extended discussions within the EURYDICE network that one participant member interpreted 'educational administration' to mean *internal* institutional administration, whilst others perceived it as the overarching national or regional organisation and management of the service. In another example, a German respondent interpreted questions about the school curriculum as referring to subject syllabuses.

Ensuring comparability of statistics is also beset with difficulties. For example, statistics on the number of students who successfully complete ('graduate from') upper secondary education are influenced by a number of factors.

Definition of categories. Because of the degree of choice open to students aged 16-18, United Kingdom statistics used for international comparisons classify students attending schools and institutions of further education as receiving general or vocational education respectively, regardless of the courses followed.

Double counting of students may occur (e.g. in Belgium) when students complete multiple programmes at a given level (CERI, 1997). Assessment may be based on attendance (thereby embracing large numbers of students) or on examinations which are intended to discriminate between students, for example, to control admission to oversubscribed higher education courses.

Involving specialists from a range of countries in the process of defining terms and criteria enriches the formulation of research instruments and the interpretation of findings, by ensuring that national particularities are, at least, discussed and recognised. The use of more than one language for negotiating the framework can also serve to highlight differences in understanding. But this process is time-consuming and therefore costly.

Data Collection and Analysis

Data are only as good as their sources. Cross-national sources present a triple challenge: access, validity and reliability. Primary sources may be inaccessible due to cost, time delays and language. Secondary sources may eliminate these problems but, as processed information, they may contain inherent mistakes or misinterpretations.

Whatever the source, researchers need to be aware of the perspective and/or objective of the author(s). Do the concepts and terminology match those of the current study? What are the criteria for selection of information? What has been excluded? How has the information been processed and interpreted and to what extent has this affected the accuracy and/or representativeness of the data? What are the intended messages of the report? To what extent does the context of the source document affect the inferences or conclusions which may be drawn? For example, the provision of information relating to student expenditure may differ, according to whether the purpose is to demonstrate commitment to education or efficiency in use of resources.

Whilst these questions apply to all research, the contextual (e.g. historic, cultural and social) and linguistic differences between countries and their systems increase the complexity of cross-national study. Two main models of data collection have been used which seek to address these problems.

In the *centralised* model, the purpose, scope and research instruments are defined, and the data collected, processed and interpreted in one country, although the countries surveyed may be invited to correct inaccuracies in drafts of the report. With the research in the hands of a single team, the criteria used for collection and interpretation are likely to be more consistently applied, but the perspective adopted may result in distortion or misrepresentation as different systems are 'squeezed' into the framework. An example of this is the artificial separation of the unitary system of compulsory education, common in Nordic countries, into primary and secondary phases. Another occurs when generalisations are made about provision in a federal system. This is a particular danger where the research report takes the form of tables or snapshot descriptions (e.g. CERI, 1997; European Commission, 1997). A second difficulty may be physical and linguistic access to information from remote locations and an imperfect understanding of the specific national contexts. Recent legislation in (Communist) Vietnam calls for the 'socialisation of education' (Republic of Vietnam Government, 1998). The interpretation of this term, to describe the willingness of all citizens to contribute financially, is not one that immediately comes to the mind of a Western reader.

The *decentralised* model relies on the participation of several or all of the countries represented in both data collection and processing. The advantages of ready access to, and detailed understanding of, local data may be undermined by potential discrepancies in the way in which researchers in different locations interpret the purpose and scope of the project and the cross-national presentation framework. An example of this is general and vocational education for adults, which may be designated as upper secondary, post-secondary, further or non-university higher education, depending on the country concerned. The challenge of finding a common, mutually acceptable, term is considerable.

The optimum strategy exploits the strengths of the central and national teams, to obtain the highest quality information within the shortest timescale.

Presentation of Findings

Researchers have a primary responsibility to present their findings to sponsors in an agreed form. Reviewers in the United Kingdom and the USA (e.g. Kennedy, 1997; Hillage et al, 1998; Tooley & Darby, 1998) criticise educational research, particularly that aimed at policy-makers, on the grounds of relevance, quality, accessibility and usability. Meeting this challenge requires careful liaison between the provider and the end user of the information, to define its purpose, content and scope. However, the publication of findings makes them available to a wider – unspecified – audience, whose unpredictable and possibly contradictory expectations may result in high levels of dissatisfaction.

A policy report requires a concise but clear summary of complex issues, understandable within a national, or cross-national, context. On the other hand, practitioners look for more details of implications and implementation. The research readership requires a full account of method, supporting evidence and reference to primary sources, so that the reliability of the information and the interpretation may be checked.

This latter requirement is particularly important to allow for accurate classification of research findings in meta-analyses and reviews.

Cross-national studies may comprise a series of country reports (e.g. EURYDICE & CEDEFOP, 1999-2000) or a single report, drawing on the contributions of numerous participants (e.g. European Commission, 1997). The demand for easily comparable information within a concise report may distort the specificities of national systems. Similar problems arise when seeking to describe education systems of countries with devolved responsibilities for education (e.g. Australia, Canada, Germany and the USA). One corrective strategy is to complement a general overview with more detailed national (or subnational) descriptions, which respect the peculiarities of different systems and elucidate aspects of the overview (for example, EURYDICE, 1997b). Although such a strategy may be unwieldy and costly for paper versions, these disadvantages are virtually overcome in electronic formats.

Scope and Balance

An attempt to reflect the diversity of numerous systems may result in a publication which, however interesting, is unmanageable and remains unread. An oversimplified text may falsely lead readers to think that, within 10 pages, they have an insight into 'what is going on worldwide', whilst nationals no longer recognise their own system.

The exclusion of information on some countries from a report may be justifiable because:

the issue is irrelevant within a particular national context (e.g. the teaching of religious education in schools would not be an issue in France, where state education is, by law, secular);
the national structure conflicts with the framework of the study (e.g. regional education policy is irrelevant in a country which does not have regions, or conversely, the role of national government in countries where all responsibility is devolved to states and provinces);
the information is not collected in a given country (e.g. specific statistics).

Language

Cross-national studies, which may be used by audiences in a number of countries, are particularly vulnerable to variations in interpretation and expectation. They need to include definitions of terms and concepts used and to ensure that readers are aware of any concessions that have been made in the interests of cross-national understanding. For example, the use of 'private education' to designate institutions which are established and managed by non-state authorities, but which receive public sector funding (as in the Netherlands and Belgium) may be confusing to a

United Kingdom reader, who interprets this term as applying to an independent, fee-paying establishment. Equally, subtle distinctions between, for example, (student) assessment, (teacher) appraisal and (school or system) evaluation may escape some readers and are better avoided.

One of the strengths of reports published by international organisations or networks is their availability in more than one language. However, the intricacies of disparate education systems can present problems, even to a specialist translator. For example, the terms used in translation to denote nursery school staff may disguise the distinction in professional training, responsibilities and employment between 'nursery teachers' and 'nursery nurses' in the United Kingdom. Sensitivity to the appropriateness, or even acceptability, of certain terms is also required. For example, a literal translation of the French *élèves handicappés* would not be suitable in the United Kingdom context, where the term 'pupils with special educational needs' is used. Even the use of 'state' to designate public-sector education may create confusion in federal countries.

Use ... and Abuse

Increasingly, findings are presented on CD-ROM and on the Internet, thereby facilitating cross-national searches, exploitation and subsequent analysis. Computer-based formats also provide scope for developing audit trails of policy and provision. For example, in each successive update of the *International Review of Curriculum and Assessment Frameworks Archive (INCA)* (O'Donnell et al, 2000), superseded policies and provisions will be placed in the annex of the relevant national description. By following the structure of the core description, it will be possible, over time, to trace the frequency and nature of educational change.

It makes sense – in terms of resources and time – to build on existing research wherever possible. This is facilitated when the original purposes and constraints of the research are explicitly stated so that the limitations of its (subsequent) applicability are clear. This is part of the process of 'managing expectations' and it reduces the risk of the uncritical use of one set of findings for a different purpose. The ill-considered use of research to draw unrelated or unsupported conclusions constitutes abuse, which serves neither researchers nor policy-makers. Four examples of such inappropriate use follow.

Design and use. The ORTELIUS higher education database provides information on institutions, courses and qualifications intended to guide students who wish to undertake part of their higher education studies in a foreign country. It has been suggested that the database can also underpin the comparisons and ranking of qualifications for recognition purposes. However, information on course duration and content may not constitute a sufficient basis for judgements of their level or quality.

Correlation and cause. There is a tendency to confuse correlation and cause. In 1987, the United Kingdom Secretary of State for Education and Science supported his proposals for self-managing schools with the argument that 98% of pupils in a similarly self-managing school in the Netherlands went on to university. He failed to mention that the Dutch school in question was part of a selective system and admitted only those students likely to proceed to, and succeed in, university education.

Fact and extrapolation. In the selection of desirable indicators for *Key Data* (European Commission, 1997), it was suggested that information on school inspectorates would provide an insight into methods for appraising teacher performance. Whilst this expectation is reasonable in the context of the French system, where teachers' professional performance is appraised by inspectors, it is misplaced in the case of England, where teacher appraisal is conducted within the school.

Simplification and misrepresentation. The desire to represent numerous systems in a simple diagram, or the propensity for 'quick fix' solutions, have led to examples of oversimplification and misrepresentation. The most common one is that of grouping a range of systems into a generalised whole ('in the States ...', 'in the Far East ...') with no regard for the differences between the individual states or countries. A second, equally dangerous error is that of attributing outcomes to a single cause, divorced from the national and cultural context and assuming that an identical outcome could be achieved in the United Kingdom if the supposed causal behaviour were adopted. For example, the emphasis on whole-class teaching underpinning the United Kingdom numeracy initiative was based on observation of this teaching style in South-east Asian countries which scored highly in the TIMMS survey. The adoption of this strategy does not take into consideration the conformist culture of the education systems and the high status enjoyed by both education and teachers in the countries concerned.

Conclusion

It could be argued that this chapter paints a discouraging picture of the difficulties and limitations of comparing education systems. However, its purpose is to raise awareness of potential problems and thereby to contribute to improving the conduct and usefulness of cross-national research. In order to achieve quality and relevance, attention needs to be devoted to three aspects of the work.

Groundwork. Sponsors and researchers should take time to define the purpose, scope and outputs of the research, and of the contributions of each research partner, so that there is a clear understanding of what the project can be expected to deliver. Researchers should define the concepts and terminology and identify their sources.

Communication. Researchers should maintain communication with both sponsors and research partners, to check the consistency and comparability of emerging findings and to resolve any problems with the data collection or interpretation that may affect the quality of the outcome.

'Health warnings'. No research can meet the needs of all (potential) users. It must primarily meet the needs of the sponsor and should include a clear statement of its purpose, scope and limitations for the benefit of other users. Whilst an indication of constraints is helpful, a long list of difficulties or defences is counterproductive.

In the longer term, the closer involvement of researchers *throughout the policy-making process* will lead to better definition of research projects and to more appropriate use of the findings.

Acknowledgements

This chapter is based on a paper presented at the Inaugural Conference of the British Association for International and Comparative Education (BAICE), 'Doing Comparative Education Research: issues and problems', at the University of Reading on 12 September 1998.

Note

[1] Dr Le Métais was Head of the National Unit for England, Wales and Northern Ireland of the EURYDICE European education information network between 1984 and 1998. Since 1996, she has directed the International Review of Curriculum and Assessment Frameworks for the Qualifications and Curriculum Authority in England. She has also conducted numerous other cross-national studies.

References

Alexander, R. (1996) *Other Primary Schools and Ours: hazards of international comparison*, CREPE Occasional papers. Coventry: Warwick University Centre for Research in Elementary and Primary Education.

Broadfoot, P. (1998) Stones from Other Hills May Serve to Polish the Jade of this One: towards a 'comparology' of education, in this volume, pp. 85-107.

Centre for Educational Research and Innovation (CERI) (1997) *Education at a Glance: OECD indicators*. Paris: Organisation for Economic Cooperation and Development.

Clarke, C. (1998) Resurrecting Educational Research to Raise Standards, *Research Intelligence* (The British Educational Research Association Newsletter), 66, pp. 8-9.

European Commission, Directorate-General Education, Training and Youth (1996) *Teaching and Learning: towards the learning society.* Brussels: European Commission.

European Commission, Directorate-General Education, Training and Youth (1997) *Key Data on Education in the European Union 1997.* Luxembourg: Office for Official Publications of the European Communities.

EURYDICE (1997a) *Measures Taken in the Member States of the European Union to Assist Young People Who have Left the Education System without Qualifications.* Brussels: EURYDICE European Unit.

EURYDICE (1997b) *A Decade of Reforms at Compulsory Education Level.* Brussels: EURYDICE European Unit.

EURYDICE (1998) *EURYBASE: the community database on education.* Brussels: EURYDICE European Unit. (Online) Available at: //www.eurydice.org

EURYDICE and CEDEFOP (1999-2000) *Structures of the Education and Initial Training Systems in the European Union*, 3rd edn. Luxembourg: Office for Official Publications of the European Communities.

Hillage, J., Pearson, R., Anderson, A. & Tamkin, P. (1998) *Excellence in Research on Schools.* London: Department for Education and Employment.

International Bureau of Education (IBE) (1998) *World Data on Education* (CD-ROM). Geneva: IBE.

Kennedy, M. (1997) The Connection between Research and Practice, *Educational Researcher*, 26(7), pp. 4-12.

Keys, W., Harris, S. & Fernandes, C. (1996a) *Third International Mathematics and Science Study, First National Report. Part 1: Achievement in mathematics and science at age 13 in England.* Slough: National Foundation for Educational Research.

Keys, W., Harris, S. & Fernandes, C. (1996b) *Third International Mathematics and Science Study, National Reports. Appendices: Additional information relating to the study in England and Wales.* Slough: National Foundation for Educational Research.

National Academic Recognition and Information Centre (NARIC) (1998) *International Comparisons* (CD ROM). Cheltenham: NARIC.

O'Donnell, S., Greenaway, E., Le Métais, J. & Micklethwaite, C. (2000) *INCA: the international review of curriculum and assessment frameworks archive*, 3rd edn (online). London: Qualifications and Curriculum Authority. Also available online at: http://www.inca.org.uk

Osborn, M. (1997) Children's Experience of Schooling in England and France: some lessons from a comparative study, *Education Review.* London: National Union of Teachers.

ORTELIUS (1998) *ORTELIUS. The database on higher education in Europe.* (Online) Available: http://ortelius.unifi.it/

Pring, R. (1998) Editorial, *British Journal of Educational Studies*, 46, pp. 357-361.

Republic of Vietnam Government (1998) *Law of Education Nr 11/1998/QH10.* Hanoi: Vietnam Government.

Tooley, J. & Darby, D. (1998) *Education Research: an OFSTED critique.* London: Office for Standards in Education.

Trow, M. (1986) Researchers, Policy Analysts and Policy Intellectuals, in T.N. Postlethwaite (Ed.) *International Education Research: papers in honor of Torsten Husén.* Oxford: Pergamon Press.

Watson, K. (2001) Comparative Educational Research: the need for reconceptualisation and fresh insights, in this volume, pp. 23-42.

Welch, A.R. (1993) Class, Culture and the State, *Comparative Education*, 29, pp. 7-27.

Woodhead. C. (1998) Academia Gone to Seed, *New Statesman*, March.

Gleaning Meaning from Case Studies in International Comparison: teachers' experiences of reform in Russia and South Africa

MICHELE SCHWEISFURTH

How do primary school teachers experience large-scale social and educational changes in new democracies? How is this expressed in their practice? And what are the factors which affect individual teachers' responses to change in these contexts? These are important questions in coming to understand what Alexander (1995) calls the 'dynamics and culture of change', which in turn can help to illuminate the processes at the interface of policy and practice. For, as many studies have shown, the mediation of reform initiatives by teachers is a critical, but often overlooked, element in determining the impact of new education policy (Broadfoot & Osborn, 1993; Fuller et al, 1994; Pollard et al, 1994; Alexander, 1995; Smyth, 1995; Villegas-Reimers & Reimers, 1996).

The empirical study which informs this chapter is a 4-year PhD project at the University of Warwick, and is based on two periods of fieldwork in Russia and two in South Africa. The first phase of fieldwork (2 weeks in each country) was exploratory, and highlighted themes which were pursued further in phase two.

Among them were teachers' definitions of democratic and student-centred practice, the extent, nature and understanding of the changes they were implementing, the constraints they perceived to these changes, and the personal, social and professional influences shaping their current perspectives and practice. In the second phase (approximately 1 month in each country), six teachers in Russia and six in South Africa were selected as case studies. Over a minimum of two school days, a series of interviews, lesson and whole-school observations, and assorted other instruments were used to explore their situations, attitudes, classroom practice and life histories, and the relationships among these. While some interesting patterns are beginning to emerge from analysis of the data, it is too soon to examine these in the depth that they deserve. Instead, the focus here will be on the methodology of the study, in particular, how to 'glean meaning' from the use of case study approaches cross-nationally, and how these principles are being applied to this research.

As Cohen & Manion (1991) point out, case studies are based on observation, the purpose of which is to 'probe deeply and to analyse intensively the multifarious phenomena that constitute the ... [case study] unit, with a view to establishing generalisations about the wider population to which the unit belongs' (p. 125). They offer the advantages of being firmly embedded in reality, with attention to the subtleties and complexities of the case, including rich detail which may at times be contradictory, depending on the perspectives of the subjects involved (Cohen & Manion, 1991).

These qualities make case study an appropriate choice of approach to address the research questions at hand. Some writers (such as Yin, 1993) object to the exclusive placement of case study research approaches within the qualitative paradigm; however, the issues in this study, with their focus on teachers' experiences and perspectives, make this a natural choice. The changes being experienced by teachers in Russia and South Africa may be welcomed by many after years of tightly centralised control. However, they are also extremely complicated and demanding, and reach beyond the structures of schooling, curriculum and pedagogy into a redefinition of teachers' roles and relationships with students, communities and authorities. I believe that understanding of the shifting subtleties of teachers' responses to the strange and stressful pressures of democratic reform demands not distant objectivity, but rather what Stenhouse (in Burgess & Rudduck, 1993, p. 72) calls 'critical intersubjectivity'. The researcher's interaction with the subjects aimed to produce in-depth knowledge, which is enhanced by being approached from two different cultural perspectives. For example, teachers may have difficulty articulating which influences from their own schooling experiences have been most profound on their practice. However, researcher and subject understanding can be mutually enhanced through a sequence of interviews and lesson observation where the teacher has the chance to think back to his or her own schooldays, to predict the progress and outcomes of a lesson, to act, to explain, and to reflect. In response to cues from the researcher, who sees the lesson through different eyes and who finds alien the details of life and schooling under communism or apartheid, the taken-for-granted is foregrounded, and memory, practice and espoused theory are triangulated. In turn, the researcher's perspective is interrogated by the emphasis the teacher places on different aspects of each of these. This process takes time, and requires a rapport with the subject which cannot easily be created in a single interview. Such intricate and embedded phenomena are not at all accessible by questionnaire. In pursuing such phenomena, it was concluded that 'it is better to have in-depth, accurate knowledge of one setting than superficial and possibly skewed or misleading information about isolated relationships in many settings' (Spindler, 1982, in Crossley & Vulliamy, 1984, p. 203).

In what ways is this a comparative study? What is often expected from cross-national studies involving two countries are generalisations about the two national units, and an analysis of the commonalities and differences between them: in this case, statements about national characteristics of teachers in Russia and teachers in South Africa. However, that is neither the aim of the study, nor an efficient use of the data about individual teachers, although similarities among case study teachers from one country may be one potential finding. This would be a comparative study even if there were only one country involved: there is more than enough variety to generate interesting comparisons among the case studies in either one of the countries. The diversity is such that some teachers could have more in common with colleagues from the other country than with colleagues from their own: the education traditions among white South Africa teachers, for example, seem to be shared as much with Russian teachers as with their black compatriots. In any event, those sorts of generalisations – 'South African teachers are like this; Russians are like that' – are not what case studies explore. They celebrate processes and the particular more than they do the fixed and the general. Therefore, the case units were individual teachers, while their schools, regions and countries were potential explanatory units for findings concerning the individual case.

However, generalisability remains an issue even if one chooses to avoid the word and to focus on the unique aspects of a particular case. Research which has no apparent meaning beyond its own boundaries has limited appeal and even less potential for application of findings, except in situations deemed very similar to those described. It was hoped that through these case studies, isolated and limited though they might be, the research could 'use the micro level to illustrate the macro' (Vulliamy et al, 1990, p. 72). In attempting this, many writers on case study variously address combinations of some of the issues of *selection, verification, cumulation, generalisation* and *application*, showing them as problematic in the process of giving wider meaning to self-contained cases (Crossley & Vulliamy, 1984; Walker, 1986; Atkinson & Delamont, 1986; Cohen & Manion, 1991; Burgess & Rudduck, 1993; Yin, 1993; Stake, 1995). Different commentators place varying degrees of emphasis on individual issues; much of the discussion in this chapter draws especially on Stenhouse's analysis of verification, cumulation, generalisation and application (in Burgess & Rudduck, 1993), Crossley & Vulliamy's (1984 and 1997) writing on cumulation and generalisation, and Yin (1993) and Walker (1986) on selection. All of these criteria could be seen as essential, and dependent on the others in a linear way. Here each of these factors will be explored very briefly, outlining issues inherent in case study for each of them. I will also attempt to show how these five challenges faced by the case study practitioner are related, with overcoming one being dependent on successfully dealing with the one before, and to explain how this study of teachers in new democracies is approaching each of them.

Selection

Selectivity on the part of the researcher is an essential dimension of case study, despite its claims to flexibility and resistance to premature closure. Cases must be chosen: what and who to be studied, and the boundaries of each case. Here, choosing to use teachers as the case unit, and choosing Russia and South Africa as the countries in which to study them, were vital first steps. Choosing the teachers themselves was another vital stage: how could a range of fairly typical experiences be conveyed within such a small study group? Within each case, decisions must be made about which issues to raise and what to observe; if these decisions are not taken consciously, preconceptions and bias will inevitably govern them. In this study, the formulation of basic interview questions from which to start the process of probing, and the methods of classroom observation, were critical. Finally, at the editing and presentation stages, researchers will discriminate among the data collected, attributing greater significance to some than to others. It is not possible to include every detail; what is selected will ultimately govern the reader's understanding of the case. Thus, selection is an inescapable aspect of case study. However, its effect may be tempered through conscious application, with integrity, of principles which expose and discipline it. If the selection process does not confront these decisions explicitly – if, for example, exceptional examples are portrayed as typical, or vice versa, or if ease of access for the researcher is the main selection criterion – the illuminative potential of the cases is severely reduced and the study is likely to fail at the first hurdle.

In the process of designing this research project, the first selection juncture came in choosing the two countries from which to select individual cases. Russia and South Africa were chosen for a number of reasons. Apart from a long-standing personal interest in the two countries (but equally, little experience of them), the nature and stages of the democratic transitions which they have been experiencing offered enough similarities to warrant comparison, with plenty of differences to help highlight the impact of contextual factors. The changes experienced in these two countries have been happening within similar time-frames and scope. In very general terms: administration and funding systems in both countries are moving away from high degrees of centralisation and regulation. New types of schools with more 'open' access are being created in both countries: in Russia, market forces are creating more specialised schools with varying admission requirements and costs (and quality); in South Africa, schools are being officially desegregated (although integration is more problematic). The numbers of private schools are increasing in both countries in response to consumer demand, which has become a greater driving force in the absence of centralist dictates. In both countries, there are moves toward the inclusion of children with special educational needs. In terms of curriculum, there has been the rewriting and refocusing of history to encompass perspectives other than that justifying the previous regime. Throughout the curriculum, the singularity of an ideological perspective has been replaced by what in Russia is called 'humanised' and in South Africa 'outcomes-based' education, attempting to cater for the needs of individuals and to encourage a more critical outlook, and teachers and schools have greater freedom of choice in content. Teachers in both countries are being encouraged to employ less didactic and more child-centred approaches to complement these curricular changes (Education Policy Unit, Witswatersrand, 1993-98; World Bank, 1995; Nkabinde, 1997, Organisation for Economic Cooperation and Development [OECD], 1998). These generalisations are admittedly sweeping. However, they do illustrate some of the common themes which emerge when one takes a long view of the changes in education in Russia and South Africa, and they create a basis for the choice of these two very different countries as the starting point before choosing the smaller units to be studied as cases and compared in a more intricate manner.

Why teachers as the unit of study for the cases? There is a considerable body of literature from various countries describing the 'constellation of factors' (Fuller et al, 1996) which play important roles in shaping the culture of teaching and the responses of individual teachers. Other studies outlining some of the cultural and more personal factors impacting upon teachers include Calderhead (1987), Nias (1989), Broadfoot & Osborn (1993), Gillborn (1994) and Hargreaves (1994). However, while the categories of influences may be similar and there are discernible patterns of response among groups of teachers, there are still critical differences at the individual level (Pollard et al, 1994; Webb & Vulliamy, 1996). Even two different teachers at one school may have quite different reactions to demands for change. Thus, teachers were chosen as the unit to be explored, while other units – schools, constituencies, regions, countries – were explanatory.

Felicitous chance and personal contacts – as they very often do – played roles in the selection of teachers to participate in the study; however, conscious research design, informed by understanding gained in the exploratory phase of the fieldwork, refined the process. The aim in selection was to represent as far as possible the range of experience in each of the countries and the process was purposive, not random. To illustrate: the South African group comprised three black, one Indian and two white teachers; teachers from three schools experiencing special training inputs related to the reforms, and three which were not; two suburban, two township, one urban and one rural school; teachers from three schools whose intake had changed little since apartheid, two which had a slightly different student composition, and one which was profoundly different; five women and one man; a newly-qualified teacher, one who had been teaching for 25 years, and a range in between. The Russian group reflected a parallel range in terms of age, experience, gender and type of school. It was felt that by studying six teachers in each country, a balance could be struck – considering the ever-present constraints of time and funding – between in-depth understanding of individual cases, and comparative potential which might help to enhance understanding of individual cases and also to reveal any wider patterns which might exist. The interview schedules were informed by the themes which emerged from the exploratory phase of the research, but the interviews remained as open as possible so that unforeseen issues could be developed.

Thus, by making controlled choices in terms of contexts, units of study and individual cases, it was hoped that the selection stage of the study was sufficiently rigorous to make the next stages feasible.

Verification

Once the researcher has controlled for the problems of selection, how can the data gathered be verified? Statistical means of verification are obviously unsuitable for case studies which are based on qualitative methodology. Here, internal validity may be strengthened through respondent verification of researcher impressions and findings. In this study, the final stage of interviews with each subject involved a feedback session in which each was given the opportunity to respond to the impressions which I had formed over the research period. In addition to talking them through a range of points which we had covered about their backgrounds, attitudes and teaching practice, I attempted to provide an idea of how I viewed their priorities relative to those of other teachers – whether they prioritised the personal, social or professional dimensions of their jobs – and how I felt they fit into the typology developed by the PACE project in England on teachers' responses to educational reform. This study by Pollard et al (1994) characterised teachers' responses to the 1988 Education Reform Act in England and Wales as: *compliance, incorporation, mediation, resistance* or *retreatism*. When there was disagreement – which was very rare – we negotiated to arrive as closely as possible to consensus. Thus, the researcher was equipped to tell a story which was phenomenologically true – that is, from the subjects' point of view – while beginning to fit it into wider frameworks. Further feedback from the subjects will be sought in the analysis stages.

Depending on what the researcher is attempting to convey, adhering rigidly to the singular and sometimes partially formed and articulated perspectives of the subjects themselves may be problematic. Inconsistencies often appear between, for example, words and actions, or between opinions of different individuals involved with each study; in fact, these discrepancies and conflicting definitions are considered by some to be essential phenomena of case study (Simons, 1987). In this study, in addition to checking my impressions against the case study teachers, I solicited contextual information from heads and teachers at the same school; these data could help to triangulate – or otherwise – the impressions gained. Is the teacher's description of their educational priorities reflected in how they spend their time in the classroom? Is the teacher's version of the dissemination of policy information within the school similar to the version given by the headteacher? Is the teacher's impression of how students behave in groups consistent with what is observed by the researcher? There may also be personal agendas among those studied, who want themselves to appear in the best possible light. Indulgence of these agendas will produce a biased and unbalanced account: 'The case study worker may produce a study which is internally consistent and acceptable to all those involved, but which in fact relates only marginally to the "truth"' (Walker, 1986, p. 197).

Judgement by the researcher is informed in part by his or her own comparative perspective. The researcher may have an intuitive sense of the authenticity of an account, in the same way that good fiction 'rings true' to an appreciative reader. Important as this verisimilitude might be to the extraction of meaning from qualitative case study research, when one wants to go beyond this 'common-sense' level, verification becomes more demanding, and meaning more elusive: 'The successful unravelling and explication of mundane beliefs and actions demand the suspension of common sense, not its uncritical endorsement' (Atkinson & Delamont, 1986, p. 246). Here, coherence with a larger theoretical framework can help to substantiate the works; thus, verification within and between case studies in one research project is best supplemented with comparison to other examples of related research, and theories generated by them. Through cumulation, individual case studies both rely on this framework and contribute to it.

Cumulation

Left in isolation, there is the danger that a case study will remain an idiosyncratic 'one-off', neither seen in the light of related research, nor contributing to the wider discussion. In discussing the process of making case study research cumulative, Stenhouse (in Burgess & Rudduck, 1993) uses the analogy of improving one's chess game by studying a large number of matches: the emergence of skills and understanding of patterns is a gradual process requiring the input of a large number of records of possible sequences and outcomes, without ever being able to predict their dynamics perfectly. This analogy might similarly be applied to the experienced comparative education researcher, whose 'protean adaptability' allows the researcher to have 'several operating cultures' (Fry & Thurber, in Crossley & Vulliamy, 1997, p. 12), and whose repertoire of cases researched has created flexible analytical frameworks which simultaneously inform new experience and are modified in the light of it. Sensitisation to context is critical here as indiscriminate 'bullying' of data into pre-existing personal, cultural, or large-scale theoretical frameworks may convince the researcher that the research is meaningful, but it will not bear up to the critical scrutiny of other perspectives. Crossley & Vulliamy (1997) recommend the use of a combination of outsider and insider perspectives in the research process to help to 'facilitate studies that are more sensitive to local contextual factors, while retaining systematic rigour and an important degree of detachment from the culture and world view being studied' (Crossley & Vulliamy, 1997, p. 3). In this study, in Russia, for example, the assistance of translators and interpreters went beyond facilitating communication; they became cultural informants, helping to place the individual cases into their wider context. A cumulation of perspectives as well as cases is demanded, during all phases of the research.

The comparative nature of the study at hand means that it has cumulation built into it: resonance and dissonance among the cases will generate a new level of data beyond the singular. In addition, it needs to be embedded in, and, in turn, illuminate new sides to theory which exists about teachers and educational reform and innovation, as found in the literature. How the findings from this study relate, for example, to Fullan's (1993) theories about educational change, or Broadfoot & Osborn's (1993) analysis of the interplay of teaching cultures and professional identity, will add another layer to the research. It is hoped that the process of progressive focusing, along with the constant comparisons within and among cases, including verification from respondents and other actors, will generate grounded theory (Glaser & Strauss, 1967). However, comparisons at these levels are not enough to arrive at robust theory with potential for application (except to situations very similar to the cases). The theories generated need to be compared with those produced in other studies, in a cumulative way, before they have been sufficiently tested (and perhaps modified) to have potential for generalisation and application.

Generalisation

Once a case study, or comparative study of cases, has been placed in the context of wider findings, issues, and theory, potential then exists for generalisation. The word generalisation is often associated with statistical validity. There are other words, sometimes applied to case study research to convey a similar message with varying degrees of credibility, which are free of this association: illumination, comparability, fittingness, resonance, allusion, vicariousness. What is the nature of 'generalisation' in the context of comparative research which employs case study approaches? In describing the potential of the case study approach they have used, Crossley & Vulliamy outline the processes of cumulation and generalisation as they perceive them:

> *This evaluation was conducted in the light of a review of literature relating to curriculum development and implementation within a conceptual framework derived from research on barriers to curriculum change, and with special reference to the environmental, historical and socio-political contexts of the innovation. Conclusions were therefore drawn from a wide range of data and the study demonstrates how case studies ... can usefully contribute to the analysis of contemporary educational problems, how macro- and micro-level research can be profitably combined and how more general conclusions can be abstracted from such work. In the latter respect, however, it should be recognised that given the epistemological foundations of case study, although findings are used to challenge certain assumptions currently held by many curriculum change theorists, no attempt is made to extrapolate general laws or universally applicable recommendations in a positivistic sense. Rather, at its broadest level, this study attempts to offer new insights and critical perspectives on the process of school-centred innovation, to generate increased awareness and understanding of the factors that influence the functioning of such change strategies. (Crossley & Vulliamy, 1984, p. 201)*

In this study too, the intention, as outlined earlier, is to give meaning to the study beyond its immediate boundaries, without arguing for the universality which is, ironically, reductionist and confining in scope. The emphasis is on insight rather than overview.

Will this study cast light on the circumstances and perspectives of six Russian teachers at one point in time? Of all Russian teachers? Of South African teachers? On specific groups within these countries, such as black South African teachers in township schools? Will I be in a position to say something about teachers in contexts of political, social and educational democratic change? Or in all contexts of change and innovation? About the interplay of personal and contextual factors with broader issues in teachers' responses to change? Or even about all teachers? The further one gets from the specifics of the case unit, the more stretched the comparability of *findings* becomes. It is hoped, however, to some extent and to varying degrees, all of the foregoing are possible: provided selection, verification, and cumulation have been done with integrity, the potential to generalise to *theory* will exist. If one is in a situation where it is possible to identify strongly with specific dimensions of individual cases, then findings are relevant; theory, however, can be more inclusive in its scope. Patterns are already emerging about the constraints that teachers are experiencing in both national contexts – patterns which resonate with other studies about teacher professionalism and the dynamics of change.

According to Cohen & Manion (1991), a case study 'reduces the dependence of the reader upon unstated implicit assumptions ... and makes the research process itself accessible' (1991, p. 150), affording the opportunity for readers to make their own generalisations. How authentic readers judge the resulting account will therefore be critical, and the issue of presentation is important, and problematic. However, a PhD thesis cannot accommodate 12 complete case studies full of thick description. The current plan is to present three to four cases which illustrate types of responses, as they emerge from the analytical framework.

Application

If cases are idiosyncratic and if no effort is made to extract universals or patterns through aggregation, then there is little hope of successful application of the isolated findings, except in a limited number of very similar situations where the specific findings have direct bearing. How can individual case studies inform policy, or help, for example, teachers and trainers experiencing similar situations in the decisions they make? 'Descriptive accounts of individual instances may be accepted as true by practitioners but they are not likely to create appropriate and convincing bases for policy or decision making' (Walker, 1986, p. 203). However, if selection, verification, cumulation and generalisation are conducted with rigour, there is scope then for the application of the results. A particular case study's findings are context-bound and not universal, but in the light of other relevant research and theory deriving from it, the patterns and insights gained may help to illuminate similar processes in contexts which have some of the same conditions. It is one source upon which to call when judgements need to be made, and it may form one strand in the complex process of educational decision-making. Stenhouse (1979, p. 6, in Crossley & Vulliamy, 1984, p. 201) advocates the potential of understanding gleaned through case study to 'tutor our judgement': a phrase which captures the non-linear, but no less important, influence that case studies might have on this process.

Case study approaches generally have the advantage of aiming to explain what is actually happening rather than what ought to be happening: information which can help to bring realistic detail to the evidence guiding judgement. Education policy reform and its implementation tactics tend to harbour assumptions about teachers' capacities and willingness to embrace changes of enormous scope. These expectations may not reflect the realities of teachers' circumstances and priorities, as other writers have noted (see, for example, Calderhead, 1987; Fullan, 1993; Campbell & Neill, 1994; Hargreaves, 1994; Smyth, 1995; Alexander, 1997). The findings from this study could help to reveal these realities, highlighting why and how teacher translation of policy affects the process, and illuminating avenues for more effective (and hopefully sympathetic) strategies. Again, the relevance of the specific findings will be greatest for contexts very similar to those in the study, but the broader, cumulative and generalised issues may have wider application, perhaps in other contexts experiencing educational reform catalysed by transition to democracy. The results of this study as they emerge are being communicated to in-service education and training providers in both countries, who may be able to use the information as one background source in the planning and design of training programmes.

Conclusion

The challenge in gleaning meaning from case studies is to appreciate the unique and intrinsic value of each specific case, while at the same time using them comparatively to give them wider significance. The value of such meaning is secured through careful application in turn of each of the principles outlined above. In this study of primary school teachers in Russia and South Africa, both context-specific detail and wider theoretical resonance are being sought. One would not employ case study approaches unless interested in the rich detail of individual experience, but one would not do 12 diverse case studies across two countries without believing that patterns might be found with the potential to illuminate wider issues.

The expression 'gleaning meaning' in the title of this chapter is used advisedly. The word 'glean' originally meant to go behind the reaper in the field, collecting and gathering together the grains that were flung about on the ground. The process of gleaning meaning in case studies is similar: starting with a wide-open field and through selection, verification, cumulation, generalisation and application, ending up with something useful.

References

Alexander, R.J. (1995) *Versions of Primary Education*. London: Routledge.

Alexander, R.J. (1997) *Policy and Practice in Primary Education: local initiatives, national agenda*. London: Routledge.

Atkinson, P. & Delamont, S. (1986) Bread and Dreams or Bread and Circuses? A Critique of 'Case Study' Research in Education, in M. Hammersley (Ed.) *Controversies in Classroom Research*, pp. 238-255. Milton Keynes: Open University Press.

Broadfoot, P. & Osborn, M. (1993) *Perceptions of Teaching: primary school teachers in England and France*. London: Cassell.

Burgess, R. & Rudduck, J. (1993) *A Perspective on Educational Case Study: a collection of papers by Lawrence Stenhouse*. Coventry: University of Warwick, CEDAR papers.

Calderhead, J. (Ed.) (1987) *Exploring Teachers' Thinking*. London: Cassell.

Campbell, R.J. & Neill, S. (1994) *Curriculum Reform at Key Stage 1: teacher commitment and policy failure*. Harlow: Longman.

Cohen, L. & Manion, L. (1991) *Research Methods in Education*, 3rd edn. London: Routledge.

Crossley, M. & Vulliamy, G. (1984) Case Study Research Methods and Comparative Education, *Comparative Education*, 20, pp. 193-208.

Crossley, M. & Vulliamy, G. (1997) *Qualitative Educational Research in Developing Countries*. London: Garland.

Education Policy Unit, University of the Witswatersrand (1993-98) *Quarterly Reviews on Education and Training in South Africa*.

Fullan, M. (1993) *Change Forces: probing the depths of educational reform*. London: Falmer Press.

Fuller, B., Snyder, C., Chapman, D. & Hua, H. (1996) Explaining Variation in Teaching Practices? Effects of State Policy, Teacher Background and Curricula in Southern Africa, *Teaching and Teacher Education*, 10, pp. 141-156.

Gillborn, D. (1994) The Micro-politics of Macro Reform, *British Journal of Sociology of Education*, 15, pp. 147-164.

Glaser, B. & Strauss, A. (1967) *The Discovery of Grounded Theory: strategies for qualitative research*. London: Weidenfeld & Nicolson.

Hargreaves, A. (1994) *Changing Teachers, Changing Times*. London: Cassell.

Nias, J. (1989) *Primary Teachers Talking: a study of teaching as work*. London: Routledge.

Nkabinde, Z.P. (1997) *An Analysis of Educational Challenges in the New South Africa*. Oxford: University Press of America.

Organisation for Economic Cooperation and Development (OECD) (1998) *Reviews of National Policies for Education: Russian Federation*. Paris: OECD Centre for Cooperation with Non-Members.

Pollard, A., Broadfoot, P., Croll, P., Osborn, M. & Abbot, D. (1994) *Changing English Primary Schools? The Impact of Education Reform at Key Stage One.* London: Cassell.

Simons, H. (1987) *Getting to Know Schools in a Democracy: the politics and process of evaluation.* London: Falmer Press.

Smyth, J. (Ed.) (1995) *Critical Discourses on Teacher Development.* London: Cassell.

Stake, R.E. (1995) *The Art of Case Study Research.* London: Sage.

Villegas-Reimders, E. & Reimders, F. (1996) The Missing Voice in Educational Reforms around the World, *Prospects*, XXVI, pp. 469-492.

Vulliamy, G., Lewin, K. & Stephens, D. (1990) *Doing Educational Research in Developing Countries: qualitative strategies.* London: Falmer Press.

Walker, R. (1986) The Conduct of Educational Case Studies: ethics, theory and procedures, in M. Hammersley (Ed.) *Controversies in Classroom Research*, pp. 187-219. Milton Keynes: Open University Press.

Webb, R. & Vulliamy, G. (1996) *Roles and Responsibilities in the Primary School: changing demands, changing practices.* Buckingham: Open University Press.

World Bank (1995) *Education in the Transition.* Washington, DC: World Bank.

Yin, R.K. (1993) *Applications of Case Study Research.* London: Sage.

Doing Comparative Historical Education Research: problems and issues from and about Hong Kong

ANTHONY SWEETING

Introduction

'Doing Comparative Education Research: issues and problems' is a deceptively worthy theme for the inaugural conference of the British Association for International and Comparative Education. On one reading, it is an attractively simple catch-all, capable of containing the most catholic range of presentations. On another, it encourages a special focus on *praxis*, perhaps, even, on the techniques of comparative education research, rather than upon theorising about it – or indulging in the modern, league-table inspired fetish for listing and categorising it. A more cabalistic reading might also consider the possibilities of ellipses: for example, doing (justice to) comparative education research or, more alarmingly, doing it (down or in).

The theme might also suggest a deliberate emphasis of the *comparative* rather than the *international* aspects of the new society's remit. In this context, international, presumably, refers to perspectives on educational practice and policy that are shared by and among nations. Most obviously, international aspects would include the educational activities of UNESCO, UNICEF, the Organisation for Economic Cooperation and Development (OECD), the World Bank, and other aid agencies that deal with the governments of various nations. They would also include cross-national trends, such as globalisation and its effects on education (e.g. McGinn, 1996). But what, precisely, are the comparative aspects? According to Cowen, 'Comparative education begins when some complex, coherent and theoretically stateable understanding of the relationship between at least two societies and their educational systems has been formed'. Current practitioners may wish to question why the understanding needs to be complex, coherent, or even theoretically stateable, and, especially, what is meant by two 'societies'. The latter question seems particularly apposite when Cowen goes on to assert that further exploration and testing is required in two other 'countries' 'if what we are talking [about] is (international) comparative education' (Cowen, 1996, p. 153). For some time, now, for example, many 'societies', whether nation-states or not, have accommodated numerous different communities and these themselves have pioneered different and comparable educational practices. Furthermore, over time, societies – and both the purpose and structure of their educational 'systems' – change. Comparison, here, within societies, would also appear to hold out promises of understanding, perhaps complex, perhaps coherent, perhaps even theoretically stateable.

There can be little doubt that comparison entails pluralities, rather than singularities. With regard to education, however, one might query whether the pluralities are essentially confined to contemporaneous nation-states, whatever their size (Bray & Packer, 1993) or constitutional condition (Carnoy, 1974; Altbach & Kelly, 1984; Birzea, 1994) or the interest being shown in the educational responsibilities of the state (Green, 1990, 1994, 1996; Turner, 1996; Whitty et al, 1998). The key question must be what is the *point* of the comparison. Only when this is satisfactorily answered can one proceed to its often hidden companion: what is the appropriate *unit* of comparison? And, whatever the answers to these questions might be, they must surely, at least at the conceptual level, allow for the possibility that the pluralities that make up the subject of comparison can be viewed in temporal as well as in locational terms. The recognition of this possibility encourages making comparisons beyond those focusing on recorded events and/or identifiable trends at specific levels of one or more educational systems (states, local authorities, schools, classrooms, etc.), i.e. what might be termed *product* comparisons. It facilitates the comparison of ideas, influences, climates of opinion, i.e. *process* comparisons.

To me, at least, it appears that efforts to stretch comparisons across places, with little or no attention paid to time, are likely to create a thin, flat, quite possibly superficial outcome. Efforts to enable comparisons to encompass time, as well as place, however, are likely to enhance the profundity of the study. It is possible, of course, that this impression is largely the product of my own inclinations as a practising historian of education. And equity demands a recognition that projects focusing almost exclusively on time, paying little or no attention to developments in any other than one place, could become detail-obsessive, parochial, and inert.

On the positive side, however, historical perspectives are likely to enhance sensitivity to context and, in particular, to a developing culture. Both international and comparative studies of education (plus Cowan's [1996] 'international comparative studies') may fail to convince and impress, especially if they do not recognise contextual factors sufficiently clearly. Moreover, their findings will be flawed if the investigators neglect sustained consideration of cultural aspects while they peddle their panaceas, their simplistic tables, and/or their tacit invitations to join cargo cults.

Clearly, some attention to both time and place will make in-depth understandings more feasible, as, for example, the recent and methodologically sophisticated study of teacher education at universities in the France, the USA and England (Judge et al, 1994) revealed. Support for this approach, especially in connection with efforts to compare structures, is offered by the conclusions of some sociological studies (Mueller & Karle, 1990, p. 26; Halsey, 1990, p. 28), as well as by theory-centred arguments about the application of postmodernism to comparative education (e.g. Green, 1994, p. 73). The purpose of this chapter is to contribute to a discussion about the issues and problems involved in doing comparative education research, by focusing mainly upon primary and secondary sources concerning education in one 'society', Hong Kong. It does not discount opportunities for comparisons with other societies, but it certainly emphasises the historical perspective. For this reason, it uses a title, which, though clumsy, may have the virtue of an appealing acronym.

Focus on CHER in Hong Kong

Over the past few years, Hong Kong itself has become subject to quite a sharp focus in the literature of comparative education (e.g. Luk, 1992; Sweeting, 1995; Bray & Lee, 1997). Many of these studies have concentrated upon the links between education and economic development and/or education and political transition. They are essentially comparative policy studies at the system level. In this chapter, the focus is avowedly methodological. A selection of problems and issues from and about Hong Kong serves as case studies (or, at least, raw material) for *meta*-level comparisons.

Problems

A problem confronting historians of education in Hong Kong, especially those seeking comparisons with other societies, is that of *periodisation*. Although merely a convention of historians, periodisation serves to provide boundaries and a perception of thematic coherence to the study of past developments. Such a service is helpful to those who seek to understand past developments in education, in the same way as it is to those exploring more general social, economic and political developments. In the case of developments in education in Hong Kong, precedents are few, because little has yet been written in this field. At least partly for the same reason, the precedents tend to echo each other, frequently adopting a top–down viewpoint. Thus, the earliest published historian of education in Hong Kong, the nineteenth-century E.J. Eitel, organised his comments around the terms of office of Governors or Acting Governors. His successors, most notably T.C. Cheng (1949), Fong (1975), Wong (1982) and Ng (1984), while not being quite so blatantly hierarchy-obsessed, sought to identify key dates and overarching themes at the systems level, usually confining their treatments to relatively short chronological spans. In 1990, I lengthened the span and modified the key dates, but retained an interest in systems-level themes. The major purpose of all these publications was to provide introductory overviews of their chosen historical span. This approach to periodisation is, therefore, unexceptionable.

An alternative scheme of periodisation appears as Table I. It essays the largest of overviews, while deliberately accommodating contributions to each *Zeitgeist* by agents other than central governments or those they commission and allowing for chronological overlap. Influenced, perhaps, by dependency theorists and/or critical analysts, this scheme may accord excessive priority to colonialism. It does, however, possess the advantages of a draft, based upon factors endogenous and exogenous to Hong Kong, and designed to provoke comparisons with other, colonial and non-colonial, societies.

Another set of methodological problems involves *agency* and *terminology*. There is an understandable tendency of writers on comparative education to concentrate upon product documents such as White Papers, commission reports, and digests of statistics rather than the type of process documents that illuminate past decision-making (and fascinate historians). This leads, at times, to a failure to distinguish between the officially designated agents of policy-making and the actual ones.

In Hong Kong, credit for policy change or clarification is usually accorded to the Executive Council, because, constitutionally, this is the highest authority and, therefore, constitutionally, it is responsible for government. In fact, however, the clarification or change is usually the outcome of negotiation, argument, and, possibly, compromise between various agents and agencies at a lower level and, even here, its provenance may not be explicit in the product document. Similar difficulties arise over assumptions about sequence and generality. This is particularly true in the case of the formulation and implementation of policy. Formulation does not, necessarily, precede implementation, as, for example, language policy in Hong Kong has frequently attested. Furthermore, the actual application of a policy may not be as generalised as the product document implies.

Dates	Period title	Further comments
c. 5000 BC – c. 1075 AD	*Prehistoric*	Problems between Yue & 'Han' Chinese; no direct evidence of schooling
c. 1075 – c. 1843	*Prelapsarian*	Written emphasis on success in Imperial Civil Service Examinations; text-based, exclusively male formal schooling, but also informal education; variations over time.
c. 1843-1913, 1941-45	*Classic Colonial*	Evils and advantages; different British and Japanese styles; slow expansion and rapid contraction; irrelevance for majority of population (?); pragmatism re language and gender issues.
c. 1914-1941, 1945-1954	*Applied Colonial*	Strengthening of Chinese nationalism; quickening of expansion; changing economy; increased importance of China and of refugees while Britain declined as a world and imperial power; non-officials more prominent in policy-making; uncertainties over language policy; minimal curriculum diversification; civic education countering legitimacy-threats.
c. 1955 – Present/ Future	*Applied Decolonial*	Sequential expansion; greater curriculum diversification, including concern for technical, special, physical, cultural aspects; beginning of centralised decentralisation; beginning of de-Anglocentrification of the curriculum; pressure groups gaining publicity; language problems bypassed or approached with variable determination; bureaucratic incrementalism.
c. 1949 – Present/ Future	*Neo-colonial*	Increasing educational activities of American foundations, etc.; piratical raids from USA, United Kingdom, Canada, Australia, etc. to capture Hong Kong students; beginning of centralised decentralisation; formal de-Anglocentrification; struggles over length of courses at tertiary level; growing importance of 'International Schools'.
c. 1984 – Present/ Future	*Post-colonial*	Politicisation of policy-making; dismantling of Anglocentric structures; increased opportunities for postgraduate students from the PRC; curriculum changes; efforts to resolve language policy; civic education to promote Chinese identity; political correctness of anti-colonialism.

Table I. Tentative periodisation of education in Hong Kong.

For example, curriculum specifications in Chinese history rarely applied to the 'Patriotic' schools in the periods before the resumption of sovereignty by China and even such radical changes as the 'reorganisation of primary and secondary education' in the 1960s did not apply to all private schools. Much has depended upon the potency of the actual policy-making agency and its capacity for being attended to, as well as on the compatibility of the policy with existing practice, or with aspirations perceived at the grass-roots level to be feasible, or with its ease of fit within the prevailing structure.

Terminological identity may disguise local variants. In Hong Kong, this has sometimes been the case with regard to the types of schools and the nature of curriculum subjects. Numerous outsiders have confused 'Government schools', for example, with the type of mainstream educational provision operating in their own countries. At the time a recent Professor of Education in Hong Kong made this mistake in connection with secondary education, fewer than 10% of secondary schools fell into the category of Government schools, the majority of the remainder being 'Aided' and, often, until recently, Private. The widespread use of the name 'colleges' for secondary schools has occasionally hoodwinked observers about the levels of education approached therein, especially when the late nineteenth-century debate over raising the Government Central school to 'collegiate status' was an early step towards the establishment of a university in Hong Kong. The existence of 'social studies' as a subject studied in some Hong Kong schools persuaded a few commentators that Hong Kong had joined an alleged trend towards the Americanisation of the curriculum. Observation of actual classroom practice, however, suggests that the link was merely verbal (Sweeting, 1996). The terms used in official syllabuses for the school subject known as world history suggest that a major trend over the past two decades has been towards the study of more recent events. However, discussions with teachers and pupils, supplemented by classroom observation, show that, in fact, largely for reasons of (political) insecurity, most teachers now conclude their treatment of twentieth-century history at an earlier and safer date (Sweeting, 1997, pp. 179-181). Curricular activities publicly known (and known in official publications) as civic, political, moral, and/or sex education range from occasional exhortations at school assemblies to rigorously timetabled and frequently examined school subjects. Secondary schools' medium of instruction policy has been obfuscated for years by the officially frowned upon, but frequently implemented, use of mixed code in the classrooms. It has also been complicated by the officially approved practice of using different languages for different subjects and even switching languages at different form-levels of the same subject. Thus, even in the period since the formulation of a 'firm' language policy (i.e. post-September 1997) and its official implementation (post-September 1998), a clear understanding of

'Chinese Medium of Instruction' (CMI) schools and 'English Medium of Instruction' schools is not guaranteed by focus upon the linguistic facility of students and teachers.

The lesson to be gained from these (and many other) examples is simple. Numerous instances (especially in the fields of curriculum, assessment, teacher education and institutional organisation) exist in Hong Kong where the push of exogenous forces and/or the pull of endogenous factors led to the adoption of practices that had originated elsewhere. At least as many instances exist, however, where the process significant for producers, consumers, and distributors of education in Hong Kong was not adoption, but adaptation. Presumably, academics and others concerned to make comparisons may avoid some of the worst pitfalls of oversimplification by acknowledging this. Similar points apply to other societies around the world. Methodologically, it is important to recognise that an appreciation of historical context is likely to enhance awareness both of borrowing and of adaptation. It may also provide illustrations of how the meanings of words change, over time as well as over place, and, thus, encourage a cautious approach to such labels as 'Western', 'Asian', 'American', 'British', and even 'system'.

The availability and reliability of *sources* raise problems in connection with the development of education in Hong Kong, as they do in many other places and with regard to most other communities. In the case of Hong Kong, both primary and secondary sources relating to what have been described as the prehistoric and prelapsarian periods are extremely sparse. Primary sources are mainly confined to archaeological and anthropological findings that require leaps of the sympathetic imagination to convert into impressions of educational provision or quality. Secondary sources are mainly restricted to brief comments in a small number of publications (e.g. Eitel, 1890-91; Sung, 1937; Ng, 1982; Sweeting, 1990; Meacham, 1996). The scarcity (but certainly not absence) of sources about these periods heightens concern for their reliability and opens opportunities for the generation, dissemination and acceptance of certain forms of myths. For later periods, scarcity is less of a problem. From the 1840s onwards, government gazettes, administrative reports, reports of committees of enquiry, newspaper commentaries, examination papers and scripts, private papers, even statistics, offer the sustenance of primary sources to the historical investigator. Within decades, photographs, school magazines, and prospectuses add further flavour. And secondary sources (e.g. Anon., 1877a, 1877b; Bateson Wright, 1908; Dyer, 1939; T.C. Cheng, 1949; Luk, 1981, 1984; Hayes, 1984; Lee, 1991; Crawford, 1991), while not profuse, open up greater possibilities for debate. Even so, comparativists and modern students of education policy, as well as historians of education, need constantly to question the reliability of both primary and secondary sources. One discovers in official documents, for example, significant dates and names mistaken

231

(Education Department, 1948, p. 5), statistical errors by a factor of 10 (Hong Kong Government Secretariat, 1981, p. 11), and, in general, what has been described (Sweeting, 1997, pp. 181-182), as a 'vanishing sense of history' with regard to education policy-making at the highest levels. The possibility that non-official primary sources are partial, in the sense of being incomplete and/or biased, is now commonly recognised, as is the danger that secondary sources are compiled according to their own agenda, which may not accord a high priority to accuracy and impartiality. In the case of pamphlets such as the two produced anonymously in 1877 and in Cheng et al's (1973) *At What Cost? Instruction through the English Medium in Schools*, the authors' agendas soon become obvious and can, therefore, be allowed for. When, however, academics accept, acknowledge and recycle the conclusions of earlier works, without apparently questioning the evidence upon which they are based (e.g. Fu, 1979; Johnson, 1983; Yuen Yau, 1984), the problems engendered are not so transparent and the potential for misunderstanding increases.

Problems over sources have quite frequently expressed themselves through the creation, dissemination, and widespread acceptance of *myths*. For reasons that probably compound cultural, ethnic, linguistic, political, and methodological factors, publications about education in Hong Kong frequently harbour myths. Some are simple outcomes of unquestioned assumptions or other forms of carelessness. This would seem to be the case with the assumptions of the Sisters of St Paul de Chartres (1909, p. 9) about the existence of the Suez Canal in 1848. The predisposition of Stokes & Stokes (1987, p. 3) to discover proof that the first colonial officials were determined to 'Christianise' young Chinese residents via school rules certainly explains the misreading of those school rules. The declaration by Fung (1986, p. 300) that there were no schools in Hong Kong before the arrival of the British is more difficult to understand, however, other than as the outcome of total blindness to evidence, reinforced, perhaps, by a deculturated and colonised mentality. Another widely held belief, even in the nineteenth century, credited the local predilection for getting and spending with the establishment of a 'cultural desert'. Taking a latitudinarian view of culture, perhaps, a social historian might consider the opening of *HMS Pinafore* in Hong Kong's City Hall only months after its world premier in London convincing disproof of this canard.

More importantly, a whole set of myths has gained credence, largely through obeisance to predetermined themes, bolstered up by a selective use of evidence. Most conspicuous are those related to colonialism, which will form the basis for further discussion in the next section of this chapter. Others include claims made, over the past several decades, about the 'transparency' of the Government and the supposed increase of public involvement in education policy-making. These appear particularly ironic at times when decision-making has been restricted to insiders (e.g. the 1977-80 committee on pre-schools and primary schools and the 1988-89 plans to increase radically undergraduate places at universities) and when public unease about the firmer language policy has been substantially ignored. Assumptions about the ever-extendible nature of teacher professionalism (Clarke et al, 1994; Education Commission, 1997) are certainly comforting and are especially compatible with projects designed to enhance 'quality' in schools. They tend, however, to ignore signs of teacher perception of overload as well as teacher perception of being ignored in important areas of innovation (Morris et al, 1996). In turn, these are creating teachers' resistance to changes considered likely to increase their loads and increasing teacher dependence on the central government, training institutions and publishers for detailed specifications of teaching strategies, tactics and materials. Perhaps the most important predetermined theme, nowadays, however, is that of 'one country, two systems'. The evidence is insufficient and, therefore, the verdict is not yet in on whether this mantra deserves the status of policy foundation stone or myth.

Issues

As might be expected, issues from and about Hong Kong concerning the comparative and historical development of education are closely linked with characteristic problems. Thus, *colonialism*, in its various guises, achieves a high profile in much of the literature. At times, it appears as almost a gut-driven response to theory-driven rhetoric (e.g. Cheung, 1987; Chan, 1991). At others, it is approached with greater moderation and sophistication (Luk, 1992; Bray & Lee, 1993; Lee & Bray, 1995). Rarely, however, are the possibilities explored that colonialisation brought with it not only opportunities within education for cultural imperialism and the exploitation of hardworking students and teachers. It was also accompanied by opportunities for socio-economic elevation (especially among females) and for the ending of the sort of isolationist parochialism that had so effectively hampered development in the rest of China and much of the rest of Asia. On a personal level, there can be little doubt that numerous colonial officials, missionaries, and other males and females from the metropole used the educational arena to display arrogance and unthinking disdain for a people and a culture with which they were unfamiliar. At the same time, however, there were also officials, missionaries and others who dedicated themselves to the educational well-being of Chinese or Eurasian students and teachers. And not a few Chinese and Eurasians devoted themselves to exploiting the opportunities that colonisation brought, enriching their families, their descendants and, sometimes, their compatriots in the process (Sweeting, 1989). On a more general level, it is worth noting that, in

Hong Kong at least, much of the heat generated about colonialism in education has been fuelled by American and some (especially in the 1940s) by Japanese commentators. It is, therefore, conceivable that colonialism, far from being the conceptual skeleton key so prized by dependency theorists and critical analysts, is instead (or also) used mainly as a distracter from relatively recent American neo-colonialist endeavours and earlier more nakedly exploitative activities by Japanese within the field of education. On the other hand, there can be little doubt that, currently, anti-colonialism has become a mark of political correctness in Hong Kong. This has been underlined not only by numerous academic publications, but also by a High Court Judge's view that an educationalist's past experience of colonial discrimination while employed at a university provided extenuating circumstances for alleged financial irregularities.

At another step up in the level of generality, studies of the links between education and politics (e.g. Cheng, 1987; Morris, 1988; Morris & Sweeting, 1991; Luk, 1991, 1992; Lee, 1996; Sweeting, 1997, Morris & Chan, 1997; Tan, 1997) have tended to emphasise exogenous factors as causes and endogenous curricular or structural developments as effects. In almost all cases, the exogenous forces have been seen as exercising a 'push effect'. The 'pull effect' of educational opportunities abroad, especially combined with the pressures of local politics, has, as yet, received relatively little attention, although the 'knock-on effect' of temporary emigration as shown by the profusion of international schools has (Bray & Ieong, 1996). The most recent publications have understandably focused upon the impact on education of the resumption of sovereignty over Hong Kong by China (e.g. Postiglione & Leung, 1991; Postiglione & Lee, 1995; Bray & Lee, 1997), have accepted the label 'transition studies', and may contribute their mite to an understanding of 'transitology' (Cowen, 1996). They vary in the extent to which they make use of archival or ethnographic evidence and in their interpretations of the potency of such agents as the Education Commission, various other government appointed bodies, the Professional Teachers Union (PTU) and the churches. They also differ in the degree of their willingness to accept the Government's own rating of the rationality and far-sightedness of its policy-making, as well as in the confidence they exhibit over the likelihood of their analyses and interpretations being heeded by officials or peers.

Connections between education and economics have provided the focus of studies at both macro- and micro-levels. Contributions, in the years immediately after the Second World War, to the requirements of a changing economy by a rapidly increasing population able to complete at least primary-level schooling have attracted widespread interest. The essentially sequential nature of educational expansion in post-war years, coupled with the probability that the lack of higher educational opportunities in the medium of Chinese encouraged able young refugees to devote their skills to economic advancement, provided a special Hong Kong gloss on human capital theory (Sweeting, 1995, p. 55). Friedman-influenced commentators choose to emphasise the Government's laissez-faire or 'positive non-interventionist' policies as explanations for both economic and educational development. Less doctrinaire analysts point out active government intervention to provide housing for workers, to adopt and, most recently, very strenuously defend, the currency peg to the US dollar, and to attempt to protect its own legitimacy while demonstrating its potency over educational concerns (Cheng, 1987; Scott, 1989). At the micro-level, studies of the financing of education in Hong Kong (Chung & Wong, 1992; Bray, 1993), although relatively restricted in historical scope, have provided valuable new data and some interpretations along the lines of analyses produced by such comparativists as Lewin (1987, 1996) and Watson (1990).

Apart from their appearance in studies of the economics and financing of education, the contribution that statistics may make to the understanding of educational development is well attested by authors using mainly census and/or enrolment, attendance, participation and qualification level figures. Luk & Wu (1983) produced a small, but classic, publication along these lines that did much to clarify post-war educational progress and problems. Pong & Post (1991), Post (1993, 1994, 1996) and Post & Pong (1998) have utilised more sophisticated statistical analyses upon data from similar sources to infer conclusions about the 'massification' and stratification of the education system, and gender and sibling effects on students' attainment. More recently and more controversially, efforts have been made to quantify quality (e.g. Clarke et al, 1994; University Grants Committee, 1996; Education Commission, 1997). Research assessment exercises and teaching quality appraisal schemes at the tertiary level, a more sustained focus on effective schooling through 'whole school inspections' at secondary level, and the eventually forceful implementation of target-oriented curricula at the primary level raise the spectre of league tables. Little, as yet, has appeared in academic publications of comparative and/or historical intent to link this latest trend with the 'payment by results' grant code arrangements of the late nineteenth century, possibly because of the ahistorical (or, at least, extremely short historical) span of the tables.

Other issues that currently exercise the energies of academic commentators on education in Hong Kong include:

the language problem;
the role of information technology;
imbalances of educational opportunity according to gender and class;
inequitable and/or ineffective provision of education for children with special needs;

accountability (of educational institutions and of the education policy-makers); and

the apparent emasculation (but continued face-enhancement) of the various advisory boards.

With the possible exception of the last-named, however, the approach to these issues has tended to be ahistorical. In many cases, these issues are treated by academic commentators as predetermined themes. Consequently, data are sometimes tailored to fit the themes. In other cases, the issues (and, therefore, themes) are seen to emerge from the data themselves. To a historian of education, these emergent themes seem the more plausible of cases and the more accessible to genuine, rather than derivative, decontextualised and superficial comparison.

Possibly the most significant issue of all may well be that of comparability. For many years, the principal point of reference for Hong Kong, at least, in the minds of many officials and academics, was the United Kingdom. Consequently, commentators on Hong Kong's educational scene frequently made comparisons with British (mainly English) standards, innovations, and opinions – or with those which were considered to be influenced by the United Kingdom, such as other colonies or former colonies. As Hong Kong achieved greater autonomy over its educational policies and practices, its system came to be more readily perceived as possessing autochthonous elements (Luk, 1992). Inevitably, perhaps, other foci for comparison attracted attention. These included the smaller states (Bray & Packer, 1993), neighbouring societies within the East and South-east Asian region (Morris & Sweeting, 1995), and, in the past few years, other societies on the Asia–Pacific Rim, especially fellow-members of the 'Four Asian Tigers' (Sweeting & Morris, 1998). A focus on China and comparisons designed to show how Hong Kong may contribute to most effective modernisation has historical (Yan, 1980; Ng, 1984) as well as future connotations. Perhaps, however, the prospect of a flexible plurality of comparisons holds out the most valuable rewards for educators, policy-makers, and academic commentators in Hong Kong.

Conclusions

Links with Theory

Data from Hong Kong have frequently been used in apparent efforts to confirm dependency theory and world systems theory (e.g. Meyer, 1992). Such uses, however, frequently provoked disclaimers from local academics. Efforts to create analyses of Hong Kong educational endeavours compatible with critical theory have variously focused on gender, race, and class (Postiglione, 1991; Friederichs, 1991; Choi, 1992; Mak, 1996). Very rarely, however, have they attempted to provide a broad chronological perspective. Therefore, they evoke comparisons with other societies at only the most general level. In some respects, Hong Kong may be regarded as the most postmodernistic city in the world, deriving much of its viability and erstwhile success from post-industrialism and an implicitly approved post-nationalism. And, has already been mentioned, a neglect of historical perspectives has characterised much of its educational planning as well as its architectural scene. Non-linear, almost random, outcomes of educational practices seem almost daily occurrences. Even so, with only one, rather self-indulgent, exception (Lee, 1993), no analysis of education in Hong Kong acceptable to sincere disciples of postmodernism has yet appeared.

Hong Kong is a society, which, at least in the past several decades, has become noted for its pragmatic adaptability. For a time, at least, in the fields of politics, economics and social welfare, the tenets of positive non-interventionism held sway. It is, therefore, appropriate, perhaps, that, in the cockpit of theory as applied to comparative and historical studies in education, what might be termed *positive eclecticism* rules the roost.

Lessons from Hong Kong

Hong Kong's experience of educational development and, especially, its typical policy-making processes, emphasise the importance of territoriality, a concept that combines both aggressive tendencies (to assert rights of jurisdiction and tenure) and defensive ones (to protect and conserve those rights). At the systems level, unease between the two main government agencies involved in public education, the Education Department and the Education and Manpower Branch of the Government Secretariat (now known as the Education and Manpower Bureau) has largely arisen over territoriality disputes. Much the same may be said in relation to higher education, where the initial response by local universities to efforts on behalf of distance learning in Hong Kong were less than warmly welcoming. At both system and institution level, it also applies in relation to the medium of instruction issue, where frequently linguists seek to preserve their authority, and to informational technology, where computer specialists wish to assert theirs. Moreover, territoriality can operate to prevent the publication of research findings in comparative research that has historical and/or political connotations. This is especially likely when an interested party in the developments being investigated commissions the original research and this party considers some or all of the comparisons made to be less than fulsomely appreciative of its efforts. In such a situation, the research consultancy relationship strongly suggests that the piper's tune should harmonise with the paymaster's expectations – or be silenced. Skills of harmonisation are accordingly rewarded.

Originality, on the other hand, does not appear to have been prized in practice, whatever lip-service has been paid to it in public. Instead, officially acknowledged 'success' – in public examinations, in teacher education and career development, in policy-making, and with regard to research proposals appears to have been awarded to rule-following, bandwagon-climbing, and, in general, a whole array of conformist (therefore unthreatening) ploys. The extent to which this feature of Hong Kong's educational practice has been influenced by colonialism, by insecurities about China, by the industrial line-worker and clerical subordinate mentality, and/or by a tall poppy mentality is open to debate. As yet, it has received little recognition.

Both the territoriality syndrome and the distrust of originality have helped create, at the various levels of Hong Kong's educational system, what might be termed the *ABC*, the Abelard-Bobbit Corollary of the Peter Principle. Perhaps because of Hong Kong's obsession with efficiency, it is rare for an education official or teacher or researcher to be promoted to the level of his/her incompetence. What happens much more frequently is that, when an individual begins to exhibit potency, s/he is (metaphorically, but in a spirit similar to that which applied to the medieval monk and the modern miscreant) emasculated – usually by being transferred away from the area of his/her genuine achievements.

Thus, lessons from Hong Kong take the form of warnings as well as stimuli. The present educational climate is, at least partly, composed of teachers decrying their lack of status and respect (*South China Morning Post*, 11 October 1998), students insecure about employment prospects, and parents unhappy about the language situation as well as about the economic downturn. It is, therefore, to historical studies in education that one might most fruitfully turn when one seeks to consider doing comparative education research that involves Hong Kong.

References

Altbach, P. & Kelly, G. (Eds) (1984) *Education and Colonial Experience*. New Brunswick: Transaction Books.

Anon. (1877) Dates and Events Connected with the History of Education in Hong Kong. Hong Kong: St Lewis Reformatory.

Anon. (1877) The Central School: can it justify its *raison d'être*. Hong Kong: Noronha.

Bateson Wright, G. (1908) Education, in Arnold Wright (Ed.) *Twentieth Century Impressions of Hong Kong, Shanghai, and the other Treaty Ports of China*, pp. 121-128. London: Lloyds Greater Britain Publishing House.

Birzea, C. (1994) *Educational Policies in the Countries in Transition*. Strasbourg: Council of Europe Press.

Bray, M. (1992) Colonialism, Scale and Politics: divergence and convergence of educational development in Hong Kong and Macau, *Comparative Education Review*, 36, pp. 322-242.

Bray, M. (Ed.) (1993) *The Economics and Financing of Education: Hong Kong and comparative perspectives.* Hong Kong: Faculty of Education, University of Hong Kong.

Bray, M. & Ieong, P. (1996) Education and Social Change: the growth and diversification of the international schools sector in Hong Kong, *International Education*, 25, pp. 49-73.

Bray, M. & Lee, W.O. (1997) Editorial Introduction, in M. Bray & W.O. Lee (Eds) *Education and Political Transition: implications of Hong Kong's change of sovereignty*, pp. 3-10. Hong Kong: Comparative Education Research Centre, University of Hong Kong.

Bray, M. & Packer, S. (1993) *Education in Small States: concepts, challenges and strategies.* Oxford: Pergamon Press.

Carnoy, M. (1974) *Education as Cultural Imperialism.* New York: McKay.

Chan, M. (1991) Series General Editor's Foreword, in G.A. Postiglione & J. Leung (Eds) *Education and Society in Hong Kong: toward one country and two systems*, pp. ix-xii. New York: M.E. Sharpe.

Cheng, K.M. (1987) The Concept of Legitimacy in Educational Policy Making: alternative explanation of two policy episodes in Hong Kong, unpublished PhD thesis, University of London.

Cheng, N.L. (1973) *At What Cost? Instruction through the English Medium in Hong Kong Secondary Schools.* Hong Kong: Shun Shing Printing.

Cheng, T.C. (1949) The Education of Overseas Chinese: a comparative study of Hong Kong, Singapore and the East Indies, MA thesis, University of London.

Cheung, H.K. (1987) History Curricula in Hong Kong Secondary Schools in the Forty Year Period since the Second World War, *Chinese University Education Journal*, 15, pp. 76-82 (in Chinese).

Choi, P.K. (1992) Education, in J.Y.S. Cheng & P.C.K. Kwong (Eds) *The Other Hong Kong Report. 1992*, pp. 260-281. Hong Kong: Chinese University Press.

Chung, Y.P. & Wong, Y.C. (Eds) (1992) *The Economics and Financing of Hong Kong Education.* Hong Kong: Chinese University Press.

Clarke, J.L., Scarino, A. & Brownell, J.A. (1994) *Improving the Quality of Learning: a framework for target-oriented curriculum renewal in Hong Kong.* Hong Kong: Hongkong Bank Language Development Fund/Institute of Language in Education.

Cowen, R. (1996) Last Past the Post: comparative education, modernity and perhaps post-modernity, *Comparative Education*, 33, pp. 151-170.

Crawford, L. (1991) Education in Hong Kong; government development of primary and secondary education, 1945-1978, unpublished PhD thesis, University of Western Australia.

Dyer, W.J. (1939) The English Language in Local Education, *Hongkong University Journal of Education*, 11, pp. 13-15.

Education Department (1948) *Annual Report.* Hong Kong: Government Printer.

Education Commission (1997) *Quality School Education*, Report No. 7. Hong Kong: Government Printer.

Eitel, E.J. (1890-91) Materials for a History of Education, *China Review*, XIX(5 & 6), pp. 308-324 & 335-368.

Fong, M.Y. (1975) *The First Hundred Years of Hong Kong Education*. Hong Kong: China Learning Institute (in Chinese).

Friederichs, J.O. (1991) Whose Responsibility? The Impact of Imminent Socio-political Change on Hong Kong Education, *International Review of Education*, 37, pp. 193-209.

Fu, G. (1979) Bilingual Education in Hong Kong: a historical perspective, *Working Papers in Language and Teaching*, 1, pp. 1-19.

Fung, Y.W. (1986) The Development of Education in Hong Kong, in J. Cheng (Ed.) *Hong Kong in Transition*, pp. 300-330. Hong Kong: Oxford University Press.

Green, A. (1990) *Education and State Formation*. London: Macmillan.

Green, A. (1994) Post-modernism and State Education, *Journal of Education Policy*, 9, pp. 67-83.

Green, A. (1996) *Education, Globalisation and the Nation State*. London: Macmillan.

Halsey, A.H. (1990) An International Comparison of Access to Higher Education, in D. Phillips (Ed.) *Lessons of Cross-national Comparison in Education*, pp. 11-36. Wallingford: Triangle Books.

Hayes, J. (1984) Education and Management in Rural South China in the Late Ching, *Proceedings of the Sixth International Symposium on Asian Studies*. Hong Kong: Asian Research Services.

Hong Kong Government Secretariat (1981) *The Hong Kong Education System*. Hong Kong: Government Secretariat.

Johnson, R.K. (1984) Language Policy in Education in Hong Kong, *Asian Journal of Public Administration*, 5, pp. 25-43.

Judge, H., Lemosse, M., Payne, L. & Sedlak, M. (1994) *The Universities and the Teachers: France, the United States, England*. Wallingford: Triangle Books.

Lee, W.M. (1993) Education, in P.K. Choi & L.S. Ho (Eds) *The Other Hong Kong Report, 1993*, pp. 193-219. Hong Kong: Chinese University Press.

Lee, W.O. (1991) *Social Change and Educational Problems in Japan, Singapore and Hong Kong*. London: Macmillan.

Lee, W.O. (1996) From Depoliticisation to Politicisation: the reform of civic education in Hong Kong in political transition, in Chinese Comparative Education Society, Taipei (Ed.) *Educational Reform: from tradition to modernity*, pp. 295-328. Taipei: Shi Ta Publishers.

Lee, W.O. & Bray, M. (1995) Education, Evolving Patterns and Challenges, in J.Y.S. Cheng & S.H. Lo (Eds) *From Colony to SAR: Hong Kong's challenges ahead*. Hong Kong: Chinese University Press.

Lewin, K. (1987) *Education in Austerity: options for planners*. Paris: International Institute for Educational Planning (IIEP), UNESCO.

Lewin, K. (1996) *Access to Education in Emerging Asia: trends, challenges and policy options.* Manila: Asian Development Bank.

Luk, B.H.K. (1981) Traditional Education in Urban Hong Kong, paper presented at the Conference on Hong Kong History and Society in Change.

Luk, B.H.K. (1984) Lu Tsu-Chun and Ch'en Jung-Kun: two exemplary figures in the 'Sishu' education of pre-war urban Hong Kong, in D. Faure, J. Hayes & A. Birch (Eds) *From Village to City: studies in the traditional roots of Hong Kong society.* Hong Kong: Centre of Asian Studies.

Luk, B.H.K. (1991) Chinese Culture in the Hong Kong Curriculum: heritage and colonialism, *Comparative Education Review,* 35, pp. 650-688.

Luk, B.H.K. (1992) Hong Kong, in W. Wielemans & Pauline Cho-Ping Chan (Eds) *The Interaction between Industrialization, Cultural Identity and Education,* pp. 111-150. Leuven: Leuven University Press.

Luk, B.H.K. & Wu, K.L. (1983) *Educational Development in Postwar Hong Kong: chronicles in graphs.* Hong Kong: Wah Fung Book Co.

Mak, G.C.L. (1996) Primary and Secondary Education, in M.K. Nyaw & S.M. Li (Eds) *The Other Hong Kong Report, 1996,* pp. 389-407. Hong Kong: Chinese University Press.

McGinn, N. (1996) Education, Democratization, and Globalization: a challenge for comparative education, *Comparative Education Review,* 40, pp. 341-357.

Meacham, W. (1996) Defining the Ancient Yueh, Proceedings of the Fifteenth Congress of the Indo-Pacific Prehistory Association, Canberra.

Meyer, J.W., Kamens, D.H. & Benavot, A. (1992) *School Knowledge for the Masses: world models and national primary curricular categories in the twentieth century.* London: Falmer Press.

Morris, P. (1988) The Effects on the School Curriculum of Hong Kong's Return to Chinese Sovereignty in 1997, *Journal of Curriculum Studies,* 20, pp. 509-520.

Morris, P. & Chan, K.K. (1997) The Hong Kong Curriculum and the Political Transition: politicization, contextualization and symbolic action, *Comparative Education,* 33, pp. 247-264.

Morris, P. & Sweeting, A.E. (1991) Education and Politics: the case of Hong Kong from an historical perspective, *Oxford Review of Education,* 17, pp. 249-267.

Morris, P. & Sweeting, A.E. (1995) *Education and Development in East Asia.* New York: Garland Press.

Morris, P., Adamson, R., An, M.L., Chan, K.K., Chan, W.Y., Ko, P.Y., Lai, A.W., Lo, M.L., Morris, E., Ng, F.P., Ng, Y.Y., Wong, W.M. & Wong, P.H. (1996) *Target Oriented Curriculum Evaluation Project: interim report.* Hong Kong: Instep, University of Hong Kong.

Mueller, W. & Karle, W. (1990) Social Selection in Educational Systems in Europe, paper presented at the Twelfth World Congress of Sociology, Madrid, 9-13 July.

Ng, L.N.H. (1982) Village Education in Transition: the case of Sheung Shui, *Journal of the Hong Kong Branch of the Royal Asiatic Society,* 22, pp. 252-270.

Ng, L.N.H. (1984) *Interactions of East and West: development of public education in early Hong Kong.* Hong Kong: Chinese University Press.

Pong, S.L. & Post, D. (1991) Trends in Gender and Family Background on School Attainment: the case of Hong Kong, *British Journal of Sociology,* 42, pp. 249-271.

Post, D. (1993) Educational Opportunity and the Role of the State in Hong Kong, *Comparative Education Review,* 37, pp. 240-262.

Post, D. (1994) Educational Stratification, School Expansion, and Public Policy in Hong Kong, *Sociology of Education,* 67, pp. 121-138.

Post, D. (1996) The Massification of Education in Hong Kong: consequences for equality of opportunity, *Sociological Perspectives,* 39, pp. 155-174.

Post, D. & Pong, S.L. (1998) The Waning Effect of Sibship Composition on School Attainment in Hong Kong, *Comparative Education Review,* 42, pp. 99-117.

Postiglione, G.A. (1991) The Decolonization of Hong Kong Education, in G.A. Postiglione & Julian Leung (Eds) *Education and Society in Hong Kong: toward one country and two systems.* New York: M.E. Sharpe.

Postiglione, G.A. & Lee, W.O. (Eds) (1995) *Social Change and Educational Development: mainland China, Taiwan and Hong Kong.* Hong Kong: Centre of Asian Studies, University of Hong Kong.

Postiglione, G.A. & Leung, J. (Eds) (1991) *Education and Society in Hong Kong: toward one country and two systems.* New York: M.E. Sharpe.

South China Morning Post (1998) People think less of us, say teachers, Internet Edition, Friday 11 September.

Scott, I. (1989) *Political Change and the Crisis of Legitimacy in Hong Kong.* Hong Kong: Oxford University Press.

Stokes, G. & Stokes, J. (1987) *Queen's College: its history 1862-1987.* Hong Kong: Queen's College Old Boys.

Sung, H.P. (1937) Legends and Stories of the New Territories: Kam Tin, *Hong Kong Naturalist.*

Sweeting, A.E. (1989) Snapshots from the Social History of Education in Hong Kong: an alternative to macro-mania, *Education Research and Perspectives,* 16, pp. 3-12.

Sweeting, A.E. (1990) *Education in Hong Kong, Pre-1841 to 1941: fact and opinion.* Hong Kong: Hong Kong University Press.

Sweeting, A.E. (1991) Hong Kong Education within Historical Processes, in G.A. Postiglione & Julian Leung (Eds) *Education and Society in Hong Kong: toward one country and two systems,* pp. 39-81. New York: M.E. Sharpe.

Sweeting, A.E. (1995) Educational Policy in a Time of Transition: the case of postwar Hong Kong, *Research Papers in Education,* 10, pp. 101-129.

Sweeting, A.E. (1996) The Globalisation of Learning: paradigm or paradox, *International Journal of Educational Development,* 16(4), pp. 201-216.

Sweeting, A.E. (1997) Education Policy and the 1997 Factor: the art of the possible interacting with the dismal science, in M. Bray & W.O. Lee (Eds) *Education and Political Transition: implications of Hong Kong's change of sovereignty,* pp. 25-39. Hong Kong: Comparative Education Research Centre.

Sweeting, A.E. & Morris, P. (1993) Educational Reform in Post-war Hong Kong: planning and crisis intervention, *International Journal of Educational Development*, 13, pp. 201-216.

Sweeting, A.E. & Morris, P. (1998) The Little Asian Tigers: identities, differences, and globalization, in Keith Sullivan (Ed.) *Education and Change in the Pacific Rim: meeting the challenges*, pp. 203-224. Oxford: Symposium Books

Tan, J.K. (1997) Church, State and Education: Catholic education in Hong Kong during the political transition, *Comparative Education*, 33, pp. 211-232.

Turner, J.D. (1996) *The State and the School: an international perspective.* London: Falmer Press.

University Grants Committee (1996) *Higher Education in Hong Kong.* Hong Kong: Government Printer.

Watson, K. (1990) Alternative Funding of Educational Systems: some lessons from Third World experiments, in David Phillips (Ed.) *Lessons of Cross-national Comparison in Education*, pp. 113-146. Oxford: Symposium Books.

Whitty, G., Power, S. & Halpin, D. (1998) *Devolution and Choice in Education: the school, the state and the market.* Buckingham: Open University Press.

Wong, C.L. (1982) *An Account of the Development of Chinese Education in Hong Kong.* Hong Kong: Po Wen Co. (in Chinese).

Yan, W.Y. (1980) Hong Kong and the Modernisation of China (1862-1911): the contribution of the Central School graduates, unpublished BA dissertation, University of Hong Kong.

Yuen Yau (1984) *A Historical Study of the Educational System of Hong Kong.* Hong Kong: Progressive Education Publishers (in Chinese).

Post-colonialism and Comparative Education Research

LEON TIKLY

Introduction

Recent years have seen the development of 'post-colonial studies' as a subdiscipline of literary and cultural studies. The emergence of this subdiscipline reflects a renewed interest in the historical legacy of European colonialism within the arts and social sciences. According to the authors of the *Post-colonial Studies Reader* (Ashcroft et al, 1995), post-colonial theory 'involves discussion of the following kinds of experience: migration, slavery, suppression, resistance, representation, difference, race, gender, and the responses to the influential master discourses of imperial Europe' (p. 2). The authors point out that discussion of these issues should include themes and perspectives of older colonial and anti-colonial texts. What is distinctive about recent post-colonial theory, however, is that it attempts to reinterpret the colonial experience in the light of developments in postmodernist and post-strucuturalist thought.

The aim of this chapter is to consider the relevance of these recent theoretical developments for comparative and international education (CIE) research. The chapter was motivated by the following concerns. First, although much valuable research has been undertaken about the colonial legacy in education, there has been little effort in recent years to develop the *theoretical* dimensions of this work. To the extent that existing texts on CIE *have* addressed the theoretical aspects of colonialism, this has often been done in relation to some variant of dependency theory, which has increasingly been subject to criticism. More recent developments, such as the use of globalisation theory in CIE, have often neglected to theorise adequately the colonial legacy.

Secondly, and related to the first point, although some writers on education have begun to incorporate a post-colonial perspective into their work, this literature has remained marginal in relation to the CIE canon, and the implications of post-colonialism for CIE (and indeed for education more generally) have not been discussed in any systematic way.

Thirdly, much of the recent literature on education in formerly colonised countries has been weighted towards economic concerns. This reflects the post-Jomtien emphases on access and quality in relation to basic education in the context of deepening austerity and structural adjustment programmes. It also reflects the hegemony of what Samoff (1992) has described as the 'intellectual-financial' complex in education research (i.e. the dominance of the research priorities, discourses and agendas of the major donors and financial institutions in education). One implication of this emphasis has been the relative neglect of 'non-economic' concerns, including those concerning race, culture, language and identity. This is despite the central role that these issues continue to play in shaping education policy, particularly in the context of the resurgence of ethnic nationalisms and conflict in Africa, eastern Europe and elsewhere.

The chapter begins with a summary of the key aspects of recent developments in post-colonial theory. The purpose here is not to provide an exhaustive account of the field, but rather to outline a theoretical approach that is useful for critical discussion of educational issues in subsequent sections. Although the work of several authors has been influential, the writing of Stuart Hall (1996a, 1996b) and of Ania Loomba (1998) has been found particularly helpful.

The Meaning of Post-colonialism

At the most general level, the term 'post-colonial' is used to describe a global 'condition' or shift in the cultural, political and economic arrangements that arise from the experiences of European colonialism both in former colonised and colonising countries. Importantly, it is used not just to describe specific developments or events related to colonialism and its aftermath, but also to signify an *epistemological* shift in the way that these events are described and interpreted. There is much debate, however, concerning the meaning of the term. These debates have centred on the extent to which colonial relations and dependency between historically colonising and colonised countries have indeed been superseded; the extent to which those at the 'bottom' in terms of class, caste and gender have witnessed any improvement in their situation in the 'post-colonial' period; and whether or not 'post-colonialism' proves too homogenising a term given the diverse experiences and histories of formerly colonised countries (McLintock, 1992; Loomba, 1998).

Rather than using the term 'post-colonialism' as a yardstick by which to compare the nature and extent of colonialism and decolonisation in different countries, however, the approach adopted here is to use the term to signify a general '*process* of disengagement with the whole colonial syndrome which takes many forms' (Hulme, in Hall, 1996a, p. 246) and as 'the contestation of colonial domination and of the legacies of colonialism' (Loomba, 1998, p. 12). If the term is understood at this level of abstraction, it is possible to keep in mind the global experience of European colonialism as a general referent whilst leaving room for the careful study of the effects of colonialism in specific contexts.

Understanding post-colonialism as a process also helps to draw attention towards an important element of post-colonial theory, namely, the move away from the modernist preoccupation with the nation state. For writers such as Hall (1996a) and Loomba (1998), post-colonialism should be seen as an aspect of the emergence over several centuries of the system of global capitalism. For the purposes of our discussion, this view of post-colonialism has three important implications. First, it serves to underline the point that colonialism is not 'over' in the sense of an epochal shift, but that its modalities and effects are being transformed as a consequence of globalisation. Secondly, it allows for a consideration of the experiences of colonialism both in former colonised and colonising countries, i.e. of the 'ways in which colonialism was never simply external to the societies of the imperial metropolis [but] was always inscribed deeply within them' (Hall, 1996a, p. 246). Thirdly, it draws attention to the central role that European colonisation of countries outside of Europe has played in defining the post-colonial condition. This is not to underplay the historical significance or contemporary relevance of other forms of colonialism (Russian colonialism in eastern Europe or Japanese colonialism in Asia, for example). It is simply to recognise that the process of European expansionism since the sixteenth century has been particularly instrumental in the development of contemporary global markets.

Implicit in Hulme's characterisation of post-colonialism as a process is a more subtle change of emphasis, not only in the content of what post-colonialism is seeking to describe but also in the way that colonialism is *understood* and narrativised. In keeping with postmodern and, in particular, post-structuralist emphases, post-colonial theory provides a critique of the 'meta-narratives' of the European Enlightenment. Thus, according to Hall:

> *This [post-colonial] re-narrativisation displaces the 'story' of capitalist modernity from its European centering to its dispersed global peripheries; from peaceful evolution to imposed violence; from the transition from feudalism to capitalism (which played such a talismanic role in, for example, Western Marxism) to the formation of the world market. (Hall, 1996a, p. 250)*

247

This 're-narrativisation' then involves a reconceptualisation of colonialism not as a subplot of some 'grander' (European) narrative, but as a violent event central to the developing new relationships of globalisation and global capitalism. Crucially, it also signals an 'epistemic shift' (i.e. a renegotiation of the ground-base of knowledge on which European, modernist accounts of colonialism were premised). This involves going beyond the 'binary oppositions' by means of which colonialism has been studied in the past, such as those between 'coloniser' and 'colonised', 'First World' and 'Third World' and 'Black' and 'White'. The consequence of this shift has been the development of a more contingent and complex view of colonial culture, politics and identities.

On the one hand, this has been achieved by focusing on the 'unstable', 'hybrid' and 'fractured' nature of colonial and post-colonial identities. Spivak's (1988) work, for example, draws attention to the implication of a variety of factors – colonialism, patriarchy and caste – in the formation of different subject positions amongst the colonised. Similarly, Hall's (1992) work provides a critique of the essentialised 'black subject' and seeks to recognise the 'extraordinary diversity of subject positions, social experiences and cultural identities which compose the category "black"' (p. 254).

On the other hand, post-colonial theory also seeks to deepen understanding of the coloniser/colonised relationship by drawing attention to processes of transcultural 'mixing' and exchange and to the complexities of diasporic identification. In *The Black Atlantic*, for example, Gilroy (1993) considers how cultural forms, identities and modalities of resistance to colonialism have developed as an aspect of the emergence of the African diaspora. Other phenomena, such as the formation of exiled and refugee communities, have contributed to this process as well. In this respect, post-colonialism is concerned with what Hall describes as the 'transverse' linkages between and across nation state frontiers in addition to the more traditional 'vertical' relationships between coloniser and colonised.

Although there are clear overlaps between post-colonialism and postmodernism in terms of the epistemological critique of Enlightenment thought, there are also important divergences. Chief amongst these is the view expressed by some post-colonial writers concerning the Eurocentric nature of postmodernism. Extending Said's earlier critique of Foucault (Said, 1978), Adam & Tiffin, the authors of the influential post-colonial text, *Past the Last Post* (1991), have argued that postmodernism represents a new form of Western global hegemony. In other words, postmodernism 'inevitably proscribes certain cultures as being "backward" and marginal' whilst presenting itself as 'a neo-universalism to which these other cultures may aspire' (Adam & Tiffin, 1991, p. 10). Eurocentrism is also demonstrated by the late recognition on the part of some postmodernists that their critique of modernist thought had long been pre-empted by anti-colonialist (and feminist) authors (Appiah, 1992; Young, 1992; Williams & Chrisman, 1994; Loomba, 1998).

Turning now to criticisms of post-colonial theory, some authors have argued that post-colonial theory neglects an analysis of the possibilities for economic and political change. For Shohat (1992), the problem lies in the tendency of post-colonial theory to 'dissolve polititical resistance' because it 'posits no clear domination and calls for no clear resistance' (p. 59). Rather than signifying a move away from political struggle, however, writers such as Hall (1992, 1996a) and Loomba (1998) have argued that post-colonial theory leads towards a more contingent and strategic view of what political struggle entails. In explicating his position, Hall gives the Gulf War as an example of a typical 'post-colonial event':

> *What the Gulf war provided was not the clarifying political experience of 'lines ... drawn in the sand' but the difficulties that arose in opposing the western war in the desert when manifestly the situation in the Gulf involved both the atrocities which the Alliance committed in defence of Western oil interests under UN cover against the people of Iraq (in whose historic 'under-development' the West is deeply implicated); and the atrocities committed against his own people and against the best interests of the region, not to speak of those of the Kurds and the Marsh Arabs, by Saddam Hussein. (1996a, p. 244)*

For some post-colonial writers, the work of Antonio Gramsci on political struggle and on hegemony has provided a means for reinserting a concern with political agency into their work. The attraction of Gramsci's ideas lies in his 'open' form of Marxism, which allows for a theorisation of the ways in which different factors, including 'race', class and gender become implicated in the operation of both hegemony and counter-hegemony (see Barrett, 1991; Hall, 1996b, for example). There are, however, dangers in assuming that one 'epoch' of political struggle according to the old binaries (exemplified by the struggles for national liberation in Africa and elsewhere) has simply been replaced by new, more subtle forms of hegemony and counter-hegemony. If, as argued earlier, one views post-colonialism as a process, then it is crucial to understand how old binaries (for example, between 'First World/Third World', 'Black/White') continue to be reinscribed upon, and to articulate with, new modalities for understanding and engaging with the political level. It also underlines the necessity of taking seriously the work of the earlier theorists of national liberation (Parry, 1995).

For Dirlik (1994), the problem with post-colonial theory is the way that he believes it grossly underplays 'capitalism's structuring of the modern world' in a way that makes post-colonialism complicitous in 'the consecration of hegemony'. Indeed, it is often the case that the emergence of global capitalism is bracketed to one side in much post-colonial literature, and this can in part at least be related to the emergence of post-colonial studies as a subdiscipline of literary and cultural studies. Some post-colonial writers, however, have attempted to engage with Dirlik's critique and to take seriously the importance of the economic domain. Loomba (1998), for example, has argued that it is debatable whether the neglect of economic considerations in the work of other post-colonial critics makes them 'agents of global capitalism'. Rather, she draws attention to the way that 'narratives of women, colonised peoples, non-Europeans *revise* our understanding of colonialism, capitalism and modernity: these global narratives do not disappear but can now be read differently' (p. 249).

Implicit in this view of post-colonialism is the denial of the post-structuralist assumption that there is 'nothing outside of the text' and the acknowledgement of the existence of the 'non-discursive' material realm. Indeed, a key concept within post-colonial theory is that of 'articulation', which is used to designate the contingent and context-bound relationship between these two spheres (Grossberg, 1996; Slack, 1996). Also related to this is a rejection of some approaches towards both post-colonialism and postmodernism that privilege the 'local' at the expense of the 'global' (exemplified in the rather glib slogan, 'think globally, act locally'). As Hall (1996a) has argued, it is not a question of the global fragmenting into the local but rather of the global and the local being repositioned in relation to each other. In this understanding, political struggle should not be confined to the sphere of immediate experience but should seek to engage with politics at the global and national levels as well.

Post-colonialism and Comparative Education

The aim of this section is to critically discuss the relevance of post-colonial theory for CIE research. Rather than claiming that post-colonial theory provides an all-embracing framework for comparison, it will be argued that it provides a new 'critical idiom' (Loomba, 1998) through which the master discourses of CIE can be renarrativised. This renarrativisation involves both a reconsideration of the content of the CIE canon and the theoretical perspectives used. The section will start with a look at how more recent post-colonial theory relates to existing accounts of colonialism in education. Attention will then turn to a consideration of some of the possibilities opened up by recent post-colonial theory for CIE research. The chapter will conclude by arguing that post-colonial theory provides a necessary basis for developing a less Eurocentric and more comprehensive account of the effects of globalisation on education.

Colonialism and the CIE Canon

There have, of course, been many attempts to write and theorise about the colonial legacy in education within CIE. Critical writing on this theme reached its apotheosis during the 1970s and early 1980s in the context of the ongoing movement towards independence in Africa, Asia and elsewhere. Much of this literature was based either explicitly or implicitly on some version of dependency theory (see, for example, Carnoy, 1974; Altbach & Kelly, 1978; Watson, 1982, 1984). The work provided a valuable critique of human capital and modernisation theory, which had treated the colonial relationship as unproblematic. It also greatly enriched understanding of the relationship between colonialism, neo-colonialism and education through providing detailed case study material. As this work developed, it began to integrate theories of the state within an overall dependency framework (Fagerlind & Saha, 1989; Carnoy & Samoff, 1990).

Important criticisms have, however, subsequently been directed at dependency theory and its use in CIE and these have been discussed at length elsewhere (see Fagerlind & Saha, 1989; Hettne, 1990; Martinussen, 1997). From the perspective of recent post-colonial work, the limitations of dependency theory may be summarised as follows. First, it is fundamentally an *economic* theory of underdevelopment and as such does not lend itself easily to an analysis of issues of race, culture, language and identity. Secondly, it tends to portray the relationship between colonised and colonisers as one of omnipotence to the extent that little attention is given to the contradictory effects of colonial education or to the development of forms of educational alternatives and cultural resistance. Thirdly, as a modernist discourse, it works exclusively within the binary oppositions of colonised and colonisers, centre and periphery, and uses as its fundamental unit of analysis the nation state. This has had further implications.

To begin with, with some notable exceptions (see, for example, Watson, 1984), work within the dependency mould has focused on the effects of colonialism on education in colonised countries and has neglected its effects on the education systems of colonising nations. In other words, little attention was paid to the ways in which the colonial legacy 'worked its way back' to the imperial centre through migration and the implications of these processes for education. Further, although dependency theory does have as a central referent a notion of global relationships, the potential opened up for understanding the transnational aspects of educational policy has often gone unexplored within the CIE literature. This is because of the tendency to examine the effects of colonial education at the national level through the use of country case studies.

There were other attempts during the 1980s to account for the colonial legacy in education that largely fell outside of the dependency paradigm. Some researchers, for example, working within a socio-anthropological paradigm, made use of a concept of 'cultural identity' in order to explain the role of education in reproducing cultural patterns in the post-colonial period. (Brock & Tulasiewicz, 1985). In contrast, Mangan (1988) used a historical approach to try to understand the contradictory effects of British imperial education on the political socialisation of both the colonised and colonisers. Like many of the dependency studies, these texts, as examples of their genre, have provided valuable case study material although they maintain the emphasis on the nation state as the primary unit of analysis and pay less heed to the transcultural and global aspects of the colonial legacy. The texts are also problematic because they employ an essentialised view of culture as a 'whole way of life' into which children are 'assimilated' through forms of socialisation. As will be discussed later, more recent approaches would contest the notion of any 'fixed' identity and would seek to examine how terms such as race, culture and language are themselves discursively constructed and are constitutive of social realities and of identities.

Post-colonialism and CIE Research

This section will explore some of the implications for research that arise from a consideration of the post-colonial condition. The intention here is to raise questions and to open debate rather than to imply closure. The choice of areas and the issues raised are therefore intended as being illustrative only.

1. *Racism and education policy.* The publication of *Orientalism* by Edward Said (1978) marked the beginning of a concern within post-colonial theory with the analysis of colonialism and of racism as discursive practice. Subsequently, writers in education have used a similar strategy to analyse changing discourses concerning race, culture and education in countries as diverse as England (Rattansi, 1992), South Africa (Tikly, 1995a, 1997), the USA (McCarthy & Crichlow, 1993) and Australia (Knight et al, 1990). Such an approach has, however, made only a limited impact as a basis for comparison between countries (Mangan, 1993a; Carrim, 1995; Gundara, 1990) despite its potential contribution to the CIE canon.

First, such an approach lends itself to an understanding of 'racism' as a category of comparative research. Traditionally, where issues of race, culture and difference have been concerned, comparativists have felt more comfortable working within a pluralist, multicultural framework based on the socio-anthropological reading of colonialism described earlier. Within this framework, inequality is rarely seen as the result of racist discourses and practices despite the centrality of these within the colonial project as a whole. The understanding of racism implied by more recent post-colonial literatures differs, however, from previous structuralist accounts. These differences have been described in some detail elsewhere (see Wetherell & Potter, 1992; Donald & Rattansi, for example). In brief, recent post-colonial theory starts from an understanding of racism as discursive practice. That is to say, it tries to understand how individual and group identities are constructed in discourse, often in quite contradictory and changing ways, and how these constructions have operated hegemonically to legitimate inequalities and the colonial project.

Mangan's edited volume (Mangan, 1993a) on the imperial curriculum provides an example of the application of such an approach comparatively and historically. The contributors to this volume discuss how racial stereotypes of the non-European Other were constructed in imperial textbooks. The book demonstrates the 'infinite diversity' of these constructions depending on the time and context of their location and also their contradictory nature (how, for example, the colonised could come in for selective praise as well as scorn in the eyes of Europeans). Of relevance here is that the book is concerned not only with the impact of racist constructions on the colonised, but also on how they profoundly influenced the learning experiences of children in the imperial centre. In his own contribution and drawing on the work of Jan Mohammed, Mangan (1993b) describes how these constructions then fed into a 'Manichean allegory' (i.e. a field of diverse yet interchangeable oppositions between white and black, good and evil, superiority and inferiority). This allegory 'functions as the currency for the entire colonial discursive project' (p. 9) and serves to legitimate the economic exploitation of the colonised.

Many commentators have remarked, however, upon a shift in the nature of European racism during the second half of the twentieth century away from an overt 'biological' essentialism (based on supposed biological differences) towards a more subtle, cultural essentialism (in which cultural differences are used as a basis for legitimating inequality) (see, for example, Wetherell & Potter, 1992; Tikly, 1995a; Carrim, 1995). In part, this shift can be attributed to the extent to which biological accounts of difference have been challenged and discredited (although such accounts still play a prominent role in 'common-sense' racism). The shift can also be related, however, to the changing hegemonic function of racist accounts of difference in these post-colonial times. In many wealthier industrialised countries for instance, cultural essentialism has been used in dominant discourse primarily to maintain the 'insider–outsider' binary or 'the alien wedge within' (Hall, 1983; Rasool, 1998).

One area of relevance, then, is to deepen understanding of how different groups are constructed in the curricula, textbooks and policy discourses of contemporary societies and how these legitimise continuing inequalities. This type of analysis need not, of course, confine itself to a consideration of how groups of European origin continue to preserve their hegemony in Europe, Australia, North America and elsewhere. If we are to take account of the complexities of the post-colonial condition, then attention also needs to be given to how non-European elites defined by ethnicity, cast, class and gender also legitimise their dominance over other groups through their control over education systems.

Besides playing a hegemonic role in relation to dominant groups within the education systems of specific countries, cultural essentialism is also apparent at the global level in many of the policy discourses of multilateral agencies and in the international media. For example, Samoff has criticised the school effectiveness paradigm adopted by multilateral funders of African education on the grounds that it is premised on a new kind of modernisation theory. According to Samoff, the discourse of school effectiveness 'insists now as it did 30 years ago that the causes of Africa's problems are to be found within Africa: its people, resources, capital, skills, psychological orientation, child-rearing practices and more' (p. 70). This observation leads him to assert that 'just as poverty is to be explained by the characteristics and inabilities of the poor, so the explanation of problems of African education are to be found within and around African schools' (1992, p. 30). The implication for comparative research arising out of this kind of analysis is to question the extent to which culturally essentialist constructions play a role in legitimising global economic arrangements such as the imposition of structural adjustment policies, the tolerance of Third World debt or uneven terms of trade between North and South.

2. *Culture, language and curriculum.* In the preceding section, the focus was on the possibilities for deconstruction opened up by the application of recent post-colonial theory to CIE. As mentioned in that section, however, post-colonial theory has also historically been concerned with the development of alternatives to colonialism. This has implications for curriculum development. The struggle against colonial domination has often involved a rejection of imposed educational patterns and the establishment of alternative forms of provision. The history of South African education provides rich examples of this. What is interesting about these examples for comparative researchers is that forms of resistance have often assumed a diasporic dimension.

For example, Kallaway (1984) draw attention to the role that Garveyism and the American school movement played in the growth of African nationalism during the first half of the nineteenth century. Indeed, the rich exchange of ideas between the African diaspora in the USA and elsewhere was an important ingredient in the ferment of black consciousness during the 1970s and 1980s. Further, in 1979, the African

National Congress (ANC) established a school for South African refugees in Morogoro, Tanzania.[1] An important goal of the school was to develop an alternative to apartheid education. The school was staffed not only by South African exiles (who had subsequently lived, and developed skills, in many other parts of the world), but by representatives of the international community. The cultural and educational forms that emerged at the school were both hybrid and global. Students and teachers from the school have subsequently directly participated in the development of education policy in the new South Africa. These examples do not fit easily with traditional ways of understanding the role of different cultures in the curriculum. Rather than present curriculum politics as a binary opposition between two opposing and essentialised cultures, as many pluralist models do, they are suggestive of more complex processes of transcultural mixing in which the boundaries between cultural forms and identities are fluid rather than fixed.

These observations are of direct relevance for curriculum reconstruction elsewhere. First, in many parts of the previously colonised world, governments are still grappling with the highly contested and complex process of developing curricula that are more suited to the cultures and histories of the local population. Some of the complexities of this process have recently been captured by Bray (1993, 1994). Exponents of curricula reform have often had to contend with the vested interests of local elites, a lack of resources and the hegemony of Western culture and forms of knowledge in an increasingly global world. This hegemony and the subsequent interpretation and hybridisation of cultural forms (processes in which education systems have been so deeply implicated) have made it increasingly difficult to define what a more culturally 'relevant' curriculum might entail.

Secondly, the example of the ANC School in Tanzania also draws attention to another dimension of the post-colonial condition that has implications for an essentialised view of culture in the curriculum, namely, the issue of refugee communities. As of January 1998, the United Nations High Commission on Refugees estimated that there were 22.3 million refugees, returnees or people displaced within their own countries (UNHCR, 1998). What the experience of the ANC school demonstrated was not only the potential benefits for curriculum development that the transcultural context of refugee education affords but also the difficulties involved in defining a common identity given the diversity represented not only by refugee community but by the host community as well.

Thirdly, during the 1980s and 1990s 'cultural restorationists' in Britain, the USA, Australia and elsewhere in the more industrialised world sought to challenge the inroads that multiculturalists had made into the curriculum and set about reinserting a 'traditional' (read

Eurocentric) view of knowledge (Knight et al, 1990; McCarthy & Crichlow, 1993; Chitty & Mac an Ghaill, 1995). Apart from heralding the triumph of a conservative, nationalistic and essentialist world-view, these events also brought into sharp relief the crisis of the multicultural movement in education. Faced with the charge of cultural relativism from the right, this crisis was in important respects an epistemological one and is worth outlining briefly.

One historical response to white, European cultural hegemony in the colonial curriculum has been one of *substituting* one conception of reality and 'truth' with another, black or non-European, view. For Steve Biko and his black consciousness colleagues in South Africa, for example, the solution to the Eurocentric curriculum lay simply in replacing existing 'White truth' based on Eurocentric norms and values with a 'Black truth' based on African humanism (Tikly, 1995b). Similar strategies of replacing parts of the existing curriculum with new material based on positive representations of black experiences and cultures were adopted by proponents of 'black studies' in the USA, Britain and elsewhere during the 1970s and 1980s.

However understandable such efforts may have been in the context of their time, they were also problematic in that they were based on the same false premise as the approaches they criticise, i.e. that it is possible to present a 'single, uncontestable, objective and accurate' representation of reality (Rattansi, 1992). (Ironically, such approaches were also unpopular in the USA with black parents because they were perceived to deny children access to the formal, academic curriculum [Stone, 1984].)

A second strategy, favoured by multiculturalists in particular, has been to *add* new multicultural material to the formal curriculum. (A similar approach has also sometimes been adopted by governments of newly independent countries.) This approach has been criticised, however, on the grounds that it actually serves to legitimise Eurocentric curricula by leaving unchallenged the underlying norms and values embedded within them (McCarthy, 1993). Rather, drawing on the related work of several scholars, (McCarthy, 1993; Said, 1994; Taylor, 1993; Giroux, 1997), it is possible to outlined an alternative approach, more congruent with recent post-colonial theory, that engages with the existing canons in the curriculum. This new approach has three interrelated aspects.

The first aspect involves acknowledging the place of black and non-European scholars within the canon and, therefore, within the school curriculum. In the words of Matthew Arnold, it is to acknowledge that the 'best that has been thought and said' within the disciplines necessarily includes work of black and non-European scholars and intellectuals. The second aspect involves understanding and engaging with the complex and interrelated process of canonisation and curriculum design. This necessarily involves focusing on the production, distribution and legitimisation (canonisation) of 'official knowledge' (Apple, 1993) across a number of institutional sites (the academy, the school, research institutes, government departments, publishing houses, examination boards etc.) It is only on the basis of an understanding of the micro-processes by which certain forms of knowledge become 'official' and others not that a politics of transformation involving the democratisation of knowledge production can be advanced. The third aspect involves demonstrating the relationality and interconnectedness of Western and other forms of knowledge, i.e. to recognise, following Bernal (1987), how the very notion of 'Westernness' is itself a construct and how Western forms of knowledge and 'civilisation' are directly indebted to older, non-European forms.

To date, research of this nature has focused largely on the USA and the United Kingdom, although Altbach's (1984) study on the 'Distribution of Knowledge in the Third World' goes some way towards identifying these processes in wider context. The key point from a post-colonial perspective, however, is that largely as a result of the colonial legacy, these processes are global in nature and need to be analysed as such.

Similar arguments to those advanced here have been made concerning language policy in education. Space does not permit a full discussion of this complex area and so only certain aspects will be highlighted. The importance of language in relation to post-colonial theory is that it is a fundamental site of struggle over meaning and, by implication, the nature of social reality and of identity. One of the most significant legacies of colonialism in education, then, has been the hegemony and subsequent globalisation of the languages of the colonisers and the underdevelopment of indigenous languages (Ashcroft et al, 1989; Tollefson, 1995).

There have been two broad responses to this hegemony within the post-colonial literature. The first response, exemplified by writers such as Ngugi wa Thiong'o (1995), has been to reject the colonial language as a medium of instruction and to promote indigenous languages in their place. As critics have subsequently pointed out, however, this approach relies on an essentialised view of traditional culture as something that can be 'restored' (Pennycook, 1995; Ashcroft et al, 1997). A second response has been to start from the recognition of linguistic and cultural identity as contested and contingent, and it is this view that is more consistent with the complexities of the post-colonial condition.

For example, Naz Rasool (1998) has described the issues surrounding linguistic human rights in the context of mass migration of peoples and the hybridisation of indigenous cultures as an aspect of globalisation. On the one hand, she describes the tremendous possibilities opened up for language choice for migrant and formally colonised groups of people in relation to ever-changing geographical demographies. On the other hand, she points to the difficulties of language planning in relation to these groups. She demonstrates how the issue of language choice for specific communities in former colonised and colonising countries is heavily contingent on a number of factors, including their social status within the country in question. Interestingly, from the point of view of this chapter, she describes how language maintenance policies and rights of migrant groups also need to be understood transnationally, i.e. as an aspect of the status of specific languages in the country of origin.

A further example of the application of post-colonial theory to language policy concerns recent responses to the globalisation of English as a colonial language. In the past, the predominant debate has been between conservatives (who have wanted to preserve Standard English within the 'traditional' curriculum) and pluralists (who have wanted to accord different versions of 'English' equal status within the education system). For more recent post-colonial scholars, however, the problem with the pluralist position is that it fails to acknowledge the relationship between different versions of the English language and discursive power. For them, the issue is more one of emphasising the *process* of reading the texts. This involves a greater sensitivity to the relationship between Standard English and global hegemonic discourses than pluralist models allow for and recognition of the relative power and position of learners in relation to these discourses. They also place emphasis on language as a site of struggle and on how English has been used 'against the grain', as a means of the empire 'writing back' to the centre (Ashcroft et al, 1989). The implication for comparative language policy research is to recognise how counter-hegemonic discourses can be 'formed in English' (Pennycook, 1995, p. 52).

Conclusion: post-colonialism and the globalisation of education

During the 1990s, globalisation theory has increasingly been used as a framework for comparative analysis. Indeed, so popular has it become that it now operates as a 'master narrative' within the CIE canon in a similar way that dependency theory did in previous decades. At a general level, as Green (1997) has observed, globalisation theory has three major elements to it. The economic element emphasises the increasing significance of global market forces and transnational corporations over national economies, the globalisation of labour markets and a new international division of labour. The political element considers the demise of the nation state as an aspect of the new power of international capital and of the development of supra-national trading blocks and organisations. The cultural element looks at 'the emergence of the borderless world where national cultures are transformed by global communications and cultural hybridisation' (Green, 1997, p. 130).

Different authors have, however, emphasised different aspects of globalisation, depending upon their particular 'take' on the theory and on the theme(s) that they have wished to illuminate. Accepting Green's account of globalisation, it would seem that globalisation theory provides a promising framework for the exploration of post-colonial issues. What is striking about this literature, however, is that very little attention is, in fact, given to the colonial legacy. This neglect has the following implications.

First, a large body of the literature on globalisation and education and, in particular, that literature informed by a postmodern reading of the world takes as its point of reference Western industrialised countries and (occasionally) their significant Others, namely, the newly industrialised countries of the Pacific Rim. Where the education systems of developing countries are mentioned, this is often as an aberration to the European 'norm' either in respect to their origins or to the extent to which they demonstrate 'postmodern' characteristics. Thus, in Green's (1997) and Cowan's (1996) work, for example, the education systems of formerly colonised countries are presented as variants on 'modern' education systems (which are defined as having their roots in the processes of state formation in Europe). Eurocentrism is also evident within this body of literature in relation to the choice of themes discussed, such as the implications of the information superhighway for learning or the crisis of the modernist (read European) curriculum and pedagogy.

Secondly, where globalisation theory has been applied to the developing world, economic concerns have often predominated (with some notable exceptions; see, for example, Crossley, 1996; Phillipson, 1998). The upshot is that many issues relating to race, culture, diaspora and identity are either ignored or marginalised. What is required, then, is a post-colonial rereading of globalisation theory in education. This would start from the perspective that the colonial legacy is central to the ongoing processes of globalisation in education rather than marginal to it. That is to say that it is impossible to understand globalisation in education without recognising the role that colonial and post-colonial education systems have played in the spread of Western cultural forms and languages and the implication of these systems in the processes of cultural mixing and hybridisation. (They have, of course, also played a key role in relation to the developing global economy and political systems, although these are aspects that have not been dealt with explicitly in this article.)

In conclusion, a note of caution. Attention has been given to the *theoretical* contribution that an appreciation of the post-colonial condition can make to the CIE canon. Clearly, however, there are also implications to be drawn for the *processes* of comparative research, although space has not permitted a full exploration of these issues. This is to acknowledge that there is a necessary dialectic between theory and research and that the development of a fuller understanding of the colonial legacy in education is intimately tied up with the politics of inclusion and exclusion within the knowledge production process itself.

Acknowledgements

I would like to acknowledge the help of a number of people who provided critical comments and advice on earlier drafts. In particular, I would like to thank Richard Sergeant, Jenny Douglas, Clare Tikly and Glen Rikowski.

Note

[1] The author worked as a science teacher at the school between 1987 and 1989.

References

Adam, I. & Tiffin, H. (Eds) (1991) *Past the Last Post.* Hemel Hempstead: Harvester Wheatsheaf.

Altbach, P. (1984) The Distribution of Knowledge in the Third World: a case study in neocolonialism, in P. Altbach & G. Kelly (Eds) *Education and the Colonial Experience*, 2nd revised edn, pp. 229-251. London: Transaction Books.

Altbach, P. & Kelly, G. (Eds) (1978) *Education and Colonialism.* London: Transaction Books.

Appiah, K.A. (1992) *In My Father's House: Africa in the philosophy of culture.* London: Methuen.

Apple, M. (1993) *Official Knowledge: democratic education in a conservative age.* London: Routledge.

Ashcroft, A., Griffiths, G. & Tiffin, H. (1989) *The Empire Writes Back: theory and practice in post-colonial literatures.* London: Routledge.

Ashcroft, B., Griffiths, G. & Tiffin, H. (Eds) (1995) *The Post-colonial Studies Reader.* London: Routledge.

Barrett, M. (1991) *The Politics of Truth: from Marx to Foucault.* Cambridge: Polity Press.

Bernal, M. (1987) *Black Athena: the Afroasiatic roots of classical civilisation,* vol. I. London: Free Association Books.

Bray, M. (1993) Education and the Vestiges of Colonialism: self-determination, neocolonialism and dependency in the South Pacific, *Comparative Education*, 29, pp. 333-348.

Bray, M. (1994) Decolonisation and Education: new paradigms for the remnants of empire, *Compare*, 24, pp. 37-51.

Brock, C. & Tulasiewicz, W. (Eds) (1985) *Cultural Identity and Educational Policy.* London: Croom Helm.

Carnoy, M. (1974) *Education as Cultural Imperialism.* New York: David McKay.

Carnoy, M. & Samoff, J. (1990) *Education and Social Transition in the Third World.* New Jersey: Princeton University Press.

Carrim, N. (1995) From Race to Ethnicity: shifts in the educational discourses of South Africa and Britain in the 1990s, *Compare,* 25, pp. 17-33.

Chitty, C. & Mac an Ghaill, M. (1995) *Reconstruction of a Discourse.* Birmingham: University of Birmingham, Educational Review Publications.

Cowan, R. (1996) Last Past the Post: comparative education, modernity and perhaps post-modernity, *Comparative Education,* 32, pp. 151-170.

Crossley, M. (1996) Issues and Trends in Qualitative Research: potential for developing countries, *International Journal of Education Development,* 16, pp. 439-448.

Dirlik, A. (1994) The Postcolonial Aura, *Critical Inquiry,* 20, pp. 328-356.

Donald, J. & Rattansi, A. (Eds) (1992) *'Race', Culture and Difference.* London: Sage.

Fagerlind, I. & Saha, L. (1989) *Education and National Development: a comparative perspective.* Oxford: Pergamon.

Gilroy, P. (1993) *The Black Atlantic: modernity and double consciousness.* London: Verso.

Giroux, H. (1997) *Pedagogy and the Politics of Hope: theory, culture and schooling; a critical reader.* Oxford: Westview Press.

Green, A. (1997) *Education, Globalization and the Nation State.* London: Macmillan.

Grossberg, L. (1996) On Postmodernism and Articulation: an interview with Stuart Hall, in D. Morley & K. Chen (Eds) *Stuart Hall: critical dialogues in cultural studies,* pp. 131-150. London: Routledge.

Gundara, J. (1990) Societal Diversities and the Issue of 'The Other', *Oxford Review of Education,* 16, pp. 97-109.

Hall, S. (1983) The Great Moving Right Show, in S. Hall & M. Jacques (Eds) *The Politics of Thatcherism,* pp. 19-39. London: Lawrence & Wishart.

Hall, S. (1992) New Ethnicities, in J. Donald & A. Rattansi (Eds) *'Race', Culture and Difference,* pp. 252-259. London: Sage.

Hall, S. (1996a) 'When Was the Post-Colonial?' Thinking at the Limit, in I. Chambers & L. Curti (Eds) *The Post-colonial Question: common skies, divided horizons,* pp. 242-260. London: Routledge.

Hall, S. (1996b) Gramsci's Relevance for the Study of Race and Ethnicity, in D. Morley & K. Chen (Eds) *Stuart Hall: critical dialogues in cultural studies,* pp. 411-440. London: Routledge.

Hettne, B. (1990) *Development Theory and the Three Worlds.* Harlow: Longman.

Kallaway, P. (Ed.) (1984) *Apartheid and Education: the education of black South Africans.* Johannesburg: Ravan Press.

Knight, J., Smith, R. & Sachs, J. (1990) Deconstructing Hegemony: multicultural policy and a populist response, in S. Ball (Ed.) *Foucault and Education: disciplines and knowledge*, pp. 133-152. London: Routledge.

Loomba, A. (1998) *Colonialism/Postcolonialism*. London: Routledge.

Mangan, J. (1988) *Benefits Bestowed? Education and British Imperialism*. Manchester: Manchester University Press.

Mangan, J. (Ed.) (1993a) *The Imperial Curriculum: racial images and education in the British colonial experience*. London: Routledge.

Mangan, J. (1993b) Images of Confident Control: stereotypes in imperial discourse, in J. Mangan (Ed.) *The Imperial Curriculum: racial images and education in the British colonial experience*, pp. 6-22. London: Routledge.

Martinussen, J. (1997) *Society, State and Market: a guide to competing theories of development*. London: Zed Books.

McCarthy, C. (1993) After the Canon, in C. McCarthy & W. Crichlow (Eds) *Race, Identity and Representation in Education*, pp. 289-305. London: Routledge.

McCarthy, C. & Crichlow, W. (Eds) (1993) *Race, Identity and Representation in Education*. London: Routledge.

McLintock, A. (1992) The Angel of Progress: the pitfalls of the term 'post-colonialism, *Social Text*, Spring, pp. 1-15.

Ngugi wa Thiong'o (1995) On the Abolition of the English Department, in B. Ashcroft, G. Griffiths & H. Tiffin (Eds) *The Post-colonial Studies Reader*, pp. 438-442. London: Routledge.

Parry, B. (1995) Problems in Current Theories of Colonial Discourse, in B. Ashcroft, G. Griffiths & H. Tiffin (Eds) *The Post-colonial Studies Reader*, pp. 36-44. London: Routledge.

Pennycook, A. (1995) English in the World/The World in English, in J. Tollefson (Ed.) *Power and Inequality in Language Education*, pp. 34-58. Cambridge: Cambridge University Press.

Phillipson, R. (1998) Globalizing English: are linguistic human rights an alternative to linguistic imperialism? *Language Sciences*, 20, pp. 101-112.

Rassool, N. (1998) Postmodernity, Cultural Pluralism and the Nation-State: problems of language rights, human rights, identity and power, *Language Sciences*, 20, pp. 89-99.

Rattansi, A. (1992) Changing the Subject? Racism, Culture and Education, in J. Donald & A. Rattansi (Eds) *'Race', Culture and Difference*, pp. 11-48. London: Sage.

Said, E. (1978) *Orientalism*. London: Routledge & Kegan Paul.

Said, E. (1994) *Culture and Imperialism*. New York: Vintage.

Samoff, J. (1992) The Intellectual/Financial Complex of Foreign Aid, *Review of African Political Economy*, 53, pp. 60-87.

Slack, D. (1996) The Theory and Method of Articulation in Cultural Studies, in D. Morley & K. Chen (Eds) *Stuart Hall: critical dialogues in cultural studies*, pp. 112-130. London: Routledge.

Shohat, E. (1992) Notes on the Postcolonial, *Social Text*, 31/32, pp. 103-132.

Spivak, G.C. (1988) Can the Subaltern Speak, in C. Nelson & L. Grossberg (Eds) *Marxism and the Interpretation of Culture*, pp. 271-313. Basingstoke: Macmillan.

Stone, M. (1984) The Education of the Black Child in Britain, in R. James & R. Jeffcoate (Eds) *The School in the Multicultural Society*, pp. 45-57. London: Harper & Row.

Taylor, N. (Ed.) (1993) *Inventing Knowledge: contests in curriculum construction.* Cape Town: Maskew Miller Longman.

Tikly, L. (1995a) Levelling the Playing Fields Whilst Moving the Goal Posts: changing discourses on race in South African education policy, in C. Criticos, R. Deacon & C. Hemson (Eds) *Education Reshaping the Boundaries, Proceedings of the Twentieth Kenton Conference Held in Scotburgh Natal in October 1993*, pp. 11-28. Durban: School of Education, University of Natal.

Tikly, L. (1995b) The Racial Interpretations of the Democratic Movement, in G. Kruss & H. Jacklin (Eds) *Realising Change: education policy research, Kenton, 1994*, pp. 67-80. Cape Town: Juta.

Tikly, L. (1997) Changing South African Schools? An Analysis and Critique of Post-election Government Policy, *Journal of Education Policy*, 12, pp. 177-188.

Tollefson, J. (Ed.) (1995) *Power and Inequality in Language Education.* Cambridge: University of Cambridge Press.

United Nations High Commission on Refugees (1998) http//: www.unhcr.ch

Watson, K. (Ed.) (1982) *Education in the Third World.* London: Croom Helm.

Watson, K. (Ed.) (1984) *Dependence and Interdependence in Education.* London: Croom Helm.

Wetherell, M. & Potter, J. (1992) *Mapping the Language of Racism.* Hemel Hempstead: Harvester Wheatsheaf.

Williams, P. & Chrisman, L. (Eds) (1994) *Colonial Discourse and Postcolonial Theory.* Hemel Hempstead: Harvester Wheatsheaf.

Young, R. (1992) Colonialism and Humanism, in J. Donald & A. Rattansi (Eds) *'Race', Culture and Difference*, pp. 243-251. London: Sage.

Confessions of a Long Distance Runner: reflections from an international and comparative education research project

SIMON McGRATH

Introduction

The nature of international and comparative education is its focus outwards. It is somewhat contrary, therefore, that this chapter concerned with the future of this disciplinary field will rather focus inwards on the context in Britain in which this practice exists. Also, the chapter is written by someone whose research activities are directed very firmly towards practical issues in Southern countries and not towards the methodological and philosophical debates about the nature of the field of study.

However, these realities are at the heart of why I have decided to write this paper. I will attempt to show that it is vital that methodological and philosophical debates about the future of international and comparative education should take account of a rigorous reading of the context in which international and comparative education is done in Britain. That reading is not yet adequately developed but it is apparent what some of the key elements would be.

As a profession, we are already becoming increasingly comfortable in discussing the impact of globalisation on the topics we study. It is also imperative that we make that reflexive and ask how globalisation impinges upon our own practices. The study of globalisation is also a study of marketisation. I will argue in this chapter that the way that universities and research are becoming increasingly subject to market forces is a crucial element that must be factored into our analysis of the future of international and comparative education. To date, we have been far more adept at talking about how this affects Southern universities and education systems than in how it impinges upon us. As aid is seen as a central element of the topography of education systems internationally, so it has become common for academics to analyse the policies and actions of donor agencies. However, too rarely have we been prepared to acknowledge that their policies and their monies are crucial determinants of the shape of international and comparative education and of our own professional biographies.

Before proceeding to the heart of the discussion, it is worth providing a little more context to the chapter. It is largely a general discussion of the future of international and comparative education within the framework I have already outlined. However, it is written from the perspective of someone who works on education in the South, and sub-Saharan Africa in particular. Moreover, the general discussion gives way in the second, shorter, section to a brief exploration of some of these issues in the specific context of one agency-funded research project. That exploration reflects the genesis of this paper in a personal attempt to fit together a concern to understand international and comparative education as a field of study with the imperatives of making a living as a junior researcher. Though the context is personal and particular, it does have a broader resonance.

The Crisis of International and Comparative Education

The very use in the title of this chapter of the term 'international and comparative education' points to part of the problem facing those of us discussing these issues. Whilst Watson (1998) shows the origins of comparative education and international education, it is evident that the reality is one of blurred distinctions. The name of the professional body, the British Association for International and Comparative Education, is in practice a convenience which allows us to get on with our work without having to spend too much time agonising over whether international and comparative education are distinct entities. Whilst the *International Journal of Educational Development* may have been established to give more space to 'internationalist' research, *Compare* is currently a major publisher of 'internationalist' articles.

In so far as forces such as globalisation undermine ossified distinctions between North and South, it can be argued that the geographical level of differentiation between international and comparative breaks down. In particular, the growing fascination with the interdependence of different nations, North and South, means that themes such as development policy become important areas of research in our field, but ones that fit uneasily in old categories. Equally, the trends evident in postmodernism and globalisation towards the reduction in importance of monolithic nations and nationalism question the future of a field of study based largely in notions of the national.

The clumsiness in current contexts of 'international and comparative education' is an element of a major challenge facing researchers in this field, in Britain and elsewhere. Watson (1998) argues that the field is growing globally, a claim apparently confirmed by the record numbers at the 1998 World Congress of Comparative Education Societies (WCCES) Cape Town Conference. However, he points to the danger of marginalisation in OECD countries because of:

downsizing;
financial constraints;
management being emphasised over theory;
lack of apparent practical focus. (Watson, 1998, pp. 8-9)

International and comparative education in Britain has also been fundamentally changed by historical shifts in its rationale. Much of the post-war growth in the field came from training British students for colonial and post-colonial service and developing country nationals for leadership posts in their national education systems. These niches are all but closed as international and comparative education looks towards the new millennium.

As this chapter will go on to argue in more detail, the current crisis of the British university is particularly evident at the margins, and that is where international and comparative education is already placed. The overall resource crisis of higher education is particularly concentrated on those less able to compete on the terms of the current market modality. Instead of a 'level playing field', competition within universities is more often characterised by asset stripping and by large departments seeking to secure their own future at the expense of weaker 'rivals'. Increased 'relevance' is a partial defence and so, as Watson notes, management studies become increasingly attractive at the expense of more theoretical work, and applied research can easily overwhelm basic work.

Whilst international and comparative education has many of its multiple origins in applied policy work (Watson, 1998), the current cult of efficiency works against the painstaking analysis of systems, cultures and histories and in favour of quick, simple and implementable solutions. Too often, the comparative is little more than a legitimation tool for domestically devised policies. Thus, the choice of countries to be studied on brief fact-finding visits, and the lessons to be learned, are frequently crudely based in the existing policy prejudices of those authorising the research. This has been seen in British readings of, for example, Japan, that tell us far more about policy aspirations in Britain than in the country being studied. East Asian fears that their education systems do not promote innovation and undermine national competitiveness are turned into a celebration of the merits of discipline and whole-class teaching through research that is unconcerned about what it apparently perceives as the irrelevancies of culture, history and society.

International agencies and many governments also have an inherent bias towards quantitative over qualitative research. This has led them into a fascination with cross-national data sets, such as those that have been produced post-Jomtien on education for all, or the international mathematics and science surveys. However, as Watson argues:

> problems arise from this kind of approach, partly because of
> the dubious methods of data collection by governments and
> aid agencies which form the bases for some of these analyses;
> partly because they ignore the complexity of different
> societies; partly because they are largely concerned with
> immediate problems and issues; and partly, perhaps largely,
> because they ignore the historical and cultural contexts.
> (Watson, 1998, p. 13)

Watson (1998), following Hobsbawm (1994) and Jameson (1988), sees a widespread popular historical amnesia as being at the heart of the problem faced by international and comparative education and academic activity more generally. This is an important argument, but it needs to be developed further. In reality, the current relationship with the past experienced in Britain, and elsewhere, is complex and varied across different groupings. As well as the kind of 'ever-present' that Watson warns against, individuals and groups operate in multiple pasts, both romantic and critical, official and popular. Part of the reason that the historical amnesia that Watson critiques is significant is that it frequently comes into contact with the histories of individuals and communities, which lead them to read different meanings into the 'objective truth' of the policy reform and to find resources for resistance and subversion.

Thus, it can be seen that the historical amnesia of much of policy and policy research is also a blindness to culture and a deafness to society in favour of the omnipotence of the individual and the economic. Whilst this allows the strengths of simplicity and certainty in the pronouncements produced, it is the failure to understand the systemic that fundamentally undermines the cherry-picking approach to comparativism, both theoretically and practically.

The future of the profession is also threatened by the effects of the resource crisis on its demography. The lack of young academics in British international and comparative education is accentuated by the paucity both of doctoral funding and of established posts on completing doctorates (Yngström & King, 1995). Moreover, the 'new resource' is likely to find itself funnelled into both doctoral and post-doctoral research that reflects the narrow geographical and sectoral interests of funding agencies. Reporting on a survey of research students in international and comparative education, Yngström & King conclude:

The research also suggested that some countries and regions were more likely to attract funding than others and more likely to attract research interest. The reasons for both are likely to be connected to British aid interests, both in terms of the previous knowledge and experiences of British teachers/educationalists looking to do research in the field, and the kind of expertise required by donor agencies and NGOs. (Yngström & King, 1995, pp. ii)

Poverty Eradication Policy

The most recent pressure on British international and comparative education comes from the changing fashion in development policy. Since the Copenhagen Social Development Summit of 1995, there has been a growing perception that a new phase of international development cooperation is emerging (King & Buchert, 1998; King & Caddell, 1998; McGrath, 1998).

Development discourse has gone through a series of stages since the inauguration of the United Nations–Bretton Woods era as the Second World War was coming to a close (Riddell, 1997). Central to reformulations of development discourse have been the relationship between poverty and growth.

Whilst there is a widespread realisation that 'it is almost impossible to distinguish between assistance that is designed to eradicate poverty and assistance that promotes growth' (Sweden, Ministry for Foreign Affairs, 1997, p. 43), much of the development cooperation thinking of the post-war era has tended towards polarisation on one side of the argument or the other. It can be argued that the period up to the end of the 1960s was one in which development did not need to be problematised. It was believed that economic growth could be planned for and would lead inevitably to the eradication of world poverty. With the collapse of the Keynesian 'Golden Age' (around 1968-73), there was a growing awareness of the inadequacies of this simplistic model. This led to a more direct focus on poverty eradication through the 'basic needs' approach. That economic growth inevitably led to poverty eradication came to be rejected by analysts as one of the most serious developmental fallacies.

However, by the late 1970s, intellectual fashions changed again. Economists and politicians of the Right developed a powerful critique of welfarism, both North and South. Instead, they called for the unchaining of the market mechanism. 'Trickle-down' or 'poverty eradication through growth maximisation' was reinstated as the mode for development, although the means of achieving it was radically different from that of the 1960s. In Africa, in particular, this approach called for the radical pruning of the state and the re-establishment of the 'fundamentals' of economies through structural adjustment programmes.

By the late 1990s, it had become clear that the power of this neo-liberal vision was waning. The World Bank began to play down its anti-statism and its critics developed a considerable arsenal of evidence against the alleged efficacy of structural adjustment. Across Sub-Saharan Africa, the world's poorest region, there are still insufficient data to conclude that either poverty or growth has been adequately addressed via adjustment. These realisations contribute to the stirrings of a new paradigm.

Poverty is once more the primary focus across the policy papers of several bilateral and multilateral agencies (e.g. Finland, 1996 and Denmark, 1998). For those of us working in international and comparative education in Britain, it is the recent British development White Paper, *Eliminating World Poverty: a challenge for the 21st century* (Department for International Development [DFID], 1997) that assumes the most significance.

The Education Director of the British Council argues that the White Paper threatens the future of British university activities in the field of international education through seriously narrowing the funding possibilities for international research (Walton, 1998). She maintains that whilst the Overseas Development Administration did have policies on what it would fund, in practice it took a relatively broad view of development-oriented research. DFID, she alleges, has become far more prescriptive and this is certainly reflected in the draft Economic and Social Research funding policy of DFID (DFID, 1998). This contains a series of proposed research themes, deliberately mimicking the Economic and Social Research Council:

  socially responsible business;
  poverty analysis, measurement and monitoring;
  global issues and poverty elimination;
  the rights based approach to development;
  participation, accountability and policy change;
  the impact of donor partnership arrangements.

As well as stressing poverty eradication quite strongly, these themes are overwhelmingly economistic and managerialist in their conceptions both of development and of useful social science. The draft policy does hold out the possibility of funding for other research but there is no comfort in the vision for those who might wish to maintain a holistic vision of a field such as international and comparative education. Of course, DFID has a core business to be concerned with. Nonetheless, for our profession, the decreasing opportunity of other income sources, in part as a result of other historic trends in development policy, means that the views of DFID about what constitutes appropriate research are particularly significant.

Peter Williams argues that there is a danger of non-basic education research being undermined by the new policy and that the poverty eradication policy could threaten the alliance-building work at the higher education level that is more akin to diplomacy than development (Williams, 1998, p. 65). He paints a grim picture of the future that is worth quoting at length:

> *Depending on the breadth of conceptualisation of the problem of eradicating poverty, it may be that only a very narrow range of actors in the developing countries and Britain will interface with each other under such a programme. It is not clear for example that university links, joint research and staff development programmes could be justified in exclusively poverty-elimination terms; and much of the high-level training and consultancy work being undertaken is connected only indirectly or hardly at all with poverty elimination. Opportunities for colleges and universities in Britain and developing countries to work together on important themes which lack an explicit poverty-orientation could be severely constricted. (Williams, 1998, p. 67)*

If the logic of the White Paper is followed rigorously, Williams argues:

> *A great many valuable programmes of educational, scientific and cultural cooperation with developing countries would have to be privately funded or would fall by the wayside, and many of the resource centres of expertise on developing countries in universities and other institutions would perish because they would be starved of budget support and, far more important these days, of training and consultancy contracts. The notion of a public interest in, and consequential public funding in support of, provision of opportunities for young people and public institutions to acquaint themselves in depth through study, travel and cooperative activity with the cultures and societies of developing countries, would receive no recognition. (Williams, 1998, p. 68)*

We are faced with a double challenge from poverty eradication policy. First, as analysts of policy and practice in the education systems of other countries, how do we respond to the new paradigm? How do we best critique it when it is growing rapidly in discursive power? Is it, in fact, something to be opposed or does it provide a way out of the failures of aid stretching back to the wave of new nations in the early 1960s? Second, as a group of professionals committed to the future of their collective endeavour, how do we understand and respond to this new paradigm's likely impact on international and comparative education in British universities? Crucially, can we make both morally and intellectually consistent our position in response to the two aspects of the challenge?

The Partnership Paradox

After its commitment to eradication of poverty, the next most striking emphasis of the 1997 British White Paper is on partnership. Again, here it is in line with broader agency trends (Carton, 1998; Cedergen, 1998; King, 1998a, 1998b; King & Caddell, 1998). As with poverty eradication, this seems to be a laudable shift in emphasis for agencies that have often been accused of cultural and economic imperialism. However, as with poverty eradication, there are a number of inconsistencies and contradictions lurking behind the attractive façade. Moreover, the implications for international and comparative education research, both North and South, are far from uniformly positive.

Partnership is more rhetoric than reality. Carton (1998) argues that it should be seen as lying between cooperation and co-management on a continuum of donor–recipient relations. He suggests that the reality is that the majority of practice has yet to reach even the level of cooperation. Moreover, he notes the close relationship in France and Sweden between development policy and immigration policy. This helps to highlight the probability that much of the new 'partnership' is aimed at the needs and concerns of the Northern participant rather than being about genuine solidarity with the Southern counterpart.

Moreover, it is the context of poverty eradication policy that will shape the new partnership:

> the British notion of partnership emphasises equal,
> consultative relationships between donors and recipients. It
> emphasises the need for both partners to share a commitment
> to the elimination of poverty. (Colclough, 1998, p. 33)

This notion of partnership, however, is in need of a critical reading absent in Colclough's position. Dower argues that:

> partners (ideally) (a) have broadly the same goals and values;
> (b) have a fairly equal input into decision-making about how
> to realise these goals/values. (Dower, 1998, p. 21)

In reality, he surmises, the form of partnership being talked about here falls far short of this ideal. Poverty eradication may in its broadest sense be shared as a goal by all governments and partners in development. However, it is the particular interpretation of its meaning that is crucial and that interpretation remains in the ownership of the development agencies. Asymmetries of money, power and knowledge make it highly difficult for both partners to 'have a fairly equal input into decision-making about how to realise these goals/values' (Dower, 1998, p. 21).

Dower argues that people choose partners as those they can work with in doing what they want to do. Given the different positions of donors and recipients, this leads to the former choosing winners from among the latter, as evidenced by the Clinton visit to Africa of 1998 (King, 1998a, p. 81).

Research partnership is a minor item on this agenda, particularly in Britain. Other nations, the Dutch, Norwegians and Canadians, for instance, historically have committed themselves to large-scale and long-term funding of major research programmes in the South (King, 1998b).[1] Britain, however, has tended towards much lighter notions of partnership, although, of course, there is an older tradition of very strong relations such as that between Durham and Fourah Bay in Sierra Leone, or between London and countless universities internationally. It is to be welcomed that the DFID's draft economic and social research funding policy makes explicit mention of the possibility of promoting international research relationships:

> *Limited funds will be made available ... for the development of*
> *research capacity in developing country research institutions,*
> *normally as part of a collaborative research project with a UK*
> *institution. Greater weight will be given in research*
> *programmes, and in the assessment of research proposals, to*
> *the quality of collaborative arrangements with developing*
> *country institutions. (DFID, 1998, para. 6)*

This, however, leaves many questions unanswered. Is this enough of an emphasis? Shouldn't collaborative *relationships*, as opposed to *arrangements*, be stressed as a fundamental priority rather than something that is likely to get a proposal a few bonus points? How will quality of collaborative arrangements be measured in any case? There certainly will be little incentive for partners to be honest. Does it matter that it is likely that collaboration will be project-specific rather than longer term? The former is certainly consistent with the powerful vision of the nature of research in the future outlined in Gibbons et al (1994) [2], but is this vision both inevitable and desirable? It is interesting to note that the next paragraph of the draft report goes on to admit that there is a tension between building such collaboration and developing new British researchers. Are we in a situation in which the new British resource is in direct competition with researchers in Southern universities? How do we face such a scenario as a profession and as individuals?

There are also many questions to be posited about the notion of partnership more generally. What are the effects of the 'picking of winners' on research choices? How can we respond to the more pernicious elements of this? What does partnership mean for Southern universities and academics? What is the relationship between academic partnership and developmental partnership? How well positioned is international and comparative education to refocus itself to simultaneously study the domestic and international dimensions of the new development paradigm?

International and Comparative Education in the Era of the Global Market

The third crucial element of the new context of comparative education is its insertion into the global market. The international intensification of commodification drives activities such as education into a closer relationship with markets and economic forces. The current phase of capitalist development, with the pervasiveness of international capital flows and the extension of short-termist and narrow economic calculation to ever-greater arenas, both seriously reorders the world which comparativists seek to study and the climate in which they attempt to conduct such study.

One immediate impact of the growth of short-termism is the threat it poses to longer lasting academic partnerships between institutions in the North and South, already vulnerable to a fundamentalist reading of poverty eradication policy. The culture of short-term contracts for staff and research programmes, and the scramble for consultancy, act against the development and sustenance of longer relationships between colleagues and institutions.

> *For partners in Britain the realities of the economic climate, in*
> *which all putative partners exist, are such that, at best*
> *medium term benefit to the university must be demonstrable,*
> *but most often immediate benefit is what is demanded. The*
> *management of any faculty will be looking for improved*
> *chances in the next research rating exercise, the possibility of*
> *paid consultancy and the possibility of attracting full fee*
> *paying students (probably coming under donor funded*
> *schemes). The investment of time is just as valuable as a cash*
> *investment and must show a return. If it does not then the*
> *activity in question will give way to something that does.*
> *(Walton, 1998, p. 59)*

DFID's avowed support for meaningful partnerships in knowledge creation and utilisation (DFID, 1998) will remain rhetoric if no concerted effort is taken to promote stable and continuing relationships across the North–South divide. In the current climate in universities, this requires a level of resourcing that makes it clear to faculty management that such relationships can pay their way.

The Research Assessment Exercise (RAE) had a major impact on academic life in the 1990s. For those working in a potentially developmental area such as education, it has led to contradictions

(Taylor, 1998). Perversely, the RAE's interpretation of the market imperative towards quality assurance and performance-related funding is to prioritise basic research, reflected in articles in 'respectable' journals and single authored books, rather than the kind of applied work that comparativists find themselves engaged upon as consultants or through medium-term agency funding through their research budgets (King, 1996). However, because the RAE also tends to favour a professionally defined mainstream and, in any case, does not bring sufficient financial rewards for the survival of departments, more marginal groups such as comparative educators must find alternative sums of money. Teaching-related money, however, is biased towards those disciplines which can teach at a larger scale. Research council funding increasingly becomes more explicitly about promoting British economic competitiveness, a contribution comparative education is poorly placed to claim.

The general financial crisis of the university and the resultant informalisation and insecurity of staff is particularly apparent in such a field. This trend threatens to undermine many of the key principles of international and comparative education:

> *Leaving research to the market, and particularly to the present global competitive market, can spell the end of a great deal of carefully built-up publicly-supported research capacity. In the industrialised world publicly-supported centres of academic excellence, large and small, cannot easily survive 'market-testing', since the product of that accumulated capacity cannot necessarily be marketed, and especially when these centres and units are identified with critical analysis, advocacy and a concern with alternative conceptualisations.*

> *Similarly in many developing countries, and especially in Africa, market forces are draining the universities of their most talented teachers and researchers, and even where there is no physical flight of intellectual capital, what remains may be deployed on a range of conceptually barren and unconnected pieces of commissioned work. (King, 1995a, p. i)*

As with partnership and the poverty paradigm, marketisation challenges us to look internationally, locally, and, indeed, within our own institutions. How far should we be studying the effects of marketisation on how we operate as academics and how far should we pay attention to ways of preserving cultural space outside the full surveillance of the invisible hand? Authors increasingly point to the breakdown of the traditional university research monopoly (Gibbons et al, 1994; Buchert, 1996; King, 1996; McGinn, 1996): what is our response to this? How do we best position ourselves so that we can promote the future of the profession and of what it holds dear? As a profession, are we in any position to lobby for the importance of valuing 'Southern' publications in the RAE, and should we be?

Consultancy and Consensus

Internationally, many education departments, schools and faculties have sought to escape their funding crisis and respond to market forces through the consultancy route. Equally, underpaid or unemployed academics have seen this as a viable means of income generation. It is evident that good work does get done in these conditions (Preston & Arthur, 1995; Preston, 1996). However, there is considerable concern about the high level of poor practice as viewed from an academic point of view:

> At present the consultancy mode for this type of applied research is dominating the research enterprise and it places a premium on the qualities required for contract work: speed, prescription, confidentiality – qualities inimical to scholarly values. (Gmelin, 1995, p. 2)

Some go further and argue that consultancy tends to reinforce a particular world-view, methodology and developmental discourse (Preston & Arthur, 1995; Samoff, 1995, 1996; Preston, 1996):

> Although there are of course debates and disagreements among those involved in commissioned research, the conjunction of external funding and research fosters a methodological orthodoxy. Quite simply, some theories and methods are deemed acceptable, while others are rejected. To be heard, to influence outcomes and to be employed again requires operating, for example, within the world of human capital and rate of return analysis. ... The presumed universalism of the accepted research canons treats efforts to depart from the mainstream in order to tune approach and method to the local setting as simply poor social science. In this way, the combination of foreign assistance and commissioned research functions to disseminate globally not only particular understandings of education and development but also how those understandings are created, revised and refined. ... In the conjunction of funding and research, scholarship becomes a proprietary process. The investors have the determining voice in the selection of topics, researchers and methods, limit access to source materials, and often control the dissemination of findings. Consequently the process of knowledge creation is obscured, mystifying the power relations embedded in the research and thereby in the programmes it supports. Perhaps not entirely aware of their

own role, scholars become advocates not only for particular
understandings of development and underdevelopment but
also for a particular sort of global order. (Samoff, 1995,
pp. 21-22)

In the North, this leads to 'schizophrenic scholars' who have to write for very different audiences. It also leads increasingly to PhD students operating as part of a larger funded project, with as yet poorly understood effects on both the student–supervisor relationship and the nature of the dissertation-as-product (Samoff, 1995, 1996). For Southern scholars, however, there is often only the single viable alternative of writing for the agencies: peer approbation and promotion being irrelevant in terms of financial survival. Thus, in Africa in particular, national scholarship is effectively dominated by agency needs (Samoff, 1995, 1996). Many authors point to the intellectual nomadism and lack of rootedness of researchers in the needs of their own societies that results from this trend (Namaddu, 1983; Kajese, 1991; Mamdani, 1993).

How far does the trend towards consultancy have to be taken for granted? How can rigorous scholarship continue to flourish? How can we ensure that the next generations of comparativists are critical and reflective practitioners?

Reflections on Personal Practice

At the heart of my personal understanding of these complex and disturbing issues are my experiences over 3 years on a large (in British international and comparative education terms) agency-funded research project. As I noted in the introductory remarks to this chapter, this reflection is not intended to be a criticism of others but rather a critique of my own practice and the context in which it is developing.

The project was staffed by two academics in Edinburgh, with four partners in the South. Of the two Edinburgh staff, one was officially only partly involved with the project, being a full professor and director of a planning unit within the university. As the other member of staff, I was officially 100% active on the project. However, this is where the informalisation and intensification processes of the market can be seen in action. With staff in a small department already overworked, an additional, junior, staff member is under great pressure to contribute to teaching, supervision and administration. When that individual is part of the insecure 'new resource', the internal pressure to conform to departmental expectations is inevitably magnified. Thus, the short-term survival of the profession puts pressures on the quality of research and on the professional development of the young researcher.

The project had four Southern collaborators. Their varying backgrounds and the process of entering into a relationship with them tells its own story. It was only in South Africa that the colleagues are university-based and where their names emerged primarily out of academic networking. In Ghana, the partner was a consultant who was identified not through asking university-based colleagues but through contacts with non-governmental organisations (NGOs) and agencies. It had originally been intended that another, university-based, colleague from Ghana would be involved. This was someone whom we had collaborated with previously but he had subsequently moved into the 'super league' of Ghanaian consultants and was beyond our price range. In the case of Kenya, the partner was the research manager of an NGO with which both we and our funders have a long relationship. In practice, these relationships are more typically with individuals than institutions. Where it is still possible so to do, academics are understandably keen to retain consultancy income as personal rather than departmental. Thus, we were quite far removed from the notion of long-term relationships with academic partner institutions.

Although we talked of partners and we had only three meetings of all project staff and funders, it must be admitted that the research proposal was written in the North and was the product of an attempt to marry the interests of a funding agency with our academic interests. We were undoubtedly fortunate to find such an accommodating funder that this was a relatively painless process, although we would do well to remind ourselves more often and more forcefully of Samoff's critique rehearsed earlier. Whilst the partners have had considerable scope for localising and operationalising the research idea, it was not radically configured by them.

The progress of the research, too, sheds light on the realities of collaboration in the current economic conjuncture. Cash flow problems and overcommitment were experienced from partners desperately trying to survive in a hostile world. Infrastructural problems such as unreliable fax and email systems made North–South communication difficult. The cost of communication also encouraged it to be overwhelmingly North–South rather than South–South.

Asymmetries in research access were also apparent. Whilst the budget, which was effectively capped by tender waiver requirements, allowed the Northern researchers to visit all three African countries, it did not allow for intra-African movement, except to a final workshop. The ability of Northern researchers to access materials and high-status individuals is also far greater than for the majority of Southern researchers. Except for the partial exception of South Africa, Internet and other research resources are massively biased in favour of the Northern researcher. However, it is more striking to note that it is the foreign academic, particularly but not necessarily if agency linked, who is far more able to access the policy community, both national and donor, than the local researcher. In part, this may be due to the local researcher's reticence in attempting to gain an interview with a 'big man' but it is, more importantly, due to the higher perceived status of the expatriate, particularly one with an agency connection.

Does the experience of this project, and of others in the field, indicate that meaningful and sustainable partnerships are being developed or are likely to be developed in the context of probable British practices, policies and resourcing? How can this context be made more favourable? How can the ability of Southern researchers to shape research agendas be augmented? What is the appropriate role of Northern researchers in collaborative international research projects? What implications does this have for the future of a new British resource?

Concluding Comments

This chapter raises more questions than it provides answers. In part, this relates to my own uncertainties about the future of international and comparative education in Britain. That itself is to a considerable extent a function of the way in which the current context reduces the space for critical thinking and reflexive practice. The dominance of intensification and commodification leaves precious little room for the kind of early career development so necessary for individuals and the future of the profession.

There is clearly some excellent comparative education research and teaching going on in Britain presently. The challenge is to sustain and extend this. We must resist the temptations brought by the external environment to become ever less theoretical and ever more practically focused. Psacharopoulos's (1990) claims that we already know the answers to the big questions in international and comparative education seems more wrong-headed with every passing day. To the contrary, we must continue to reassert the importance of reflective practice built on a sound theoretical basis and critical analysis of the material and cultural contexts in which we are operating. As well as the contexts of the research fields that we are addressing, we are increasingly called to analyse our own contexts in the North. We are faced with the challenge of critiquing development policy both as it impinges on the South and on the North. We are impelled to ask how the dominance of the global market shapes our institutions. Methodological and philosophical debates about our field of study are essential but they must be underpinned by a political economy of international and comparative education as a disciplinary area.

BAICE came into existence at a point when the future of international and comparative education in Britain seemed to be threatened by a particularly unfavourable conjuncture. However, this is also a time when it is evident that we are faced with the imperative to reassess our practices and priorities. It is in addressing these challenges that the future will become clearer.

Notes

[1] These programmes were primarily state funded. As McGinn (1996) notes, American universities were also encouraged into long-term relationships through the support of the big foundations, such as Ford and Rockefeller.

[2] Gibbons et al posit a shift from what they call Mode 1 research to Mode 2. Mode 2 is transdisciplinary and brings together research teams on a case-by-case basis in order to answer specific research and practical problems. It envisages relatively small core university staffs with large 'clouds' of part-time consultants that can be brought in for specific activities. It also sees the university as increasingly only one of many players in the research field.

References

Buchert, L. (1996) The Interface between Research and Consultancy: some conditions and issues, in L. Buchert & K. King (Eds) *Consultancy and Research in International Education*. Bonn: German Foundation for International Development (DSE)/Northern Policy Research Review and Advisory Group (NORRAG).

Caddell, M. (1998) Beyond the White Papers: an overview of the debate, in K. King & M. Caddell (Eds) *Partnership and Poverty in Britain and Sweden's New Aid Policies*, Occasional Paper 75. Edinburgh: Centre of African Studies, University of Edinburgh.

Carton, M. (1998) Poverty, Solidarity and Globalisation: a Swiss perspective, in K. King & M. Caddell (Eds) *Partnership and Poverty in Britain and Sweden's New Aid Policies*, Occasional Paper 75. Edinburgh: Centre of African Studies, University of Edinburgh.

Cedergen, J. (1998) Partnerships in Development: a realistic proposition, in K. King & M. Caddell (Eds) *Partnership and Poverty in Britain and Sweden's New Aid Policies*, Occasional Paper 75. Edinburgh: Centre of African Studies, University of Edinburgh.

Colclough, C. (1998) Bilateral Aid to the South: notes on partnership and development, in K. King & M. Caddell (Eds) *Partnership and Poverty in Britain and Sweden's New Aid Policies*, Occasional Paper 75. Edinburgh: Centre of African Studies, University of Edinburgh.

Denmark, Ministry of Foreign Affairs – Danida (1998) Guidelines for Sector Programme Support: final draft. Copenhagen.

Department for International Development (DFID) (1997) *Eliminating World Poverty: a challenge for the 21st century*. London: HMSO.

Department for International Development (DFID) (1998) Draft Economic and Social Research Strategy, 1998-2001. London: DFID.

Dower, N. (1998) Global Ethics, Global Citizenship and Governments' Policy on Combating Poverty, in K. King & M. Caddell (Eds) *Partnership and Poverty in Britain and Sweden's New Aid Policies*, Occasional Paper 75. Edinburgh: Centre of African Studies, University of Edinburgh.

Finland, Ministry for Foreign Affairs (1996) *Decision-in-principle on Finland's Development Cooperation*, The Cabinet, 12 September, Helsinki.

Gibbons, M., Limoges, C., Nowotny, H., Schwartzman, S., Scott, P. & Trow, M. (1994) *The New Production of Knowledge*. London: Sage.

Gmelin, W. (1995) The Scope for Alternative Paradigms in External Support of Educational Research, *Norrag News*, 18, pp. 1-2.

Hobsbawm, E. (1994) *The Age of Extremes*. London: Abacus.

Jameson, F. (1988) Postmodernism and the Consumer Society, in E.A. Kaplan (Ed.) *Postmodernism and its Discontents*. New York: Verso.

Kajese, K. (1991) African NGO Decolonisation: a critical choice for the 1990s, in Centre of African Studies (Ed.) *Critical Choices for the NGO Community*. Edinburgh: Centre of African Studies.

King, K. (1995a) Editorial, *Norrag News*, 18, pp. i–ii.

King, K. (1995b) New Markets in Higher Education: casual labourers and consultants, *Norrag News*, 18, pp. 2-6.

King, K. (1996) From Analysis to Advice and from Counsel to Consultancy: the challenge to educational research, in L. Buchert & K. King (Eds) *Consultancy and Research in International Education*. Bonn: DSE/NORRAG.

King, K. (1998a) New Challenges to International Development, in K. King & M. Caddell (Eds) *Partnership and Poverty in Britain and Sweden's New Aid Policies*, Occasional Paper 75. Edinburgh: Centre of African Studies, University of Edinburgh.

King, K. (1998b) Links as Bridges in International Education, *Journal of International Education*, 1, pp, 39-43.

King, K. & Buchert, L. (Eds) (1998) *International Aid to Education: global patterns and national contexts*. Paris: UNESCO/NORRAG.

King, K. & Caddell, M. (Eds) (1998) *Partnership and Poverty in Britain and Sweden's New Aid Policies*, Occasional Paper 75. Edinburgh: Centre of African Studies, University of Edinburgh.

McGinn, N. (1996) Changing Paradigms, Not Sources of Finance, as an Explanation of Changing Research: the US experience, in L. Buchert & K. King (Eds) *Consultancy and Research in International Education*. Bonn: DSE/NORRAG.

McGrath, S. (1998a) Education, Development and Assistance: the challenge of the new millennium, in K. King & L. Buchert (Eds) *International Aid to Education: global patterns and national contexts*. Paris: UNESCO/NORRAG.

Mamdani, M. (1993) University Crisis and Reform: a reflection on the African experience, *Review of African Political Economy*, 58, pp. 7-19.

Namaddu, K. (1983) Uganda: educational research capacity and environment in Uganda, 1970-81, in S. Shaeffer & J. Nkinyangi (Eds) *Educational Research Environments in the Developing World*. Ottawa: International Development Research Center.

Preston, R. (1996) Consultancy, Knowledge and Human Development, in L. Buchert & K. King (Eds) *Consultancy and Research in International Education*. Bonn: DSE/NORRAG.

Preston, R. & Arthur, L. (1995) *Knowledge Societies and Planetary Cultures.* Coventry: International Centre for Education and Development (INCED), University of Warwick.

Psacharopoulos, G. (1990) Comparative Education: from theory to practice or are you A:/neo* or B:/ist? *Comparative Education Review*, 34, pp. 369-380.

Riddell, R. (1997) The Changing Concepts of Aid and Development, in W. Cummings & N. McGinn (Eds) *International Handbook on Education and Development.* Oxford: Pergamon.

Samoff, J. (1995) The Structural Adjustment of Educational Research, *Norrag News*, 18, pp. 21-23.

Samoff, J. (1996) The Structural Adjustment of Educational Research: reflections, in L. Buchert & K. King (Eds) *Consultancy and Research in International Education.* Bonn: DSE/NORRAG.

Sweden, Ministry for Foreign Affairs (1997) *The Rights of the Poor: our common responsibility: combating poverty in Sweden's development cooperation.* Stockholm.

Taylor, D.W. (1998) Science against Poverty: where and when can we have an impact, in K. King & M. Caddell (Eds) *Partnership and Poverty in Britain and Sweden's New Aid Policies*, Occasional Paper 75. Edinburgh: Centre of African Studies, University of Edinburgh.

Walton, R. (1998) Higher Education Links and the New DFID Agenda, in K. King & M. Caddell (Eds) *Partnership and Poverty in Britain and Sweden's New Aid Policies*, Occasional Paper 75. Edinburgh: Centre of African Studies, University of Edinburgh.

Watson, K. (1998) Memories, Models and Mapping: the impact of geopolitical change on comparative studies in education, *Compare*, 28, pp. 5-31.

Williams, P. (1998) Can We Avoid a Poverty Focused Aid Programme Impoverishing North–South Relations? in K. King & M. Caddell (Eds) *Partnership and Poverty in Britain and Sweden's New Aid Policies*, Occasional Paper 75. Edinburgh: Centre of African Studies, University of Edinburgh.

Yngström, I. & King, K. (1995) International Education Research: a survey of the new British resource. Edinburgh: United Kingdom Forum for International Education and Training (UKFIET)/University of Edinburgh.

A Dance on Six Floors: some issues of ownership and collaboration within the MUSTER (Multi-site Teacher Education Research) Project

JANET S. STUART

Foreword

This chapter comprises an outline of, and some brief reflections on, the Multi-site Teacher Education Research (MUSTER) Project, and was first presented at the BAICE conference in 1998.[1] It has been slightly revised for this book, but still remains a 'work in progress' report; a list of fuller accounts of the research can be found in the appendix. The chapter takes as its theme the English proverb 'he who pays the piper calls the tune' in order consider some of the issues arising when researchers from several countries, north and south, try to work together within certain constraints of resources, time and place.

Origins and Rationale of the Project

The Centre for International Education (CIE) at the University of Sussex Institute of Education has over the past few years built up links with Universities in a number of developing countries. Among the common interests which emerged was a focus on teacher education, an area which we found to have been neglected and underresearched.

In 1997 the CIE approached the British Department for International Development (DFID, formerly Overseas Development Administration [ODA]) with a proposal for collaborative and comparative research into teacher education in five countries. The partner institutions were:

Institute of Education, University of Cape Coast, Ghana
Institute of Education, National University of Lesotho
Centre for Educational Research and Training, University of Malawi
Faculty of Education, University of Durban-Westville, South Africa

Janet S. Stuart

School of Education, University of the West Indies, Trinidad & Tobago.

The Overall Aims of the Project

It was hoped that the study would:

enhance understanding of how new teachers can most effectively acquire the skills needed to teach in different systems, and of what it means to be(come) a teacher in different cultural contexts;

categorise different types of pre-service provision leading to initial qualification in each system, identifying the associated patterns of overall costs and costs per qualified teacher;

reach policy level conclusions both at country level and for international agencies;

build local research capacity focused on issues in teacher education using both quantitative and qualitative techniques.

Research Design

The study looked at teacher education from four different but complementary aspects. The intentions were to:

Analyse the curricular processes by which new teachers acquire and learn to apply the understanding, skills and attitudes needed to become effective professional practitioners in their local schools.

Study the identity and role of the teacher, with particular regard to the transition from 'entering student' to 'newly qualified teacher' in different cultural contexts.

Explore the varied patterns of initial qualification, costs, and benefits. Gain a deeper understanding of the training colleges, their development and organisation, and the career patterns and perspectives of their staff.

Research Implementation, Timescale and Outputs

Each institution appointed a Lead Researcher who organised the local study. Four faculty members and a research fellow from the Centre for International Education worked on the project in Sussex and paid a number of short visits to each country. The project also supported three doctoral students at Sussex undertaking research related to the MUSTER questions in Ghana and Malawi. The study initially covered the three years from January 1998-December 2000, and was extended for a further year to allow for the dissemination of the findings through local workshops and through publications. These will eventually include: a detailed report from each country, a synthetic report for DFID, discussion papers, articles in local and international journals, one or two edited books, and a collection of resource materials for teacher trainers. Most of these are being written collaboratively.

Ownership: the paymaster, the piper, the tune and the dancers

Our intention was that the research should provide comparative data within an agreed overall design, while responding also to local research needs and agendas. For this to happen negotiations had to take place at several levels, among different people, and in the light of what could realistically be achieved.

The paymaster. DFID agreed to fund the research and in response to their suggestions the project was expanded. It had started as a small-scale comparative study into how new teachers acquire professional knowledge and how they develop their identities as teachers in different cultural contexts, but it has grown into a larger policy-oriented project that attempts, in addition, to analyse and compare the effectiveness of different kinds of pre-service training in terms of both quality and cost.

The piper. CIE at Sussex was the initiator, and undertook tasks of co-ordination, support and consultancy, as well as participating in some of the fieldwork. Money was disbursed in lump sums to the country sites on receipt of specific research products: baseline studies, detailed research plans, interim analyses and final reports. The details of what was produced were agreed by CIE and then were worked out separately for each site.

The tune. In March 1998 the country team leaders came together at Sussex for two weeks to agree an overall design. The original three main research foci were distilled into a series of sub-studies and the framework divided into three arenas: input, process and output. Each leader then adapted this design to their own context and wrote a 'Country Research Plan' to a common format. Sussex researchers added a fourth focus: the teachers' colleges and their staff. Further collaborative workshops, at Durban in July 1999 and at Sussex in July 2000, allowed for review, revised planning, discussion and drafting of reports.

The dancers. However, each plan was implemented in different ways, not only because of the different kinds of teacher education institutions and programmes, but also because of a number of personal, institutional and contextual factors.

Experience. Of the five team leaders, three had doctoral degrees and two had a masters' degree, and their colleagues' expertise also varied; Sussex support and advice was therefore focused more in some places than in others.

	ARENA 1: INPUTS	ARENA 2: PROCESS	ARENA 3: OUTPUTS
Culture/ identity	◊ What are the characteristics of entrants in terms of prior experience, attitudes, motivation?	◊ How are the trainees socialised by the college experience? ◊ How do they experience it?	◊ What are the characteristics of the graduates, in terms of self-perception, motivation, attitudes? ◊ How have they been changed by the course?
Curriculum	• How was the college curriculum developed and what influenced it? • According to the documents, what is to be taught, and how? • What knowledge and experience do entrants bring with them, in terms of academic qualifications and previous job record?	• How is the curriculum, including the practical elements, delivered, in terms of pedagogy, assessment, teaching/learning materials, and how far are the stated aims and objectives achieved?	• What are the competences, in terms of knowledge, skills and attitudes, of the graduating NQTs? • What happens in their first year of teaching in terms of utilisation or washout of the course?
Costs	• Who applies and how are they selected? • What are the sources of funds for the course? • What are the national levels of supply and demand for primary teachers?	• What is the annual budget and how is it allocated? • How efficiently are the human and physical resources of the college used?	• How many NQTs graduate, where are they utilised, and how long do they stay in teaching? • What was the overall average cost per NQT? • What benefits have accrued from the costs, and to whom? • To what effect have the resources been used?
College	• How did the college develop, and what influenced it? • What are the characteristics of the lecturers, in terms of experience, qualifications attitudes, beliefs and motivations?	• How do the lecturers teach? • What is the college like in terms of culture, management, vision and ethos?	• How far do the college graduates fulfill the demands of the primary school system, in terms of 'effective' teaching?

NQT = newly qualified teachers

Figure 1. Figure 1. MUSTER: an overall view of arenas and strands with some of the main research questions.

Workload and cascades. Only one of the leaders was a full time researcher; three others combined their research roles with teaching and administration, and the fifth had normally a full teaching load. This, combined with personal styles of leadership, led to a kind of 'research cascade' in all but one of the sites, with the lead researcher delegating some or most of the research to colleagues and/or graduate students. Some participants hoped to use the exercise as a step towards their own post-graduate degrees. While this enhanced local ownership, at the same time it led to some of the studies being carried out in different ways, making it less easy to compare studies across the sites. For example, in Lesotho, 7 teachers college lecturers were involved and one said of her proposed study: 'This may not be what MUSTER wants, but it will help the college know what's going on'.

Institutional pressures. As the above implies, the leaders were working under different sets of pressures. Some were relatively free to organise the research as they saw fit, others were constrained by work pressures, by demands from above, or by bureaucratic systems. For example, in two cases the local university accounting procedures made it necessary to draw up very precise budgets, and delays in money transfers sometimes held up the fieldwork.

Research cultures. In all five countries, the positivist research paradigm has, until recently, been the predominant approach. Several aspects of MUSTER involved working in an interpretative paradigm, and in some places research training was required to orient members of the local teams. A wide range of both qualitative and quantitative methods of data collection were used, but not all the researchers were familiar with all of them, and more support would have been welcome in this area.

Theme and Variations?

The project sought to balance comparability with the desire to respond to the local agendas, and as fieldwork proceeded, certain dilemmas emerged. The aim of comparing across sites called for a certain amount of central direction over the collection and analysis of data from the five countries. In the case of qualitative data, it was appropriate for it to be collected in slightly different ways and analysed on site, so that emerging themes and preliminary findings could be fed back into the next stage of the research, before trying to look later for wider patterns. However, in the case of quantitative data, common instruments, coding and analysis methods were needed. Thus during the second workshop a survey instrument was drawn up, for use with large samples of student teachers at different points in their careers, that would provide a common framework for comparisons.

Collaboration

Cross-fertilisation. Clearly there was enormous potential for learning from each other. The Sussex team who travelled around the sites had the advantage here over the lead researchers who only met at annual intervals. The final workshop, although it was mainly devoted to report-writing, did allow for more sharing of findings, and for some in-depth discussions on common topics.

Insider-outsider perspectives. The combination of external and internal views has greatly enriched the study. Outsiders bring wider comparative frameworks, and can ask questions about things taken locally for granted; sometimes data (e.g. financial) is more readily released to someone perceived as neutral. Insiders bring cultural understanding and insights and, most importantly, they can collect data using two or more languages.

Joint authorship. The final test of both ownership and collaboration is how far the publications are joint productions, both in the sense of reflecting the findings, ideas and experiences of everyone involved and also in the sense of sharing the tasks of writing and editing (see Appendix).

Postscript 2001

A Solo Turn and a Foursome Reel

It quickly became apparent that teacher education in South Africa was in such a state of flux that a different design and different methods were needed. The research in South Africa therefore took off on a different trajectory, involving several researchers in different institutions.[2] Continuing dialogue with this team, however, provided very illuminating perspectives for comparison.

In the remaining four sites the research matrix (see Figure 1) proved a strong but flexible heuristic. Data relevant to each cell was collected and analysed in all the countries, albeit in different degrees of breadth and depth. It is now possible to make some generalisations, for example, about the kinds of students who enter primary training, the types of curriculum laid down, and how that curriculum is enacted by tutors and experienced by trainees, both in the colleges and on teaching practice. We can compare the costs, and ways that colleges operate in different countries. We know more than we did before about the careers and perspectives of college tutors, and how these vary between contexts. Unsurprisingly, the most tentative answers are about the effectiveness of the training, as the 'Impact' arena proved the most difficult to research.

In terms of local agendas, each country team foregrounded different issues. For example, while Malawi undertook a general evaluation of the current mixed-mode initial training programme for unqualified teachers, Lesotho looked at the way the new pre-service Diploma was being implemented. Trinidad and Tobago, *inter alia,* researched teaching practice in great depth, and Ghana explored some of the mismatches between current models of training and those that might be more relevant to local classrooms.

What have We Learnt?

Overall, the project has been a very enriching experience for the participants as well as producing results. In many places, not least in Sussex, there were steep learning curves to survive, and the positive outcomes are described above. For those who wish to follow us on to the dance floor, here are some preliminary reflections on what we might do differently next time.

Fitting the Resources to the Context

As always happens, the project required far more energy, time and resources than had been envisaged, putting at times almost intolerable burdens on some participants. The lesson here, I think, goes beyond warning against over-ambition or weak planning, to considering in more detail how the research context in the South differs from that in the North. Leaving aside political instability – South Africa invaded Lesotho in the project's first year – there are many practical and psychological factors that make research more time-consuming. First, the infrastructure is limited and/or unreliable, and communication takes much longer: papers have to go several miles away for photocopying; when the phones don't work, one goes for a meeting to find it has been cancelled or one may have to drive to consult a colleague – such apparently trivial examples multiplied many times can extend the work by weeks or months. Secondly, when research is a relatively new undertaking, the methods are unfamiliar, and there are no established routines in place, so the whole process takes longer. Thirdly, the institutional context may not be conducive to research: it may not be recognised for career progression, research time may not be adequately costed, or people are expected to fulfil external contracts while still carrying administrative duties, which may include, for example, being at the beck and call of the Vice-Chancellor. Library facilities are often poor, and Internet access still expensive or only intermittently available if at all. 'Building research capacity' effectively involves diagnosing the specific local needs, and paying attention to physical, personal and institutional factors – and costing them adequately. Paymasters, please take heed.

Dilemmas between Direction and Democracy

A big research project needs strong leadership and guidance, but also sharing of ideas and the participation of team members in decision-making. The MUSTER team met together only three times – 6 weeks out of 156. Though there was much intra-team communication, most of it went on, perforce, between the centre at Sussex and the periphery elsewhere, with far fewer exchanges – and only one individual visit – along the rim. The potential for much valuable sharing, and perhaps for a greater sense of ownership, was thus underutilised, and the expertise among the lead researchers was not fully exploited. Many important issues only emerged at the final workshop, though the ideas had been developed earlier in one or other of the sites. Perhaps keeping projects less ambitious, building in more time for cross-site visiting, making more imaginative and determined use of electronic media for consultation, might allow for maximum participation. The piper must play his tune, but must also take cues from the dancers and respond to their requests and initiatives.

Sharing Research Frameworks

Collaborative research brings together individuals with different experiences, assumptions and personal conceptual frameworks. For successful collaboration, these need to be made explicit, shared, heard and accorded mutual respect. This can be crucial enough between members of one academic institution; it is even more difficult across geographic distance and cultural spaces, particularly if there are perceived differences of status. Discussing key texts, for example, and talking through the different assumptions, orientations and perspectives of the group, are but some of the essential prerequisites for developing a shared sense of what the research is about, what questions are important, and how to answer them. This takes yet more time and effort, but the dancers need to hear the same beat if they are to move in unison.

Notes

[1] The MUSTER project was coordinated in Sussex by Professor Keith Lewin, Dr Yusuf Sayed (from 1999), Dr David Stephens (1997-99), Dr Janet Stuart. Research fellows/officers for all or part of the time include Dr Julie Coultas, Alison Croft, Dominic Furlong, John Hedges. The lead overseas researchers were: Dr Kwame Akyeampong (Ghana); Pulane Lefoka (Lesotho); Demis Kunje (Malawi); Dr Michael Samuel (SA); Dr June George (Trinidad and Tobago). Although this chapter draws on common themes and has benefitted from discussion among the team, the views expressed here are those of the author alone.

[2] Reports are being prepared in the form of an edited book rather than as Discussion Papers.

APPENDIX. Discussion Papers Produced by the Multi-Site Teacher Education Project (MUSTER)

These papers have been produced to show preliminary findings, and are published by the Centre for International Education at the University of Sussex. They are grouped here by theme or country.

Baseline Studies

No. 5. *Malawi: a baseline study of the teacher education system* (December 1999) D. Kunje & J. Chimombo

No. 6. *Trinidad & Tobago: a baseline study of the teacher education system* (July 1999) L. Quamina-Aiyejina, J. Mohammed, B. Rampaul, J. George, M. Kallon, C. Keller & S. Lochan

No. 7. *Ghana: a baseline study of the teacher education system* (April 2000) K. Akyeampong & D. Furlong

No. 8. *Lesotho: a baseline study of the teacher education system* (April 2000) J.P. Lefoka et al

Comparative Analyses

No. 1 *Counting the Cost of Teacher Education: cost and quality issues* (January 1999) K. Lewin

No. 3 *Primary Teacher Education Curricula as Documented: a comparative analysis* (July 1999) J.S. Stuart

No. 16 *Careers and Perspectives of Tutors in Teacher Training Colleges: case studies of Lesotho and Malawi* (September 2000) J.S. Stuart with D. Kunje & J.P. Lefoka

Sub-study Reports

a) Ghana

No. 4 *'On the Threshold': the identity of student teachers in Ghana* (April 2000) K. Akyeampong & D. Stephens

No. 13 *The Importance of Posting in Becoming a Teacher in Ghana* (June 2000) J.P. Hedges

No. 17 *Learning to Teach in Ghana: an evaluation of curriculum delivery* (July 2000) K. Akyeampong, J. Ampiah, J. Fletcher, N. Kutor & B. Sokpe

No. 18 *The Costs and Financing of Teacher Education in Ghana* (January 2001) K. Akyeampong, D. Furlong & K. Lewin

b) Malawi

No. 2 *The Costs and Financing of Teacher Education in Malawi* (Rev. April 2000) D. Kunje & K. Lewin

No. 11 *The Malawi Integrated In-Service Teacher Education Project: an analysis of the curriculum and its delivery in the colleges* (February 2000) J.S. Stuart & D. Kunje

No. 12 *The Malawi Integrated In-Service Teacher Education Programme and its School-based Components* (June 2000) D. Kunje & S. Chirembo

No. 14 *Gender Gaps in Schools and Colleges: can teacher education policy improve gender equity?* A. Croft

c) Trinidad and Tobago

No. 9 *Teacher Education in Trinidad and Tobago: costs financing and future policy* (July 2000) K. Lewin with C. Keller

No. 15 *Newly Qualified Teachers: impact on/interaction with the system* (March 2000) J. Morris & A. Joseph

No. 19 *On-the-Job Training (OJT): pre-service teacher training in Trinidad and Tobago* (August 2000) J. George, J. Fournillier & M-L. Brown

No. 20 *Becoming a Primary School Teacher in Trinidad and Tobago, Part 1: the curriculum in the teachers' colleges* (August 2000) J. George, J. Rampersad, P. Worrell, B. Rampaul & J. Mohammed

Janet S. Stuart

No. 21 *Becoming a Primary School Teacher in Trinidad & Tobago, Part 2: teaching practice experience of trainees* (October 2000) J. George, P. Worrell, J. Rampersad & B. Rampaul

d) Lesotho

No. 10 *Costs and Financing of Teacher Education in Lesotho* (November 1999) K. Lewin, V. Ntoi, H.J. Nenty & P. Mapuru

PART FOUR

International Agencies, Data and Globalisation

The Evaluation of Education Development Projects and Bureaucratic Cultures: prospects for the education sector within the context created by the White Paper on International Development

COLIN LACEY & ANGELA JACKLIN

Introduction

The 'New Labour' Government, within 6 months of being in office, radically changed the direction of United Kingdom policy with respect to overseas aid. There is a new optimism and purpose associated with overseas aid and a promise to halt the decline in the proportion of gross national product (GNP) devoted to overseas aid, and eventually to increase it, once a basis for the expansion of the programme has been achieved. This new purpose and optimism is expressed in the Secretary of State's foreword to the November 1997 White Paper.

> *This White Paper sets out the Government's policies to achieve the* sustainable development *of this planet. It is first, and most importantly, about the single greatest challenge which the world faces* – eliminating poverty ...

> We can *succeed. The* overall successes of development *in recent decades have been remarkable. ... There are good reasons for optimism. But to succeed we need to mobilise greater* political will *across the international community.* (emphases added)

It must seem churlish to immediately set about criticising the kind of White Paper which many people working in the development field have been waiting for, for the last two decades. However, that is what we intend to do. We do so because, despite its undoubted strengths, the White Paper has some important omissions, and glosses over some very important problems within the Ministry itself which could result in a failure to implement the policy or learn from the results of previous failures and successes.

We will argue our case from our experiences in the education development sector. We will leave it to others to take up the debate in other sectors. Nevertheless, there is evidence that other sectors are affected by the issues that we will describe and attempt to substantiate.[1]

The Political Context

During the run up to the May 1997 election, Tony Blair committed New Labour to produce a government in which the three top priorities would be 'education, education and education'. It therefore seems a strange omission within the White Paper that the 12 strands of the Government's policy for overseas aid do not include a mention of education at all. Instead, education emerges within the general discussion. However, despite acknowledging the importance of education and hinting at a positive connection between economic development and education in Asia, there is no evidence presented in the paper of a body of research which establishes the strategic importance of education, nor is there any real indication about how the targets set for education will be achieved (see p. 31). For example, universal primary education by 2015, and eliminating gender inequalities in primary and secondary education by 2005 are worthy goals but very unlikely to be achieved without far more knowledge and commitment than we currently possess. The major goals are followed by a wish list of educational 'goods' which excludes one major plank of domestic policy – the promotion of competition between schools (based on test and inspection results) for pupils and resources. The list of educational goods includes the following.

Access – for girls as well as boys, rich or poor, rural or urban and those in socially or ethnically disadvantaged communities.

Quality – to prepare children for the life ahead.

Equity – to remove all barriers to opportunity and achievement.

We also intend to strengthen and extend partnerships to support a range of innovative strategies.

In short, we will argue that the White Paper can be seen as an attempt to reach out to the poor, the undernourished and undereducated, but also to cover up the lack of knowledge of how to achieve this and the lack of a policy for learning about development, based on previous experience in the field. In other words, Claire Short, the Minister for Overseas Development, is faced with a substantial shortfall in technical ability and professional expertise within the government department that will be responsible for delivering her espoused policy.

We do not suggest that this problem is the fault of individual staff members of the department; we argue instead that it arises out of the historical constraints and regulatory functions of the department, which have given rise to an internal culture which relies heavily on bureaucratic evaluation (MacDonald, 1977; Lacey & Torrance, 1998). In turn, this internal culture makes it difficult for the Department for International Development (DFID) to fully utilise the expertise of outside groups or individuals brought in as consultants. Nor do we argue that DFID is unique in experiencing this problem, although in DFID's case the contrast between performance and the recently espoused policy highlights the issue.

The Need for Evaluation

The minimum requirement for the improvement of educational systems is that new policies are based on the researched and evaluated outcomes of previous policies. This may be expressed as a virtuous spiral (Lacey & Jacklin, 1999):

1. the setting up of schemes based on the best evidence from past experience, adapted to the new context and the new circumstances that prevail;
2. the rigorous evaluation of the scheme, during and after its existence, (formative and summative evaluation);
3. the evaluation of the long term effects of the scheme: a test of the sustainability of any success that has been achieved and an analysis of the reasons for any deterioration;
4. the setting up of new schemes based on the best evidence (and so on for the next cycle).

This can be achieved through the evaluation of whole systems or experiments established via projects. This simple and apparently obvious truth can, however, be extremely difficult to achieve in practice. The list of things that can and do go wrong is very long and it is at times very difficult to decide precisely where an apparently functioning system is actually failing.

The 'real world' in developing countries does not always respond in the way that bureaucrats and experts from Western countries expect it to.

It follows that 'blueprint' projects devised in great detail and in consultation with bureaucrats and experts from developing countries do not often proceed according to plan. Instead, they begin to founder on problems that were not part of the knowledge base around which they were planned. If these problems are not uncovered by competent process evaluation within the life of the project, they not only jeopardise the outcomes of that project, but are likely to remain undiscovered by a summative evaluation and remain outside the knowledge base of the bureaucrats and experts who devise the next generation of projects.

This analysis makes a clear distinction between a formative or process evaluation, in which the outcomes and problems encountered at various stages of the project are made available to the project management in time for the management to respond and take corrective action, and the reliance on summative evaluation, which is restricted to viewing the project as a 'black box' from which the outcomes emerge as a justification or a failure to justify the money spent on the project. In the first case, the process evaluation leads to a summative evaluation which builds on and enhances the understandings developed during the project; in the second case, the summative evaluation is often superficial and unreliable. In the first case, management makes space and resources available to a sustained, independent and professional evaluation; in the second case, evaluation is a bureaucratic requirement to be squeezed in-between other pressures and made subservient to the politics of the controlling organisations. The first case or scenario we will call 'professional evaluation' and the second scenario will be referred to as 'bureaucratic evaluation'. It is our view that bureaucratic evaluation dominates the scene with respect to education development projects funded by DFID. In addition, we argue that a strong professional evaluation is an essential element in setting up a learning culture within an administrative organisation to enable it to succeed in the complex task of improving education.

Our thesis is an attempt to clarify a complex problem and focus attention on the government departments that are responsible for informing and carrying out policies. Our major focus will be DFID in the United Kingdom. It is important to note that we do not wish to imply that the problems we describe are special to, or more developed within, DFID. These issues occur within all major development agencies (Hancock, 1991). They need to be recognised, debated and the organisation concerned needs to take radical reforming action. The thesis, stated simply, is that in order to carry out its function, DFID should possess a learning culture where intelligence is cultivated and where knowledge and expertise of the practical functioning of education systems is a top priority. Our experience [2] of DFID as an organisation is that this is not the case. Instead, there is a culture of ignorance in which worthy political and ideological goals are pursued without the expertise or the organisational structures that can deliver them. The result is a massive bureaucratic subterfuge in which large sums of money are wasted on projects which achieve little. However, more important than whether a project is a success or failure, the department seems insufficiently oriented to learn from its successes or its failures.

It is our intention to use the terms 'culture of ignorance' and 'culture of learning', with caution and precision. We present them as ideal types. For example, we do not suggest that, because individuals work in an organisation dominated by bureaucratic procedures with a poorly developed culture of learning, they are individually unwilling to listen or unable to learn. Cultures of learning and cultures of ignorance coincide within most organisations, they are frequently in conflict and where cultures of ignorance become dominant, they result in individuals making decisions based on limited or misleading information. In highly uncertain and complex situations, poor decisions (unsuccessful projects and wasted resources) can then be covered up or downplayed by a series of devices, for example, working parties, delays, reports which are endlessly revised or shelved and the maintenance of a public front which emphasises successes or new policies and approaches and keeps all criticism out of the public debate.

The concept of a culture of ignorance derives from a strand of organisational research which began in the 1960s. It focused on the dysfunctions of bureaucratic cultures and the clash between bureaucratic values and democracy. It stems from work by Merton (1936, 1965) in which he highlighted the 'trained incapacity' of bureaucrats. It includes studies by Blau (1955) and Burns & Stalker (1961), who looked at the tensions between collegiate, professional relationships and bureaucratic structures, and was extended by Gouldner (1955), who focused on issues of democracy and grass-roots cultures and clashes with the 'top–down' emphasis within control-centred bureaucracy. The concepts therefore have 'classic' antecedents and should not be interpreted as narrow, empirically derived concepts, although we would claim that they are 'grounded' in our investigation of DFID (Glaser & Strauss, 1967).

A culture of ignorance within a bureaucracy can be strengthened and become dominant if the following features of bureaucracy are allowed or encouraged to develop without corresponding counter measures to strengthen a culture of learning.

1. A general stress on procedures and bureaucratic rules without a countervailing emphasis on the purpose of the procedure. This can be the result of an overworked staff or powerful individuals emphasising procedure for other reasons.

2. Promotion based on seniority or the opinions of a powerful senior management, without countervailing emphasis on suitability as measured by professional and technical competence or expertise.

3. An organisation dominated by a small senior group, giving rise to a 'top–down' structure with few individuals able to put alternative views, for fear it could damage their career prospects.

4. An organisation which demands and gets 'loyalty' from its staff. No public digression from espoused policy is allowed, no matter how improbable or unattainable that policy might be. Within this context, even outsiders, brought in to do specific 'expert' tasks, are controlled by the ethos or are not re-employed.

5. An organisation in which the provisions for a learning culture are undermined by points 1-4 and this undermining is contributed to by other factors, e.g. the regular movement of staff so that they cannot build up an expertise in a particular area and a lack of openness so that public debates are manipulated to prevent important but critical issues from emerging into the public arena.

Clearly, the establishment of these dimensions in relation to any organisation is a difficult and complex task, open to personal judgement and bias. We present them here as a guide to future inquiry and debate. We do not claim within this article to have established them in all aspects of work carried out within DFID. Instead, we present our evidence as deriving from our own experience within evaluation, our survey of the literature and from the experience of a limited number of fellow consultants, as a challenge within the debate about facilitating development. We see our article as a stimulus, not the final word on a complex and contentious matter.

The Evidence

The evidence reported in this chapter comes from three sources.

The published literature on the evaluation and sustainability of education projects funded by donor nations in developing countries. This includes some general texts on the success or failure of development aid and literature published by DFID.
Interviews with 10 consultants/researchers [3] from a variety of backgrounds who have worked in development and have a first-hand experience of DFID and aid programmes.
The long-term experience of one of the authors, who has worked on two projects, the Seychelles BEd and the Andhra Pradesh Primary Education Project (APPEP) for periods of 5 and 10 years respectively. On both of these projects, he worked within a team. The views expressed here should not be seen as necessarily the views of any other team member.

The evidence presented in this chapter is illustrative and partial. Nevertheless, it is substantial enough to justify an attempt to initiate a public debate on the central issue of the competence of DFID to deliver the ambitious policy described in the White Paper.

It will be important to begin this chapter with a look at the literature to see what previous evaluations of projects can tell us about the successes and failures; long-term sustainability of projects; and, most importantly, the Overseas Development Administration (ODA)/DFID's record in learning from the evaluation of past projects.

How the Literature Summarises Previous Experience of Development Projects Designed to Improve Educational Provision

In the early 1980s, Watson examined what he referred to as the 'enormous gulf between the earlier [1950s] expectations and subsequent achievements' (Watson, 1984, p. 30) in relation to education. He argued that there needed to be far more research and analysis to address this gulf, especially in relation to the social and cultural contexts of schooling as well as the factors which influence educational developments. Most importantly, he called for international aid agencies to 'take this more difficult and long-term approach'. But have they?

By the end of the 1980s, it appeared that little progress had been made. References were still being made to the often disappointing impact of education projects (e.g. Stephens, 1990; Bray, 1991; Jones, 1992; Verspoor, 1993). Stephens (1990), for example, commented that:

> *Quite often worthy projects, heavily funded by the large aid organisations, have failed to have any impact because at each stage of the development of the project scant regard has been paid to the involvement of local people in the decision-making process. (p. 25)*

He highlighted the need for informed coordination and cooperation at all levels of decision-making. Quoting Freire, Stephens warned of the propensity of international aid to engender passivity in recipients but also that the effects of changes in control of decision-making may be seen as an attack on the vested interests of the privileged. He went on to argue, 'By keeping each role and activity separate we are in danger of both wasteful duplication of effort and a misuse of existing scarce resources' (p. 25).

Like Stephens, other independent researchers began to highlight similar key factors in relation to project sustainability, notably, the development of human resources and the improvement of institutional infrastructures (e.g. Morrison, 1990; Leach, 1991). There were calls for aid agencies to work together and arguments for a more critical consideration of the contribution of the aid to planned developments (Bray, 1991). Crucially, there were also arguments for the importance of project monitoring and post-project evaluation to inform decision-making (Lockheed & Hanushek, 1988; Jones, 1992).

In 1990, ODA's policy for British aid for education in the 1990s (ODA, 1990) argued that it was not possible to aim for both quantity and quality. Within the context of universal primary education (UPE), their stated priority was to be the promotion of quality provision. At about the same time (early 1990s), the ODA commissioned a review of research evidence on school effectiveness in developing countries and, most importantly, 'hence to indicate possible priorities for education aid' (Pennycuick, 1993, p. 2). The 'way-in' to quality? The review was comprehensive, but yet again, what was clearly highlighted was the 'paucity of research evidence' in relation to effectiveness and efficiency of schooling as well as a methodological caution which related to the stronger preponderance of quantitative studies and corresponding lack of qualitative research. Despite this, Pennycuick argued:

> *None of these caveats mean that existing research evidence*
> *should be rejected; it is the best evidence we have. However, it*
> *is important that it should not be applied blindly or*
> *prescriptively, but rather used to* assist *decision making, with*
> *due attention to context. On the other hand, it can be said*
> *with confidence that policy-makers who* ignore *the research*
> *evidence take a considerable and unjustifiable risk.*
> *(Pennycuick, 1993, p. 4; original emphasis)*

Sustainability in relation to educational developments (e.g. Havelock, 1970; Fullan, 1982) is without doubt of crucial importance. It takes on an even more heightened importance where there is a reliance on external aid and a need to target often scant resources. Increasingly, emphasis has been placed on the importance of evaluation of aid for education developments (King, 1991; Dyer, 1994; Torrance et al, 1997), but unfortunately, as Hopkin (1994) pointed out, evaluations have tended to be neither consistent nor uniform. One example of good practice, however, was highlighted by Hopkin (1994) in his analysis of aid and education in Botswana. He described the country's use of aid as exemplary and 'a model to other developing countries' (p. 393). Importantly, he highlighted one of the key factors in Botswana's success as ongoing research and evaluation of the education programmes. An example of this, and of what we would call 'professional evaluation', may be seen in the Primary Education Improvement Project (PEIP), which had 6-monthly evaluations in order to 'identify the accomplishments of the last half year, to point out the major problems being encountered and to present plans for PEIP for the next six months' (Botswana Ministry of Education & US Agency for International Development, 1990, p. 1). Commitment and funding from both the Government of Botswana and donor agencies, expressly for ongoing research and evaluation, were arguably important factors in the project's sustainability.

If we consider what has been learnt from examples of good practice such as this, it is questionable whether lessons have been carried forward. The ODA/DFID clearly have a stated commitment to research and evaluation (e.g. Foreign and Commonwealth Office, 1997; White Paper, DFID, 1997). Since the early 1990s, they have periodically issued a series of education papers (Education Research Serials).[4] Each 'represents a study or piece of commissioned research on some aspect of education and training in developing countries' (Brock & Cammish, 1997). Although most of the studies were undertaken to 'provide informed judgements from which policy decisions could be drawn' (Brock & Cammish, 1997), they have been published as of interest and value to a wider audience. These 'serials' clearly provide a welcome and important addition to the field, but what of research and evaluation in relation to the individual funded projects themselves?

On this, DFID's policy is fairly clear (e.g. Foreign and Commonwealth Office, 1997). In relation to funded projects, evaluations and reviews are carried out, taking different forms at different levels. Project Completion Reports (PCRs) are required for all projects which cost in excess of £500,000. In addition, approximately 15 projects a year, covering all sectors, have 'full retrospective impact evaluation' on the basis that 'project impact may not become fully evident until some time after completion' (Foreign and Commonwealth Office, 1997, p. 81). Findings from small clusters of projects on similar themes are then drawn together in a synthesis study.

In an attempt to reconcile the rhetoric of impact evaluation with the reality of development projects, Oakley et al (1998) consider how the long-term impact of social development programmes may be evaluated by development agencies. They conclude that although there is no easy answer, a range of methods and approaches to evaluation is needed to explore complex social processes. It should be noted that this was the approach used in the APPEP evaluation.

Building on earlier advice, e.g. in relation to moves to more people-centred development strategies (ODA, 1995; ODA, 1995-96, cited in Oakley et al, 1998), DFID (1997) suggests that impact should be understood in terms of both outputs and effects. Thin et al (1998), in a multi-agency review to inform ODA/DFID about approaches to developing and implementing social policy systems, is critical of impact assessments which he argues are still too biased towards 'outcomes'. He calls for assessments of *change* as being more significant for planning, rather than assessments of *impact*. He highlights the rarity of evaluation studies conducted substantially after project completion, despite unanimous agreement on the importance of long-term sustainability. He argues that:

> *Most of the interesting and potentially useful information on*
> *social policy outcomes takes the form of illustrative case study*
> *material and its interpretation, as opposed to the*
> *'measurement' and 'products' anticipated in the scientistic*
> *metaphors and rhetoric which pervades aid agencies'*
> *evaluation guidance. (p. 4)*

We find here the emphasis on understanding social processes relevant to development projects.

Eyben (1998) and Thin (1998) call for increased development cooperation, with partnerships between agencies. Thin argues that there is still too much concern with individual agencies focusing on their own 'outcomes' rather than a wider generation of understandings. He believes that good use of information is dependent on 'patterns of relevance and ownership' (p. 2). Cassen et al (1994) make a similar point as they highlight that their report frequently discusses 'the failure to learn from mistakes' (p. 12). Thin quotes an example of good practice where Danida's evaluation reports are made available and widely disseminated, including on the Web: 'The self-critical rather than promotional nature of these documents is a clear example of good practice in transparency and willingness to learn' (p. 20).

Moving from policy to practice, and using the ODA/DFID's own data, we have been able to trace 22 [5] evaluations that were carried out in the Education and Training sector between 1987 and 1998, of which three were synthesis studies. That is, 19 projects were evaluated over the 12-year period. Accessing the data did not prove to be as straightforward as might have been anticipated. Different 'lists' of evaluations (obtained directly from DFID as well as accessed from their web-site) contained slightly differing information and it also became apparent that there were additional evaluation reports which we were not able to trace. As the total number of evaluations was relatively small, the omission of a report from a list represented a significant omission.

Considering what we have learnt from these project evaluations, the most striking feature is, perhaps unsurprisingly, the reiteration of the same themes as have appeared in the more general literature. For example, there have been fairly constant references to the involvement and the role of recipients in education developments. These have tended to identify the need to take into account the wishes of the recipients (e.g. White & Stewart, 1987) as well as their involvement in implementation (e.g. EVSUM 403, 1988). More recently, references have shifted slightly to focus on the importance of local ownership, for example, EVSUM 585 (1996) argues that 'encouraging local ownership among all key stakeholders is essential to develop commitment to implementation and to ensure sustainability'. Also apparent are references made to the need to take into account the developing country context, e.g. 'ideas which are excellent in the UK context, will not always be applicable elsewhere'

(EVSUM 579, 1996). All of which makes us question whether we are really progressing or whether the bureaucratic nature of the project evaluations carried out by the evaluation department actually invites repetition of previous mistakes and militates against a learning culture. In a paper which discusses experiences from European Agencies, Thin (1998) makes a similar point. He draws attention to evaluation reports 'typically listing generic "lessons" which are in effect truisms that could have been found in any number of introductory guides to aid and development in the 1970s or earlier' (p. 13). He also highlights how evaluators frequently reiterate their importance, all of which are the 'most basic requirements in social planning which all developers should be aware of without having to be reminded by evaluation findings' (p. 13).

The importance of organisation, preparation and planning to make most effective use of resources is a second key theme (EVSUM 566, 1995). This covers what King et al (1998), in their higher education synthesis study, refer to as 'operational lessons', which relate to such things as project objectives, design and implementation. It is interesting to note that King et al point out that their study tends to 'reflect those insights about project development already gained from other DFID syntheses' (p. 5).

The third and perhaps strongest recurring theme to emerge from the evaluations referred to the importance of monitoring and evaluation. Comments such as 'Simple monitoring systems, in place from the start, are essential' (EVSUM 586, 1996) were typical. Reference to the lack of monitoring, evaluation and/or appraisal, evident in early reports, was still to be found in more recent reports. For example, in 1980, Griffiths & Ackroyd highlighted the 'lack of rigorous appraisal' by ODA and in 1982, Ball pointed to the fact that 'no system of monitoring or reporting was prescribed by ODA' (Ball et al, 1982, p. 30). Sixteen years later, King et al's (1998) synthesis report noted:

> The need for effective monitoring to be built into the project's design and implementation emerged strongly from the projects considered. Neglect of this aspect was commented upon in a number of the PCRs. (p. 28, para. 3.30)

More important, perhaps, there has been a noticeable change from initial references simply to the lack of monitoring and evaluation towards a clearer focus on the *type* of evaluations felt to be necessary. Archer & Cottingham (1996), for example, present the results of a 2-year action research project designed to monitor and evaluate pilot literacy projects (REFLECT) in three countries.[6] They argue for the need for continued close monitoring and evaluation of these pilot projects to determine both the longer term impact and sustainability of initial gains as well as 'the relevance and effectiveness of REFLECT in new contexts' (p. 93). Lubben et al (1995) also strongly advocated the importance and value of longer term qualitative evaluation methods. In relation to their evaluation of in-service support, they comment:

> *A strength is that data is collected over time and so there is a greater chance that an evaluator can gain a sense of the reality of understanding and implementation of a curriculum innovation in a natural teaching context rather than capture the after-glow of a positive INSET [in-service education and training] experience orchestrated by enthusiasts and usually (in our case) away from the reality of schools and pupils. (p. 27)*

The importance of research and evaluation of education programmes cannot be overstated and has been clearly exemplified in the case of Botswana. DFID has stated a commitment to investment in research as well as its dissemination in relation to development (DFID, 1997, para. 2.42). In addition, it is stated that they shall 'measure the effectiveness of our efforts, alongside others, against the targets' (DFID, 1997, Summary, section 2), going on to highlight the importance of knowing 'what will work and what will not work' as well as 'how best to tackle the problems of development'. The section of the White Paper (DFID, 1997, pp. 40-41) entitled 'Research: the new approach' is concluded with the statement that 'The Government sees continued investment in knowledge generation as a key element in achieving its aims and objectives for international development'. What we need to question is the extent to which this policy commitment translates into practice. The evidence points to a lack of lessons learnt and to a culture of bureaucratic evaluation which needs to be challenged by a call for a more professional approach to evaluation. We need to move beyond ideology, build on what we have achieved and identify *how* the ideology may be translated into practice. As Watson (1997) pointed out, education development is 'far more complex than politicians and aid agencies would have us believe' (p. 120). There is clearly a need for formative evaluation which is integral to project design, so that aid and development money is not wasted. The lack of progress in relation to this is evident in the literature. We turn now to a consideration of the experiences of 10 consultants/researchers.

The Experience of Overseas Consultants
Employed by ODA/DFID and British Council

The role of the consultant is far from simple. Of key importance are the skills of cross-cultural communication as well as competence in negotiation and diplomacy (Fry & Thurber, 1989; Leach, 1994; Chambers, 1997). This is clearly in addition to the obviously essential technical and professional skills required of education consultants. Cassen et al (1994) go further by highlighting the particular sensitivity of education, spanning as it does 'huge cultural differences' between school systems (p. 148).

There are a number of factors which impact on the effectiveness of consultants. Hills (1979, cited in Fry & Thurber, 1989) argues that we need to consider three dimensions: the recipient country context and attitudes; the donor's organisational context and attitudes; and the attitudes, qualities and competencies of the individual consultants. The interaction between the dimensions is complex. Arguably of crucial importance to the overall quality of the work carried out is the quality of the relationship between the consultant and the various stakeholders (Arthur & Preston, 1996). This relationship often takes time to build and Arthur & Preston (1996) warn of the problems of consultants who are 'caught in institutional relationships which may be obstructive to the consultancy' (p. 7), a point also made by Leach (1995) and Cassen et al (1994, p. 12). Chabbott (1998), drawing on work by Haas (1989, 1992), further argues that the consultants' effectiveness also lies in their ability to avoid becoming 'self-interested bureaucrats intent on securing resources for their organisations' (p. 215).

Within the context of an increasing number of organisations engaged in development work (Chabbott, 1998) as well as an increasing demand for education consultants, the nature of the role itself is changing. Arthur & Preston (1996) highlight moves to commercialisation and more short-term contracts. A key finding of their study is how tensions arise as market forces militate against the time and commitment necessary to ensure the quality and effectiveness of the consultancy. Within what they describe as a 'culture of cash driven haste' (p. 5), Arthur & Preston highlight late and restricted periods of contracting, pressures of time and multiple contracting within individual projects.

Some of the problems that have been highlighted in the literature were evident in the interview data obtained from the consultants/ researchers.

The experience of overseas consultants employed by ODA/DFID has always been difficult to obtain. The first impediment is the contract they sign. This contract ensures that they sign away the rights to the contents of the reports that they write. The reports are submitted to the department and rarely seen again. They rarely give rise to publications in academic or professional journals. However, the movement into print has become more frequent in recent years and should become even more frequent in the future, although at any stage the terms of the contracts could be enforced and permission to publish withheld.

The second impediment is the need not to publish anything that could embarrass or damage the reputation of any senior DFID officer or even the sensitivities of foreign governments. To do this might severely affect that consultant's employment and future income. The reluctance of any of our interviewees or informants to be identified testifies to the importance of this consideration.

The third major impediment is the lack of any incentive to publish. The exceptions to this are academics who are employed as consultants and are pressured by their academic departments to publish. The lack of incentive is nevertheless both real and important. It arguably derives partly from the almost complete lack of a 'learning culture' within DFID itself, the need to control the process of project development and evaluation as well as the contempt in which research is sometimes held by some senior DFID officers (see the examples that follow).

It follows that in order to get material from consultants, we have had to promise complete anonymity. The examples that follow are therefore altered in some respect to avoid the project or any person associated with it from being recognised. All except one (example 2) are derived from consultants who specialise in education.

Example 1

A newly arrived 'consultant' was in conversation with a senior ODA official at a reception organised by the High Commissioner in a developing country. When asked about his/her brief, he/she began to describe the part of it which involved initiating some small-scale research projects. The ODA official made clear that he had 'no time' for research. When asked why, he replied that it never told him anything that he did not know already. The consultant asked if that meant that he already knew all there was to know about all the problems associated with [the country in question]. The official turned abruptly and walked away.

Later, the consultant was reprimanded by his/her project director because he/she did not want any researcher unnecessarily affecting the outcome of the project. The complaint had come from the ODA official via the High Commissioner (1994).

Example 2

At a presentation/reception in the United Kingdom given to consultants by DFID officials to explain their new policies, a consultant asked what must be construed as a serious and important question: 'What structural and organisational changes had DFID in mind, in order to ensure the implementation of the new policies?'

The answer, given by a senior DFID official and presumably not intended as a joke, was as follows: In the past when there was a need for, say, an air traffic control tower, we built an air traffic control tower. In the future, we will carry out a survey to show how the air traffic control tower will alleviate poverty and then build the air traffic control tower (1997) – the clear implication being that the new policies to eliminate poverty would not entail much change within DFID. A new bureaucratic requirement would suffice.

Example 3

A consultant recently returned from an overseas assignment and having given some thought to the way projects were managed and evaluated, asked for talks with DFID officials to facilitate improvements. His/her attempts to make a contribution met with a polite refusal to do anything. However, more surprising for the consultant, it was revealed that there was little interest in evaluation within DFID beyond the formal bureaucratic requirement that an evaluation was reported on. In addition, it was made clear that a well-designed, properly carried out field evaluation (essential for process management) was rarely carried out. Indeed, it was an exception.

When officials were asked how they reported on a project that did not have a proper evaluation, the reply was that 'it was difficult'. It involved sifting through the paperwork, making use of what there was, and 'telling a story' (1997).

Example 4

A consultant brought in to carry out a post-factum assessment of a major project (it involved tens of millions of pounds) found that DFID's ability to support even a desk exercise was deeply flawed. There had been four major evaluation reports written on the project, but only one was available within DFID. There had been numerous consultants' reports written on the project, as many as three per year. Only a few were available. There had been a large number of case studies carried out 'in-country' and none were available within DFID.

All of this material had been produced during the life of the project, which had been wound up. DFID had had plenty of time to accumulate and make use of it. Even the bureaucratic job of assembling the material had not been accomplished satisfactorily and the consultant had the somewhat embarrassing job of recontacting the originators of the material and borrowing their copies. He/he was both astonished and embarrassed to have to proceed in this way but as he/she pointed out, at least the evaluation had been carried out and material was available. Some consultants working on parallel tasks had found that no comparable material existed on which to base their assessments (1997).

Example 5

An evaluator called to evaluate a medium-sized (£2 million) English language teaching project found that there had been *no* thought given to evaluation until a short time before it became due. He/she was sent project documents as a brief, expected to design his/her own evaluation and spend two periods of 2 weeks in-country collecting data before returning and writing an evaluation report. The project had failed to achieve many of its goals. Indeed, there were very few indications that there had been a need for the project in the first instance. There were several major structural problems within the project regarding the relationship between the regions and the centre, which also predictably militated against the project's success. Finally, the time sequence within the project meant that those returning from training in the United Kingdom with the language skills required to sustain the project had only at most 6 months to establish themselves. They had no training for the considerable organisational and managerial demands that were placed upon them. Moreover, one of the early trainees with an earmarked role in sustaining the project was almost immediately poached by another DFID project and sent back to the United Kingdom for more training totally unrelated to the first project.

These examples were obtained from interviews and conversations with a small number of consultants; they could be multiplied many times over from these interviews alone. If the sample were to be expanded, it is our feeling that the case could be strengthened beyond reasonable doubt.

It is important to realise the significance of the real effects of the lack of a culture of learning within DFID. In the first example, the illustration is representative of what happened to a badly designed, incompetently monitored and administered project. No evaluation took place during the project; bureaucratic delays and lack of control from DFID meant that some £2 million of taxpayers' money was wasted on the main part of the project, which produced none of its planned outcomes.

In the second example, an experienced and talented person resigned from their job which would have involved working with DFID and went to work elsewhere, with people who 'show some signs of understanding development work'.

In the third example, a considerable amount of work and experience, which should have been made available to people working on major projects funded by the British taxpayer, will probably be shelved and, to all intents and purposes, lost. The third and fourth examples illustrate the inner culture of DFID, which we have called a culture of ignorance, and which must be reformed before the kind of major effort to eliminate poverty envisaged in the White Paper has any chance of success.

The fifth case illustrates what we have described as bureaucratic evaluation. The evaluation was carried out because a new project director realised that very little had been achieved in the first year.[7] However, there was no management system made known to the consultant to take account of the evaluation report. In any case he/she considered that the evaluation report was too late to do any good. There had been no initial commitment to designing and planning a sound and useful process evaluation which could inform both the project management and DFID.

Contracting, Briefing and Reporting; some general points

The process of being contracted by the ODA/DFID was characterised by most interviewees as ad hoc, short term and usually with no follow-up after submitting the all-important final report. The process was typically described as follows:

> *The contracting officer obviously keeps a list of people who have worked for him in the past and adds to it on the recommendation of others. When a request for a consultant crosses his desk, he simply goes down his list until they find a suitable one. If they can't do it, he goes on to the next or takes a recommendation on a new face from the person who could not go. The problem is that it is ad hoc and short term. You could be asked to go to Vietnam for 6 months or Kenya for 2 weeks and be expected to leave tomorrow. (This is a composite quotation)*

The briefing by ODA/DFID as reported by consultants varied enormously in its detail, accuracy and the degree to which it was up to date. In the worst case, a senior ODA/DFID official mistook both the consultant and the country.

> *'Mike isn't it?'*
> *'No, Brian.'*
> *'Zambia, isn't it?'*
> *No, Zimbabwe.'*

The official then sent her/his secretary to find the required papers. She/he returned with material 18 months out of date and the official proceeded to brief the bewildered consultant on project issues that were no longer current. Fortunately, the consultant had already spoken (unofficially) with the project director. In the event, he/she was sent out to the project 6 months too late to have an effect on crucial decisions which determined the scope and success of the project. Soon after his/her delayed arrival, he/she realised that the major objectives of the project were unattainable.

In the best cases of induction/briefing, conferences/workshops were organised and all the known major issues were aired. Most examples fell well below this, and nearly all consultants reported simply receiving a selection of the relevant project documents which they might or might not have discussed over the telephone with the contracting official before leaving.

Whatever the quality of the induction or initiation of the consultant, the end of the contract was in almost all cases final: end of contract, end of contact. The final report disappeared into the files of DFID and no information was passed back about action taken as a result of the report, or indeed, if anyone took any notice of the report.[8] Generally it seemed consultants were brought in, given specific evaluation tasks and then expected to deliver and wait for their next contract.

In concluding this section of the evidence, it is possible to notice that the way DFID tends to treat evaluation consultants amounts to a peripheralisation. At the same time, the reservoir of available evaluation consultants means that DFID does not recruit a strong internal team of experienced evaluators. This absence means that evaluation reports can be shelved or used where convenient by powerful officials within the internal politics of DFID. As we have seen, there is no consistency even in storing reports that they have commissioned. These factors are all consistent with the notions of 'bureaucratic evaluation' and a culture of ignorance within DFID as an organisation.

Our third source of evidence derives from the experiences of one of the authors on a major education development project over a 10-year period.

The Andhra Pradesh Primary Education Project

Introduction

The Anhdra Pradesh Primary Education Project (APPEP) came to an end in 1996. It was widely accepted as a major project which had been successful and which had been competently and thoroughly evaluated. Nevertheless, it is unlikely that many of the major lessons learned from the evaluation will be incorporated into the design of future projects or that the successful strategies for evaluation will be incorporated in future policies. The APPEP evaluation is unusual in another respect. It has been written up in two journal articles and a chapter in a major collection of articles (Lacey et al, 1993; Cooper et al, 1996; Torrance et al, 1997). In addition, an evaluation handbook (Lacey et al, 1998) based on the experience of evaluating APPEP has been published. This chapter will therefore draw on and refer to this published material to establish the major parameters of the project and the part played by the evaluation.

The following account describes, in a nutshell, the project and its evaluation. In addition, it highlights the lessons learned from the evaluation and the relationship between the project, the evaluation, the British Council's field management and ODA.

The Project

The APPEP constituted the largest intervention into the provision and conduct of primary education in a developing country ever funded by the ODA. Including the pilot phase, it lasted for nearly 10 years (from 1984), with a gap of nearly 2 years, the 'bridging period', between phase 1 and phase 2.

Its major features were:

a school building programme (schools, classrooms and teacher centres);
a rolling programme of in-service education for all primary 1-5 teachers in the state and many district level officers;
a yearly distribution of materials for the construction of classroom teaching aids in line with the project philosophy;
a programme of professional development conducted via bimonthly Teachers' Centre meetings.

In the last 2 years of the project additional elements were added:

the preparation and publication of modern texts and readers for pupils, starting with year 1;
the start-up of a 'Social Project' to benefit underprivileged groups based on local democracy, the Village Education Committee (VEC);
the strengthening of Teachers' Centres through the provision of more resources and more teacher services.

The essential central strand of APPEP was to improve the traditional classroom practices of Andhra Pradesh primary schools, with their heavy reliance on rote learning methods and remote texts. To this end, the intention was to inject a powerful drive towards active learning, pupil participation and group work. At the core of this effort were the six APPEP principles:

the development of activity-based learning;
the use of practical work;
the use of small group work as well as whole-class teaching;
the recognition of individual differences in learning;
the use of the local environment for teaching materials and as a teaching context;
the display of children's work and the creation of an interesting classroom environment.

The Experience of Evaluation and Lessons Learned

The evaluation of the scheme was begun by Lacey in 1984, and Cooper and Torrance joined him for phase 2. They therefore represent a continuous consultancy on evaluation for the whole of the project. Despite this continuity and the obvious importance of experience and good ongoing relationships with the Indian project team, and despite requests from the British Council field management, the whole of this period was managed on the basis of 1-year contracts in which the uncertainties, delays and straightforward mistakes by ODA, associated with each contract, were a constant source of worry and distraction. The continuity of the evaluation depended on the insistence of field managers in India, who valued its products, rather than any ODA policy or strategy.

The early experience of evaluating the pilot phase of the project had shown that there were a number of substantial problems to be overcome before a reliable evaluation of such a large project could be achieved. These problems and some of the lessons learned can be listed as follows.

The lack of evaluation experience of local academics, education researchers and the available education service personnel meant that the existing levels of skill would need substantial upgrading and support.

Existing bureaucratic methods for collecting basic statistics on, for example, enrolments were deeply flawed – there were many documented cases of unreliable data.

The usual methods of large-scale baseline data collection could not provide a reliable or methodologically robust way of evaluating the effects of APPEP. The evaluation would need to rest on a comparative, over-time design within which there were many opportunities to cross-check and test data reliability and outcomes.

The evaluation would need to employ a wide variety of data collection methods from tests of achievement through interviews and questionnaires to case studies and participant observation.

The result of this review and early visits meant that a close collaborative association grew up between the evaluation cell of the project, the project directors, the British Council's field management team and the evaluation consultants. Within this arrangement, the evaluation consultants became responsible for the overall design of the evaluation, the design of the major instruments for collecting data, the design of the analysis of the results and for planning and guiding the writing of reports. In addition, the evaluation consultants provided a fail-safe system for much of the computer analysis so that when major errors occurred (as they did) or major data sets were lost (as they were), the consultants were able to get the evaluation back on the road.

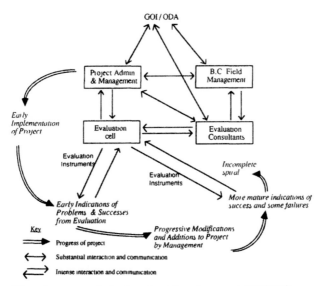

Figure 1. The virtuous spiral of project development (APPEP).

This description highlights the role of the consultants. The evaluation was nevertheless a genuine collaboration and team effort. The input of the Indian evaluation cell was local knowledge, a remarkable effort of organisation which at times involved the training and coordination of 92 lecturers from District Institutes of Education and Training (DIETs), collecting data and all the hard work of checking, coding and entering the data. In addition, some members of the evaluation cell carried out case studies along with over 20 DIET lecturers and workers from non-governmental organisations (NGOs). Finally, the drafting and production of evaluation reports was the responsibility of the project evaluation cell, although early drafts were usually the work of the consultants. This collaboration produced a viable system in which reports were on time, they were accurate and they addressed the major issues that the stakeholders expected. In short, they were useful and influenced the direction and planning of the project.

The evaluation was able to show that the project was taken up and practised in 30-40% of schools, a further 30% took it up partially and a further 30% made almost no attempts to implement it. In schools where it was taken up, pupils enjoyed school more and parents became aware of the project and the new learning experiences of their children. As the project became consolidated in schools and further developed in teacher centres, there was evidence of improved learning and better pupil attendance and enrolment. In fact, schools that were high on 'APPEPness' were protected against the encroachment of private schools, which were gaining ground in the state at that time. Finally, the evaluation was able to point to more substantial learning gains when a new textbook and readers were introduced, starting in year 1.

It is therefore possible to portray the development of the APPEP as a virtuous spiral in which the evaluation of the project played a crucial role.

It is important to point out that the 'success' of APPEP depended centrally on the very able and responsive British Council field managers and their teams, the hard work and dedication of the project personnel, and the responsiveness of ODA and the Government of India to the needs of the project. The role that we claim for 'evaluation' is a catalytic role. Without the catalyst, the reaction would have been very much weaker.

It is perhaps useful to illustrate some of the feedback from the evaluation that influenced the project's policy and implementation and development.

> It was pointed out that training materials were sometimes more suited to urban schools than rural situations.
> Training materials were initially narrow and repetitious; more room was required for diversity and innovation.
> The same schoolchildren, drawn from local schools, were used time and time again for demonstration lessons, with devastating effects on their keenness.
> The innovation did not contribute directly to solving rural poverty or specifically the education of underprivileged groups.
> There was a substantial demand from teachers for training in assessment that was in line with APPEP principles.
> Teacher mobility and absenteeism during training courses meant that 'untrained' teachers sometimes taught in 'trained' schools. This significantly reduced the effectiveness of the project (outcomes). 'Mop up' courses were targeted on these teachers.

It is also important to illustrate some of the technical and professional problems that needed to be solved before a reliable, ethical and robust evaluation could be produced.

> Freeing evaluation cell personnel from routine administrative monitoring so that they could concentrate on the designed, purposive evaluation (i.e. professional evaluation).
> Maintaining the integrity of the evaluation cell by preventing sideways transfers of experienced evaluation cell personnel (if the transfers were against their wishes) and working towards a professional role and status for cell personnel.
> Ensuring the confidentiality of individuals and individual schools and a professional commitment to accuracy and reporting relevant 'truths'.
> Fighting for suitable training for the evaluation cell against powerful bureaucrats who wished to promote their own candidates – not always successfully.

Jettisoning the traditional design of large-scale baseline studies with follow-ups and supplanting it with a robust, comparative, over-time design. The design expanded as the project progressed and allowed multiple comparisons synchronically and diachronically (trained v untrained, 1 year v 2 years after training, etc.)

Jettisoning the traditional dependency on official statistics or data collected in a similar way on enrolment and attendance, and replacing it with observations and data collected by trained fieldworkers.

Uncovering through case study work many of the reasons for inaccuracies within and falsification of attendance and enrolment data, for example, private schools.

Formulating data collection procedures (observations of classrooms, interviews of parents and pupils as well as teachers) that enable comparative data to be triangulated, thus guarding against the presentation of a 'rosy' picture.

Developing indices of implementation that summarised the many strands of APPEP and allowed comparison.

Developing attainment tests that were more in line with the aspirations of the new APPEP approach.

Creating a heuristic model of the innovation which helped simplify the presentation of complicated issues and helped to explain how the findings of the evaluation could be interpreted.[9]

Judged from the above list and a critical perspective, the APPEP evaluation had produced more useful information than most previous project evaluations, and it was now important that the lessons learned should be passed on through publications and ODA/DFID workshops and seminars to other projects, in particular, DPEP (the District Primary Education Programme), which was to replace APPEP in Andhra Pradesh. This was also the view of ODA/British Council officials who had worked closely with the project and made funds available for the writing of the evaluation handbook. In addition, workshops in India were promised, funds to secure the APPEP database in Hyderabad were recommended, and once again, there was optimistic support for training evaluators and funding research studentships for Indian graduates. The evaluation handbook was produced on time but the officials that supported the recommendations moved on to other jobs and none of these recommendations came about. Instead, there followed a slow process of death by a thousand delays, broken undertakings, misrepresentation, and finally, an attempt to shelve the whole experience. It is important to try to understand why this came about.

Discussion

The APPEP evaluation had been an unusual case. The field management of the project had been handled by the British Council.[10] The British

Council field managers had brought in the Sussex team to underpin the Indian evaluation and ensure a technically competent, professional evaluation. The evaluation of the pilot project ensured that the evaluation of phase 2 (the main project) was designed on previous experience and the long period of cooperation and team work ensured a deep learning and well-established relationships for all participants. This enabled findings to be fed-back to management, enabled management to respond and finally enabled the evaluation to produce new findings, based on the improved project procedures and practices. However, this had been achieved through a number of factors fortuitously coming together. The ODA officials most closely associated with the project, and the British Council field managers (only two during the life of the project) had a good working relationship and an understanding of the role of evaluation. The British Council field managers were responsible for the project budget, which included a budget for evaluation. They were therefore able to protect the evaluation team from the worst aspects of ODA bureaucratic regulation and short-term contracts. They ensured sufficient funds, negotiated flexible contracts that enabled the consultancy needs of the Indian Evaluation Cell to be met in full, ensured freedom of publication and made full use of the evaluation findings. Most important of all, they ensured that a 'culture of learning' pervaded the APPEP and all who became associated with it became aware of the power and potential of the project.

In contrast to this arrangement, many projects do not have an independent budget for evaluation. In fact, some projects are not evaluated at all although all projects are bureaucratically monitored.[11] In a substantial number of cases, where project evaluations take place, they are organised and funded by the Evaluation Department. However there is a strong tendency, in DFID and other similar agencies, for project development to be given priority and for evaluation to take second place, or to be totally neglected. Within DFID, a small Evaluation Department has the enormous and probably impossible task of monitoring and coordinating the evaluation of projects across the full range of departments. In this context, evaluation becomes a bureaucratic procedure with 'accountability' as its major function. The issue of learning about project development through evaluation becomes an almost impossible task. The broader issues of evaluation and sustainability can and do remain important concerns for some individuals but the central organisation cannot support them and sporadic initiatives are not sufficient to give them a prominent place within the culture of the organisation.

In the absence of a cultural or organisation platform within DFID for an evaluation team (such as APPEP) to feed back their experiences or lessons learned, the attempt to achieve an organised feedback was likely to be doomed to failure. The bureaucratic procedures governing evaluation have their own pace and in the absence of an open learning culture based on evidence, powerful individuals can play an important role in defining success, failure and relevance.

This process by which the department creates its own internal definition of success and relevance was first encountered by the APPEP evaluation team when a team member gave a paper to a seminar within ODA. The paper concentrated on the major evaluation issues and how they were solved or at least 'understood'. The subsequent discussion completely ignored these issues. Instead, the most senior person at the seminar pointed out that the evaluation had been 'expensive', 'too complex' and had taken 'too long'. It had been a 'Rolls Royce' of an evaluation when in fact the department needed 'Model T Ford' evaluations. Instead, they should look to techniques like 'rapid rural appraisal', which had been so successful within the agricultural setting, and apply these cheaper, quicker techniques to education. This intervention completely changed the nature of the seminar as each official then criticised the *project* (not the evaluation) and explained how their *projects* met these criticisms and then added a rider on how 'rapid rural appraisal' could be used to evaluate them. It was clear that 'rapid rural appraisal' was now 'flavour of the month', and it was important for career progression within ODA/DFID to be seen to be conversant with its rhetoric.

The APPEP evaluation has, subsequently, been subjected to two evaluations by independent consultants (Montgomery et al, 1996; Steward & Felton, 1998), funded by the ODA/DFID. It is impossible to uncover the motivations for these evaluations but it is surprising that DFID needed to fund two evaluations of an evaluation to find out the 'lessons learned' when they were clearly stated in the original evaluation and management reports.

The following quotations summarise the findings of the first evaluation of the evaluation on points relevant to the major criticisms.

APPEP's main surveys were based on an elaboration of the basic principles of robust impact designs. The strengths of the study were partly due to careful preparation (of design features, data collector training) and a pilot survey.

The main surveys were directly useful to project management. They identified shortcomings at the level of project outputs at various stages.

The results of the class 2 textbook impact assessment is a good example of how a small but robust study can influence policy.

These case studies injected some realism into the evaluation process, thereby tempering over-optimistic expectations ...

319

> *APPEP's evaluation system is estimated to have cost approximately 1.1% of the total cost of £27m. These costs appear low in relation to the importance of the information provided for both project management and those at policy level. (Montgomery et al, 1996)*

The second evaluation of the evaluation was similarly supportive.

> *APPEP II had a strong evaluation component built into the project. This seems to make it very different from other ODA-funded education projects, and it is not clear why there was such a significant difference in approach. For example, the cost of the evaluation of APPEP amounted to about 1.5% of the total project cost. This may be compared with 0.04% allocated to monitoring and evaluation for SPRED (Kenya). This raises the issue of a possible lack of consistent policy about the role of monitoring and evaluation in ODA education projects during the late 1980s and early 1990s ...*

> *Although there was a substantial lead time between the collection of data for the Main Surveys and the publication of results [approx. 1 year], it seems clear that information obtained by means of evaluation was available to the project and field management in good time. This enabled those responsible for the implementation of the project to review and reflect on the quality of implementation and make changes, where feasible and appropriate. (Steward & Felton, March 1998)*

It will be interesting to see how DFID responds to the final post-factum evaluation. Certainly, in the 3 years since the APPEP evaluation effectively ended, the team that undertook the evaluation has experienced complete peripheralisation. The evaluation recommendations, particularly those relating to the training of evaluators and the sustainability of the project, have been ignored. The proposed workshops have not taken place and more importantly, the handbook on evaluation remains a neglected asset not useful to the DPEP evaluation. The ODA/DFID have almost willed the dust to settle on the APPEP evaluation by countenancing never-ending delays in an interminable process.[12] The culture of bureaucratic evaluation remains dominant and it seems that few lessons will be learned from the APPEP evaluation.

Conclusions

The review of the literature relating to education development projects makes it clear that they have not been credited with very much success. The literature describes a history of failure. The ODA/DFID as an organisation seems to be more bound up with the practice of bureaucratic evaluation and its own internal politics than 'learning' through the evaluation of projects. The issue of learning through evaluation has not been taken up and a culture of learning does not seem to have been created. As a result, DFID is not in a position to make use of constructive criticism within the literature, which therefore exhibits a pattern of recommendations which repeats itself every 3 or 4 years.

The evidence from the consultants confirms this view. Consultants are brought in on an ad hoc basis. They rarely achieve a close long-term relationship with a project, which is an important ingredient in a successful evaluation. The policy of the department, as illustrated in the literature review and evidence from consultants, has been to peripheralise these 'consultants'. The effect has been to exclude them from planning and from seeing through competent evaluations by bureaucratising the process and making individual consultants dependent on frequent short-term contracts with no promise of future employment. They are brought in late, their reports are separated from them and used by the department or ignored.

The issue becomes, what can be done to ensure that the lessons learned from present-day projects are translated into policy and improved project design? Some steps have already been taken within DFID. There is a willingness to espouse the notion of process managed projects, there is a commitment to monitoring project progress and there is a commitment to impact evaluation via the log-frame and consultants brought in to evaluate a proportion of the projects. Unfortunately, these provisions do not amount to a coherent system, sufficient to maintain a culture of learning. This is especially the case in a government department that, by its nature, has to operate across a wide range of different cultures and languages in an area (development) where there are few certainties and massive political difficulties (issues of power and wealth distribution). These are formidable difficulties.

In addition, a large government department, like DFID, has inherited a bureaucratic structure and culture, many elements of which militate against the emergence of a strong culture of learning. The issues of learning through evaluation are not adequately provided for, through the provision of monitoring and log-frame evaluation, which becomes a predominantly bureaucratic form of evaluation. This bureaucratic perspective ensures that the consultants remain peripheral and their evaluation reports are used largely to justify expenditure and satisfy bureaucratic procedures. It will be extremely difficult for individuals working within DFID to overcome these difficulties without substantial reform to internal processes and a new set of priorities within the organisation. This in turn requires political action and a full realisation of the problems faced by DFID. This is unlikely to happen unless there is a full and open public debate about these issues.

This chapter has not been based on a rigorous research design. It gains its strength from examining evidence from three disparate sources, the research literature, interviews with a small number of ODA/DFID employed consultants and the in-depth experience obtained through one large-scale evaluation. Nevertheless, those three sources point to substantial difficulties (in at least one important sector) in the way of implementing the goals of the new government White Paper. These problems are deeply imbedded in the bureaucratic culture of DFID, which we have characterised as a culture of ignorance. This represents a strong critique of an aspect of development that has hitherto remained relatively unchallenged. We argue that the evidence to support this critique is substantial and hope that it will release the energy for reform that will be essential if the Department for International Development is to meet the challenges that it presently confronts.

Acknowledgements

The authors wish to acknowledge the help of a large number of individuals, who have read this chapter or who have helped in other ways but who wish to remain anonymous. Since delivering the original paper at the Inaugural Conference of the British Association of International and Comparative Education, we have received support and useful criticism from a number of unexpected quarters, including ex-DFID staff, all of whom have been anxious that our promise of confidentiality be rigorously applied. In particular, the authors would like to thank Professor Harry Torrance and Dr Janet Stuart, who made helpful comments on an earlier draft.

Notes

[1] There is substantial literature on development aid and much of it is critical. The critical literature ranges from writers like Seers (1983), Myrdal (1970, 1982), Mende (1973) and Madeley (1995), who do not abandon the moral argument for aid but who argue for substantial structural change affecting policies and institutional competence, to writers like Hancock (1991) who directs his criticism directly at the institutions who manage aid, for example, ODA, the EEC and the UN. He argues for stopping aid in its present form and ousting the 'lords of poverty'. His criticisms focus on the way that much aid ignores the interests of the poor and contributes to poverty. He is particularly scathing about aid officials who are too closely associated with the interests of international firms, who are arrogant and ignorant about the lives of the poor and who enjoy high salaries and a luxurious lifestyle. He argues that official aid agencies who employ them are not directly accountable to the public and are not transparent, open and honest in their dealings. His book is packed with evidence and case studies, much

of it derived from his own travels and experience. In contrast to the critical literature, Cassen et al (1994) argue that the great majority of aid for development work is successful in meeting its objectives.

[2] This 'experience' involves the results of interviews and conversations with 10 consultants/researchers, who have had a first-hand experience of projects funded by DFID, and 10 plus years of consultancy with ODA/DFID.

[3] These interviews represent an opportunity sample. There is no readily available information about the total population of education consultants employed by DFID. Hence, there is no basis for constructing a random or stratified sample. The interviews are nevertheless with a group of senior and experienced people who have had a wide range of experience – some of it outside the education sector. In addition to these interviews a number of DFID staff were spoken to about these issues. They were not formal interviews. Nevertheless, these conversations inform our analysis and include individuals from a range of departments, for example, Education, Evaluation and Statistics.

[4] The first by Pennycuick (1993), the latest at the time of writing, number 24 (Williams, 1998).

[5] The main data sources were DFID's Evaluation and Statistical Departments as well as their web site. Each department cooperated fully with requests, supplying data they had available on project evaluations and the former providing copies of (available) evaluation summaries (EVSUMS). However, the lack of coordination between the two departments contributed to an inability to achieve a complete data set, e.g. to establish the percentage of education projects evaluated each year. The difficulties described in this footnote and the paragraph illustrate the apparent lack of importance of these evaluations to ongoing planning and design of new projects.

[6] The REFLECT programmes were developed with the help of the NGO ACTIONAID and were conceived of as starting points, to be evaluated for their effectiveness and used as a source of learning for other literacy programmes in other countries and regions.

[7] It is interesting to note that new project directors sometimes call for an evaluation. A new director taking over a project which is in serious trouble will wish for this to be known at the earliest possible date so that they are not blamed for the failure. There were two examples of this phenomenon in the interviews.

[8] There has been one notable exception to this pattern but it is difficult to know if this has happened because of initiatives within DFID or because a consultant wrote and made representations about 'the end of contract, end of contact' policy.

[9] This is not an exhaustive list. It does, however, illustrate the substantial contribution made by the evaluation team in finding solutions to obdurate problems that had confounded many previous evaluations.

[10] There are a variety of avenues for commissioning evaluations. The most common is for evaluators to be brought in at a late stage in the project and commissioned by ODA officials. This practice severely limits the contribution that even the most talented evaluation consultants can make. It is interesting to note that even APPEP consultants had to 're-apply' each year for a new contract. This bureaucratic requirement added substantially to the stress and workload of the Sussex team.

[11] We have made a clear distinction in this chapter between bureaucratic evaluation and professional evaluation. The term 'bureaucratic monitoring' refers to the process of monitoring visits carried out by DFID staff as a routine method of checking the progress of projects and facilitating development and accountability.

[12] The final report on the APPEP evaluation, with recommendations, will be written by yet another external consultant who will have the benefit of the Steward & Felton evaluation and three other project evaluations.

References

Archer, D. & Cottingham, S. (1996) *Action Research Reform on REFLECT: regenerated Freirean literacy through empowering community techniques: the experiences of three REFLECT projects in Uganda, Bangladesh and El Salvador.* Serial no. 17. London: Overseas Development Administration (ODA).

Arthur, L. & Preston, R. (1996) *Quality in Overseas consultancy: understanding the issues.* British Council Professional Services.

Ball, J.G., De, A.K., Geddes, W.G., Gopalan, K., Hunting, G.A. & Stevens, J.N. (1982) *Evaluation of IIT Delhi/British Universities Research Collaboration: a joint British Government (ODA/FCO) Indian Government (Ministry of Education) evaluation of the research collaborations by departments of UK universities and the Indian Institute of Technology in New Delhi.* EV 265. London: ODA.

Blau, P. (1955) *The Dynamics of Bureaucracy.* Chicago: University of Chicago Press.

Botswana Ministry of Education & US Agency for International Development (1990) *Botswana Primary Education Improvement Project: Phase II: 1986-1991. Seventh Report, September 1 1989–February 28 1990.* Gaborone: University of Botswana.

Bray, M. (1991) *Making Small Practical: the organisation and management of ministries of education in small states.* London: Commonwealth Secretariat.

Brock, C. & Cammish, N. (1997) *Gender, Education and Development: a partially annotated and selective bibliography.* Serial no. 19. London: Department for International Development.

Burns, T. & Stalker, G. M. (1961) *The Management of Innovation.* London: Tavistock.

Cassen, R. & Associates (1994) *Does Aid Work?* (2nd edn). Oxford: Clarendon Press.

Chabbott, C. (1998) Constructing Educational Consensus: international development professionals and the World Conference on Education for All, *International Journal of Educational Developoment,* 18, pp. 207-228.

Chambers, R. (1997) *Whose Reality Counts? Putting the First Last.* London: Intermediate Technology.

Cooper, B., Lacey, C. & Torrance, H. (1996) Making Sense of Large-scale Evaluation Data: the case of the Andhra Pradesh Primary Education Project, *International Journal of Educational Development,* 16, pp. 125-140.

Department for International Development (1997) *Project Impact on Livelihood and Farming Systems.* New Delhi.

Department for International Development (1997) Eliminating World Poverty: a challenge for the 21st century, White Paper presented by the Secretary of State for International Development.

Dyer, C. (1994) Education and the State: policy implementation in India's federal polity, *International Journal of Educational Development,* 14, pp. 241-253.

Eyben, R. (1998) *Poverty and Social Exclusion: north-south links.* London: Department for International Development (DFID).

Foreign and Commonwealth Office (1997) *Foreign and Commonwealth Office including Overseas Development Administration 1997 Departmental Report. The Government's Expenditure Plans 1997-98 to 1999-00.* London: HMSO.

Fry, G.W. & Thurber, C.E. (1989) *The International Education of the Development Consultant. Communicating with Peasants and Princes.* Oxford: Pergamon Press.

Fullan, M. (1982) *The Meaning of Educational Change.* Ontario: OISE Press.

Glaser, B. & Strauss, A. (1967) *The Discovery of Grounded Theory.* London: Weidenfeld & Nicolson.

Gouldner, A. (1955) *Patterns of Industrial Bureaucracy.* London: Routledge & Kegan Paul.

Griffiths, I. & Ackloyd, P.J. (1980) *Evaluation of the Birkbeck/Bangalore Chemistry Link.* EV 231. London: ODA.

Haas, P.M. (1989) Do Regimes Matter? Epistemic Communities and Mediterranean Pollution Control, *International Organization,* 43, pp. 377-403.

Haas, P.M. (1992) Knowledge, Power and International Policy Co-ordination, *International Organization,* 46(1).

Hancock, G. (1991) *Lords of Poverty.* Mandarin.

Havelock, R.G. (1970) *A Guide to Innovation in Education.* Ann Arbor: Center for Research on Utilization of Scientific Knowledge, University of Michigan.

Hills, R.C. (1979) *Technical Assistance: towards improving the underlying framework.* Development Studies Centre, ANU, Occasional Paper no. 14.

Hopkin, A. (1994) Aid, Education and Development in Botswana: a qualitative analysis, *International Journal of Educational Development,* 14, pp. 393-407.

Jones, P.W. (1992) *World Bank Financing of Education: lending, learning and development.* London: Routledge.

King, K.J. (1991) *Aid and Education in the Developing World: the role of the donor agencies in educational analysis*. Harlow: Longman.

King, K., Ashworth, R. & Girdwood, A. (1998) *Higher Education Synthesis Study, Evaluation Report EV602*. London: Department for International Development.

Lacey, C. & Jacklin, A. (1999) Training teachers for a small island system: short term and long term outcomes, *International Journal of Educational Development* (forthcoming).

Lacey, C. & Torrance, H. (1998) Evaluating Education Development Projects: technical competence and political agendas. Paper prepared for the UK Evaluation Society Annual Conference, 3-5 December 1998.

Lacey, C., Cooper, B. & Torrance, H. (1993) Evaluating the Andhra Pradesh Primary Education Project: problems of design and analysis, *British Educational Research Journal*, 19, pp. 535-554.

Lacey, C., Cooper, B. & Torrance, H. (1998) *The Evaluation of Large Scale Education Development Projects: a handbook for evaluators based on the evaluation of the Andhra Pradesh Primary Education Project (APPEP)*. Brighton: University of Sussex Institute of Education.

Leach, F. (1991) Perception Gaps in Technical Assistance Projects: the Sudanese case, in K. Lewin & J. Stuart (Eds) *Educational Innovation in Developing Countries. Case-studies of Changemakers*. London: Macmillan.

Leach, F. (1994) Expatriates as Agents of Cross-cultural Transmission, *Compare*, 24, pp. 217-231.

Leach, F. (1995) Development Projects and their Host Institutions: are they compatible? *International Review of Education*, 41, pp. 459-479.

Lockheed, M.E. & Hanushek, E. (1988) Improving Educational Efficiency in Developing Countries: what do we know? *Compare*, 18, pp. 21-38.

Lubben, F., Campbell, B. & Dlamini, B. (1995) *In-service Support for a Technological Approach to Science Education*. Serial no. 16. London: ODA.

MacDonald, B. (1977) A political classification of evaluation studies, in D. Hamilton et al (Eds) *Beyond the Numbers Game*. Basingstoke: Macmillan.

Madeley, J. (1995) *When Aid is no Help*. London: Intermediate Technology Publications.

Mende, T. (1973) From Aid to Recolonisation: lessons of a failure. London: Harrap.

Merton, R.K. (1936) The Unanticipated Consequences of Purposive Social Action, *American Sociological Review*, 1(16).

Merton, R.K. (1965) Bureaucratic Structure and Personality, in A. Etzioni (Ed.) *Complex Organisations*. New York: Holt, Rinehart & Winston.

Montgomery, R., Davies, R., Saxona, N.C. & Ashley, S. (1996) Guidance Materials for Improved Project Monitoring and Impact Review Systems in India, presented at a Workshop, 14-15 March.

Morrison, J. (1990) Sustaining Education Projects Overseas through Training in Britain, in K. Watson (Ed.) *Educational Quality and Educational Development Issues in the 1990s*. Reading: Faculty of Education and

Community Studies, University of Reading in association with Education for Development.

Myrdal, G. (1970) *The Challenge of World Poverty.* London: Allen Lane, Penguin.

Myrdal, G. (1982) Relief Instead of Development Aid, *Scandinavian Journal of Developing Countries,* 1(4).

Oakley, P., Pratt, B. & Clayton, A. (1998) *Outcomes and Impact: evaluating change in social development.* Oxford: INTRAC.

Overseas Development Administration (ODA) (1990) *Into the Nineties: an education policy for British aid.* London: ODA.

Overseas Development Administration (1995) *Project Monitoring and Impact Systems in India.* London: ODA.

Overseas Development Administration (1995-96) *Record of the Working Group Discussion on Monitoring and Impact Review Systems.* London: ODA.

Pennycuick, D. (1993) *School Effectiveness in Developing Countries: a summary of the research evidence.* London: ODA.

Seers, D. (1983) 'Time for a Second Look at the Third World', *Development Policy Review,* 1(1) May.

Stephens, D. (1990) The Quality of Primary Education in Developing Countries: who defines and who decides? in K. Watson (Ed.) *Educational Quality and Educational Development Issues in the 1990s.* Reading: Faculty of Education and Community Studies, University of Reading in association with Education for Development.

Steward, J. & Felton, A. (1998) *Evaluation of the Andhra Pradesh Primary Education Project* (Draft) March 1998. London: Department for International Development.

Thin, N. with Good, T. & Hodgson, R. (1998) Social Development Policies, Results and Learning: a multi-agency review. London: DFID.

Thin, N. (1998) *Social Development Policies, Results and Learning: experiences from European agencies.* London: DFID.

Torrance, H., Lacey, C. & Cooper, B. (1997) The Role of Evaluation in Large-scale Educational Interventions: lessons from the Andhra Pradesh Primary Education Project, in J. Lynch, C. Modgil & S. Modgil (Eds) *Education and Development: tradition and innovation. Vol. 1. Concepts, Approaches and Assumptions.* London: Cassell.

Verspoor, A. (1993) More than Business-as-Usual: reflections on the new modalities of education aid, *International Journal of Educational Development,* 13, pp. 103-112.

Watson, K. (1984) External and Internal Obstacles to Educational Development, in K. Watson (Ed.) *Dependence and Interdependence in Education: international perspectives.* London: Croom Helm.

Watson, K. (1997) Editorial, *International Journal of Educational Development,* 17, p. 120.

White, J. & Stewart, I. (1987) *Joint ODA British Council Evaluation of the English Language Component of Moharrem Bey Technical School Project in Alexandria, Egypt. EV 451.* London: ODA.

Williams, E. (1998) *Investigating Bilingual Literacy: Evidence from Malawi and Zambia.* (Serial No. 24). London: DFID.

EVSUM Reports Available

1987

EVSUM 497 Training in Britain for the Indian Coal Industry

EVSUM 451 Egypt: English Language Component of Moharrem Bey Technical School Project

EVSUM 420 Abbassai Biomedical Training Project, Arab Republic of Egypt

1988

EVSUM 442 Indonesia LAN/RIPA Training Project

EVSUM 403 English for Yemen Textbook Project

EVSUM 436 Evaluation of the Low Priced Book Scheme (LPBS)

1989

None

1990

EVSUM 487 Eastern and Southern Africa Management Institute

EVSUM 472 Indian Railways: Training project for the modernisation of workshops

EVSUM 499 ODA's Caribbean Training Programme

EVSUM 525 Training Synthesis Evaluation Study

1991 and 1992

None

1993

EVSUM 551 Uganda Public Administration, Training and Institutional Development Project (PATID)

EVSUM 545 Aga Khan Foundation's School Improvement Programme

1994

EYSUM 559 Synthesis Study of Institutional Strengthening Projects

EVSUM 511 Baseline Study of English Language Teaching, Guinea

EVSUM 485 Role and Design of Baseline Studies in the Evaluation of English Language Teaching: the case of Nepal.

1995

EVSUM 566 HM Customs & Excise's Overseas Training Programme on Drug Law Enforcement

1996

EVSUM 586 Ghana Literacy Project

EVSUM 585 ODA Support to Strategic Management Inputs, University of Zambia

EVSUM 581 ODA Support to the Faculty of Engineering, University of Zimbabwe

EVSUM 579 Evaluation of ODA Assistance to Indira Gandhi National Open University (IGNOU)

1997 and 1998

None

Classifying Out of School Education

ROY CARR-HILL,
GABRIEL CARRON & EDWINA PEART

The International Standard Classification of Education (ISCED) was designed in the early 1970s to serve as an instrument for assembling, compiling and presenting statistics of education both within individual countries and internationally. The classification was essentially developed within the schools and college system. This institutional bias ignored attempts to broaden access. However, there have been several changes over the last quarter century, such as:

the multiplication and growth of different forms of vocational education and training;
the increasing diversity of education providers; and
the increasing recourse to distance education and other modalities based on new technologies.

The purpose of this chapter is to document the range and variety of terms used to describe and classify 'out-of-school' education (inverted commas indicating that we are not pre-empting the whole issue of definition by using such a term), and suggest ways in which some adaptation of these classifications can be made compatible with ISCED 1997.

I Background

I.1 Summary of Theoretical Debates

There has been a very long theoretical debate about the nature and appropriate ways of classifying education taking place outside the 'standard' school or college system, These debates can be summarised as follows.

'Non-formal' versus formal and other distinctions. The term 'non-formal', was introduced by Coombs et al (1973). It seemed a useful way of characterising those learning activities which were organised – and therefore distinct from the 'informal learning' which takes place all the

time in the family and social environment without being 'formally' recognised as education – but distinct from the 'standard' programmes in school and college especially because, at the time, the latter tended to be organised in a very formal and hierarchical fashion in most countries.

On the whole, there has been no serious disagreement that it is appropriate to distinguish between informal learning and all other educational activities simply by the fact of organisation. However, subsequent authors have shown that the label 'non-formal' education (NFE) is unhelpful and unsatisfactory in that the activities cannot be systematically distinguished in terms of the degree of 'formality' – or indeed along any other dimension (e.g. strength of links with the local community, extrinsic or intrinsic nature of programme). Several other terms have been suggested but they have all encountered a similar set of problems: there are too many overlaps between the types of education proposed in such classifications to be useful for collecting data or for use internationally. For example, the proposed distinction between 'adult' and 'regular' education made by the previous ISCED in the mid-1980s proved unsatisfactory in practice because many of those enrolled in programmes outside the 'regular' education system were of school-going age (Carr-Hill & Lintott, 1985). Indeed, the International Institute of Educational Planning adopted the formulation 'the diversified educational field' in the mid-1980s to describe its research programme precisely so as to avoid the confusions surrounding the definition of NFE.

Does the fact of enrolment distinguish? Whilst the argument here is, therefore, that the ISCED division between adult and regular is not helpful, it might be thought that the distinction drawn by the UNESCO Office of Statistics – rather confusingly – between formal and non-formal adult education, where the dividing criterion is not the degree of formality (or any other theoretically-based division) but the presence of absence of registration, is a valuable one. For the point can be generalised: different types of programmes collect, record and transmit different sets of data, and, for the purposes of compiling an inventory of programmes or of stocktaking the level of activity, types of programmes need to be differentiated by their relationship to organised data collection instruments as much as by any educational or even management criteria.

The problem is that, on this basis, an inventory of NFE programmes or a compilation of data from institutions would be dominated by the threefold division into programmes for which enrolment or registration data are systematically reported, programmes whose existence is recognised, and others. In consequence, any subsequent classification, however potentially interesting for policy purposes, is unlikely to provide reliable information because this original division is arbitrary in educational management and policy terms. For example, the next most coherent division would probably be by type of sponsor because they are the reporting agencies (at least for data on programmes). Generally – although not universally – those programmes organised by branches of the Ministries of Education or by parastatals will collect, record and transmit relatively detailed registration data, whilst programmes organised by voluntary agencies are likely to transmit only summary registration data to any central agency, and there will be overlaps as well as many omissions. A breakdown by 'type of sponsor', will, therefore, be restricted to the summary level of information and even then with incomplete coverage.

This demonstrates the difficulties of devising a unified *approach* to, let alone a unified *system* of, classifying NFE. This should not be surprising, for one of the presumed characteristics of the range of NFE programmes is their flexibility and independence from centralised control. In a certain sense, one should talk not in terms of a diversified educational field, but diversified fields of education. These issues all have implications for the kind of information base which should be developed (reviewed in Carron & Carr-Hill, 1991).

Proposed solutions. It may be sensible to group together out-of-school educational activities under one rubric. It probably makes sense to exclude casual learning which accompanies some other activity, such as the educational value of participating in a cultural event (whether that be a football match, initiation rites or an opera). But the basic point is that the various components of education have arisen in different contexts for different reasons and with different social referents.

Hamadache (1993) also argues that the concept of NFE is broad and can only be defined in each specific context: 'It would be impossible, indeed pointless, to give this concept a single, universal definition, as what distinguishes NFE is the variety of forms it can take on in response to the different demands and needs of different individuals or groups' (p. 113).

Different contexts, different concerns. The concerns are different in developing and 'over-serviced' countries. In developing countries, on the whole, there are three basic types of NFE: those which are a complement of formal education, targeting those who for various reasons have 'failed' or are excluded, e.g. drop-outs or adult illiterates; those which are alternative in that they were based on the unwillingness or inability of the colonial educational administrators – and often the administrators of the early independence period – to accept and recognise that there had been pre-existing teaching and learning structures; or a supplement because of the failures of the educational system to respond sufficiently rapidly to changes in the global economic environment.

In over-serviced countries, basic education has been guaranteed to the vast majority of the population by the state school system, so that what has come to be called NFE has focused on complementary activities such as vocational and, increasingly, cultural education and learning.

Household surveys. An alternative approach to documenting the diversified fields of education is to develop client-based data collection exercises of the sample household surveys type. They respond to a precise and important need of the central policy-maker to know about the pattern of expressed demand for the various components of the diversified educational field. They are not a substitute for the institution-based data collection systems but should be seen as complementary.

However, the essential preliminary for such a survey is a reasonably reliable sampling frame. In many developing countries, this poses a problem. Even assuming an adequate sampling frame exists, a dedicated survey to estimate adult participation in educational activities would obviously be expensive. However, several (over-serviced) countries have now experimented with one-page add-ons to the labour force surveys.

I.2 Organisation of this Chapter

The purpose of the next section is to move beyond these 'sterile' definitional debates to examine how, in practice, educational systems in different countries have been changing and reforming in the last decade. This is a preamble to a review of how countries have gone about the problem of classifying out-of-school education in country publications and statistical reports in section III. The chapter concludes with an initial discussion of the possibility of developing a classification of the types of education in the diversified field of education.

II Developments during the Last 10 Years

II.1 The Experiences of Different World Regions

II.1.1 Industrialised (OECD) countries. A Report from the Centre for Educational Research and Innocation (CERI) (part of the Organisation for Economic Cooperation and Development) (OECD/CERI, 1995) suggests that adult education and training have been given new priority because of economic changes. Other aims should not be ignored, such as education's role in facilitating participation in society. Areas that currently concern governments include making citizens more effective consumers of services, better able to support the education of their children, and demographic trends which show that the proportion of children is shrinking.

The economic context. Tabbron & Yang (1997) also argue that the shift towards the tertiary sector:

*has close association with several other changes. Firstly, the
economy becomes more knowledge intensive. Secondly, more
and more employees become involved directly with customers.
Thirdly, new technologies such as information technology, are
playing a more important role. (Tabbron & Yang, 1997, p. 324)*

Growing importance of 'adult' education. These changes, coupled with
the changing demographic situation and lasting unemployment, mean
that:

*No longer can industry select its workforce and leave the rest
for low-skilled jobs. Many companies are likely to be forced to
look for workers among groups they once ignored. (Tabbron &
Yang, 1997, p. 326)*

These projections suggest that 'adult' education will become a bigger
priority (inverted commas because, regardless of the legal age of majority
in these countries, many of those taking these courses have peers who
are following 'standard' track courses); and that new types of skills are
also identified as becoming more important:

*Education and training systems in the developed countries are
facing tremendous pressures to equip the human resources
urgently demanded by the economies. (Tabbron & Yang, 1997,
p. 328)*

Individual countries have presented a variety of responses to these
issues. For example: attempts to combine general and vocational
education, and to ease the transition between the two; training for
generalisable skills (Atchoarena, 1996). In general, this has tended to
lead to a reduction in the range of technical and vocational education
and training (TVET) and a preference for more generalised TVET.

At the same time, however, cooperation has been growing between
education and employment authorities; and, in some countries – for
example, Australia and the United Kingdom – the education and
employment ministries have been merged. In addition, the overall
societal trends towards decentralisation and privatisation have also had
their impact, with delivery systems for public sector provision being
decentralised and the funding, curriculum development, and delivery for
adult retraining shared between public and private sectors.

II.1.2 Middle income countries. One of the areas identified by Jomtien is
that of adult literacy and continuing education. These examples illustrate
the trend.

In Thailand, functional literacy programmes for adults have been
established, run by the department of non-formal education, which
developed from the adult education division. It has three major sections:
adult general and basic education, providing formal equivalency from

basic literacy to upper secondary level; vocational and interest programmes, to improve existing knowledge and skills; and the development of a news and information base, which provides enriched learning and supports the cultural environment.

Within Botswana, the national policy (1992) does not specify a role for adult education. However, it does have a department of non-formal education and this is defined as 'educational and training programmes generated outside the formal institutionalised education system for the whole population or specific groups' (Ministry of Education, 1992, p. 25). In defence of the lack of centralised planning, it states, 'It is the government's belief that the impetus for a great deal of NFE must come from the people' (Ministry of Education, 1992, p. 25). The 1994 revised national policy includes a new category of out-of-school education. This area is not defined very clearly:

> *Out of school is a complex area in view of the wide variety of client groups it caters for. The current situation reveals that the various providers operate parallel to each other and the quality of the programmes is uneven. This sector lacks the status and recognition it usually enjoys in developed and some developing countries. The sector also lacks a comprehensive policy as it was left out of the government paper no 1.*
> *(Government of Botswana, 1994, p. 10)*

In Papua New Guinea, the community-run non-formal pre-schools (*tok ples*) are no longer in operation. There is a literacy and awareness council which has been formed to oversee aspects of Education For All (EFA). The national plan of action includes public awareness campaigns for remote areas, and adult literacy to be increased to 95%.

It is difficult to assess the general progress made across countries in literacy and continuing education. There are problems with definition, and with generating accurate and comparable data.

II.1.3 Poorer countries. The focus of external aid has been on the development of basic education provided in state 'standard' schools. However, in conditions of extreme poverty, the formal state school often collapses and the community has to rely on alternative patterns of provision.

> *In Kenya non-formal schools managed by local communities do not qualify for the type of assistance and support which formal schools get from the government. These non-formal schools are not officially recognised, and therefore not even registered. The students do not have access to means of being granted a certificate or further schooling opportunities.*
> *(Wright & Govinda, 1994, p. 66)*

Countries of the Sahel. In Mauritania, about 20% of children only have access to 'l'enseignement originel' (Mahdras), which also teach men and women and several nationalities. Efforts are needed to integrate this teaching with the 'formal' sector. In Burkina Faso and Niger, there are permanent literacy centres which concentrate on 'functional literacy' courses and programmes. These initiatives are difficult to evaluate in terms of the benefits provided against the effort and resources which go into them precisely because of the lack of formal accountability. Moreover, there is no clear mechanism for transition: 'Out of school and NFE programmes do not have adequate links with the mainstream of formal education' (Wright & Govinda, 1994, p. 66).

II.2 The Education of Street Children

Whilst all the aforementioned developments can be seen as extensions of preceding trends and therefore absorbed within the same classification system, there have been other innovations which are much more difficult to capture within the 'traditional' scheme. One such example is the growing movement to provide some form of education for 'street children'. It should be emphasised that this is not a phenomenon restricted to poor shanty town areas in developing countries, as the following examples illustrate.

Anthony Swift: children for social change. The project that is documented works with socially excluded children. Swift makes the point that at the time of writing, the numbers of pupils excluded from British schools is rising. He cites newspaper reports of:

> *a threatened strike by teachers demanding the exclusion from*
> *their school of violent and uncontrollable pupils. In the past*
> *year alone we learn 13,419 children were permanently*
> *excluded from schools in the UK. (Swift, 1997, p. i)*

The project was conceived within a religious framework but has moved beyond that. Initially, children were organised into work cooperatives. Out of this:

> *a vigorous national movement of street boys and girls has*
> *emerged, whose members – poor community children and*
> *educators – have taken a prominent role in defining*
> *children's rights and responsibilities, securing legal rights*
> *and developing an educational experience through which*
> *both educator and child learn to exercise citizenship.*
> *(Swift, 1997, p. i)*

In this instance, both the educational goals and methodology are different from those of standard school education.

UNESCO: Working with Street Children. This is a collection of articles describing various initiatives in developing countries. The point is made that intervention is usually left to individuals, non-governmental organisations (NGOs) and religious organisations:

> *As a result there are thousands of small, uncoordinated but nevertheless highly effective projects throughout the world. (UNESCO, 1995, preface)*

> *Among the varying services offered to children by civilian society, education appears to be the most difficult to implement, manage and finance within the rehabilitation structure. (UNESCO, 1995, p. 17)*

Education is seen as a traditional way of reintegrating those outside of societies institutions of social control and socialisation. The projects are divided into three groups: those that use education for reinsertion; those that use work for reinsertion; and those that use the experiences of the street.

Overall commentary. Educational initiatives such as this highlight the difficulties of applying any simple classification scheme. This is for several reasons:

(a) the problem of relying on statistics from official sources, which limits information to those projects where registration takes place and returns are made to a central authority;
(b) the levels, duration, and field of study are based on the formal system of education and are often inappropriate for analysing these programmes;
(c) the objectives of this type of programme and its style of functioning cannot be adequately grasped aňd described by the categories available.

In fact, those enrolled in most of these 'street programmes' would be omitted from national statistical returns. Although the numbers involved may not be very large, similar activities for out-of-school youth often include very large numbers of teenagers (in back street colleges etc.) The range of programmes included in statistical returns for that age group is therefore only a very partial selection of what could be included and omits a very important subgroup of artisan or 'vocational' training.

II.3 The Growing Rhetoric about Lifelong Education

There has been a growth of interest in lifelong education:

> *Lifelong education describes the processes for promoting, supporting and improving learning that (a) last a lifetime; (b) lead to the systematic acquisition of skills, attitude and knowledge necessary in changing conditions of modern life, (c)*

emphasise self directed learning, (d) acknowledge the contributions of non-formal and informal educational influences. (Atchoarena, 1996, p. 177)

The following examples provide illustrations; note that they are not all industrialised countries.

Germany

In accordance with short and medium term labour market initiatives, government attitudes to lifelong education are currently overshadowed by the urgency of internal economic and social alignment. (Kunzel, 1995, p. 28)

Although the development of strategies for lifelong learning has come under the influence of new political priorities, the overall emphasis on labour related premises and objectives has been even further strengthened. (Kunzel, 1995, p. 31)

India

The debate about lifelong education/learning is not restricted to industrialised countries. For example, India's National Education Report details an example of an NFE initiative in India:

The department conceptualised a non-formal stream of education for social justice by mobilising the university system itself. ... The non-formal education stream differs from the formal stream in the fact that an individual can join at any age at any level and at any time of the year to achieve a level of education at his own pace. He can rejoin the stream at any point of interruption without having to repeat a class. Instruction and evaluation in this stream is at the convenience of the group of people involved and based on problem solving and application to daily life situations. (pp. 543-544)

Japan

Law concerning the Development of Mechanisms and Measures for the Promotion of Lifelong Learning enacted in 1990 including the establishment of a National Council for Lifelong Learning and similar bodies at Prefectural levels. Four issues to be tackled were:

promotion of recurrent education;
fostering of and support for volunteer programmes;

enrichment of out-of-school programmes for youth; and
enhancement of learning opportunities dealing with contemporary
issues.

Although there continues to be a substantial body of exciting rhetoric
surrounding the notion of lifelong learning, there is very little which
provides the basis for a classification of types of education implied by
such a policy.

III Approaches to Classification
Used When Collecting Data in Practice

III.1 Surveys by International Organisations

(a) *Surveying NFE in Africa.* Sheffield & Dejomah (1972) included all
training and education used outside the regular school system. The
summary by Mariko (1976) distinguished between industrial and
vocational training prior to employment and those who were on-the-job
or skill upgrading; between training programmes for out-of-school youth
and for adults in rural areas; and finally, multipurpose training
programmes.

(b) *South East Asian Ministries of Education Organisation (SEAMEO).*
The SEAMEO study classified 60 literacy programmes as:

mass literacy campaigns;
basic literacy courses;
literacy as part of development projects;
functional literacy;
post-literacy courses and programmes; and
programmes supporting literacy.

They classified the 47 NFE programmes/projects in vocational/technical
skill development according to:

the sectors of the economy, whether industrial, commercial or general;
mode of delivery, whether training in the training centre, on-the-job
training or industry or both;
sponsoring agency, whether government, semi-governmental or
private.

Commentary. Within the limited range of programmes considered,
SEAMEO suggested using different approaches to classification
according to the particular subsector (agriculture, literacy,
technical/vocational programmes) considered. Whilst there are
disadvantages (e.g. of comparability), the flexibility of this approach
seems to reflect more faithfully the kinds of programmes available.

(c) *USAID.* Four US Agency for International Development (USAID) appraisals of the education sector were considered. In Liberia, NFE was conceptualised as a residual:

> *The assessment ... covers the formal education system ...*
> *Remaining sections concern vocational and technical*
> *education and training, health education, agriculture, adult*
> *based education and management training. (Ministry of*
> *Planning and Economic Affairs, Liberia, 1983, p. 1-1)*

Implicitly, therefore, NFE was defined as agricultural extension, health education and literacy and this was mirrored in similar assessments in Botswana, Morocco and Somalia; indeed, the only assessment which contains an explicit chapter on NFE – that of Botswana – does *not* have chapters on health education or agriculture (and livestock) education, as do the others.

(d) *The World Bank.* No clear breakdown of the component parts of the educational system is presented. What we are given is a list of messages, issues and approaches that relate to educational policy options. Thus:

> Formal education consists of primary and secondary schools that focus on basic general skills, which are 'language, science and mathematics, and communications ... [and] ... the development of attitudes necessary for the workplace' (World Bank, 1995, p. xi).
> In terms of what constitutes NFE, or any type other than formal, the only reference made is to adult education: 'Outside the formal system, programs are necessary to deal with the problem of adult literacy, but these are not the subject of this report; they will be discussed in a future World Bank paper devoted to adult education' (World Bank 1995, p. xi).

III.2 Terms Used in Country Publications/Statistical Reports

It was obviously impractible to examine the reports from all the member states of UNESCO. We have therefore attempted to examine the official publications and statistical reports (or recent analyses) of a representative sample of countries from each of the major world regions.

In order to cover as much variability as possible, we have chosen large and small countries and relatively wealthy and relatively poor countries from within each of the world regions (within constraints of document availability).

There are a number of possible dimensions for analysing the wide range of non-formal or out-of-school educational possibilities that have been observed: distinctive administration, which kind of programmes are involved, who are the main target group, and what is the relationship between these and the formal educational system. It is also useful to examine how these reports have set out to differentiate the diversified field.

Separate administration. In some countries, there are identifiable administrative or legal definitions of non-formal or 'out-of-school' education. For example:

> *Botswana*: has a separate Department of Non-Formal Education but believes that the impetus for NFE should come from the people;
>
> *Brazil*: the Education Reform Law of 1961 was focused on vocational education and training and 10 years later on Supplemental Education;
>
> *Ethiopia*: there was a separate Department of Adult Education which has now been disbanded;
>
> *Iran*: a Bureau of Continuing Education has been established, emphasising the literacy programme, which, however, has a technical and vocational slant.

The existence of a separate administration or legal framework is very important: if these examples are representative, they appear to have been established to regulate vocational education and training, outside the structure of formal primary and secondary schooling. In other words, they have different aims and objectives from those that the formal education system in that country was designed to accomplish.

A set of discrete programmes. Yet another group of countries appear to define non-formal or out-of-school education ostensively, i.e. in terms of what is included in their country. Thus:

> *Germany*: non-vocational continuing education provided or regulated by the *Länder*; voluntary organisations are recognised as performing a public function; and there is public sector provision most commonly administered by *Volkshochshulen*;
>
> *Jamaica*: the section on NFE details the work of JAMAL (the movement for the advancement of literacy), the public library service and the national information system;
>
> *Hong Kong*: adult education includes both courses for personal development and to update knowledge and skills.

Once again, it is clear that the programmes are designed so that those who have 'missed out' can catch up. They tend to be provided by a variety of agencies.

Targeting. For some countries, the crucial aspect of NFE is that it caters for specific (marginal) population groups. Thus:

> *China*: workers' education, farmers' education and cadres' education;
>
> *Ethiopia*: non-school-going children and adult population;
>
> *India*: 'The policy emphasises the need for making available non-formal, flexible and need based vocational programmes to school drop-outs, neo-literates etc.' (Ministry of Education, 1995, p. 13).

In this case, it is clear that the programmes have been defined by reference to what the formal school has failed to do for certain groups or for particular kinds of clientele.

A residual. Finally, although most countries in fact treat non-formal or out-of-school education *in policy terms* as a residual, some countries appear to have defined NFE *only* as a residual (e.g. Bangladesh, Egypt).

III.3 Making Distinctions between NFE and Other Out-of School Educational Activities

Some countries categorise non-formal education as a subset of education outside the formal system. Thus:

Argentina: NFE is mainly for adults, essentially part-time, not following the educational ladder; and distinguished from para-formal, including professional terminal schools and adult formal education;

Australia: a range of possibilities for classification; institutional type, course type, organisational and funding structures, historical origins, user characteristics, and delivery methods are advocated.

Haiti: distinguishes NFE from vocational and technical education so that, 'a training programme to prepare professional artisans is considered vocational or technical, while an income generating project in which rural people learn a craft is considered NFE' (USAID, 1987, p. 111).

Some countries distinguish between various types of non-formal or out-of-school education. Thus:

Bangladesh: separates out madrasah (a form of Koranic education) education and adult education which deals with literacy;

China: elimination of illiteracy, school education, in-service professional training, examination through independent study, etc.

South Africa: distinctions made according to the providers (state-run programmes, industry-based programmes, and non-profit project work);

Sweden: labour market training, personnel education or in-service education, popular education with the objective of developing basic democratic values.

In addition to vocational programmes, there are catch-up programmes, courses oriented only to the individual, and programmes with a societal objective. The distinctions made depend upon culture, economy and history.

IV Developing a Classification of Types

The OECD/CERI report referred to earlier suggested that adult education could be categorised in terms solely of the motivation of the learner by dividing it into personal development, professional development and family development. A similar argument is advanced by Tennant (1990): 'Ultimately it is the learner's application of his or her knowledge and skill which determines whether an educational experience is vocational or non-vocational' (Tennant, 1990, p. 117).

These arguments, which are mainly in terms of learner motivation, do not appear to be consistent with the approach underlying ISCED, which involves laying a template on national education systems based on levels and objectives of different programmes. Moreover, they do not 'fit' with the variety of descriptions of non-formal and out-of-school education documented in the previous section. However, learner characteristics should probably form part of the classification system. In a publication for the International Institute for Educational Planning (IIEP) (Carron & Carr-Hill, 1991), discussing the problems of classifying the diversified educational field, we suggested a fourfold classification where types of education would be distinguished according to:

    their aims and objectives (to what purpose);
    the kinds of clientele they serve (for whom);
    the organising agency (by whom); and
    the relationship with the formal educational system.

Initially, the development of NFE was largely inspired by a welfare approach aiming to satisfy the demands of groups who for many reasons could not benefit from the standard school or college system. Although this approach has not disappeared, it has been largely overshadowed by a 'market approach' whereby different courses are being sold 'either for direct consumption as is the case of artistic expressive courses or as human capital investment as is the case of vocational courses' (Gallart, 1989, p. 63). The growing popularity of the business of private tutoring of students is part of the same trend.

As for the relationships between non-formal vocational courses and formal or standard schooling, the studies show a similar evolution in different countries. During a first phase, formal school systems have systematically tried to recuperate the non-formal initiatives:

> *Many initiatives that began as non-formal or para-formal*
> *education particularly in vocational training, tend to become*
> *formal and melted into the dominant educational system.*
> *(Gallart, 1989, p. 15)*

But gradually, school and college planners have realised that they can no longer answer the wide variety of educational needs and that given their highly bureaucratic organisation, they have a limited capacity to react quickly to technological changes and new demands. Consequently, it is necessary to have a multiplicity of training mechanisms.

The material reviewed in this chapter suggests that these are indeed the correct dimensions. The applicability of the fourfold classification proposed – para-formal, professional, personal development and popular – is considered in the following sections.

IV.1. Para-Formal Education

Some of the different types of education define themselves. One obvious example is the set of programmes designed for educational equivalencies to officially recognised primary, secondary, or higher educational diplomas. Indeed, some authors (e.g. Verhine, 1993) claim that these should be considered as not being part of NFE, which term should be reserved only for those *not* aiming at a school or college diploma.

Case studies (e.g. Bibeau, 1989; Gallart, 1989) also demonstrate that there has been a progressive tendency for the formal educational system to absorb 'innovations' from the NFE sector as part of the standard curriculum. This further complicates the attempt to draw the boundary or borderline between formal and non-formal education; it also suggests that despite the rhetoric about the relative flexibility of NFE as against formal education, formal school systems have demonstrated more flexibility in adapting their organisational modes of delivery and teaching methods to the changing needs of the clientele, at least in the medium term, than is generally recognised.

In addition to these 'second chance' para-formal education programmes, there has been a rapid expansion in the private tutoring of regular formal school students. It has grown with the massification of formal education as elite middle-class parents, who perceive their previous privileged position to be disappearing, have sought ways of retaining the competitive edge for their children. At the same time, for formal school teachers in many developing countries, where civil service salaries have been seriously eroded over the last decades, the private tutoring system has been a welcome opportunity to increase their income. Demand and supply factors have therefore been reinforcing each other to create a real market for individual student coaching.

We have given this the label *para-formal* education:

Definition: educational programmes which provide a substitute for regular full-time schooling. The main objective of these programmes is to offer a *second chance* to those who, for various reasons, could not benefit from the regular school system at the ordained moment.
Examples: evening classes, official literacy programmes, distance education programmes, some of the programmes for street children.
Relationship to formal schooling: some of these programmes are only a condensed form of full-time day schooling, while others are more flexible and more innovative in design and implementation. A central issue for this segment of the educational field is to guarantee

equivalences with the certificates and degrees awarded in the corresponding levels of the formal school system.

IV.2 Professional and Vocational Education

At first sight, another obvious grouping is *vocational education and training*. But the well-known documented explosion in qualifications which has led to the growing demand for vocational training to garner additional skills qualification poses a problem. For whilst the increased skills among the population may indeed make real contributions to economic growth – in which case, the training should be classified carefully according to the particular field of study (as, for example, in the present ISCED) – several authors have argued that the major explanation for the increased demand for skills qualifications is not the content of the qualification but is more to do with screening (Arrow, 1973; Dore, 1980) or worker socialisation (Bock & Papagiannis, 1983; Bowles & Gintis, 1976).

Whilst none of the authors would want to claim that there is one unique answer, the evidence that the human capital theory cannot be the total answer is compelling. On this basis and given the implications of both the screening hypothesis and the worker socialisation theory, that at least some of the training which is apparently 'vocational' is, in fact, part of a general preparation for the harsh world of paid work rather than for any particular kind of job, it would seem sensible to make a distinction in vocational education and training along the lines of the more traditional distinction between academic disciplines (general) and vocational courses (specific) or between formal education (general) and informal, on-the-job learning (specific).

Following this line of argument, *general vocational education* would refer to the transmission of skills, knowledge and behavioural traits which are broadly relevant to performance in all or a considerable number of occupational roles (learning to work), whilst *specific instruction* is concerned with the performance of a single task (or set of tasks) within a single job or occupation within a single institutional locale (learning to do), which is limited in scope and non-portable in application.

Staley (1971) proposes four phases of job preparation: general education, pre-occupation education, job-entry training, and career-long training. Castro (1975) contends that course duration is a reliable indicator of the generality or specificity of a course: 'longer courses give more attention to the teaching of general principles' (p. 439). On this basis, four types could be distinguished:

General Extra-school Education, including adult literacy courses and preparatory courses for school equivalency examinations (such efforts are substitutes or partial substitutes for traditional schooling);

Semi-specific Pre-employment Job Training focuses on basic skills and the teaching of industrial discipline. A typical course lasts 2 years focuses in a broadly defined blue-collar occupation stressing the 'theoretical dimensions of the subject';

Specific Career-long Job Training for workers with previous industrial experience normally lasts from 2 to 6 months, usually focusing on a very specific occupation or aspect of that occupation;

Highly Specialised In-firm Job Training – normally very short (less than 2 months or 100 hours duration). This does not include all in-firm courses because some firm's offerings are not specifically job-skills oriented.[1]

Staley then lumped all other types of education and training under the rubric 'Miscellaneous Non-vocational Extra-School Education (ESE)', covering a wide variety of programmes ranging from courses for industrial workers in fire prevention and first aid to Church-sponsored offerings on topics such as marriage and baptism.

On the whole, whilst appreciating the purpose of the fourfold distinction advocated by Staley, it appears unlikely that one could make similar gradations in respect of training for other sectors of the economy (even other industrial sectors). However, many other authors – and employers – have made the distinction between education and vocational training programmes (possibly organised around a specific skill) with the principal objective of demonstrating general trainability; and education and vocational training leading to a particular skill qualification that is (intended) to be used.

(a) *Definition:* in this case, the proposal is that there should be two subgroups:

general vocational education would refer to the transmission of skills, knowledge, and behavioural traits which are broadly relevant to performance in all or a considerable number of occupational roles (learning to learn);

specific instruction is concerned with the performance of a single task (or set of tasks) within a single job or occupation within a single institutional locale (learning to do) which is limited in scope and non-portable in application.

(b) *Examples:* programmes of professional and vocational training organised by firms, trade unions, private agencies and also by 'formal' professional and vocational schools.

(c) *Relationship to formal schooling:* depending on the extent to which vocational courses are included in secondary schooling.

IV.3. Personal Development

The rapid expansion of personal development activities is one of the most significant common trends in the diversification of the educational field. Learning for personal development regroups a wide variety of activities which may differ from one country to another. For example, in Quebec, the sector of personal development activities is as important as the sector of professional learning, and the same is true in Argentina:

> *a more individualistic concept of the role of the individual in the social development process, a concept which is reinforced by recent changes in the functioning of the labour market and by questioning of the role of the State in social development. (Bibeau, 1989, p. 83)*

Individual demand is the regulating factor of the expansion of this type of education.

(a) *Definition:* education programmes which cover a range of learning practices, organised by cultural institutions promoting leisure time activities. It includes a market approach whereby different courses are sold either for direct consumption, or as human capital investment.

(b) *Examples*: learning organised by cultural institutions (museums, libraries, cultural centres), by clubs, circles, associations promoting lesson-time activities.

(c) *Relationship to formal education:* most of the participants are seeing their participation in this activity as 'making up' for what they missed at school.

IV.4. Popular Education

Finally, there is another separately identifiable example in the type of education used as a means of consciousness-raising, practised, for example, by the Catholic communities in Latin America during the 1980s. This was obviously linked to the general line of argument that NFE served to perpetuate colonialism (e.g. De Kadt, 1976). The model of collective promotion – perhaps via popular education – appears to have weakened in favour of the spectacular emergence of personal development activities (although some of the latter have tried to repackage collective sentiments), but there are still situations where a liberating form of education is seen as an essential vehicle for a movement – for example, in the existence of Catalan education.

The point is that – in this mode – education is being used as vehicle for a totally different perspective on society in contrast to the 'standard' form of school and college education, or any vocational education or training which takes the social arrangements as given, or the personal development kinds of education which are individually and collectively based.

It is important to note the inverted commas around 'standard' in the previous paragraph. Thus, Torres (1990) follows previous authors in claiming that NFE in Latin America is an integral part of governmental attempts to legitimise existing order; but Torres (1991) – the same author 1 year later – says that in Cuba, Nicaragua and Grenada, ESE has served as 'a quick and effective response of revolutionary governments to pressing need of the adult population' (p. 120) and has helped 'to enhance the readiness of the labour force to adjust to changes in the economy and job market' (p. 122).

(a) *Definition*: educational initiatives explicitly directed towards the marginal groups of the population and including political mobilisation and community developed activities.

(b) *Examples*: some of the programmes for street children are similar; Catalan education.

(c) *Relationship to formal schooling:* this type of education is seen as antithetical to the education provided by the state in the formal school and college system; indeed, the 'radicalism' of its contents is *defined* by reference to how state education is organised.

*****

At the same time, we have to be realistic about the possibilities of collecting data. The extent to which any further extension of ISCED could take account of these different forms/types of education depends in practice upon the countability of each of the different kinds of educational activities – and hence the importance of the distinction made in terms of whether or not enrolment is recorded. In Table I, we have separated the various strands of the non-standard (or non-formal or out-of-school education) into two groups:

> those where the providing institution would probably hold enrolment and/or registration data and which could therefore be captured in principle through a census survey of institutions; and
> those where the most practicable way of obtaining estimates would be through a sample population survey.

Whilst the former sounds appealing as it is effectively only an extension of the more traditional school questionnaire, the experience reported in (Carron & Carr-Hill, 1991) and summarised in section I suggests that such surveys are not without problems; and they would in any case exclude a substantial chunk of activities in several countries on a rather arbitrary basis. Instead, the recommendation here is to decide which categories one wants to include within the ISCED framework and then to investigate the feasibility of designing a simple one-page add-on to the Labour Force Surveys.

Level	Name	Standard	Non-standard	Suggested classification	
		State	Collectable from institutions	Collectable via household surveys	
1	Pre-primary	Nursery	Playgroups	Childcare	Para-formal
2	Primary	Primary	Evening classes	Street children	Para-formal
3	Secondary	Secondary	Evening classes	Youth groups	Para-formal
4		Further education colleges	Industry	Youth groups, back street colleges	TVET General/specific
5	Tertiary	University	'Open' universities	Auditing	Personal development
6	Post-doctoral	University	'Open' universities	Auditing	Personal development

Table I.

Note

[1] Other authors have drawn attention to the distinction between learning that is job-specific and that which is firm-specific (see, for example, Bowman [1988] and Shaw [1984]); but that seems a refinement too far!

Selected Bibliography

Arrow, K.J. (1973) *Social Choice and Individual Values*. London: Routledge & Kegan Paul.

Atchoarena, D. (Ed.) (1995) *Lifelong Education in Selected Industrialised Countries*. Paris: International Institute for Educational Planning.

Bacquelaine, M. & Raymaekers, E. (1991) Non-formal Education in Developing Countries, *International Journal of Educational Management*, 5, pp. 15-24.

Bibeau, R. (1989) *L'education non-formale au Quebec*. Paris: International Institute for Educational Planning (IIEP)/UNESCO, IIEP Research Report No. 78.

Bock, J.C. (1976) The Institutionalisation of Nonformal Education: a response to conflicting needs, *Comparative Education Review*, 20, pp. 346-367.

Bock, J.C. & Papagiannis, G.J. (1983) Some Alternative Perspectives on the Role of Non Formal Education: a critique and suggestions for a new research direction, in J.C. Bock & G.J. Papagiannis (1983) *Issues in Nonformal Education*, pp. 1-39. Amherst, MA: Center for International Education, University of Massachusetts.

Bowles & Gintis (1976) *Schooling in Capitalist America*. New York: Basic Books.

Bowman, M.J. (1988) Links between General and Vocational Education: does the one enhance the other? *International Review of Education*, 34, pp. 149-171.

Brennan (1997) Reconceptualising Non-formal Education, *International Journal of Lifelong Education*, 16, pp. 185-200.

Brookfield, S. (1995) Lifelong Education in the United States of America, in D. Atchoarena (Ed.) *Lifelong Education in Selected Industrialised Countries*. Paris: International Institute for Educational Planning.

Burnett (1996) Priorities and Strategies for Education: a World Bank review: the processes and the key messages, *International Journal of Educational Development*, 16, pp. 215-220.

Carr-Hill, R.A. (1988) *The Information Base for Planning of the Diversified Educational Field*. Paris: International Institute for Educational Planning (IIEP)/UNESCO, IIEP Research Report No. 68.

Carr-Hill, R.A. & Lintott, J. (1985) *Comparative Adult Education Statistics for Eighty-Four Countries*. Paris: UNESCO (ST 85/S/6).

Carron, G. & Carr-Hill, R.A. (1991) *Non-formal Education: information and planning issues*. Paris: International Institute for Educational Planning (IIEP)/UNESCO, IIEP Research Report No. 90.

Case, H.L. & Nichoff, R.O. (1976) *Educational Alternatives in National Development: suggestions for policy-makers*. East Lansing, MI: Institute for International Studies in Education.

Castro, C.M. (1975) Academic Education versus Technical Education, in T.J. LaBelle (Ed.) *Educational Alternatives in Latin America*, pp. 434-461. Los Angeles: UCLA Latin America Center.

Centro Multinacional de Educacion de Adultos (1981) *Educationa Extraescolar en Cost Rica 1980 Repertono*. San Jose: Ministerio de Educacion Publico.

Christie, P. (1996) Globalisation and the Curriculum: proposals for the integration of education and training in South Africa, *International Journal of Educational Development*, 16, pp. 407-416.

Coombs, P.H. (1976) Non Formal Education: myths and realities and opportunities, *Comparative Education Review*, 3, pp. 290-293.

Coombs, P.H., Prosser, R.C. & Ahmed, H. (1973) *New Paths to Learning for Rural Children and Youth*, pp. 9-13. New York: ICED.

Coombs, P.H. (1988) Comparative Studies in Nonformal Education, in T.N. Postlethwaite (Ed.) *The Encyclopaedia of Comparative Education and National Systems of Education*, pp. 72-75. Oxford: Pergamon.

Creative Associates (1981) *The Non-Formal Education Assessment/Analysis Model*. Washington, DC: Creative Associates.

Creative Associates (1982) *Non-Formal Education in Botswana: an assessment*. Washington, DC: Creative Associates.

Creative Associates (1983) *Non-Formal Education in the Cameroons: an assessment.* Washington, DC: Creative Associates.

De Grauwe, A. & Bernard, D. (Eds) (1995) *Developments after Jomtien: EFA in the South East Asia and Pacific Region.* Paris: International Institute for Educational Planning/UNESCO.

De Kadt, E. (1976) Is Non-formal Education Any Better, *Ciencia e Cultura*, 28, pp. 1442-1458.

Department of Education (1995) *Annual Report, 1994-95. Government of India.*

Dore, R.P. (1980) *Diploma Disease Revisited.* London: Routledge.

Evans, D.R. (1985) The Learning Opportunities Inventory in International Institute for Educational Planning, *Educational Planning in the Context of Current Development Problems*, vol. II, pp. 185-206.

Gallart, M.A. (1989) *The Diversification of the Educational Field in Argentina.* Paris: International Institute for Educational Planning (IIEP)/UNESCO, IIEP Research Report No. 73.

Garrido, J-L. G. (1992) Open and Non-formal Education: new paths for education in a new Europe, *Comparative Education*, 28, pp. 83-89.

Government of Botswana (1994) *The Revised National Policy on Education.* Paris: Centre for Research and Innovation, OECD.

Griffin, C. (1987) *Adult Education as Social Policy.* Croom Helm.

Hamadache, A. (1991) Non-formal Education: a definition of the concept and some examples, *Prospects*, XXI, pp. 111-124.

Hoghielm, R. & Rubenson, K. (Eds) (1980) *Adult Education for Social Change.* Stockholm: Liberlaromedel Lund.

Inkei, P. with Konic, G. & Poeze, G. (1988) *The Diversification of the Educational Field in Hungary.* Paris: International Institute for Educational Planning/UNESCO.

Kahn, M. (1996) Five Years Gone: a case study of educational policy implementation in the transition to democracy in South Africa, *International Journal of Educational Development*, 16, pp. 281-289.

Kouptsov, O.V. (1990) *Diversification of Education in the USSR*, mimeo. Paris: International Institute for Educational Planning/UNESCO.

Kunzel, K. (1995) Lifelong Education in Germany, in D. Atchoarena (Ed.) *Lifelong Education in Selected Industrialised Countries.* Paris: International Institute for Educational Planning.

La Belle, T.J. (1982) Formal, Non-formal and Informal Education: holistic perspectives of life long learning, *International Review of Education*, 28, pp. 159-175.

Lauglo, J. (1995) Banking on Education and the Uses of Research: a critique of World Bank priorities and strategies for education, *International Journal of Educational Development*, 16, pp. 221-223.

Mariko (1976) *Examples of Work Components in HFE in Africa.* Paris: UNESCO (ED, 76/CONF/807 110).

Ministry of Education, Botswana (1992) *Pulling Together to Do Better*, Third Biennial Report, 19989-91. Botswana: Ministry of Education.

Ministry of Education, India (1995) *National Education Report.*

Ministry of Planning and Economic Affairs, Liberia (1983) *Education and Training Secotor Assessment.* Government of Liberia and USAID.

Narang, R. (1992) Social Justice and Political Education through non-formal training, *International Review of Education,* 38, pp. 542-546.

Oxbby, R. (1997) Barriers to the Provision of Cost-effective Technical Education in Bangladesh, *International Journal of Educational Development,* 17, pp. 91-99.

South East Asian Ministries of Education Organisation (SEAMEO) (1975) *Beyond School Walls: a study on non-formal education on the SEAMEO Region 1973-74.* Bangkok.

Sheffield, J.R. & Dejomah, V.P. (1972) *Non-formal Education in African Development.* New York: Afro-American Institute.

Staley, E.F. (1971) *Planning Occupational Education and Training for Development.* New York: Praeger.

Swift, A. (1997) *Children for Social Change: for Citizenship of Street and Working Children in Brazil.* Nottingham: Education Heretics.

Tabbron, G. & Yang, J. (1997) The Interaction between Technical and Vocational Education and Training (TVET) and Economic Development in Advanced Countries, *International Journal of Educational Development,* 17, pp. 323-334.

Torres, C.A. (1990) *The Politics of Non-formal Education in Latin America.* New York: Praeger.

Torres, C.A. (1991) The State, Nonformal Education, and Socialism in Cuba, Nicaragua and Grenada, *Comparative Education Review,* 35, pp. 110-130.

UNESCO (1995) Working with Street Children. Paris: UNESCO.

UNESCO, Office of Statistics (1985) *Manual for Statistics on Adult Education.* Paris: UNESCO (ST 85/WS/14).

US Agency for International Development (1987)

Verhine, R.E. (1993) *Educational Alternatives and the Determination of Earnings in Brazilian Industry.* Peter Lang.

Wolhunter, C. (1997) Classification of National Education Systems: a multivariate approach, *Comparative Education Review,* 41, pp. 161-177.

World Bank (1995) *Priorites and Strategies for Education: a World Bank review.* Oxford: Oxford University Press.

Wright, C. & Govinda, R. (1994) *Three Years after Jomtien: EFA in the Eastern and Southern Africa Region.* Paris: International Institute for Educational Planning/UNESCO.

International Examinations, National Systems and the Global Market

JOHN LOWE

The focus of this chapter is international examinations, the use that is made of them by students learning in their home country (as distinct from expatriates) and their role in a global qualifications market. There are, perhaps, two distinct types of examinations that could be thought of as 'international'. First, there are those used to make international comparisons of achievement across nations, with the International Association for the Evaluation of Educational Achievement (IEA) studies being the most well known example. There is a growing literature on the impact or potential impact on national education policy of these international league table exercises (Kellaghan, 1996), and they certainly have the potential to encourage considerable global convergence in curricula and pedagogy, but they are not the concern of this chapter. Second, there are international examinations that assess and certify individual achievement: examinations such as the International Baccalaureate (IB) or International General Certificate of Secondary Education (IGCSE). These are commonly used by mobile expatriates – the global nomads – but it is their apparently increasing use by students at school within their own national borders that is the concern here.

This chapter will first report on some of the international qualifications that are available, and the organisations that produce and administer them. There will then be a brief look at some schools in different parts of the world where indigenous students are taking these examinations, before going on to consider some substantive and theoretical issues that arise. Two points should be made early on. The first is that from the vast number and range of international qualifications available globally, it is those of a general academic, rather than vocational nature that are the focus of this chapter: those that are primarily intended as assessments of school-based learning. The second point is that this chapter reflects the early stages of a research interest that is characterised so far by a lot of questions, a few hypotheses, and only preliminary empirical data. It is written in the hope that it will stimulate responses and criticism that will further an ongoing research process.

International Examinations and Qualifications: who produces them?

Two key players in the international examinations (and consequently, curricula) business have been chosen for particular attention: the International Baccalaureate Organisation (IBO) and the University of Cambridge Local Examinations Syndicate (UCLES). There are many others, and amongst these the US-based Education Testing Service (ETS) will be mentioned later, but the IBO and UCLES are particularly significant because of their global coverage and particularly interesting because they represent significantly different approaches to the marketing of their products. There are other United Kingdom-based examination boards whose academic examinations are available overseas. The UCLES to some extent can be seen as representative of these boards, but it has been chosen because of the scale of its overseas involvement and because it appears to be concerned to expand its overseas market share through new products.

The IBO grew out of and was originally intended to meet the needs of international schools serving geographically mobile students. Its founders were driven by a particular educational philosophy and an ideology of 'internationalism'. Though European in its origins, and retaining its main offices in Switzerland and Wales, it now has regional offices right across the world and its governing body is expected to reflect its global presence. The official rhetoric of the organisation is that an educational philosophy and the promotion of international understanding remain the twin driving forces behind the organisation; but it is also clear from conversations with IBO staff that, despite being a non-profit foundation, the IBO is increasingly aware of its position in a global education market. Its originally intended constituency of international schools has now broadened to include many schools in national systems and the organisation is frequently called upon in a consultancy capacity by national system representatives (Fox, 1998; Drennen, 1998). (The difficulties with the use of the term 'international schools' and the blurring of the distinction between national and international schools is recognised, but has no real significance for this chapter – see Hayden & Thompson [1995] for a discussion.)

Until quite recently, the only course offered by the IBO was that for the International Baccalaureate Diploma, which professes to be both a preparation for international citizenship and a university entrance qualification, accepted in the most prestigious universities in a wide range of countries. The Diploma originally offered assessment of its curriculum in two languages, English and French, but Spanish was later included. English and Spanish now dominate out of these three, giving some indication of where the expansion of the programme has been greatest (and least). It still accounts for the majority of the IBO's resources, but over the last 5 years, two new programmes have been developed: the Middle Years Programme (IBMYP) for children aged 9-16, and the Primary Years Programme (IBPYP) for children between 3 and 12. IB curricula now, therefore, cover the whole range of pre-university education. Neither of these two programmes includes an external examination, although there is external moderation of a school's assessment standards. The IBO now provides curriculum and assessment services individually to some 800 schools in almost 100 countries, as well as the assistance to state systems mentioned earlier.

The UCLES presents something of a contrast to the IBO, having its administration firmly based in one country and, indeed, using its association with that country for promotional purposes. The UCLES has been offering overseas examinations and certification for more than 130 years, originally very much associated with British colonies and, later, Commonwealth countries. Indeed, until relatively recently, 'Cambridge' was immediately recognised by students from across much of the world as shorthand for the Cambridge Overseas School Certificate (COSC). This examination is still administered by the UCLES in some countries (Lesotho, for example), though the majority of its former clients have now developed indigenous examinations systems, often with training and support from the UCLES, so that the legacy of 'Cambridge' is still visible in many of these systems. Several countries now issuing their own qualifications still rely on accreditation by the UCLES as a way of ensuring international comparability of standards and recognition of these qualifications.

International versions of the English O level and A level examinations are offered and are used as part of national qualifications systems in some countries (Singapore and Mauritius, for example), as well as by individual independent schools. The flagship of the UCLES, however, in the contemporary international qualifications market is probably the International General Certificate of Secondary Education (IGCSE). This is marketed on its technical and educational merits, where the latter are defined through its English qualifications comparability: it is advertised as being based on the English GCSE system, intended for 16 year-olds, but not tied to the English National Curriculum. Though intended for the same age-group, it differs significantly from the O level examinations in that it includes coursework, which demands that teachers involved in its marking have to be trained and accredited by the UCLES. The syndicate does not publish the number of candidates taking the IGCSE but a figure of between 20,000 and 30,000 is a reasonable estimate from the figure of almost 200,000 subject entries that is given for 1997, in 106 countries (UCLES, 1997). This is comparable with the figure of 30,000 candidates quoted by the IBO for its examinations (IBO web site), suggesting that the 'market share' of the two bodies is similar (although it is possible that the IBO figure includes those who are not taking the full Diploma but are simply obtaining certificates for some courses within it). It is important to remember, however, that the IB Diploma and the IGCSE are intended for different age groups.

Admittedly limited contact with schools taking international examinations in a range of countries suggests that the IGCSE at about 16, followed by the IB Diploma 2 years later is a common curricular pattern in these schools. In view of this, recent developments in both the IBO and UCLES invite speculation. The introduction of the Middle Years Programme by the IBO has already been mentioned, and it is tempting to see this partly as a response to the popularity of the IGCSE from a 'rival' body. For the clients, one of the key differences between IBMYP and IGCSE is that the former does not offer externally set and marked examinations. (In a few countries – Egypt, for example – the IGCSE certificate is accepted for university entrance, giving it extra value.) A Middle Years Programme certificate certifying individual achievement is available to schools that request it, but annual IBO moderation of a school's grading standards is mandatory in such cases. It will be interesting to see whether pressure from the market will in future lead the IBO to offer some form of external examination.

Meanwhile, the UCLES has introduced a new product to tap further the market for university entry credentials by offering (from 1996) the Advanced International Certificate of Education (AICE). Once again, this is presented as equivalent in standard to the English A level examination, but is distinguished by demanding a more broadly based curriculum than is common in England at this age. Thus, candidates must take at least five full-time credits, not the three that are common in England, and, in contrast to the pattern of specialisation in particular fields that characterises English schools, these must include at least one from each of three groups of subjects: mathematics and science, languages, and arts and humanities. It is very tempting to see this programme as a response to the broad-based IB Diploma programme – as a market challenge. As the newcomer, it cannot claim the same market share as the IB Diploma, being offered in only around 100 schools worldwide by 1997, but this figure still represents a rapid growth. An interesting aspect of this expansion is the use of the AICE in a few schools in the USA. The IB has had a considerable presence in that country for some time through what amounts to a franchising organisation, IB North America.

One important difference between the IBO and UCLES programmes is that the latter offers courses and examinations in English only, in contrast to the three language options available with the IBO. This reflects a fundamental difference in the programmes: the underpinning notion in the IB of education for an internationalism growing out of the individual's own culture (and language) is absent from the UCLES courses. Both organisations emphasise the international acceptability of their courses for university entrance, although the IBO is ahead here too, since it has been in the field for longer. The UCLES depends heavily on both its own international reputation gained over the last century or so and an assumption that English education retains high prestige. It is interesting to note that for the AICE, the only language, other than English, which is offered at first language status is Spanish. It seems that Latin America is seen by both the UCLES and the IBO to offer an expanding market.

One further point about language that is worth noting is that the IBO is now offering its Middle Years Programme in a fourth language: Mandarin Chinese (Drennen, 1998). There appear to be no plans to offer the IB Diploma itself in Mandarin but both the MYP and the Diploma are being offered by schools in China and, given the scale of opportunity that the country presents, future responses to an expansion there are difficult to predict. China is, of course, seen as the market of the future for so many Western producers and it would be surprising if educational concerns were not to follow. It should be noted that the IBO is dealing with individual schools in China, not with regional or national education authorities. This is the way the IBO works in general, but it seems particularly significant when the clients are schools that are part of the Chinese national system.

These two, then, – the IBO and UCLES – are two of the more significant players in the global school-level qualifications market. Both are keen to establish international credibility for their qualifications, particularly for university entrance, and there is considerable overlap in their target markets. Each, however, relies on different marketing attractions: philosophies of a complete, all-round education and internationalism from the IBO, and a technical expertise coupled with associations with English education for the UCLES. A third group of players in the international assessment market is worth considering here: those based in the USA. Amongst these, the largest and most significant is the Educational Testing Service (ETS). ETS has had an international presence for some considerable time, but this was primarily concerned with meeting the assessment needs of those seeking entrance to colleges and universities in the USA. This remains their central concern and in this respect, there is only limited market overlap with IBO and UCLES. A key difference between ETS and these other two is that ETS is essentially concerned with the production and administration of tests for other clients, such as the College Board or Graduate Record Examinations Board: it is in the business of testing, not curriculum production, and many of the tests it offers are 'curriculum-free'.

Recent developments in one of the ETS administered examinations suggest that competition with bodies such as the IBO and UCLES may increase. These developments are in the Advanced Placement (AP) Program that ETS assesses on behalf of the College Board. This programme was originally intended to support high-achieving students seeking college entrance in the USA but has broadened its scope significantly over the 40 or so years of its existence to include, *inter alia*, access to universities outside the USA. In 1995, when some 11,000 overseas students in 65 countries were participating in the AP, an Advanced Placement International Diploma for Overseas Study was introduced, specifically to meet the needs of students applying to non-North American universities (ETS, 1995). As with the AP, in general this International Diploma is based on specific curricula, and an interesting similarity with both the IB Diploma and the AICE is that candidates for APID must follow a broad curriculum, taking examinations in at least two languages, one science or mathematics and a history, social science or art course.

The significance of this development for the global qualifications market is increased further when one considers three points about ETS, the agency responsible for AP assessment. The first is its sheer size: a revenue of US $310 million by 1991 and an annual growth rate of some 11%, making it the largest private testing company in the world (Madaus & Raczek, 1996). The second is that ETS already has a considerable international presence, though largely through its involvement in other tests such as the GRE (Graduate Record Examination) and TOEFL (Test of English as a Foreign Language). In 1996-97, for example, test centres for the GRE were listed in over 150 countries outside the USA (ETS, 1996). The third and potentially most intriguing point about ETS is its experience with computer-based assessment (or computer-adaptive testing, as it calls it). Both the IBO and UCLES offer only traditional paper-based assessment modes, which are both expensive and time-consuming to process. By 1996, ETS had computer-based test centres in some 44 countries and planned expansion to more than 170 countries within 3 years (ETS, 1997). To date, the AP examinations are not available in computer-adaptive form, but should they become so, the ETS network would be available to support this worldwide, at only marginal cost.

In many countries, it seems likely that US-based qualifications are often less attractive than those based on European education systems. Part of this may be unfamiliarity coupled with none-too-high a reputation for school-level education in the USA. A further element has been the US predilection for multiple-choice testing, often seen as inappropriate elsewhere for higher school-level assessment in particular. The AP assessment includes both multiple-choice and free-response items and it is worth noting that ETS are experimenting with more open response type questions that can still be computer-based. This may be partly under pressure from the home education market for more 'authentic' forms of assessment, but it would also help enormously with any expansion into the international market. It is difficult to assess the relative position of ETS in this market at present, but given its size and access to technology, I am inclined to say 'Watch this (hyper-)space'.

Schools and Students in the International Market

Two key questions in this field appear to be: 'Who are the students who sit for international examinations?' and 'Why do they do so?' Collecting data to provide some sort of answer to these questions is likely to be difficult for a variety of reasons. Even the first question would not be answerable in anything like sufficient detail from information held by the respective examinations bodies – even if they were prepared to release it. Data would have to be collected at source: in the schools themselves. Choosing a geographically representative sample would be possible using examination board data, but the logistics of then collecting adequate information from the schools and students themselves could be horrendous. In any case, it is not yet clear whether geography will be the most significant dimension in any analysis and the most suitable basis for sampling. It is hoped that electronic communications may be useful in the initial stages of data collection, but this has yet to be explored in full.

Opportunities to collect some initial data have been presented by the quite extensive contacts between the Department of Education at the University of Bath and schools offering international qualifications in many countries worldwide. These contacts arise from teaching visits made by university staff and through an annual Summer School that attracts teachers from such schools. A large proportion of these schools deal largely, or even entirely, with expatriate children, who are not a concern here, but I have been able to interview teachers from several schools that attract a significant proportion of national students. The sample of schools thus investigated is entirely opportunistic and the information so far obtained, though undoubtedly quite reliable, is far from complete. Nevertheless, it does provide a useful outline of the field that can inform future investigations. A summary of the information obtained follows, for selected schools, which are identified only in terms of country of location.

School A: El Salvador

Around 90% of the students are local, mostly from upper- and middle-class urban backgrounds, as the school fees are relatively high. Some students do have a struggle to find the fees as they come from poorer, but by no means poor, backgrounds. Children of professionals, the local business community, landowners, and a few teachers predominate. Tuition is bilingual, in English and Spanish. The English National Curriculum is followed up to IGCSE, although with local variations demanded by law: local history and an element of community service. IGCSE is followed by the IB Diploma. IGCSE is preferred to the IB Middle Years Programme because 'Cambridge' has status amongst parents, who are very status conscious. The IB is relatively unknown to Salvadorean society but is slowly gaining acceptance. In practical terms, the IGCSE serves no external purpose, its main use being by the school, to select for IB courses. A local graduate certificate with honours bearing this school's name is probably more valuable for access to local society and local universities than either the IGCSE or IB. Almost all students do go on to university somewhere, with about 30% of them going overseas, mostly to the USA, where the IB offers a reduction in the length of a university course similar to the AP Programme. Courses related to business and commerce are particularly popular, even amongst the children of rich landowners who, presumably, would rely on inherited estates for their future livelihood.

The attractions of the school are only partly due to its 'international' curriculum. The use of English is particularly valued, both for the status it confers and because English gives access to the business and commercial world. Other attractions would appear to be the presence of expatriate teachers and the school's reputation for discipline (a nearby American school, for example, is considered too lax in this respect).

School B: Sudan

This is a small, English-medium school with about 80% of the students Sudanese. IGCSE and A levels are offered, not AICE. The school is seen as giving access to overseas universities, especially in the United Kingdom, and science subjects are almost the only ones taken at A level. For this reason, the 'balanced' programme of AICE (or IB) is not seen by the students to be appropriate to their needs. Sudanese universities are not highly regarded by the students and their parents, so access to overseas universities through internationally recognised qualifications is the chief attraction, together with the predominance of expatriate teachers. Parents of the students used to be largely from professional backgrounds but with changes in the local economy, the business world now dominates, except for those professionals who are in private practice and can afford the high fees.

School C: Jordan

Jordanian children are not allowed to attend schools which call themselves 'international' without government permission, which is rarely granted (although a recent Memorandum of Understanding between the UCLES and the Jordanian Government will allow Jordanian students to take the IGCSE). This appears to be due to a concern for education to promote Jordanian 'national identity'. This high-fees, kindergarten to grade 12, bilingual school has about 85% of its intake Jordanian. It offers IGCSE and IB Diploma but makes some adaptations to its curriculum to meet national regulations, such as the teaching of Arabic, when this does not compromise preparation for these international examinations. The students have special dispensation not to sit the local national examinations, which are compulsory for all other Jordanian students. The school manages to survive its very lax interpretations of national educational regulations through very powerful connections. Not surprisingly, the intake is largely of children from very rich and influential backgrounds in politics and commerce, although almost one-eighth of the students are the children of teachers in school taking advantage of a huge fees reduction.

Some 80% of the graduates go on to overseas universities, increasingly in the USA rather than in the United Kingdom, which was the previously favoured destination. A small number use the school to gain access to local universities, with the IGCSE and 1 year of post-IGCSE study being sufficient for this purpose. Most overseas university graduates return to Jordan after their university courses since their family wealth and interests mean they are not dependent on seeking employment overseas. The US universities' attraction seems to be their broader-based courses, but the United Kingdom retains a reputation for a more 'solid' education. Similarly, the IGCSE is preferred to the IBO alternatives because it is part of middle-class Jordanian educational culture, gaining status through its United Kingdom and 'Cambridge' connections, but the IB Diploma is seen to offer a more balanced education than A levels. The educational quality of the IBMYP and PYP is recognised and they are used as a framework around which to build the IGCSE work, but the absence of a certificate for the MYP is seen as a weakness.

School D: Thailand

As policy, this school ensures that the Thai students remain a minority, so as not to swamp its desired international character, although the demand from Thais is much greater than the number of places available. Once again, because of relatively high fees, these students are drawn from wealthier families from various professional and commercial backgrounds. Since the early 1990s, the Thai Government no longer places any restrictions on Thai nationals wishing to attend such schools or take international examinations, but Thai language and Thai studies are compulsory in this school, for all students.

Although the school is introducing the IB Middle Years Programme, students obtain an external certificate by taking the IGCSE, followed 2 years later by the IB Diploma. Only a minority of those who go on to university go overseas, mostly to the USA. United Kingdom universities are popular but are considered expensive and the current state of the economy is an important influence on university choices. Thai universities accept the international qualifications for entry, but my respondents did not know whether these offered any advantage. Apart from the attraction of access to foreign universities for a few students, the school's main attractions are probably the perceived quality of the education offered and the opportunity to learn English to a high standard.

School E: Argentina

The school has a student population that is over 80% Argentinian, drawn from the local middle classes. Argentinian law demands that 50% of teaching in such a school for local children must be in Spanish, but an education in English is one of the main attractions of the school. As a result, Spanish is used for lessons such as art and games, while some lessons in other subjects are given in Spanish and repeated in English. IGCSE and the IB Diploma are offered and are used by some students to gain access to overseas universities. A large number of graduates from the school, however, go on to local universities, in which Spanish is the only medium of instruction. Indeed, many students are obliged to take a Spanish entrance examination for university in addition to the IB or other international examinations. For these students, perceptions of educational quality and the social status and international access provided by English appear to be the key attractions.

Some Analysis and Discussion

Can any general points be extracted from these accounts? (The accounts have been chosen from a larger pool to be representative of certain patterns, but there is also considerable detail variation in the pool.)

One point is immediately obvious, and could have been predicted in advance: it is primarily the various elites within the countries concerned which make use of international curricula and examinations.

The nature of the elites involved varies from country to country, but the fact that schools offering international curricula almost always charge comparatively high fees ensures that such curricula will be accessible only to the relatively wealthy. There are examples of a few schools around the world which are part of a local national system, offering international examinations and not charging fees that are significantly higher than usual, but these are few and, as yet, I have little information about them. Some, at least, of these appear to be highly selective in their intake and therefore elitist in a different sense (although the meritocratic and economic elites commonly overlap).

It has been suggested that international qualifications may represent the next phase in the onward march of the Diploma Disease (e.g. Little, 1998). In this respect, a thesis might be that as increasing numbers obtain local qualifications, such that these become devalued in giving access to scarce but desirable opportunities, overseas qualifications could provide a competitive edge for any individual holding them. My initial response to this is that the scope for such an effect is likely to remain fairly limited in most countries, if only because access to international qualifications at school level remains largely limited to the wealthy, those who are already significantly advantaged. Such qualifications, therefore, may be used for the maintenance of existing advantage in the face of growth in locally based education and numbers obtaining local certificates. There are considerable regional and national variations in this generalisation, however. Some countries in Latin America, for example, have a large enough middle class for international qualifications to play a part in intra-class competition. Access to overseas, or to the more prestigious local universities, rather than directly to the labour market, may be the key dimension of this competition. Whether international certificates do offer an advantage in the local labour market remains to be investigated (Little, 1998) and it may be the status of the school rather than the certificate which is more important for local employment, as suggested by the El Salvadorean example given earlier. There may be a perception amongst students and their parents that overseas qualifications are more acceptable to employers in multinational companies, but both the existence and validity of this perception are also uncertain at this stage.

An alternative effect to that of local qualification inflation, which may contribute to the use of international qualifications to give access to jobs, is the perception of decreasing standards in local education and local certification in some countries. Note that it is the perception of such decreasing standards that is important, not any objective measure. This appears to be happening to some extent in South Africa, where overseas examinations are being taken by some students in parallel with local ones, as a form of insurance against perceptions of decreasing local standards. Where this is happening, the choice of overseas certificates is likely to be influenced by perceptions of sustained educational quality in their country of origin. A hypothesis is that examinations based in a country with a high international educational reputation, such as those offered by the UCLES, will be more attractive for this purpose than IB examinations, which are not linked to any national system. Anecdotal evidence suggests that the Scottish Examination Board has been identified in this way in South Africa.

The use of international certificates to gain access to an overseas university is another pattern which emerges from the school accounts presented earlier, and this access is certainly a marketing point used by the IBO, UCLES and ETS. This can be seen against a backdrop of universities in some countries, such as the United Kingdom, actively – even aggressively – trying to recruit overseas students as a means of increasing revenue. It is also interesting to note, however, that many graduates from schools offering international curricula go on to local universities. Again, this seems to be particularly true in Latin America. Since access to a local university often demands sitting an entrance examination based on the local curriculum, attending a school that offers a different curriculum might seem to be a disadvantage. In such cases, it appears that an international curriculum is seen to offer advantages other than university access and the international qualification *per se* may not be the prime motivation.

Two common attractions of international schooling are perceptions of the quality of the education available and the use of English. It does seem that many parents are concerned about the quality of the education their children receive, and not just the certificates that they may obtain. Two issues tend to become conflated here: expectations of higher quality education bought through private schooling and perceptions of the educational quality of international curricula. It seems that international curricula are often valued for their educational content and the schools that offer them may have a high reputation for their teaching and their discipline. When they can afford to, people are using these schools as an alternative to poor quality education and curricula available in the national system. Where the international curriculum is delivered in English, there is an added bonus from the status that the use of English confers and from the access it provides to the international community.

In some small states in particular, local access to international qualifications is simply not an option. In such cases, the children of the wealthy may be sent overseas for at least the later stages of their schooling. From Solomon Islands, for example, children of the elite are often sent to secondary school in New Zealand or Australia. This is seen to give access to a higher quality education and to metropolitan qualifications (rather than the more strictly 'international'), which may offer an advantage in obtaining an overseas university place. Such children should be distinguished from those of the global nomads, and are more akin to those that are the focus of this chapter.

An interesting phenomenon is that several countries attempt to bar their citizens from attending international schools and sitting for international qualifications: Malaysia, Singapore and some African countries, for example. In practice, these attempts may be circumvented by various means, including loose interpretation of the regulations, political influence and even straightforward bribery, so that the elite nature of access is accentuated even further. (As well as the Jordanian example included earlier, a Malaysian school offering an education based on the English National Curriculum and with over 80% of its intake Malaysian nationals was described to the author but is not included in the aforementioned examples because it is a primary school and does not, therefore, offer international examinations.) To understand this mistrust of international schools, it is useful to divide the fundamental purposes behind national mass education rather crudely into two: the promotion of national coherence and identity on the one hand, and the promotion of economic development on the other. It is easy to see that where national identity is emphasised, opposition to externally oriented curricula can be expected. This is likely to be the case in Malaysia, for example, where inter-ethnic tensions are a cause for concern and there is a deliberate effort to develop a Malaysian identity. A similar situation is found in some African countries, although not all may go so far as to ban attendance at international schools. An alternative to an outright ban is to impose some minimum curriculum elements such as the national language, a civics course, or teaching of religion. The last of these appears in some Middle Eastern international schools that are dominated by indigenous students, although this region is rather heterogeneous in its responses to international curricula. More conservative countries, notably Saudi Arabia, ban attendance at international schools whereas in others, such as Kuwait, such attendance is common. It is possible that these latter countries value the quality of the education that is on offer, particularly in the sciences and business-related subjects, and then safeguard national culture, religion and identity either through curriculum legislation or by ensuring the 'business' of the school is restricted to less culturally sensitive areas.

Where the emphasis in education is on its role in national economic development, there may be less opposition to international curricula. Indeed, they may be welcomed as providers of high quality education in economically important areas such as science and technology. Opposition may still arise, however, if the presence of such schooling is seen as a threat to the central planning of economic expansion or manpower provision. It would be interesting to discover whether there are different attitudes at an official level to the curricula offered by the IBO and UCLES. The former is explicitly concerned with 'culture', and although it claims to reinforce an individual's national and cultural identity as a starting point for the development of greater understanding and tolerance of other cultures, this very explicit involvement in such matters may arouse some suspicion. The UCLES, on the other hand, tends to avoid explicit cultural and ideological references and sells itself in terms of an 'objective' notion of educational quality and technical expertise.

The avoidance of national restrictions on access to international curricula that was mentioned earlier is a reminder that there may be considerable conflict between state and individual perceptions of the role of education. National culture and identity are likely to take second place to economic advantage when individuals make educational decisions. As outlined earlier, the nature of this economic advantage may be unusual in that we tend largely to be dealing with an elite which is already advantaged within the national economy. A question that presents itself at this stage is whether international curricula and qualifications serve a purpose – or are perceived to serve a purpose – in gaining access to an international elite. This is simply posing at the level of the individual the broader question about a possible role for international qualifications in processes of internationalisation or globalisation. To begin to provide an answer to this would need both more empirical data and a model of the processes of globalisation in the economic, political and cultural spheres. At this stage, a useful theoretical question may be whether an extension of some form of dependency theory might be fruitful, or adequate, to further understanding and analysis, given that we are dealing with national elites and their relationship with the international community. Or do we need to move away from seeing these elites as national, see them instead as part of a globalised elite, and turn to models of globalisation for greater understanding?

A key methodological difficulty in taking this study further relates to the most appropriate level of data collection and analysis. The classic unit of analysis in comparative or international studies is the nation state, and the location of all of the schools used as examples was given, and used in the limited discussion that followed. The significance of the country in which a school is located was almost taken for granted and seemed to offer some possible insights. At the same time, it must be noted that we are looking here at individual schools that deal directly with transnational organisations. The state may appear as an intervention of more or less significance in this interaction and the national context may be important in understanding the possibilities open to individuals, the constraints under which they act and the purposes with which they approach international qualifications. This involvement of the state does not establish its primacy as the unit of analysis and it is important not to be led into a particular analytical framework based on an assumption of this primacy. If, as was hypothesised, international examinations are at least perceived as a gateway to something global, then a global context suggests itself as a potentially more useful analytical framework.

Bray & Thomas (1995), in making a case for more multilevel approaches in comparative studies, suggested a model in the form of three dimensions of analysis, each dimension being multilayered. This has been criticised by Watson (1998) for ignoring important dimensions, but my own uncertainty about its usefulness in this case is that it seems to suggest both a privileged status and a hierarchical structure to the politico-geographical dimension: from global to regional to country to school to individual. In the case of international curricula, interactions seem to be between non-adjacent layers in this model: the global and the school, or even the individual. One must further question whether 'geographical location' is always so important, or whether it is the most appropriate space in which to locate an analysis. The advent of instantaneous global communication of vast amounts of information undermines the significance of geography, and other forms of space may become more significant: economic or cultural space, for instance. Should the schools, or their students, be located in one of these alternative 'spaces' for an initial analysis? Is such a location possible, or will we find ourselves returning to geographical location as a priority?

Yet another approach to the whole issue is from an investigation of the roles of the producers of international curricula and qualifications: the IBO, UCLES, ETS and others. These can be seen not just as servicers of global capitalism through the certification of human resources for the global market, but as a component of that same capitalism. Through them, education becomes another commodity in the global market place and both they and their product will be influenced by market forces. To see them as agents of globalisation is to see just one half of the process that is taking place. It is to take them as a given and not to problematise them. The term 'Glocalization' was very cleverly coined by Roland Robertson (1995) to describe the way in which global forces are translated into local realities, but the reverse process seems to be less commonly examined. What is commonly missing from analyses of the global is the way in which globalising forces themselves are formed and reformed through this process of interaction with the local, the way in which they must accommodate themselves and become, even if only incrementally, transformed. Thus, in the context of this emerging study, the producers of international curricula and examinations can be seen as both agents and recipients in the process of globalisation.

References

Bray, M. & Thomas, R.M. (1995) Levels of Comparison in Educational Studies: different insights from different literatures and the value of multilevel analyses, *Harvard Educational Review*, 65, pp. 472-490.

Drennen, Helen (1998) Seminar presented to EdD students at the University of Bath, 14 July. (Helen Drennen is Director of Academic Affairs at the IBO Curriculum and Assessment Centre, Cardiff.)

Education Testing Service (ETS) (1995) AP International, *ETS Developments*, 40(3), p. 8.

Education Testing Service (ETS) (1996) *Graduate Record Examinations 1996-97. Information and Registration Bulletin.* Princeton: Educational Testing Service.

Education Testing Service (ETS) (1997) *Through Technology, ETS is Providing Better Services to Growing Number of International Students.* Web site: http://www.ets.org/aboutets/china1.html

Fox, Elisabeth (1998) The Role of the International Baccalaureate in Educational Transformation: Chile as a case study, in Mary Hayden & Jeff Thompson (Eds) *International Education: principles and practice.* London: Kogan Page.

Hayden, M.C. & Thompson, J.J. (1995) International Schools and International Education: a relationship reviewed, *Oxford Review of Education*, 21, pp. 327-345.

International Baccalaureate Organisation (IBO) Web site: http://www.ibo.org/diploma.htm

Kellaghan, Thomas (1996) IEA Studies and Educational Policy, *Assessment in Education*, 3, pp. 143-160.

Little, Angela (1998) Qualifications, Globalisation and Livelihoods: towards a research agenda, paper presented at the World Congress of Comparative Education Societies Conference, Cape Town, 12-18 July.

Madaus, George F. & Raczek, Anastasia E. (1996) A Turning Point for Assessment: reform movements in the United States, in Angela Little & Alison Wolf (Eds) *Assessment in Transition: learning, monitoring and selection in international perspective.* Oxford: Pergamon.

Robertson, Roland (1995) Glocalization: time–space and homogeneity–heterogeneity, in M. Featherstone, S. Lash & R. Robertson (Eds) *Global Modernities.* London: Sage.

University of Cambridge Local Examinations Syndicate (UCLES) (1997) *Annual Review 1997.* Web site: http://www.ucles.org.uk/corp/rev_97/ar97_3.htm#int

Watson, Keith (1998) Memories, Models and Mapping: the impact of geopolitical changes on comparative studies in education, *Compare*, 28, pp. 5-31.

POSTSCRIPT

Developing the Discipline

The Development of a Discipline: some reflections on the development of comparative education as seen through the pages of the journal *Compare*

J.H. HIGGINSON

The purpose of this survey is to examine the development of the concept and scope of comparative education as it can be gleaned from a study of early *Newsletters* initiated by the Comparative Education Society in Europe (CESE) and the British Comparative and International Education Society (BCIES), which ultimately led to the publication of the journal *Compare*. This journal has had a succession of editors who made significant personal contributions to comparative studies. As a consequence, they have influenced the shaping and expansion of the concept of comparative education by their editorial selectivity, some examples of which will be noted.

To this survey I propose to add some account of an experiment that was made, in the course of the evolution of the discipline, to 'apply' comparative education in a school situation, with its implications for the training of teachers and indicating a potential line of development to be considered by the new organisation, the British Association for International and Comparative Education.

Recently, whilst cleaning up my study, I came across a folder containing the *Newsletters* issued by CESE and BCIES. I was reminded by these early *Newsletters*, in English, French and German that:

> *The CESE Newsletter is the official information bulletin of the* Comparative Education Society in Europe, *but it is also YOUR* Newsletter. *Do not hesitate to send us any information of scientific value in the field of Comparative Education, or submit texts about interesting studies, major projects, changes*

> *in Comparative Education, curricula, new courses. Send us an*
> *offprint of your latest article or a copy of the book you have*
> *just published.[1]*

Such was the encouraging invitation from CESE, which had its headquarters in Brussels. And a *Newsletter* headed *British Comparative and International Education Society* entitled *Bits and Pieces*, opens:

> *This* Newsletter *is a collection of items rather than a*
> *continuous commentary on current events. We hope,*
> *nonetheless, that the information will prove useful.[2]*

From this somewhat haphazard state of affairs, a decision was made to change from a society newsletter in duplicated form to a printed journal, which would take its place in 'line with the growing international practice'. So *Compare* was born as a *Journal of the Comparative Education Society in Europe: British Section.*

CESE, the parent organisation, was founded in 1961. Membership of this society was limited to those who, through their writings or research, were considered to have made significant contributions to the progress of comparative education. Subsequently, to accommodate the growth of interest in comparative education as an educational discipline in the United Kingdom, especially in university departments and colleges of education, the British Section of the European Society came into being at a conference held at the University of Reading in September 1965. Leon Boucher, of Chester College, steered the new publication through its early years and when his successor, Peter Raggatt, took over the editorship in 1981, he put on record this tribute to the pioneering of Leon Boucher:

> *For the past eight years Leon Boucher has edited this Journal.*
> *During that time the Journal has developed from a small, in-*
> *house news sheet to a publication which is widely used by*
> *teachers of Comparative Education in many countries.*
> Compare *is a testament to the effort and dedication which*
> *Leon has invested in his Editorship.[3]*

Peter Raggatt uses his first editorial to survey the situation of comparative studies in education as he sees it and this issue carries an article on 'Curriculum Issues 1970-1990: contents, policies and practices'. He opens his survey with the observation:

> *Comparative studies in Education have increased markedly*
> *since the CESE 1963 Hamburg Conference when it was noted*
> *that 'the different social sciences which are interested in*
> *education make more and more use of international*
> *comparison'.[4]*

He suggests that there is an older tradition in British comparative education in which education 'is the art of reflection, reflection that is concerned with gaining knowledge – not data'. In this approach, comparative education begins with speculating and theorising about education within and beyond the United Kingdom. He sees it as a liberalising tradition extending from Michael Sadler through Nicholas Hans and Joseph Lauwerys to Vernon Mallinson and Edmund King and Brian Holmes. Thus, the Editor identifies at this time two traditions as continuing to occupy a central position in comparative education. From this older tradition, Raggatt foresees a fuller development of comparative studies as a significant dimension of social science activity. Cross-national testing, in his view, is the only way in which hypotheses about the relationship between education and society can be adequately examined. Such hypotheses may be formulated after initial cross-national observation and then be stringently examined in two or more countries.

Arising from the invitation of Leon Boucher, Volume 11, No. 2, 1981, presented a special issue conceived as a *Festschrift* in honour of Edmund King, the editorial being by Harold Noah. As was appropriate for such an occasion, in addition to a selected bibliography of Edmund King's studies of comparative education, there was an assembly of tributes which included the names of the outstanding practitioners of the early 1980s: Jean Auba, Nigel Grant, W.D. Halls, Brian Holmes, Aharon F. Kleinburger, Vernon Mallinson, Sixten Marklund, G.W. Parkyn, Juan Tusquets. Standing out in this male galaxy with her contribution on 'Foundations of Moral Education: a comparison of possibilities' was Margaret Sutherland.

Volume 12, No. 2, 1982 carries an advertisement for the Fifth World Congress of Comparative Education to be held in Paris. It announces that the World Council has entrusted the Francophone Association of Comparative Education with the preparation of this international event, with Professor Michel Debeauvois carrying the major organisational responsibility. This preliminary announcement states:

Previous Congresses had been held in Toronto (1970), Geneva (1973), London (1977) and Tokyo (1980). The 5th Congress *will be attended by several hundreds of members of constituent societies, as well as specialists from countries where Comparative Education societies do not exist as yet: a particular effort will be made in order to allow specialists from the Third World to participate in the discussions on the topic* Dependence and Interdependence in Education, *which is of particular relevance for educational policies in developing countries.[5]*

Once again, in Volume 13, No. 1, 1983, there is a special issue devoted to 'Educational Transfer'. In his editorial, Peter Raggatt points out that all the articles deal with the movement of ideas, of institutional models, and of practices from one country to another. He claims that as the various contributors draw on a number of different theoretical perspectives and research traditions, they all serve to illustrate the importance of an international dimension when analysing educational transfer. The examination of economic, social, political and educational change in low-income countries is surveyed within the framework of dependency theory. An important factor in this theory is that the centre exercises its power through an indigenous elite at the periphery. In this special issue on educational transfer, there is a harvest of information and thoughtful interpretation about what is postulated as the Third World.

There is, as yet, an absence of any study from what at this time were known as countries beyond the Iron Curtain (though there are analyses of the impact of Marxist ideas upon the countries of the Third World). It has been suggested that the reason for omitting studies from the USSR and Eastern Europe was that they were regarded as Second World rather than Third World countries. With the collapse of the Communist system, it has become apparent how Third World, in fact, was the state of these social structures. The days when another survey of educational transfer will include only three countries in western Europe (England, France, Spain) and a harvest from the former Iron Curtain lands are still more than a decade ahead.[6]

By Volume 14, No. 1, 1984, we find the Editor, Peter Raggatt, once more considering 'Comparative Education: its condition and future', and the British Comparative and International Education Society is advertising its annual conference, to be held at Chester College, on the theme *Technical Change and Cultural Adaptation*. In surveying the state of play in this issue, the editor begins with an assertion that 'Comparative education is not in a healthy state'. He explains:

> *That there has been a decline in Comparative Education in the 1970s is quite clear. It has been documented by Keith Watson on behalf of the BCIES, and has been apparent in the absence of familiar faces and lower numbers at the Annual Conferences. The decline has been closely associated with cuts in teacher education experienced during the decade. The numbers tell the story. In 1971/2 some 130,000 students were enrolled in colleges of education with nearly 6,000 in universities; by 1980/81 college enrolment had fallen to some 38,000 while the university figures had remained almost constant. In the process teacher education was re-structured. About one in three colleges were closed, a further third merged with polytechnics, or, unusually, with universities, and almost*

all others diversified with a reduction in their teacher training
components.[7]

After analysing the consequence of these changes, the Editor attempts to
indicate some lines of future development. He draws attention to the
change proposed in the name of the society so that in the future it would
be identified as the British Comparative and International Education
Society (BCIES). A second essential change suggested is the need for
educationists to stress the *applied potential* of the field. As examples of
opportunities, he points to multicultural studies, gender discrimination,
education and training of young people, special educational provision,
technical and vocational education. He is careful to warn that such
emphasis on applied studies should not result in the work being any less
intellectually rigorous, and he ends on a final note of optimism. The next
issue of *Compare* [8] carries this plea for applied studies further and
Peter Raggatt's own contribution deals with 'Young People,
Unemployment and Other Matters'. There are informative articles on this
theme from West Germany and data making use of comparative studies
from France, England and Wales, and Papua New Guinea.

A new editor enters the scene in 1985 with Martin McLean from the
University of London Institute of Education. He announces an interesting
principle at the outset and begins his editorial:

A journal's contents are determined by what the Editor
receives unsolicited through the mail and by what invited
contributors can be persuaded to produce.[9]

He pays a warm tribute to his predecessors, Peter Raggatt and Leon
Boucher, for what they have achieved in raising the quality and
relevance of the articles in *Compare*. He suggests that from the firm
foundation established by these predecessors, he now proposes to be a
little more adventurous since 'Risk-taking has been one of the
characteristics of successful comparative educationists'. The contents of
Volume 15, No. 1 bear out this promise: new names of contributors
appear and themes range from a discussion, for example, of 'Mass
Schooling: a tool of capitalist domination', to 'Gender, Ideology and
Education: implications at the Ecuadorean periphery'.

The next issue in Volume 15 [10] reproduces three papers given at
various comparative education conferences and the Editor makes the
point that all these papers fall within the classical comparative education
tradition because they start, not from the question, 'Which country has
adopted the best educational policy?' but from the point, 'How do
attitudes to work differ in various cultures and how well are educational
provisions articulated to these cultural norms?' In his next editorial in
Volume 16, No. 1, in 1986 [11], Martin McLean draws attention to the
fact that in several past papers in *Compare* there has been a
preoccupation with 'educational transfer between metropoles and

peripheries'. He notes how the developing relationship between China after Mao and Western countries is likely to challenge older propositions about 'educational dependency'. The paper by Ruth Hayhoe, which gives rise to this speculation, is a foreshadowing of the distinctive contribution she will make to Chinese studies, culminating in her being invited to undertake the amalgamations of four institutions of higher education in Hong Kong, as Director of the new Institute of Education in 1997 when China resumed control of Hong Kong.[12]

To mark the retirement of Brian Holmes from his Professorship of Comparative Education in the London University Institute of Education in September 1985, all the papers in Volume 17, No. 1, 1987 are presented to form a *Festschrift*. On this occasion, Martin McLean's editorial virtually provides a concise history of the development of comparative education by locating Holmes within a number of circles that made up comparative and international educational studies in the first half of the twentieth century. Thus, McLean writes:

> *Holmes can be seen as a member of a generation of*
> *comparative educationists including Bereday in the USA and*
> *King in Britain but also many more in both west and east*
> *Europe ... it was a generation which emerged in the 1950s and*
> *was concerned with the reconstruction of education in*
> *response to the end of the Second World War, the*
> *democratisation of educational access which followed and the*
> *end of colonial empires.[13]*

A perceptive statement of the many aspects of Brian Holmes's comparative educational activities continues, and this issue contains six detailed pages of his publications. As if this were not God's plenty, there follow six pages of titles and details of PhD theses completed under his supervision, with a number of asterisks indicating where he had shared the tutoring with Joseph Lauwerys. As one who frequently had the privilege of being External Examiner with Holmes, I found myself recalling his meticulous scholarship and dislike of pretentiousness.

Volume 18, No. 2, 1988 saw Martin McLean's final issue as Editor. He took the opportunity of assessing the position of comparative and international education, as he sees it, in the late 1980s. He discerns two significant changes: first, the decline of comparative education in initial teacher education, and secondly, educational policy-makers and educational researchers are more international in outlook than in the 1970s. As evidence of this, he indicates influential statements in major countries, such as the *A Nation at Risk* (1983) report in the USA, the 1988 Education Reform Act in England and important recent statements in Japan. He notes how the entry of the People's Republic of China into the international education arena has stimulated comparative studies for China, as is exemplified by an article from Cuilin Xiaxo, published in this issue. These changes have had their impact on *Compare* and on its editorial policy, and McLean claims that the journal has gone more 'up-market'. There are fewer readers in exclusively undergraduate teaching institutions, but a greater number of major centres of educational policy-making, and research in a wider range of countries, now compose the contributions to the journal. In brief, 'The research paper which communicates original ideas or data is more appropriate to the present position of *Compare*'.

Following the editorship of Martin McLean, the task was taken over by the partnership of Nicholas Beattie and Colin Brock. In defining their principles of educational policy, they observed that:

> Compare *has its own part to play in this complex exchange of information, this unpredictable and often unnoticed patterning of thought, of decision-makers and classroom practitioners. As editors we cannot be complacent about the journal's impact.[14]*

Reacting to some criticism published in a paper by Wenhui Zhong on 'The Involvement of Chinese Scientists in International Scholarly Publishing', the joint editors of *Compare* comment:

> *We note with regret the 'imbalance and inequality' of publication which Zhong describes, and acknowledge that our journal too inevitably forms part of the industrialised world's domination of intellectual production and therefore of people's thoughts. We can only ask our readership to help us to start overcoming that historic distortion.[15]*

By the time we come to Volume 21, No. 2, in 1991, the joint Editors are murmuring about the number of competent contributions they are receiving, the problems of selection, and they fly a kite for moving to a pattern of three issues a year for the journal so as to give more contributors the chance of sharing their work and investigations. This particular volume ranges across a wide sweep of key issues in the field of comparative and international education. Thus, from a global discussion by Keith Watson on 'Teachers and Teachers in an Interdependent World' we are taken to the individual world and role of the *metapelet* in the Israeli kibbutz and how this is changing with the evolution of modern Israeli society. Harriet Harman contributes an article on 'Changes in Kibbutz Education: linking macro and micro'. There is a substantial research report by Hangli Shu on 'Sex Role Socialisation of Children in Chinese and American Cultures: a comparative study of elementary school language textbooks'.[16]

A special issue of *Compare* devoted to Europe was planned at least 2 years before it went to press. At the time, the joint Editors were thinking mainly in terms of 1992, the next great formal step towards the single market in Europe, which was due to take place on 1 January 1993. However, since this issue was initially planned, a darker side of Europe became increasingly apparent. Freer movement combined with outstanding economic inequalities of people inevitably throws different nationalities and ethnic groups into contact, and often conflict, with each other. This volume on Europe ultimately appeared as Volume 22, No. 1, in 1992. The volume makes fascinating reading in the way it informs and articulates the problems of integrating 'Europe'.

The very titles of the articles forecast the complexity of identifying the concept of a 'Europe' that will comprehend both the familiar Western, and the emerging Eastern, identities from the USSR. Thus, the themes dealt with are as follows:

'Higher Education and Western European integration'
'The Internationalisation of Higher Education and Problems of Improving the Institutional Infrastructure'
'Common Trends in Teacher Education in the European Community'
'Religion and Schools: are the issues still of interest and concern in France today?'
'Education in Present-day Germany'
'Education in the Soviet Union: the last phase'
'Multicultural Education in the Former Soviet Union and the United Kingdom: the language factor'

As the joint Editors say, 'all these studies must be read as courageous attempts to freeze movements into a snapshot'.

An announcement is made in Volume 22, No. 2 in 1992 that for the first time *Compare* will be published three times a year, in March, June and October from 1993. Reference is again made by the Editors to the abundance of contributions accompanied by 'a buoyant profile of subscriptions from individuals and institutions world-wide', factors which have led to the decision to publish three issues per annum. This issue is notable for the methodological discussions and the Asian/Pacific contributions.

The complementary articles on aspects of education in Hong Kong, together with the review of a book surveying, as the subtitle has it, 'Towards One Country and Two Systems', foresee what may well prove in the future to be a fertile ground for comparative studies. Tribute is paid in this issue to Vernon Mallinson and Richard Goodings, whose deaths are reported, noting that 'Each made a distinct and valued contribution to the development of Comparative and International Education'.

One of the helpful features of *Compare* as the years go by has been the evaluative reviews of literature and books relevant to comparative studies. In Volume 23, No. 2, 1993, Nicholas Beattie produces a review article on a publication by a professor who was almost unknown in English-speaking circles. It was entitled 'Across the Divide: an article review of Lê Thành Khôi's *L'éducation: cultures et societés* and *Culture, créativité et developpement'*. The author of these two works began as a historian and an economist with particular experience in South-east Asia. Subsequently, he turned to educational studies. At the time of these publications, he was Professor of Comparative Education and Development at the Sorbonne in Paris. Nicholas Beattie communicates vividly the social challenge presented by of Lê Thành Khôi and he comments:

> *At one level,* L'éducation: cultures et societés *is an analytical tool, a checklist even to guide researchers in the study of education. At a later date, as from within a different intellectual tradition, it is the same kind of book as the group of 'Anglo-Saxon' introductions to Comparative Education which appeared in the 1960s and 1970s (e.g. Bereday, 1964; Holmes, 1965; Noah and Eckstein, 1969).[17]*

When Volume 23, No. 3, 1993 appeared, it presented a bumper issue that according to its joint Editors had its inspiration from a report on *The School in Russia Today and Tomorrow*. In this report, V.A. Karakovsky, himself the principal of a Moscow school, describes a project or game played by his pupils. Each team received from the famous Captain Nemo and Dick Sand a large envelope which contained a note with coordinates of a point somewhere on the globe to which they had to travel – Alaska, Spitzbergen, Greenland, Tibet, etc. Little known regions were chosen. For a month, the class was expected to survive in the place named, and then later to report to the whole school their adventures and what had happened to them on this imaginary journey. The offshoot of this task was that it brought in many people beyond the pupils to help. People who had spent time in these regions were sought out, and the help of parents was invited. In fact, the entire community was drawn into the game and teachers became as absorbed as the pupils. After drawing attention to this inspiration, the joint Editors comment:

> *A journal like* Compare *is in some ways similar to such a game. This issue presents 'sealed envelopes' containing information about the eastern part of Germany, Britain, the Netherlands, Switzerland, the western part of Germany, Canada, France, Russia, Tanzania.[18]*

The emphasis turned out to be predominantly European, whereas the previous issue of *Compare* was oriented towards developing countries.

The Editorial in Volume 24, No. 1, 1994 opens with reference to the death of Professor Brian Holmes and the pioneer contribution he made to comparative studies. In drawing attention to this being the final year of their joint editorship of *Compare*, Nicholas Beattie and Colin Brock put in a special plea for more entries to be made in the BCIES Essay Prize and they remark that had this constitution existed whilst Brian Holmes was still in his post, they are sure that he would have encouraged his students to submit entries. In contrast to the disappointing response to the *Essay Prize*, the Editors note that they continue to receive far more publishable submissions than they can accommodate even with the extension of publication to three issues a year.

Nicholas Beattie and Colin Brock launched their final joint editorial with a challenging quotation from Irving Epstein:

> *Probably the most important choice comparative educationists*
> *make is the decision to pursue the 'other', to investigate*
> *phenomena grounded in contexts demonstrably different from*
> *those with which we are most familiar, and in so doing, play*
> *the role of outsider.[19]*

This theme is developed in the first article of Volume 25, No. 1, in Epstein's discussion of 'Comparative Education in North America: the search for other through the escape from self'. Other articles in this issue raise questions of what, in a democracy, constitutes a proper professional autonomy for teachers. How can that be reconciled with the need for teachers to be democratically accountable? Contributions on 'the tidal changes affecting South Africa or Germany' exemplify approaches to these questions. The joint Editors note that they welcome contributions from teachers in schools.

With the take-over of the joint editorship by Colin Brock and Ruth Aedo-Richmond, certain administrative changes in the production of *Compare* are indicated. The number of copies of manuscripts required from potential contributors becomes three. Then it was also decided to make Volume 26, No. 2, a special edition devoted to *Education in Latin America*. In fact, when this special issue appeared in June 1996, it was edited by Ruth Aedo-Richmond, and in her editorial she draws attention to the fact that this particular issue, along with others in the *International Journal of Educational Development* in 1987 and 1995, reflects the mounting interest that British universities are showing on the subject of Latin American education. She writes:

> *I particularly hope that comparative educationists whose*
> *area(s) of specialisms lie outside Latin America may find this*
> *issue's offering both useful and stimulating.[20]*

The papers composing this issue cover four countries: Mexico, Venezuela, Peru and Chile. An article by Ruth Aedo-Richmond & Mark Richmond continues their collaboration on the study of Chilean education. A valuable selected Bibliography enhances this issue.

In a retrospective search covering the last three decades, I have grown aware of how *Compare* has tabulated world trends and reflected significant societal changes, moving out of the Iron Curtain etc. into increasing awareness of and information about the countries of the former Soviet Empire, and about cultures in Africa, Asia, India and Latin America. Volume 26, No. 3, 1996 takes up this theme of increasing globalisation. The joint Editors, in selecting their material, point out that whilst the early contributions to this issue consider aspects of cultural tensions provoked by the forces of globalisation, the later articles focus on multicultural problems 'at international scale'. The Netherlands is thus surveyed as something approaching an exemplar in its approach to the provision of education in a plural society. A special research report by Seriema Lumelume, of the University of the South Pacific, and Elizabeth Todd, of the University of Newcastle-upon-Tyne is entitled 'Ready to Read: a long-term literacy project in the South Pacific'. When the Chairman gave his annual Report to the BCIES for 1994-95 he commented:

> Compare *has been successfully steered by Colin Brock and Ruth Aedo-Richmond into a new style of working, with more elaborate and impersonal procedures for vetting papers submitted – necessary in the late 1990s for maintaining the prestige of the journal.*

Compare, Volume 28, No. 1, 1998 is somewhat in the nature of an epilogue. In future, the journal will be owned by the new British Association for International and Comparative Education (BAICE) though it will continue to be published by Carfax. The Educational Board is being modified and enlarged. A major contribution to this issue, especially helpful in tracking the development of comparative education as a 'discipline', is the reprint of the farewell address by Professor Keith Watson entitled 'Memories, Models and Mapping: the impact of geopolitical changes on comparative studies in education'.[21] This address offers a penetrating survey and analysis of geopolitical changes and their implications for education: the assessment of postmodernism, and the identification of globalisation, is profound in its scope.

I note in what is proposed as Symposium 1 of the BAICE Conference the title *Reconceptualising Comparative and International Education*. This strikes me as a possibly relevant title for the journey I have made through the issues of *Compare* from its beginnings. A succession of editors can be detected grappling with the task of definition, from the days of *Auslandspedagogik* through the splintering into specialisms referred to by Professor Watson in his address. I was fascinated to see where we had arrived in 1997 with the publication of the *Festschrift* celebrating the seventieth birthday of one of comparative education's most assiduous pioneers, Wolfgang Mitter.[22] This two-volume study bears the suggestive title, *Comparative Education: challenges–intermediation–practice*. In this collection, 59 authors from 20 countries provide a panorama of where we stand in comparative education today. This detailed overview could well be taken as a reference text for the BAICE Conference.

It will not be deemed irrelevant, I hope, if I conclude this commentary on *Compare* with some reflections and conclusions that have grown in my mind as I have reread through the issues. I had the privilege of being a founder member of the Comparative Education Society of Europe and, subsequently, arising from personal contributions, was awarded honorary membership of CESE, and later of BCIES. By chance, equipped with many personal papers of the pioneering Michael Sadler, as the first Warden of Sadler Hall in the University of Leeds [23], I witnessed the gradual defining of comparative studies as a discipline in its own right. This evolution was focused in 1965 when Lionel Elvin published his book entitled *Education and Contemporary Society*.[24]

At this time, there was a strong reaction prompted by the philosopher, Richard Peters, to what he termed 'the mish-mash' that was prevalent under the label *Education*. There was a somewhat self-conscious effort to identify 'the disciplines' of Education. Commonly accepted were the areas of history, philosophy, and sociology. Somewhat more cautiously, comparative education began to be approved at examiners' meetings (though I well remember some of Professor Bernstein's caustic comments). Chapter V in Lionel Elvin's book is devoted to the case for including comparative studies, pointing out that 'so far Comparative Education has hesitated to be explicitly comparative'. On the eve of this amalgamation of the two societies, it is worth reading the 16 pages of Elvin's argument once again, in relation to future shaping, function and scope.

In the *Compare* editorials over the years there are recurrent suggestions that in addition to research and theoretical analysis, there was a need for 'applied' studies. Isaac Kandel, one of Michael Sadler's most appreciative students in his Manchester days, once wrote:

> *The greater part of the world thus constitutes today a species*
> *of laboratory in which, so far as Education is concerned,*
> *various types of solution are being attempted for the same*
> *general range of problems.*

Michael Sadler, in many attempts to define the function of comparative studies in education, always included an emphasis on 'practical' application. In one of the lengthy memoranda justifying his work to his government critics in February 1903, he crystallised his thinking by stipulating that the chief work of his office was:

> *(1) ... to collect, summarise, and publish various kinds of*
> *educational experience, with a view to getting what is sound*
> *and true from a number of discrepant opinions; (2) informing*
> *the nation how it stands in regard to Educational efficiency as*

compared with other nations; (3) promoting, as far as possible,
general consent and agreement as to the wisest and most
fruitful line of development in national education.[25]

It is characteristic of Sadler that the theme of his best known piece of
writing, the lecture he gave in Guildford in 1900, bears the title: 'How
Far Can We Learn Anything of Practical Value from the Study of Foreign
Systems of Education?'

In Volume 14, No. 1, 1984, the Editor drew attention to the decline
in comparative education courses associated with the cuts in teacher
education. The dissolution of teacher training colleges also meant that
there was an 'absence of familiar faces and lower numbers at the Annual
Conference'. That this situation developed without much concern was
another illustration of the fact that comparative education had not had
much influence or been regarded as an essential constituent in the
upbringing of a post-war generation. The public confusion about fuller
participation in 'Europe' has also exposed the shortcoming of this
potential enlightenment in our contemporary society.

It was with a conviction about the need to experiment in 'applied'
comparative education, and an awareness of the inadequacy of the
prevailing provision in teacher education and schools in which a new
generation was growing up, that led me to make a decision – to leave the
academic world where I had been tutoring in comparative studies, and
return to school. I had the opportunity of bringing to life a new school for
720 teenagers, the joint product of the then Ministry of Education and a
local education authority. The physical structure of this new school is set
forth in the *Building Bulletin* No. 17, published by HMSO in August
1960.[26]

With my belief in the importance of comparative education, how
could I apply this to the initiation and development of a new secondary
school, which would have an entry of 220 boys and 173 girls, aged 11-15
years? The experimental structure of the buildings allowed us to
reinterpret the traditional English 'house' concept and to create six
locations, each of which we linked with a largish area of the world –
Africa, Europe, India, China, USA and USSR. Each unit was guided by a
'Warden' and in the course of 5 years we built up a considerable network
of personal pupil contacts and exchanges. The seal was set on this
attempt to apply comparative education when Vijaya Lakshmi Pandit, at
the time High Commissioner for India in London, gave the address at the
opening of the school. In the course of this address to the assembled
pupils, staff, parents and governors, she said:

We in India are faced, today, with many problems; one of the
greatest is in Education. We have a vast population of many
people who are illiterate. We have not only the problem of
building more schools, both primary and secondary schools to

> teach children, we have the big problem of adult illiteracy,
> teaching adults how to read and write. We have to do it
> quickly because unless we can achieve something in this field,
> our great experiment in democratic living will be a failure.[27]

She continued with a brilliant analysis of the problems confronting India, and promising that she would establish links for our pupils, with schools in India. She concluded a memorable address:

> I look forward to the time when free countries can visit each
> other more easily, so that by seeing India, and meeting people
> different from themselves, they can really come to an
> understanding of their neighbours. It is not good enough to
> read about them in a book, that is second-best, first-best is
> always to be able to see people, their weaknesses and their
> strengths, and to be able to judge what they are like ... I want
> you all to feel that India is something very close. It is a distant
> country, many thousands of miles away, but the closeness
> exists in these links that are being created every day. I want to
> assure you that when I tell the people in India about this
> occasion, I know that the children of India will wish me to say
> to you that they wish you well, and that they will hear with
> interest what happens to you, and about you.[28]

Subsequently, her words were translated into a living reality and links with India were made. A multitude of linkages, with much visiting by overseas people, younger and older, became the established practice over the next 5 years. An interesting midday meal organisation, of which 90% of the pupils partook, made it possible for many of these visitors to be entertained at table by the pupils themselves. And when the schemes for interplay began to extend to parties of pupils going abroad, these were preceded by periods of study of the area to be visited. Well-prepared visits were an essential tool to our 'applied' comparative studies. We were not primarily concerned with organising large numbers of young people to tour 'famous places'. At its best, pupils and teachers lived, on a one-to one-basis, in the homes of their European contemporaries.

Such interplay between school and local community had several dimensions. At Parent Evenings, overseas visitors would deal with current issues in their own countries. There were occasions when well-prepared pupils gave talks arising from their studies, on the people and problems of the area to which their 'house' was linked. This background to the normal functioning of a secondary school resulted in the teachers becoming involved in further study, and in some cases, they made outstanding contributions. I had the cooperation of a keen, stimulated, sometimes sceptical, staff, in what was, though we never gave it such a grandiose name, 'in-service training'.

A comment in Professor Watson's address set me thinking further about the experience in the secondary school where we tried to give an 'applied' factor to comparative education. He remarked:

My own understanding is that it is probably fair to say that Comparative Education is research based whereas international education makes practical use of comparative data.[29]

It seems to me that in our practice in the secondary school, we were feeling towards a reconciliation of these two points of view. My teachers would have been enabled, had they had comparative education studies included in their initial training, to foster an *attitude of approach* to knowledge of international education. We made a school which had considerable linkages with six large areas of the world. What went on in the context of those six house areas could be called international education (incidentally, the interplay in such six units led to a form of 'globalisation'). But I had to rely on the knowledge and imaginations of the teachers to foster this context and, in some cases, they skilfully communicated the research approach.

Finally, I should like to offer, as a matter for further consideration, this pointer to the importance of securing studies in comparative education as an integral element in the new schemes for the education of teachers that are under discussion. There is clearly an area of development of this discipline which could be nurtured by the new British Association of International and Comparative Education. I recall, with gratitude, that it was an editor of *Compare* who, in reviewing my book, *A School is Born*, identified it as descriptive of a significant, if unusual, mode of research into comparative education 'applied'.

Notes

[1] See, for example, *Newsletter 6*, edited H. Van Daele, June 1980. *Comparative Education Society in Europe*, Brussels.

[2] *See British Comparative and International Education Society Newsletter No. 3*, February 1984, edited Trevor Corner, Glasgow.

[3] Peter Raggatt, *Compare*, 11(1), 1981, p. 5.

[4] Peter Raggatt, *Compare*, 11(1), 1981, p. 3.

[5] *Compare*, 12(2), 1982, p. 2.

[6] Elmer Lechner (1997) *Pädagogische Grenzgänger in Europa*. University of Klagenfurt: Peter Lang, EuropäischerVerlag der Wissenschaften.

[7] *Compare*, 14(1), 1984, p. 3.

[8] *Compare*, 14(2), 1985.

[9] *Compare*, 15(1), 1985, p. 3.

[10] *Compare*, 15(2), 1985, pp. 109, 121 and 129.

[11] *Compare*, 16(1), 1986, pp. 65-80.

[12] Ruth Hayhoe (1996) *China's Universities 1895-1995: a century of cultural conflict*. New York and London: Garland. Republished by the Comparative Education Research Centre, University of Hong Kong, 1999.

[13] *Compare*, 17(1), 1987, p. 3.

[14] *Compare*, 21(1), 1991, p. 314.

[15] Ibid.

[16] *Compare*, 21(2), 1991, pp. 199-207.

[17] *Compare*, 23(3), 1985, pp. 187-191.

[18] *Compare*, 23(3), 1993, pp. 314.

[19] *Compare*, 25(1), 1993, pp. 3, 16.

[20] *Compare*, 26(2), 1996. A special issue on *Education in Latin America*, edited by Ruth Aedo-Richmond.

[21] *Compare*, 28(1), 1998. 'Memories, Models and Mapping: the impact of geopolitical changes on comparative studies in education', pp. 5-31.

[22] See also *Akademische Feier für Wolfgang Mitter*, published 1997 by Deutsches Institut, Schloss Strasse 28, Frankfurt-am-Main; ISBN 388494 193 3.

[23] See J.H. Higginson (1979) *Selections from Michael Sadler*, published by International Publishers Ltd, 83-101, The Albany, Old Hall Street, Liverpool; ISBN 09056 0301 X.

[24] Lionel Elvin (1965) *Education in Contemporary Society*, The New Thinker's Library. London: Watts.

[25] J.H. Higginson, *Selections from Michael Sadler*, p. 52.

[26] Building Bulletin No. 17, *Secondary School, Arnold*. London: HMSO, August 1960.

[27] The full text of the address by Vijaya Lakshmi Pandit, High Commissioner for India, is printed as Appendix A, in *A School is Born*, by J.H. Higginson, published by The Book Guild Ltd, Sussex, 1987; ISBN 086332 199 X.

[28] Ibid.

[29] See *Compare*, 28(1), 1998, p. 11, in the article 'Memories, Models and Mapping' by Professor Keith Watson.

Notes on Contributors

Patricia Broadfoot is currently Dean of the Faculty of Social Sciences and Professor of Education in the Graduate School of Education, University of Bristol and was Head of School between 1993 and 1997. She directed the School's Centre for Assessment Studies for 11 years from 1987 to 1997. She is the author of a number of books and articles in the fields of assessment and comparative education. She is the editor of both *Assessment in Education* and *Comparative Education*. She was a co-director of two ESRC-funded research projects: the Quality in Experiences of Schooling Transnationally (QUEST) project from 1995 to 1997 and is currently directing a comparative study of pupil learning and identity in secondary schools in England, France and Denmark. She was president of the British Association for International and Comparative Education from 1997 to 1998.

Sylvia van de Bunt-Kokhuis is a consultant to international firms such as KLM and Ahold in the field of education, culture and multimedia. At Tilburg University, she completed her PhD thesis on international staff mobility (1996), she is currently a lecturer in Culture and Leadership at the Free University of Amsterdam and is a member of the Supervisory Board of Compu'Trian a European company for training IT specialists. She formerly directed the Office for International Relations at Tilburg (1988-93). She has co-published three books and various articles in international journals.

Roy Carr-Hill carried out his original research on criminal careers and sentencing patterns at Nuffield College, Oxford between 1968 and 1971. He then taught social statistics at the University of Sussex between 1971 and 1974. From 1974 to 1977 he was an Administrator to the Social Indicator Division of the Secretariat of the Organisation for Economic Cooperation and Development. Between 1978 and 1981 he was Professor of Mathematics in the Universidade Eduardo Mondlane in Maputo, Mozambique. Returning to the United Kingdom in 1981, he worked at the MRC Medical Sociology Unit in Aberdeen. Professor Carr-Hill is currently self-financing, working half-time at the Centre for Health Economics at the University of York as a contract researcher on a variety of research projects since 1983, and half-time at the Institute of Education, University of London, under the same conditions since 1992.

Michael Crossley is Vice Chairman of the British Association for International and Comparative Education (BAICE) and a Reader in Education at the University of Bristol where he is Director for MPhil/PhD Studies for the Graduate School of Education. Dr Crossley was previously Associate Dean (Planning) in the Faculty of Education at the University of Papua New Guinea. He has taught in England, Australia and Papua New Guinea; was Editor of the *Papua New Guinea Journal of Education* from 1985 to 1990; and is currently a member of the Editorial Board for *Comparative Education*, an Executive Editor for the *International Journal of Educational Development* and a Corresponding Editor for the *International Review of Education*. He is a Founding Series Editor for the 'Bristol Papers in Education' and recently published *Qualitative Educational Research in Developing Countries* (New York: Garland, 1977) (with Graham Vulliamy) and *Educational Development in the Small States of the Commonwealth* (Commonwealth Secretariat: London, 1999) (with Keith Holmes). Current research interests include methodological and theoretical studies on the future of the field of comparative and international education; evaluative and capacity building research in Kenya and Belize; and educational development.

Anastasia Economou is a research student in the Department of Educational Studies, University of Oxford. She is completing a study of the implementation of the 'European dimension' in education in England, Wales and Scotland.

Claudius Gellert was Professor of Education at the University of Reading until 2000. He studied Sociology, Philosophy and Psychology at Munich, Frankfurt and Sussex Universities. He received his MA from Munich, a PhD from Cambridge, and his *habilitation* (sociology) from Humboldt University Berlin. He held teaching appointments at the universities of Cambridge, Harvard, Munich, Klagenfurt and Humboldt (Berlin), and was Research Director at the European University Institute, Florence. He has published widely on higher education and research matters. He is now based in Munich and involved in setting up an accreditation agency for universities in several German states and Austria.

Remedios de Haro is a research assistant in the research group, 'Special Education and Educational Psychology' and Assistant in the Didactic and School Organisation Department, School of Education, at the University of Murcia, Spain. He has a PhD in Pedagogics and is an expert in multicultural education. He has published numerous articles in the field.

J.H. Higginson was first Warden of Sadler Hall in the University of Leeds for a decade. During his time he was able to make special study of the contribution of Sir Michael Sadler to the development of comparative education. On leaving this post, he became first headmaster of the Arnold County High School, an experiment in secondary education sponsored jointly by the then Ministry of Education and the Nottinghamshire Local Education Authority. He became first Head of Education in the new Christ Church College in Canterbury in 1964 and retired from this post in 1976. In recognition of his contribution to the study of comparative education, he was awarded an honorary membership of the Comparative Education Society of Europe and later of the British Comparative and International Education Society.

Angela Jacklin is a lecturer in education at the University of Sussex. She taught for 13 years in primary and special schools before moving to the University of Sussex. Research interests in primary and special education have developed more recently into the fields of teacher education and the use of research and evaluation in education development.

Colin Lacey is Professor of Education at the University of Sussex. Major research interests have developed from the sociology of schools and teaching to problems of development, especially those associated with use of evaluation.

Joanna Le Métais is Head of International Project Development at the National Foundation for Educational Research. Her main area of work is comparative analysis and evaluation of education policy, implementation and reform in the United Kingdom and overseas. She directs the International Review of Curriculum and Assessment Frameworks, an ongoing study of education systems and organisation in 20 countries, sponsored by the Qualifications and Curriculum Authority and is currently leading a review of the primary curriculum in Vietnam, for the World Bank.

John Lowe is currently a lecturer in the Department of Education at the University of Bath. His professional life began as a science teacher in Kenya and then Solomon Islands, and he retains a particular interest in aspects of science education. More recently, he has worked in curriculum development, teacher professional development and assessment issues in a range of countries. He has a variety of research interests within a general concern for the role of education in national development.

Simon McGrath is a research fellow of the Centre of African Studies, University of Edinburgh. His professional interests include international education and training policy; education–economy links, particularly related to African micro-enterprises; development cooperation; and the methodological challenge of African studies. He is currently researching knowledge and policy transfer among development cooperation agencies as part of the ESRC's Future Governance programme.

Juan Navarro is a research assistant in the research group, 'Special Education and Educational Psychology' at the University of Murcia, Spain. He is responsible for compensatory education in the area of Murcia.

Marilyn Osborn is Reader and Director of the MPhil/PhD programme in Education in the Graduate School of Education, University of Bristol, and co-director of the Centre for International and Comparative Studies in Education. She has written extensively on teachers' work and professional perspectives, both in a national and international context, and on pupil perspectives in a comparative context. She is currently directing an ESRC-funded study, Education and National Culture: a comparative study of attitudes to secondary schooling (ENCOMPASS).

Edwina Peart is a researcher, currently at the Institute of Education, University of London. Her main interests are international aid to education, non-formal and adult education, the impact of HIV/AIDs on education systems and gender and development.

David Phillips is a Fellow of St Edmund Hall and Professor of Comparative Education in the University of Oxford. His main research interest is in education in Germany, and he has published many books and articles in this area. He is Editor of the *Oxford Review of Education* and served during 1998-2000 as Chair of the British Association for International and Comparative Education.

Rosemary Preston directs the International Centre for Education in Development, University of Warwick, United Kingdom.

Pilar Arnaiz Sánchez is a lecturer in special educational needs at the University of Murcia (Spain) and since 1999 has been Director of the research group, 'Special Education and Educational Psychology' at the University of Murcia, Spain.

Michele Schweisfurth lectures in international education at the University of Birmingham, United Kingdom. She has worked as a teacher and teacher educator in Sierra Leone, Indonesia and the Turks and Caicos Islands, and has researched educational transition for her PhD thesis 'A Tale of Twelve Teachers: education and democratisation in Russia and South Africa' (University of Warwick, 2000).

Janet Stuart is lecturer in education at the Centre for International Education at the University of Sussex Institute of Education. Originally a secondary teacher of social studies in Inner London, she has travelled widely in sub-Saharan Africa, and spent 6 years training teachers of development studies at the National University of Lesotho. Other teaching and consultancy work included Seychelles, Namibia, Malawi and South Africa. Her main interests are in teacher education, action research, and textbooks appropriate for a local context. She currently coordinates the MUSTER project.

Anthony Sweeting is currently a member of the Comparative Education Research Centre, an honorary research fellow of the Centre of Asian Studies, and an honorary professor in the History Department of the University of Hong Kong, having retired recently from that University's Department of Curriculum Studies. Most of his publications are in the fields of history of education, education policy, and comparative education. In retirement, he has enhanced opportunities for comparisons of all sorts by dividing his time each year between Hong Kong, Cebu, and Oxford.

Leon Tikly trained as a science teacher in London. He has taught in London comprehensives and at the ANC school for South African refugees in Morogoro, Tanzania. He completed his MPhil in comparative education and PhD at the University of Glasgow. His PhD thesis was on 'Education Policy in South Africa since 1957'. Between 1993 and 1995, he worked as a policy researcher at the University of the Witwatersrand in Johannesburg, where he helped to develop policy for the new provincial and national governments in South Africa. Since returning to the United Kingdom, he has taught international management and policy in education at the University of Birmingham before taking up his present position as a lecturer in education policy and management, University of Bristol.

Keith Watson is Professor of Comparative and International Education and Director of the Centre for International Studies in Education, Management and Training at the University of Reading. He is the Editor-in-Chief of the *International Journal of Educational Development* and was Chair of the UK Forum for International Education and Training

(UKFIET) from 1990 to 1991. He is a former Secretary, Chairman and President of the British Comparative and International Education Society. His publications include *Educational Development in Thailand, Issues in Comparative Education, Educational Dilemmas: debate and diversity* (Ed.) (4 volumes), and numerous papers on comparative and international education.